Everyday Life
in
Southeast
Asia

EDITED BY

Kathleen M. Adams and
Kathleen A. Gillogly

INDIANA UNIVERSITY PRESS
BLOOMINGTON AND INDIANAPOLIS

This book is a publication of

Indiana University Press
601 North Morton Street
Bloomington, Indiana 47404–3797 USA

www.iupress.indiana.edu

Telephone orders 800–842–6796
Fax orders 812–855–7931
Orders by e-mail iuporder@indiana.edu

⊛ The paper used in this publication meets the minimum requirements of
the American National Standard for Information Sciences—Permanence of Paper
for Printed Library Materials, ANSI Z39.48–1992.

Manufactured in the United States of America

Library of Congress Cataloging-in-Publication Data

Everyday life in Southeast Asia / edited by Kathleen M. Adams and Kathleen A. Gillogly.
p. cm.
Includes bibliographical references and index.
ISBN 978-0-253-35637-6 (cloth : alk. paper) — ISBN 978-0-253-22321-0 (pbk. : alk. paper) 1.
Ethnology—Southeast Asia. 2. Southeast Asia—Social life and customs. 3. Southeast Asia—
Religious life and customs. I. Adams, Kathleen M., [date] II. Gillogly, Kathleen.
GN635.S58E94 2011
959—dc22
2010053606

1 2 3 4 5 16 15 14 13 12 11

CONTENTS

ACKNOWLEDGMENTS

Our heartfelt thanks go to each of our contributors, who not only provided us with their wonderful essays, but many of whom also offered us valuable suggestions as the volume developed. In addition, we wish to acknowledge and thank the students in our Southeast Asia classes in the 2009–2010 academic year. They were the trial audiences for many of the chapters in this volume, and their thoughtful comments and feedback were invaluable to us in the preparation of this book. We would also like to express our gratitude to Rebecca Tolen of Indiana University Press. She was the impetus for this volume and her patience and encouragement were appreciated. In addition, our home institutions (Loyola University Chicago and the University of Wisconsin-Parkside) deserve recognition for their financial and logistical support of this project. At the University of Wisconsin-Parkside, Jeremy Topczewski of University Graphics, under the direction of Don Lintner, patiently drew and redrew the maps for this book.

We especially wish to thank our family members for their endless support and patience as various writing and editing deadlines removed us from the joys of everyday family life. Kathleen Adams's husband, Peter Sanchez, offered both intellectual and emotional support in addition to making much-appreciated runs for gelato as crucial deadlines approached. Her eight-year-old daughter, Danielle, offered lively distractions from the more tedious aspects of editing and Danielle's questions about whether Indonesian, Singaporean, and Vietnamese children also liked *Star Wars* and pizza helped us keep in mind the book's focus on "everyday lives." Kathleen Adams also wishes to offer special thanks to Loyola University Chicago's Office of Research Services for its assistance in the form of a book subvention grant. That grant enabled us to hire our talented indexer, Mary Mortensen, whom we also wish to thank.

Kate Gillogly thanks The Center for Southeast Asian Studies at the University of Wisconsin-Madison for granting her a Faculty Access Grant in June 2009 that enabled her to connect with a wide range of Southeast Asianists and thoroughly ransack their wonderful Southeast Asia collection. She particularly thanks Michael Cullinane, Marguerite Roulet, Larry Ashmun, Mary Jo Wilson, and Peggy Choy for their support while she was in Madison. She especially thanks her partner, Charles Wilson, who has been as patient as he was during the writing of her dissertation, which is saying quite a lot, and has delighted her by becoming a good cook.

NOTE ON TRANSLITERATION

There are over eleven official national languages in Southeast Asia, and there are many hundreds of smaller language groups and dialects spoken in the region. In addition, many people of Southeast Asian speak more than one language. Given this diversity of languages, we have opted to use accepted conventions for transliterations. Many names of people, places, deities, and texts appear without diacritics in this volume. We have, however, accommodated various contributors' preferences as best we could, which means there are some variations in the pages that follow. Some of our contributors have opted to use diacritics in their translations for greater precision. Others prefer not to employ diacritics at all, sticking to English spellings that closely approximate the term's pronunciation. For greater accuracy, we have opted to spell the names of some important Southeast Asian cities and regions as Southeast Asians are currently spelling them.

Everyday Life
in
Southeast
Asia

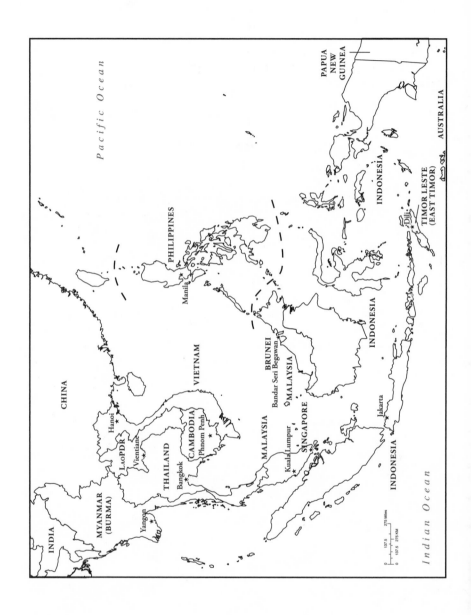

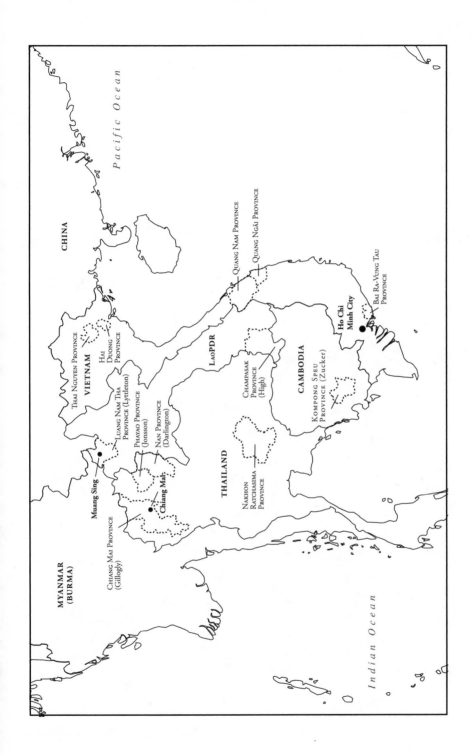

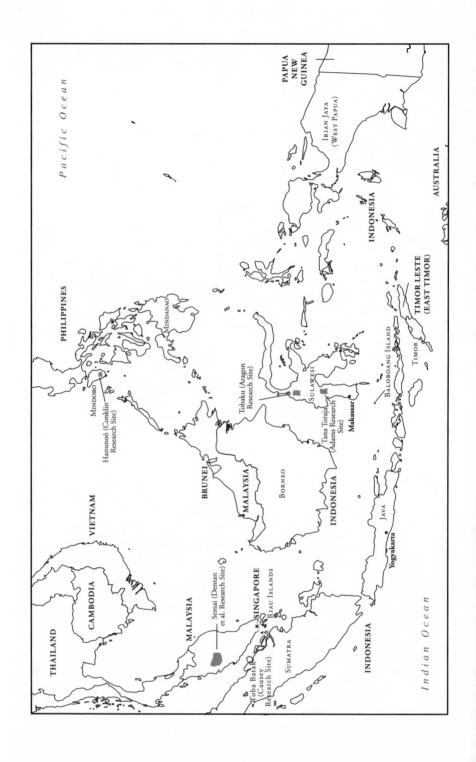

Southeast Asia and Everyday Life

Kathleen A. Gillogy and Kathleen M. Adams

Southeast Asia is one of the most dynamic, complex, and fascinating areas of the world. And yet, for most Americans, it also remains one of the world's least understood regions. Often, people lump it into the category of *Asia* (along with China, Japan, Korea) and are unaware that Southeast Asia includes eleven very diverse countries. American news media portrayals of Southeast Asia tend to present it in sensational terms: as the setting for some of our major wars (World War II, the Vietnam War); as an incubation zone for militant Muslims; as a natural disaster–prone "Ring of Fire"; or as a region that generates despotic leaders, refugees, and labor migrants. Alternatively, travel media and some tourist blogs present more "seductive" visions of Southeast Asia: as an exotic tropical vacation zone, surfers' heaven, bargain shopping Mecca, sex tourism destination, homeland of lovely "mail order" brides and delectable spicy cuisine. There are some truths here, but these are partial truths. There is far more to Southeast Asia than these extreme and often problematic stereotypes belie.

This volume represents our efforts to convey some of the richness and complexity of Southeast Asia via explorations of the daily lives and experiences of diverse people living in this region. In approaching contributors for this volume, we requested essays featuring the everyday practices of ordinary people rather than purely theoretical pieces. Highlighting the minutiae of everyday life—dressing, conversing, schooling, seeking livelihoods, rituals, recreational activities, and so forth—offers a provocative lens for reflecting on more abstract cultural principles and transformations. People's ordinary everyday activities, even when apparently distinct from other dimensions of life, are invariably tethered to broader social, economic, and political processes. Our "everyday life" approach is grounded in a now established tradition of scholarship, dating back to Henri Fernand Braudel's 1949 treatise on the long-term social history of the Mediterranean. In his now classic work, Braudel illustrated that the everyday practices and techniques of ordinary people, the farmers, fishers, and potters, the migrations of flocks of sheep, and the tides that carried sailing vessels, were all important to understanding the longer-term flows of history in the Mediterranean. A number of celebrated anthropologists of Southeast Asia similarly focused on the rhythms and microdramas of everyday life with an eye to revealing broader cultural themes. Many of Clifford Geertz's classic writings on Indonesia embrace this approach (for instance, see his "Notes on the Balinese Cockfight" or "Ritual and Social Change: A Javanese Example" [Geertz 1973]), and his work has had a profound effect on anthropology as a whole.[1] Likewise, many of anthropologist Harold Conklin's early writings on the Philippines embody the "everyday life" approach embraced in this volume. One of his articles, which follows the daily activities of a young girl from a shifting agricultural society in the late 1950s, is included in this volume as it gives us insights into a way of life that is increasingly rare in contemporary Southeast Asia.

WHAT IS SOUTHEAST ASIA? ROSE, UNICORN, SPONGE, JIGSAW PUZZLE, OR COLLAGE?

Southeast Asia is generally held to be composed of Burma, Thailand, Laos, Cambodia, Vietnam, the Philippines, East Timor, Indonesia, Singapore, Malaysia, and Brunei. This is a region of considerable geographic, social, linguistic, and cultural diversity, so much so that an earlier generation of Southeast Asia scholars wondered whether the region could be considered a natural "unit" akin to a rose (re: Shakespeare's famous line in *Romeo and Juliet,* "That which we call a rose by any other name would smell as sweet"), or if the region was not an invented fiction without any intrinsic unifying cultural characteristics—a kind of geographical unicorn (Emmerson 1984, Waddell 1972). Still others depicted Southeast Asia as a border zone: a spongelike region that absorbed the cultural and religious influences of more powerful neighboring areas (i.e., China, India). An example of this sort of analysis is Coedes's *The Indianized States of Southeast Asia* (1968), which traces the influence of Hinduism and later Buddhism in the rise of early states such as Angkor (Cambodia) and Srivijaya (Sumatra). More recently, the Filipino scholar Fernando Zialcita underscored that the concept "Southeast Asia" has been continuously evolving and is gradually cohering (albeit in different sorts of ways) in the minds of Southeast Asians. He points out that although Southeast Asians themselves did not have a common term for their realm until Western names for the region began circulating in the twentieth century, the twentieth-century advent of unifying, pan–Southeast Asian political and cultural organizations enabled a contemporary search for symbols that Southeast Asians feel differentiate them from the rest of the world (Zialcita 2003: 36). Zialcita argues that although we tend to conceive of the world as an enormous jigsaw puzzle wherein each region has its unique defining essence, in fact it is more realistic to conceive of Southeast Asia as a collage. By this metaphor, he means that Southeast Asia is best thought of as a "configuration of cultural traditions of different shapes and textures overlapping with and interconnected with each other" (37). We find Zialcita's approach to Southeast Asia, as a realm of intersecting continuities and discontinuities, particularly useful.

DIVERSITY

One fundamental divide in the region is between island (insular) and mainland Southeast Asia. Regional specialists tend to focus on one or the other of these zones; we have joined together in editing this book in part to unite our personal regional specializations. This divide between mainland and island Southeast Asia is more than a disciplinary convenience. The mainland has long had ties of commonalities in culture and language, overland trade, and population movement with the peoples of southern China. In fact, this region of the northern mainland and southern China has often been recognized as a unique economic and cultural region in its own right, with a range of names devised for it, the most recent being "Zomia," coined by Willem van Schendel and popularized by James Scott (2009). Similarly, the islands of Southeast Asia share a variety of features. Some of these features, such as language family and a tendency for traditional houses to embody social groups' identities and visions of the world, stretch beyond island Southeast Asia through much of the Pacific (cf. Fox 1993).

In addition, although linguistic similarities exist along broad swathes of Southeast Asia, no single language family unites the entire region, and language families often cross national boundaries. As one might imagine, this has presented an ongoing problem in state policies. The dominant language family in island Southeast Asia is Austronesian, which extends from Madagascar through Indonesia, Malaysia, and the Philippines, east all the way through the Pacific up to Hawaii (excluding certain pockets on islands such as Alor in eastern Indonesia and the island of New Guinea). Mainland Southeast Asia's diversity is also linguistic in basis. Outside of the widespread Austronesian languages in southern regions of mainland Malaysia, mainland Southeast Asia is home to several language families. Tai languages are found throughout northeast India, northern Burma, southern China, Thailand, Laos, and northern Vietnam. In contrast, the language of the people of Cambodia (Khmer) is not a tonal language, and belongs to a different language family (Mon-Khmer). Vietnamese is again entirely different (and while tonal, has very different tones from those of the Tai languages). Upland minority peoples speak a range of languages from unrelated language families, such as Hmong-Mien and Tibeto-Burman (Lisu, Lahu, Akha, possibly Karen) (Matisoff 1983). These linguistic differences underlie variations in cognition and culture, and yet these boundaries are ephemeral in that many people of Southeast Asia speak multiple languages and in fact can shift their ethnic identities by switching languages.

The colonial histories of the countries that comprise Southeast Asia differ dramatically as well: Burma was a part of the British Empire in India and so tied to Malaysia and Singapore; Indonesia was a Dutch colony; Vietnam, Laos, and Cambodia formed French Indochina; the Philippines was a colony of Spain, then the United States; and East Timor was a Portuguese colony, and later colonized and incorporated for a time by Indonesia. That Thailand maintained its independence was in part due to its role as a buffer state between British and French colonial territories, as well as due to the astuteness of its ruling kings in assimilating Western technologies of governance such as mapping, as Thongchai Winichakul demonstrated in *Siam Mapped* (1994).

Given Southeast Asia's complexity and the dichotomies it embodies, it is not surprising that scholars have debated how we might best conceptualize this region. Scholars periodically revisit the issue of what makes Southeast Asia a region (cf. King 2005). At the core of this is the debate about whether Southeast Asia is an invented fiction or an actuality based on shared cultural and geographic features (unicorn vs. rose). As Donald Emmerson pointed out, the naming of the region simultaneously described and invented a reality (Emmerson 1984). Although the term *Southeastern Asia* most likely debuted in an 1839 travelogue, it was not until the 1920s that the field of Southeast Asian studies was founded (ibid.). Emmerson observed that the region of Southeast Asia was constructed in the Cold War culture of designating "area studies" as a means of collecting security information on world regions (see also Cumings 1997), a perspective that implies that "Southeast Asia" is an invented fiction. The illegitimacy of regions as bounded units for analysis (the "jigsaw puzzle" model) has been further eroded by the rise of globalization and by post-modern rejections of notions of cultures as bounded discrete units. That is, the idea of Southeast Asia as an entity unto itself is seen as based on false premises.

CONTINUITY

Yet there is a "there" there. At the very least, the last sixty years of independence have seen the rise of associations such as ASEAN (the Association of South East Asian Nations) that express the common political, economic, and social interests of these countries vis-à-vis the rest of the world. This contemporary cooperation in itself justifies a textbook covering the region of Southeast Asia. There is also a history preceding colonialism, one in which premodern kingdoms traded goods and ideas. Although some might frame the region in terms of the very different historical influences of India and China, we contend that Southeast Asian society and cultures cannot be understood simply as a mere backwater reflection of India and China. This is a unique place—one that received, reformed, and restructured influences from China, India, and beyond. It is a region separate and distinct from East Asia and South Asia, replete with its own internal, regional variations.

We are not original in making this point. Others have argued that there are widespread cultural traits that unite Southeast Asia as a cultural region (cf. Wolters 1999; Reid 1988). External influences were (and continue to be) localized within a matrix of existing belief systems. (In today's language of globalization this would be called "glocalization" or "hybridization.") The long history of trade within the region and thus exchange of cultural ideas, political models, and economic linkages gives it cultural coherence. It is also united by histories of migration, with seafaring groups such as the Buginese settling along the coasts of many of the islands of insular Southeast Asia and, especially in the mainland area, by a traditional style of warfare that aimed to "gather people" and tributary alliances rather than to conquer land and establish territorial boundaries (the style of warfare more familiar to students of European history).

There are also consistent ecologically based cultural themes in Southeast Asia that set the region apart from East Asia (China, Japan, Korea) and South Asia (India, Bangladesh, Nepal). Southeast Asia is largely tropical and depends on monsoons for agriculture. It is a region where rice cultivation dominates, whether as irrigated rice or dry rice cultivation in mountainous or heavily forested regions. This basic pattern of lowland wet rice cultivation and highland dry rice cultivation has played an important role in the area's cultural history. Whereas highland communities historically tended to be smaller-scale subsistence agriculturalists and foragers, lowland communities on the coastal plains had their own patterns. The wet rice fields of the coastal and lowland valley regions supported denser populations and gave rise to early states that were involved in maritime and overland regional trade.[2]

Through these trade networks came religious influences from other regions (Hinduism and Buddhism from South Asia, Buddhism and Confucianism from China, Islam from trade networks extending to the Middle East, and Catholicism from Spain and Portugal). These influences were generally incorporated as an overlay on fundamental Southeast Asian cultural ideas of ritual power that can still be discerned in certain practices found in modern states. For instance, consider the Emerald Buddha of Thailand, a sacred relic with a history that captures some of the power dynamics in pre-colonial Southeast Asia. This key relic was captured from a Lao king by a Thai king and has since served as a marker of the Thai monarchy. Like other sacralized objects, it both represents and embodies the king of Thailand's power. Likewise, consider the *kris* (alt. *keris, kalis*) found in much of the Malay world, ranging from Indonesia to the southern Philippines, Brunei, and Thailand. A distinctive, often wavy-bladed ancestral knife that is both weapon and mystical object, a sacred *kris* is traditionally thought to be embodied with a unique, spiritlike essence and it was important that this essence mesh positively with the personality of its owner or the results could be disastrous. Some *kris* were traditionally thought to carry legendary powers and potencies, and in certain courts, a particular royal *kris* was seen as a symbol of a ruler's mandate to rule (cf. Pederson 2007). Despite the influences of Islam and Christianity, many educated Southeast Asian urbanites still retain respect for the legendary powers of certain ancestral *kris*, and several recent Indonesian presidents, including former president Suharto, reportedly went to great measures to ensure control over their sacred ancestral *kris* (Bourchier 2010: 89). These ideas of ritual power and concerns with control over the symbols of cosmological legitimacy are congruent with what Wolters (1999) called a cult of "men of prowess," people who were able to concentrate spiritual power into themselves.

Another related, recurrent theme in Southeast Asian cultures is how pre-colonial states were based on a central powerful core supported by an ideology of sacred power, the mandala-style polity, rather than a focus on containing and controlling on the basis of borders. This concept has dynamically changed as modern nation-states have been created in Southeast Asia. This has been an anthropologically significant theme addressed in the literature by scholars from Benedict Anderson to Thongchai Winichakul.

Southeast Asia was also critical in introducing the now common concept of "situational" definition of identity and shifting ethnic identity, starting with the work of Edmund Leach in northern Burma (1954) and further developed by Judith Nagata in her classic tracing of situational selections of Malay identity in Malaysia (1974). In kinship studies, work in Southeast Asia on the widespread dominance of flexible kin structures allowed anthropologists to deconstruct the idea of descent as a permanent identity based on "blood."

In short, despite its "crossroads" location between China and India in a realm that has long attracted traders and travelers from continents as distant as Europe, these and other studies suggest that Southeast Asia has its own unique characteristics: there *is* a "there" there.

THE IMPORTANCE OF REGIONAL STUDIES IN A GLOBAL ERA

Why study a culturally particular region in this age of globalization? Are we not all becoming one world? Not only is Southeast Asia one of the most linguistically, culturally, and religiously heterogeneous areas in the world, but it is also a region undergoing dramatic transformations in the face of globalization. For instance, the Philippines, Thailand, Vietnam, and islands off the coast of Singapore have become major centers for global manufacturing and outsourcing. Bangkok, Thailand is Southeast Asia's banking center. Singapore has recently become a high-tech hub as well as a center for medical technology and pharmaceutical production. And Indonesia is a major oil producer (in addition to being the world's largest Muslim nation and the fourth-most-populous nation in the world). Given that Southeast Asia is hardly a backwater of globalization, we believe it is essential to develop a richer, more nuanced appreciation of this region. Understanding the processes by which global forces (such as Western corporate expansion, the spread of Middle Eastern forms of Islam, or the growth of foreign markets for Southeast Asian fish) play out in different local settings requires that we have a detailed and intimate knowledge of particular places, as well as of past and present relationships among the different societies within the region. That is, there remains a need for place-based studies.

NOTES

1. As Geertz's writings on Bali and Java tend to be readily available online, we opt not to include them in this volume, thereby enabling us to make space for chapters by a new generation of scholars.

2. Upland peoples were generally autonomous of lowland states until colonialism and the rise of independent nations; nevertheless, lowland states and upland societies relied on each other politically, economically, and culturally. Although some of the popular imagery of historical lowlands–uplands relations portrays uplanders as victims of periodic lowlander raids for slaves and valuables, in reality relationships between lowland peoples and upland peoples were much more complex, and also included intermarriages, trade, and collaborations between elites of both zones. One theme in this book, then, entails examining these lowland–upland relations.

PART ONE

Fluid Personhood: Conceptualizing Identities

We begin with a section on "Conceptualizing Identities" because the definition of the "self" in Southeast Asia is one of the startlingly different elements that intrigue observers from other regions of the world. In the West,
particularly the United States, there is a pronounced emphasis on the self
as a bounded unit, autonomous, self-actualizing, and independent. We are
taught (if not completely or successfully) not to define ourselves in terms of
others but to be "our own selves." This is not the dominant norm in Southeast Asia. For instance, Kathleen Gillogly vividly remembers the ways in
which her "self" was redefined by friends in Vietnam over the years. When
they understood her to be married, they expected one kind of personal style;
when they later found her to be single, their conversational assessments of
her changed. As a "single" woman, she was to be an open, vivacious person,
sporting dangling earrings and bright colors, and wearing her hair down.
As a "married" woman, she was held to a standard of quiet calm and reticence, and was to have her hair bound and wear darker colors. She was
the same person—but what had changed? Her social role vis-à-vis the social group.

This fluidity of self is marked in Southeast Asian cultures in many ways,
as discussed in the readings in this section. More often than not, in this region conceptions of the self entail multiple aspects: the self, traditionally, is
not a unitary concept. This can be seen in underlying (pre–world religion)
cultural ideas of the soul, as well as in language and behavior. The notion
of multiple and overlapping identities is a theme in Andrew Causey's essay (chapter 2) on the Toba Batak of Sumatra, Indonesia. As Causey notes,
the Toba Batak idea of the person entails several different dimensions: the

"self," a complex conflation of individual personality, the particular spirit, and the collective group. The "individual personality" is based on a combination of one's physical quirks and character, whereas one's particular spirit (or *tondi*) has a will of its own and must be respected and humored lest it wreak havoc on one's well-being. Finally, the collective group dimension of the Toba Batak self pertains to one's membership in an array of broader groups: family, peer group, profession, clan, ethnicity, and nation.

Naming is one marker of personhood, beginning the process of incorporating a child into the community. In chapter 5, by Harold Conklin, we see one example of this when the new baby is not named immediately at birth; rather, the family waits for the grandparents to come from another village to name him. Traditionally on Bali, there are only four names for children, based on birth order. If a family has more than four children, the cycle of names is repeated again, and it is possible to have several children with the same name in a single family. The names can be assigned to girls or boys; what is important to mark is one's birth order. Lisu children are named by birth order and gender—which caused Gillogly much confusion (since there are many people named "First Daughter" and "First Son" in the village) until she discovered each person's personal nickname. Balinese also use nicknames to navigate the vagaries of these birth-order names. However, on Bali both nickname and birth-order name recede in importance once one becomes a parent. At that point, one is called "Mother of Wayan" or "Father of Ketut," a practice known as teknonymy. This name shift reflects both a change in status and the idea that all are expected to become parents. Finally, when one becomes a grandparent, one's name changes yet again, to "Grandmother of Made" or "Grandfather of Wayan." In her language-oriented contribution to this volume, Lorraine Aragon (chapter 1) also notes the importance of teknonymy among the Tobaku people of Central Sulawesi, Indonesia.

Just as the practice of teknonymy in many Southeast Asian societies underscores the importance of being immersed in webs of kinship, and of linguistically underscoring one's connections to others, so do everyday conversational styles convey similar themes. Aragon's contribution cogently illustrates that the absence of indigenous words for *please* and *thank you* in Central Sulawesi languages reveals much about social relations. Among other things, she underscores that the fact that so many indigenous languages in the archipelago lack these words does not mean that people do not experience gratitude. Rather, these words are not deemed necessary, as to utter words of thanks would be akin to preventing much valued interpersonal bonds of indebtedness to develop. In these island societies, she suggests, people see identities not as isolated, but rather as contingent on sociality. As Aragon writes, "Debts of significance cannot be released with a few fluffy words. . . . Obligations are a state of being and a means to create relations anew."

Southeast Asian relationships are often marked by mutable, ephemeral identities. Judith Nagata (chapter 4) underscores the fluid dimensions of identity in the Malay world. Focusing on Malaysia over a great span of history, she illustrates how being defined as Malay is generally based more on the language one opts to speak and the adoption of Islam. In a part of the world where many are multilingual, identities can shift depending on expediency, the need to craft bonds with others, or for other often pragmatic reasons. Speaking Malay and becoming Muslim are both equated with "becoming Malay." As Nagata points out, under Malaysia's constitution "a Malay is defined as one who habitually speaks Malay, practices Malay customs (*adat*), and is a Muslim. This is not a genealogical but a cultural profile, which technically could be adopted by anyone, including foreigners."

The emphasis on shifting identification in the anthropology of Southeast Asia has its origin to a great extent in Edmund Leach's *Political Systems of Highland Burma* (1965), a historical study of the Kachin people in which he discussed the oscillation between egalitarian and hierarchical political forms, as well as occasional shifts in which the hierarchical Kachin assumed Shan (a Tai-speaking group) identity. People often define their ethnic identity or membership in a cultural group in relation to neighboring peoples and polities, so these self-definitions shift with social context. As Leach wrote, "language groups are not therefore hereditarily established, nor are they stable through time" (1965:49). Many anthropologists have further developed these insights, particularly Lehman (1963) and Moerman (1965). Moerman, who worked with the Lue (another Tai-speaking group who have settled in northern Thailand, northern Burma, and southwestern China), recounts that he had to ask himself, "Who are the Lue?" and ultimately concluded that this ethnic identity was a category of self-ascription. Language, culture, and political organization were not necessarily congruent with each other. Ethnicity was impermanent; various ethnic groups used labels for other groups differently, and members of groups did not always use the same terms for themselves—how one labeled oneself was situational (Moerman 1965).

Theravada Buddhist ideas of the self are also fluid in a cosmological sense. As will be seen in Part 2, on Family, Households, and Livelihoods, social relations are contextualized in terms of the relative status (gender, age, class or rank, education, or occupation, depending on the particular culture) of the people involved with each other. In Theravada Buddhist societies, this is grounded in religious concepts of merit and karma. Buddhism holds that the soul transmigrates and is reborn again and again on the Wheel of Life until the achievement of enlightenment. Nirvana, therefore, is nothingness—not being reborn. But in everyday life, people think in terms of their own immediate caches of merit and sin. As Steven Carlisle points out, karma is understood and assessed individually; if bad things happen to a person, this is interpreted as evidence of transgression in a past life. There is also social monitoring of the reward of good acts and punishment of bad acts (Carlisle

2008). While people see themselves as having a particular backstory that can explain their station in life, Holly High (chapter 3) points out that the Lao people she knew believed they were able to take action to improve their station. Like High in Laos, Gillogly was amazed to be the object of discussion for her skin color and to have friends assess their own beauty on the basis of such color. But this is a marker of status and, as High points out, it is a flexible and manipulable element of status. Wealth allows one to achieve lighter skin by not obligating one to do manual, outdoor work. People can accumulate merit through working hard, making charitable donations, and religious behavior. (Moreover, as we will see in Sue Darlington's essay, chapter 11, the definition of kinds of meritorious acts can be reinterpreted in different settings.) Merit and sin will both be evident in the physical conditions of a person's life; the implication is that those who are beautiful, successful, or wealthy have a store of merit; that is, there is a cosmological foundation and legitimation of status.

Southeast Asia is also known for what has appeared, to Western eyes, as extraordinary gender egalitarianism. As noted in "Maling" (Conklin, chapter 5), families desired male and female children equally; the family had lots of girls, but wanted a boy to hunt with his father. "It would be nice to have the same number of both boy and girl children" says Maling. Outsiders have also noted the number of female presidents and leaders in Southeast Asia. We must be careful about how we interpret this female leadership, as many of these leaders have been daughters or spouses of past leaders. This, perhaps, tells us that the connection to power is more important than gender in and of itself.

Gender parity and complementarity were relatively pervasive in precolonial Southeast Asia. Long before most European women had legally sanctioned property rights, Southeast Asian women could not only own property but could also attain prestige as healers and spiritual specialists. In contemporary Southeast Asia, women are often allocated responsibility for managing household budgets. Thai, Lao, Filipino, and Vietnamese colleagues earnestly informed Gillogly time and again that men could not be trusted to handle money wisely, so that women needed to do it. Nevertheless, household economic power does not translate into political power, nor to large-scale public economic power in states.

These elements of gender fluidity and egalitarianism are not necessarily typical of Vietnam, however. The gender role of women in Vietnam is to some extent structured by the predominance of patrilineal organization. The Confucian ideal of family organization is decidedly patriarchal. Does this mean, in practice, that women have little power in Vietnamese society? The more important question may be whether Vietnamese women have status comparable to that of women in the rest of Southeast Asia—evidenced by their significant roles in patrilineal rituals—or whether they are subject to Confucian law and therefore have roles more akin to the more subordinate ones East Asian women are presumed to occupy—as evidenced by Vietnamese law that did not allow women to inherit land. Debates on this point continue.

While none of the chapters in this book discusses this, many Southeast Asian cultures are also notable for recognizing a different set of gender categories beyond the simple binary opposition between female and male. There are third and fourth gender categories. For instance, the famous "ladyboys" of Thailand are in fact a modern transformation of a traditional gender role of *kathoey*. Such male-to-female transgender persons are accepted and often admired in Thai society—but, as with women's roles in Thailand, there are limits to the degree of public power accessible to such people. Interestingly, in parts of island Southeast Asia, third and fourth gender category people were historically often assigned special, socially recognized ritual roles. In Sulawesi, some played essential roles in Buginese weddings, and others played roles in highland harvest rituals. However, world religions and the absorption of Western attitudes toward nonbinary gender categories have eroded these special roles.

Colonialism, postcolonial migrations, and nation-building have also brought about the reworking of other dimensions of indigenous ideas pertaining to gender, as Aihwa Ong and Michael C. Peletz have underscored (1995:2). For instance, the arrival of Spaniards and Catholicism in the Philippines ultimately diminished the spiritual potency accessible to indigenous women. Missionization and colonialism generally meant that the Filipina's role became conscripted to that of church and home. And today we find that globalization, labor migration, and other current dynamics have not been uniformly empowering for Southeast Asian women (or for those who are gay or transgendered, for that matter). While globalization offers new possibilities for Southeast Asian women to seek livelihood and mates abroad (cf. Constable 2003), not all these possibilities offer Cinderella-type outcomes. For instance, although the wages may be better than what one could earn at home, the positions Filipina, Indonesian, and Malaysian women take as overseas domestic workers may entail emotionally challenging long-distance parenting, long hours of confinement, or even abuse at the hands of bosses (cf. Salazar Parreña 2001; Robinson 2000a; Constable 2007). As Michele Ford and Lenore Lyons (chapter 23) note in reflecting on women migrants they interviewed in the Southeast Asian Growth Triangle (some of whom were working in the sex industry), the border zone presents new prospects they would not have elsewhere, but also imposes risks and other costs.

1

Living in Indonesia without a Please or Thanks: Cultural Translations of Reciprocity and Respect

Lorraine V. Aragon

"Can I take a sip of your drink, Dad?" I recently heard a seven year-old American girl ask in a public waiting room.

"Yes, but you didn't say 'Please'," her father chided gently.

"Please. . . . Thanks!" The little girl chanted these two magic words in quick succession as she eagerly reached for her father's can of soda pop.

It is easy to watch these remarkably powerful words being taught to young children in any home or public arena in the United States. Those of us who speak English or other European languages generally take these words for granted. But we know that their deployment brings politeness, persuasion, and permission to what might otherwise be unacceptable requests.

The power of these words also can be made visible by their absence. Try living a day in the company of others without ever saying "please" or "thank you," and see what happens. Social psychology experiments devised in the 1970s tested the boundaries of U.S. social norms through their intentional violation. Those studies, briefly in vogue, were termed *ethnomethodology*. The experiments were easy to design once the formula of nonchalant rule violation was conceived, but their popularity among psychologists and sociologists was short-lived because of the ill will they produced. Similar discomfort often arises when we travel innocently to distant places where customary rules of politeness differ. Even with our best efforts, our attempts to translate our own polite forms often seem to fall awkwardly flat.

That said, it may seem unimaginable that societies in Indonesia, a region known for its intricate forms of politeness, would lack such basic terms as *please* and *thank you* to oil the wheels of harmonious social interaction. As the anthropologists Clifford Geertz (1976) and James Peacock (1987) describe, the language, cosmology, politics, and aesthetics of Indonesia's most populous ethnic group, the Javanese, revolve around a dualism that contrasts the refined (*alus*, Javanese; *halus*, Indonesian) with the coarse or crude (*kasar*, Javanese and Indonesian).

We therefore would expect verbal expressions of gratitude to be prominent among peoples who are anxious about proper speech and social refinement. But, in fact, most of the more than three hundred indigenous languages spoken in the Indonesian archipelago do not include synonyms for terms such as *please* and *thank you*. Most languages in Indonesia borrow some "thank you" phrase from European languages or the national language, termed *bahasa Indonesia*, to cope with contemporary cosmopolitan expectations. When local people speak to one another in their native tongues, by contrast, they can make do without these phrases.

So, the cross-cultural puzzle arises. How does one live smoothly and politely in a society without a generic word like *please* to make your demanding requests upon others tolerable, and no phrases like *thank you* to express gratitude for help and kindness? Is gratitude simply assumed in small Southeast Asian communities of equals? Are the messages our European words contain perhaps encoded alternatively in nonverbal gestures?

The answers are more complicated. We must think in unfamiliar ways about what these kinds of words actually do—or, sometimes, cannot do—for us and others. Ward Keeler (1984:xvii) notes that "a critical part of learning a language is to learn not to want or need to say what one says in English, but rather to learn to say what people say in the culture of the language one is learning." In essence, then, studying a region's language in situ is much more about learning to intuit the logic of meaningful local categories and patterns of social expectations than it is about memorizing one-to-one linguistic translations. We are informed not only about technical language usage and conversational routines, but also about widespread Southeast Asian cultural practices of economic exchange and hierarchy. Keeler writes that Java is

> full of small talk, and polite conversation draws on a large store of stereotypical remarks. To use them is not thought stultifying, as some Westerners find, but rather gracious, comfortable, indicative of the desire to make every encounter smooth and effortless for all concerned. (Ibid.)

Given these concerns, it has surprised many observers that Indonesians, including the notoriously manners-obsessed Javanese, make little use, or very different use, of the kinds of terms we take as the mainstay of our polite interactions in most European languages. In what follows, I will show that the English term *please* is a rather diffuse word, one that maps onto many different kinds of requests in Indonesian languages. And, *thank you* has implications about intimacy and economy in Indonesia that we would never imagine. Before exploring these linguistic alleyways, though, we should consider what the Indonesian language is, and how it came to be the youthful nation's twentieth-century communication highway.

INDONESIAN NATIONAL AND LOCAL LANGUAGES

Most languages spoken in Indonesia fall into the Austronesian language family, comprised of more than one thousand languages. The result of maritime migrations starting roughly five thousand years ago, Austronesian languages span a vast reach across the Pacific Ocean from Madagascar in the west to Hawaii in the east. Only twenty-five of those Austronesian languages— Indonesian being one—have more than one million native speakers (Sneddon 2003:25).[1]

The current geopolitical boundaries of Indonesia, like those of many former European colonies in Asia, Africa, and the Americas, essentially were created by colonial conquests between the seventeenth and twentieth centuries. What is now Indonesia was ruled by the Dutch as the Netherlands East Indies. The adjacent nation of Malaysia was ruled by the English as the British East Indies. These were boundaries on a political power grid, not natural ethnic divisions.

In 1928, Malay was selected to become the national language of the Dutch East Indies by a youth congress of pro-Independence nationalists. Indonesian is essentially a dialect of Malay. Thus the national languages of Malaysia and Indonesia are, for the most part, mutually intelligible. A quick glance at a map of Southeast Asia shows that the westernmost Indonesian island of Sumatra, especially the Riau area, is separated from the Malay Peninsula by just a narrow strait. Parts of Sumatra are much closer ethnically and linguistically to western Malaysia than they are to many of Indonesia's eastern islands such as Sulawesi, Maluku, Timor, or New Guinea. These latter islands, by contrast, are closer in linguistic, genealogical, and geographical features to the Philippines, or to the Pacific island region called Melanesia.

Although only about 5 percent of the Netherlands East Indies population spoke Malay in the 1920s, it was selected to be Indonesia's national language for political and social reasons (Sneddon 2003). While Dutch was used by the educated elite, it also was the language of the colonial oppressor and did not offer the international advantages of more widely dispersed European languages such as English or Spanish. Javanese was spoken by the largest population of Indies residents, roughly 40 percent, but this seemingly obvious choice was rejected. Nationalists were interested in a language that would unite an ethnically plural nation, and the Javanese were feared to be too dominant. Even most Javanese leaders found their language unsuitable for national status because of its dauntingly hierarchical character. Javanese often is considered the purest example of a language in which the relative status of the speaker and the listener is encoded within the vocabulary of different speech levels. Every word in some sentences must vary according to the relative status of the speakers (Geertz 1976; Wolff and Poedjosoedarmo 1982). Such complexity and feudal leanings were not considered promising for the national language of a modern, twentieth-century nation of equals.

By contrast, Malay had been used as a trade language along island Southeast Asian maritime routes, spread for centuries, first by seafaring merchants and later by the Dutch colonial administration. Thus, Malay's rudimentary conversational forms—greetings, travel or market bargaining, family-life questions, and the like—already served as a basic lingua franca in coastal regions of colonial Southeast Asia. Finally, Malay seemed the best choice for the new nation's governmental and educational purposes because it had been transcribed in the Latin alphabet and increasingly was adopted by popular journalists and literary writers (Anderson 1991).

In much of Indonesia, however, children still grow up speaking regional languages, most of which are significantly different in grammar and vocabulary from Indonesian. Indonesian is thus a second language learned in primary school and through exposure to the mass media. That was the situation in highland Central Sulawesi, where I conducted anthropological fieldwork first from 1986 to 1989. My academic preparation for fieldwork was to study Indonesian, but I needed to learn a very different local language when I settled in Sulawesi.

Another quick glance at a map will show why Sulawesi languages are closer to Philippine languages than they are to Malay. The Central Sulawesi language spoken where I lived is technically known as Uma, named by colonial European missionaries after the word for *no*, which varies throughout the island. The language also sometimes is called Pipikoro (meaning "banks of the Lariang River") or, more broadly, a Kulawi District language. Uma is an unwritten language spoken by an estimated 17,000–20,000 speakers. The Pipikoro dialect was studied thoroughly by a linguist translating the Bible (Martens 1988), but no study guides existed when I went there. So, after I arrived in the Tobaku highlands, I composed lists of words and sentences, which I initially asked Tobaku people to explain to me in Indonesian. My aim was to use Indonesian as little as possible as quickly as possible.[2]

Numerous Tobaku people told me that the two things they most appreciated about me as a visitor was that I could eat their local food and that I spoke (or tried to speak) their language. For me, partaking of the local cuisine, even at its most challenging, was by far the easier of those two enterprises. Being human, I was frequently hungry. In truth, I was thankful that eating required no special talent or hard-learned skills. By contrast, mastering a mostly unwritten language that differed grammatically from any language I had previously studied was exponentially more daunting.

Most Indonesian government and church mission visitors arriving in the highlands from the provincial capital expected to be fed large portions of specially cooked meats—no pork if they were Muslims, and different, generally less spicy, cuisine if they were Christians. By contrast, I was a grateful and "unfussy" guest with a strong stomach for the highlanders' mounded plates of hill rice with side dishes of hot chilies and seasonal vegetables. While their cuisine and language seem to embarrass Tobaku people, they also serve as points of local pride. Just as U.S. travelers often expect everyone else in the world to learn English, most Indonesians visiting the Sulawesi highlands expect residents to speak Indonesian. In the 1980s, Tobaku people always spoke to each other in Uma, even if they knew Indonesian fluently and their guests did not. Their language was a source of local ethnic identity, a litmus test of responsible membership and moral knowledge that few outsiders could ever pass.

Tobaku people jokingly call their language *basa mata'*, which literally translates as the "green," "unripe," or "raw" language. With this phrase they imply that their language is unrefined (*kasar*, Indonesian) and not as sophisticated as Javanese or Indonesian languages.[3] But the lack of a "please" or "thank you" in Uma is not the result of its rural speakers' self-conscious coarseness or lack of educational refinement. Nor, as it turns out, is the absence of these words just a local linguistic or cultural phenomenon.

MAPPING THE MANY INDONESIAN WORDS FOR *PLEASE*

Learning to say *please*, even in the Indonesian national language, turns out to be much less straightforward than one might imagine. Translating *please* from English (or other European languages) into Indonesian can only be done indirectly because our one word *please*, and its other European equivalents such as *s'il vous plait* ('if you please," French) map onto several Indonesian words that are deployed differentially in specific contexts.

Indonesian *please* terms can be divided roughly into request or invitation categories. Indonesian speakers use the word *tolong*, which literally means "help," when making a request, such as "please help by doing X." Thus Indonesians can say, *Tolong bawa piring*, meaning "Help [the listener or others besides the speaker] by bringing the plate," or *Tolong bawakan piring*, meaning, "Help [me] by bringing the plate." A somewhat more submissive request or supplication would use the word *minta*, which means "ask for," or, alternately, *mohon*, (a very polite synonym for *minta*, used in more formal contexts). Thus, *Minta piring*, meaning "Asking for the plate," would be another way to translate the English phrase, "Please bring the plate."

Other Indonesian words that map onto our uses for *please* include *mari*, which is an invitation word meaning "please, I invite you to do X," or *silakan/silahkan*, which is a polite or more formal synonym for *mari*. A casual Javanese synonym for *mari*, widely known and used nationally, is *ayo*. Thus Indonesians can say *mari makan*, *ayo makan*, or *silahkan makan*, all meaning "Please eat," but with the last phrase being the most formal and polite. All these phrases, which express "help me," "I ask for," or "go ahead and do X," usually are matched with appropriate honorific or kinship terms of address such as *Bapak* ("Father" or "Sir") or *Ibu* ("Mother" or "Madam") to show additional respect for one's elders.

Each form of Indonesian request or invitation entails a matching grammatical mood, including the imperative, interrogative, and affirmative. One Javanese expert's list of English versus Indonesian "please" forms follows, with the Indonesian "please" equivalent set in bold:

1. "Please pass the salt" (**Tolong** *ambilkan garam*, request/imperative)
2. "Please come in" (**Silahkan** *masuk* or **Mari** *masuk*, invitation/imperative)
3. "Could you please tell me where she lives?" (**Maukah** *anda memberitahu saya di mana dia tinggal*? request/interrogative)
4. "Will you please shut the door?" (**Tolong** *tutup pintunya*, request/ interrogative but less formal and polite)
5. "Yes, please" (*Iya* **terima kasih**, acceptance/affirmative)
6. "Third floor, please" (**Tolong** *lantai ketiga*, request/affirmative)
7. "Please . . ." (*Saya* **mohon** . . . or **Tolonglah** *saya*. . . , elliptic request or begging/imperative)[4]

Clearly, many of these Indonesian terms work rather differently than our generic word, *please*. The Indonesian phrasings make it more explicit than the English equivalents, whether the speaker is asking for assistance or compliance. Indonesian also is clearer than English about specifying whether what is being requested is considered to be for the speaker's, the listener's, or a third party's benefit. Requests generally designate either an elder or superior's rightful demand or a social inferior's more humbling request. In the latter case, extra elements may be added, such as honorific titles of address, or the suffix *-lah* after the verb, which softens any request. Paralanguage, such as tone of voice, relative height of body positioning, or eye direction, also are involved in what we might call Indonesian requirements for sensitivity to hierarchical positioning in communication.[5]

The differential deployment of terms to connote respect makes Indonesian a deceptively difficult language for many foreigners to master. Because Indonesian (or Malay) lacks several of European languages' most complicated features (such as verb tenses, gendered words, and consonant clusters), it is often described as an easy language to learn. In terms of very basic sentence construction or "survival proficiency," this is accurate, and those who study Indonesian are well supported by the kind tolerance of Indonesians toward non-native speakers, who may be complimented as fluent after uttering just a few introductory sentences. But less-familiar linguistic features such as semantically generative verb forms and hierarchical or formal registers ensure that advanced study of Indonesian languages presents unexpectedly complex challenges.

BEING ASKED FOR THE CLOTHES OFF MY BACK

In highland Central Sulawesi, I frequently found myself being asked for my possessions with a "please-type" word. The Uma language synonym for *minta* is *merapi*, and I heard this term used often in my first three years of fieldwork. During visits to many villages, I was asked to leave what Indonesians call a *tanda mata*, a phrase that literally means "sign for the eye" but is better translated as a visual sign or souvenir. I was well aware that I was indebted to both Tobaku individuals and communities for hosting me for days or weeks at a time during my fieldwork, and I did make a conscientious effort to compensate households where I resided with locally appropriate gifts. But, sometimes, young people I hardly knew, as well as older individuals I knew better, asked me for personal possessions or items of clothing before I departed their village. I initially tried to cope with these requests by bringing extra new clothes as gifts for my hosts, but the requests for my used garments continued unabated. One day the requests reached a point where I began to think I was destined to depart the island naked.

My concern over these pleas continued until one of my closest friends, Tina Eva, a Tobaku woman who had migrated in her youth to the provincial capital, exhibited her strategy for coping with what I then discovered was not special treatment reserved for foreigners. When we arrived in the highlands after a three-day hike, we presented our hosts—Tina Eva's parents and extended family—with numerous gifts of city supplies, packaged food, and new clothes. We spent a convivial two weeks in the highlands and then prepared for our departure, receiving bundles of local produce to take back with us to the city.

I then was disarmed when Tina Eva's sisters, nieces, and cousins began to request the clothes she had been wearing during our visit. Without missing a beat, Tina Eva cheerfully began unpacking the requested skirts, blouses, and slacks—all but the outfits she needed for our three-day journey home. I followed suit, so to speak. Tina Eva's family was delighted. On the way home, Tina Eva revealed that this had been her plan all along. She had saved up what she considered her least-flattering outfits and deliberately worn them during our visit for her family members to see. Then her family helped her unload this sartorial baggage just before her return hike through the mountains. Her generosity created more room in her backpack for the gifts of fresh produce her farming relatives sent home for her family. It was a win-win game.[6]

But why, I still wondered, did local people want, even seem to prefer, our "fragrant" used clothes, rather than the brand new ones? Tobaku friends later explained that they preferred the clothes we had worn when visiting their villages because these items indeed were "signs of the eye," linked in their collective visual memory of our visit. Clothes worn by honored guests and family are considered to hold some essence of the wearer. There is a meaningful social history there, analogous to how we might treasure our grandfather's watch or our grandmother's lace shawl. I gradually became used to hearing the "please give me your shirt" requests, and rather than thinking that these needy people were begging for hand-me-downs, I realized instead that they were establishing a material memory of our relationship, showing their affection, and also helping me, in a small way, to mitigate my continuing obligations as a long-term visitor and adopted relation in their communities.

SPEAKING ABOUT FAMILY, AGE, AND GENDER

In all Indonesian languages, social hierarchy becomes quickly displayed by a deft combination of word selection, honorifics, terms of address, and general tone of voice. In the Tobaku highlands, adults most often are addressed by their "teknonyms"—kinship titles in the form of "mother of X," "husband of Y," or "grandparent of Z"—rather than by any given personal or family name. As a Tobaku person goes through life, her or his name changes from a generic term for "female/male child," to a childlike personal nickname, to "wife/husband of X," to "mother/father of Y," to "grandparent of Z." Outsiders find this naming system impossibly confusing, but local community members have little trouble keeping track. Knowing these changing monikers is simply part of knowing a consociate's life story, and people love to talk about family relations. Throughout Indonesia, kinship titles are used not only for relatives, but also for new acquaintances one wishes to respect or humor. Bus drivers often are called *Om*, meaning "Uncle," a strategy that reminds the driver that you respect his position of authority, and also that you expect him to care for your well-being on the journey as if you were cherished kin.

Indonesian terms denoting hierarchy emerge through contextual interactions. Early in my fieldwork, I met with a young professional Indonesian woman who worked at a university office in Central Sulawesi's district capital. Before we had completed two minutes of opening chit-chat, the woman inquired about my age. I found this a striking question, especially since we appeared to me to be roughly the same age. The woman explained patiently that, in Indonesia, we needed to know each other's exact age in order to establish which one of us would be addressed as "older sibling" (*kakak*) and which one as "younger sibling" (*adik*). This practice contrasts sharply with U.S. conventions where, as my son's fourth-grade teacher advised, "The three questions you should never ask a woman are her age, her weight, and her natural hair color."

Note that the Indonesian terms *kakak* and *adik* are gender neutral, applying to elder/younger sisters *or* brothers. In this respect, the Indonesian language suggests that age ranking is more critical for organizing Indonesian social relations than gender ranking, which indeed generally proves to be the case. One's age always must be known in Indonesia to enable elders to act beneficently and parentally toward their juniors, and juniors to act helpfully and respectfully to their elders. Similarly, visitors to Indonesia can expect to be asked quickly about their work roles, marital status, and children because bosses, spouses, and parents—who bear more responsibility—warrant more respectful language use. The concepts and family terms wielded (mother, father, aunt, uncle, grandparent, etc.) ideally allow Indonesians to recreate the familiarity, caring, and protectiveness of families beyond the household into the public sphere.

This extended deployment of kinship metaphors also affects national politics. Indonesian citizens called their first two presidents "father" (*bapak;* also, "mister" or "sir") for twenty and thirty-two years respectively. In response, first President Sukarno and second President Suharto called Indonesian citizens their "children" (*anak*). These linguistic practices at times instill a cozy family solidarity to Indonesian politics, but they also sometimes aid the surrender of political authority to some less-deserving father figures, who reciprocate with patronizing paternalism (Shiraishi 1997).

WHEN A VERBAL EXPRESSION OF THANKS JUST WON'T DO

Initially, it seems more straightforward for an English speaker to translate the phrase *thank you* with the Indonesian synonym (*terima kasih*) than to learn all the different ways that Indonesians say *please*. *Terima kasih* literally means "receive love," which allows the speaker to verbally declare the receipt of a kindness or gift from someone else. Many of the hundreds of indigenous languages in Indonesia, however, do not have such a phrase, so they often borrow the Indonesian expression. Central Sulawesi highlanders repronounce the Indonesian "receive love" phrase as *tarima kase.* Similar borrowings are found in the languages of other outer island Indonesian groups: *terimo kasih* (Mandailing, Sumatra); *tarimo kasi* (Angkola, Sumatra); *terimong geunasih* (Aceh, Sumatra). The list goes on and on.

In Dutch-influenced regions such as Ambon and North Sulawesi, people rephrase the informal Dutch *Denk je* ('Thank you") as *danke.* Similarly, in the former Portuguese (and later, Indonesian) colony of East Timor (now an independent nation), Portuguese words for *obliged* are used (*obrigado* for men and *obrigada* for women). This idea of expressing one's sense of obligation brings us closer to answering the puzzle of what is going on in the vast majority of Indonesian places where "thank you" has no synonym. In those regions, local people respond to kindnesses by expressing their positive emotions as raw appreciation rather than using a boilerplate catchphrase of verbal gratitude. Like the Toba people of North Sumatra who say *mauliate* (literally, "feeling good in my heart"), Uma speakers often simply say "I am happy" (*Goe' ama*) after receiving a gift. Sometimes they add a phrase that translates "but one of my arms is long," implying that they are receiving at that moment but not reciprocating. Sometimes they further engage in self-deprecation, asking for pity because they have nothing to give in return, even when they clearly do, or even just did! Essentially, their words explicitly mark the asymmetrical state of being a receiver, who exists with a future obligation to the giver.

In my study of Tobaku indigenous cosmology and Protestant revisions, I noted how foreign missionaries and church leaders frequently reminded highlanders to say *please* and *thanks* to God in their prayers for their health, crops, meals, and all life's blessings. By contrast, before Christian conversion, the Tobaku made oaths of request directly to their deities, oaths that promised offerings in return for those same benefits of life. Although the new *please* and *thank you* words were added dutifully as verbal ornaments, I suggest that "Tobaku prayers still wrap these recent and inherently empty words around the material solidarity of sacrificial offerings to instill efficacy" (Aragon 2000:248). Essentially, in the hierarchical or ritual relations among humans, and between humans and deities, words do not exist apart from material goods and deeds in constituting "signs of recognition" (Keane 1997).

Ward Keeler (1984:109) illuminates an interesting Javanese twist on the issue by describing a Javanese term, *matur nuwun* ("saying thank you"; *hatur nuhun* in Sundanese), that traditionally was appropriate only for superiors, and during formal situations. The term had been perceived as unsuitable for social inferiors and even hurtful in personal encounters. Keeler writes that a speaker at a large ritual gathering will repeat the phrase "ceaselessly." But, traditionally, a superior does not use phrases at this formal and humbling Javanese speech level (*krama andhap*) while addressing an inferior. More significantly, Keeler suggests that rather than strengthening a bond of friendship, the use of the "thank you" phrase *matur nuwun* in response to an act of kindness "short-circuits" the good feeling that gifts or kindnesses are intended to promote. Keeler writes:

> If one says "matur nuwun" to a friend, it implies both distance and a denial of reciprocity—and one can watch his or her face fall as a result. It is telling that people do often say "matur nuwun" when . . . money changes hands, since monetary payment is also a cancellation of further implications of debt and exchange. (Ibid., 109)

Keeler astutely notes here how "thank you" words seem to cancel, or deny the promise of, future reciprocation for a gift.

When writing the acknowledgments section of my first book, I struggled for a way to avoid Indonesian words, to use local Uma terms to express my gratitude and sense of obligation for all the help I received from Central

Sulawesi people. I wrote, *"Lentora rahi kai ompi' ompi' omea dipo tahi,"* or, "I greatly miss all my siblings across the sea." That was the best I could do to say "thank you" in Uma to an indigenous people who have no local words for this expression.

George Aditjondro (2007), an Indonesian social scientist who has worked in both northern Sumatra and Central Sulawesi, notes that the absence of indigenous words for "thank you" in many areas of western and eastern Indonesia "has surprised many outsiders, Indonesians and westerners alike." But, Aditjondro agrees that "the absence of the expression 'thank you' in so many ethnic languages in this archipelago does not mean that the speakers of those languages lack a sense of gratitude." Aditjondro writes:

> Different forms of gratitude are known and practiced by these peoples, different from the Western, or, for that matter, Indonesian forms of gratitude. Basically, material and non-material forms of gifts develop a sense of gratitude among the receivers of the gifts. Or, probably, a sense or feeling of indebtedness. *Utang budi* ("a debt of character" or "a moral debt") we say in Indonesian. *Utang na loob,* in Tagalog in the Philippines.
>
> One can only be relieved from this feeling once one has responded in kind or after providing a service for the person from whom one has received the material or non-material gifts. In other words, underlying the absence of words for "thank you" is the need to maintain reciprocity, or, reciprocal ways of returning the favors we have received by providing services or goods needed by the initial givers of gifts.
>
> Reciprocity, is the key word. This reciprocity is a form of exchange, prior to the Western or Malay way of trading, which maintains the internal relations within the ethno-linguistic groups, or between the ethno-linguistic groups. (Aditjondro 2007)

What Aditjondro refers to here is what anthropologists, following the economist Karl Polanyi (1944), call "delayed reciprocity," a kind of noncommodified gift exchange process, whose worldwide variations were described and theorized in the 1920s by Marcel Mauss (1990). Aditjondro contrasts this kind of long-term reciprocity with capitalist trading (the "Western or Malay way"), which follows an alternative (and to us more familiar) "tit-for-tat" or "balanced reciprocity" exchange policy between people who have no necessary or long-term relationship once the exchange is transacted. Without a sense of mutual debt and obligation, there is not necessarily any future to a social relationship. When we hand our payment to the store cashier and she says "thank you," our interaction is completed and our relationship closed.

As it turns out, the cross-cultural puzzle of why many Indonesian languages have no synonym for *thank you* is solved not by thinking about which alternate words or behaviors would be "good enough" to replace our own verbal expressions of gratitude. Rather, it is solved by recognizing that for people engaging in delayed forms of social and economic reciprocity, words themselves are not enough to balance deeds. Additionally, compensation must occur at a later date so that a period of indebtedness prolongs, and thereby strengthens, the relationship. Thus, at the moment when a first good deed is enacted, often the best thing the recipient can do is simply acknowledge pleasure and a state of asymmetry or obligation in the "gift-exchange" relationship. Both parties then may part with a sense of indebtedness and responsibility to nurture the relationship later.

Keeler (1987) notes that the Western custom of always saying "thank you" in response to any kindness seems to Indonesians to be rather jejune, in the sense of being both unsatisfying and immature. I, too, try to explain this in my ethnography about the Tobaku region:

> Debts of significance cannot be released with a few fluffy words floated for a moment in the air. Gifts require continuation of the exchange process, not its cessation through attempted compensation. Obligations are a state of being and a means to create relations anew. (Aragon 2000:vii)

Hence, when visiting Indonesia, feel free to express thanks, gratitude, and happiness for all the kindnesses Indonesian people undoubtedly will grant you. But be prepared for gifts to change your relationship, and to unleash expectations that you will make relationships continue through future, and sometimes unexpected, forms of reciprocity.

ACKNOWLEDGMENTS

Despite the irony of verbally thanking anyone after this essay, I would be remiss not to acknowledge the work of this volume's editors and to mention the names of other scholars whose contributions have directly affected my thinking on this subject. I am grateful to Ward Keeler for contributing so much to Javanese linguistic issues; to Mohammad Thoiyibi for enlightening me further on contemporary Javanese and Indonesian usage; to George Aditjondro for documenting *thank you* and reciprocity terms across the archipelago; to Michael Martens for always graciously sharing his extensive knowledge of Uma; to Nancy Eberhardt for her insight on transforming status and wealth distribution through requests; and to Liz Coville, with whom I shared early conversations about experiences of *minta* on Sulawesi. Finally, again, I remember with happiness the many kind people I met in the Tobaku highlands (*Goe' ama!*) and feel the absence of their good-natured companionship (*Lentora rahi kai*).

NOTES

1. Austronesian languages sometimes are termed "Malayo-Polynesian."
2. At that time, no one in the region spoke English, so working through English was not an option.

3. The apostrophe at the end of many Uma words (for example, *mata'* or "unripe") represents a glottal stop, as heard in the middle of Americans' common expression of chagrin, "oh-oh."

4. My thanks to Mohammad Thoiyibi of Universitas Muhammadiyah, Surakarta, for this list.

5. Showing respect in Indonesia entails keeping one's head physically lower than the heads of others, often a challenge for tall or ignorant foreign visitors. During the Southeast Asian monetary crisis that began in late 1997, a widely published newspaper photograph of an International Monetary Fund officer, who stood towering over the seated President Suharto as he signed a new loan-restructuring agreement, was considered a national disgrace, indicative of the aging president's growing political weakness in the international community, and hence at home.

6. As Nancy Eberhardt (2006:98–99) describes, this rural Southeast Asian pattern of cheekily requesting anything exceptional that anyone else visibly has allows people with "less stuff" to initiate a hierarchical personal relationship simply through the asking. This technique compels those daring to practice conspicuous consumption to be generous and caring in exchange for public prestige. The requirement of extreme magnanimity as the price for incrementally higher social status also acts as a leveling mechanism, pushing individuals toward egalitarianism (or at least minimal differences in material wealth) and other more spiritual or community-oriented forms of prestige-seeking.

2

Toba Batak Selves: Personal, Spiritual, Collective

Andrew Causey

Who is "me"? For the Toba Bataks of North Sumatra, Indonesia, probing that question might take a lifetime. My first experience with the complexity of a Toba Batak notion of self occurred when I was listening to my carving teacher's wife, Ito, talk about one of their sons, a young man who had serious learning difficulties and who was recalcitrant and mischievous. Their son always played with children much younger than himself, or played by himself; he spent hours toying with kittens, often chatting with them. The other children liked him, but it was clear that he was unlike the others. When Ito spoke about him, she had a kindly and bemused tone, and once told me, "Yes, he is different, but we have to be careful because his spirit is very strong." I was not certain what she meant, so she gave me an example.

She told me that some years earlier he had repeatedly asked her for a red plastic toy car from the market. The only toys her eight children owned were homemade, constructed out of drinking straws or rubber bands, and Ito explained that the family could not afford such an extravagance, especially not for a young man who was too old for such things. He persisted, not begging or cajoling, but simply stating over and over that he wanted the toy car. She refused. He persisted. After a month of this, she told me, he fell out of a tree and broke his arm in such a way that required an expensive trip to a specialist. They had to ask her husband Partoho's sister to sell her only gold necklace and then they borrowed the money she received. "After that," Ito continued, "it was clear I had to buy the toy for him." Her husband Partoho nodded his head in agreement as she stated the conclusion to the story.

I did not understand the tale, and wondered if I had misunderstood something along the way. Perhaps sensing the confusion in my face, Partoho said, "That's the way it is! After that, we could see that in the days to come, we should not resist his will—we must give in to it. Such is the strength of his spirit." Still confused, I asked about the connection between the toy car and the son's fall. It seemed hard for either of them to clarify something so patently obvious, but they tried to find words to explain it. Ito said, "You see, his spirit had *menjatuhkan* him . . ." (that is, it had "felled" him—caused him to fall) "because it was not being treated as it wished; his spirit is so strong it can make him fall."

To make sense of this story, we need to try understanding Bataks' notion of "self," a complex conflation of individual personality, the particular spirit, and the collective group. Understanding how other cultures construct their notions of the self has been of interest to social scientists since the beginnings of the discipline of anthropology. In the early years of the twentieth century, scholars investigated connections between the self and society, from Freud's (1918) and Frazer's (1910) work on totemism[1] to Levy-Bruhl's on the "soul" (1966 [1922]), which unfortunately seemed to imply that people from non-Western cultures possessed only a group identity. Other scholars, such as Ruth Benedict (1934), Margaret Mead (1937), and Cora DuBois (1944), proposed that personality and culture were inextricably bound, creating a culturally shared identity called the "modal personality" (DuBois 1944:2); some critics rejected these concepts as being too mechanistic and difficult to support. Anthropological research on differential constructions and notions of the self continue, ranging from works on the philosophical explorations of "technologies of the self" (Foucault 1988) to those that introduce notions of a cyborg self that is postgender, polymorphic, and disembodied (Haraway 1991). This chapter presents information about Toba Bataks' senses of self not to support a theoretical position but rather to help illuminate some of the complexities of everyday life in this part of Southeast Asia.

The Bataks are one of Indonesia's many ethnic groups, and are divided into six subgroups, of which the Toba are among the most numerous (about two million). Although they have migrated widely across Indonesia's islands, they consider their homeland to be the North Sumatran lands that surround Lake Toba, including the island in the center of that lake, Samosir.

I studied with the Toba Bataks living near the shore of Lake Toba for a year and a half. Some of my first impressions were that they were entrepreneurial, passionate about exploring ideas, ready to laugh, and individualistic. As an American who had lived in the state of Texas for more than a decade, I found the character of many Toba Bataks to be completely familiar: they were spirited, independent, brash, opinionated, and self-possessed. The longer I lived on Samosir Island, the more I began to understand the Toba Bataks' sensibilities concerning the "self." Far from being simply "individualistic" or "independent" (as they are sometimes described by other Indonesians), I learned to see that most everyday social interaction required Batak individuals to constantly balance—you might even say juggle—a number of different notions of "self" that were constructed both by themselves and the social-cultural world around them.

I should underscore that I am a student of the Bataks' cultural life, not a spokesperson for them; just as Americans have varied conceptions of personhood, not all Bataks think or feel the same way about the topic of self.

In addition, Toba Bataks' notions are not entirely unique: there are other groups in Southeast Asia (indeed, the world) with similar or comparable conceptions of self. For example, Ward Keeler (1987) writes of the various ascetic efforts a person can undergo to strengthen the self, noting further that the potency of the self ". . . does not simply stand prior to speech, seeking expression by means of it, but rather is constructed in the play of speech itself" (37), while Michael Peletz (1996), in describing the lives of Malaysians from Negri Sembilan, notes that the notion of self is strongly relational: personhood is equally grounded in social relations, the physical body and character, and the spiritual essence (Peletz 1996:202–209). It might even be tempting to see the Bataks' conception of self as a part of a larger Austronesian[2] belief system, for similar notions of a segmented self and soul are found in the Solomon Islands (Fox 1925:240).

BATAK NOTION OF THE INDIVIDUAL (PERSONHOOD)

I discovered that Bataks consider each person to have an individual personality; in this respect, the Bataks are not unlike Westerners in holding a concept of the self. This aspect of the person is based partly on their physicality and partly on their character (I: *sifat*), and it is considered unique and particular in the world. In fact, a person's *sifat* is often spoken of in terms of their "differences" (colloquial Indonesian: *lainnya*): a person's behavioral quirks and physical imperfections are both parts of their sifat or character.[3]

Because Partoho, Ito, and I were all considered to be "humorous," we shared a sifat characteristic, but we also each differed: Partoho's sifat was creative and hard-working, Ito's was gregarious and engaging, and mine was bookish and curious. In addition, Partoho and Ito told me that my sifat tended toward plumpness while theirs tended toward wiriness and toughness. To further illustrate the notion of sifat, I recall that the Bataks I knew often brought up the term when discussing a person's appropriate soulmate (using the Indonesian word *jodoh*). Finding a *jodoh* results from a search for someone whose sifat "fits" with one's own: a person who meshes with one's thinking and opinions, who suits one's personality and heart, and who becomes a "friend for life" (Sihombing 1986:53–63). Religious training or academic education might alter a person's outlook on life, but their sifat is believed to be inherent and mostly unchangeable.

BATAK NOTION OF THE SPIRITUAL SELF: *TONDI*

The Toba Bataks I worked with are staunch Christians (mostly Lutheran, but some are Catholics or Evangelical); accordingly, religion was an ever-present topic in my conversations with them. In day-to-day behaviors and social interactions, though, one might also notice a vibrant indigenous (that is, pre-Christian) belief system working alongside the professed religion. One aspect of this older system is the belief that all persons have within themselves a "life-force" called *tondi*. Many students of the Batak culture, both insiders and outsiders, have tried to define *tondi*, using terms such as. *spirit, soul material*, or *soul-stuff*.[4] However, none of these terms seems to accurately delineate the Bataks' lived experience.

The terms *spirit* or *soul* as we tend to use them in the West do not do service to a concept often seen as a driving force that is separable and sometimes at odds with the physical human being (Pedersen 1970:26).[5] As conveyed in Ito's story of her son's fall from a tree, the material self is sometimes at the whim of this immaterial being and its desires. That the two are inextricably connected is clear to Bataks, for the boy's spirit tondi was eager to have its sensual urges satisfied with little regard to the costs that such a desire might have to the physical body.

Anicetus Sinaga, a Toba Batak scholar and Catholic bishop, says that because it comes from the realm of God, the tondi has a quality of sacredness and can seem like a deity (that is, it is prayed to or beseeched for help) (1981:102–106). However, Sinaga adds that the tondi is different from God in that it only *represents* godliness in man.[6] In essence, Sinaga regards the tondi as the "numen" or living essence of the human. Paul Pederson, who lived with the Bataks for many years, reports that they believe that when a tondi is ready to enter the material world, it picks a leaf from the heavenly world tree on which is written the fate (I: *nasib*) of a single human (1970:26). Sometime before actual birth, the tondi joins a chosen fetus, bringing the child's future with it.[7]

Throughout childhood, the tondi and the human have a tenuous relationship. The tondi might create havoc if it does not get what it wants, and may even decide to leave the body permanently if favorable conditions do not exist (a situation that, I was told, would result in death). Parents must treat young children with deference and kindness until the bond between tondi and human is dependable and firm. With this in mind, parents I knew refrained from ever hitting their children, fed them indulgently if they could, and gave in to their desires whenever possible.

As people grow older, they must be sensitive to signs that might indicate their tondis are not happy, secure, strong (hard), or "cool" (Parkin 1978:145): one's conscious self must always be aware and attentive to the tondi's desires and needs. Since I had been told that these desires were difficult to understand directly, I asked how people knew for sure what their tondis wanted. Partoho was the only one willing or able to talk about the topic in any detail. But rather than provide me with his own personal examples, he reminded me of a recent event in my own life. I had made plans to travel many hours to the south, but when the day and time came to leave, I began to feel slightly nervous about the rain-slicked roads and the possibilities of rock slides. He reminded me, "Your tondi didn't want to go, and yet you still made plans to leave. You felt conflict inside, right?" What I might have called trepidation or cold feet, my teacher framed as a conflict between my material self and my tondi. Had I been Batak and sensitive to such feelings, I would not have left then (since the departure date was flexible) and would have engaged in activities that would have strengthened my tondi.

How does one "harden" the tondi? According to Bataks who were willing to discuss this matter, the process involves constant experimentation, including, but not limited to, actively engaging in *adat* (that is, traditional values or behaviors such as participating in ritual dances or wearing the identifying fabric called *ulos*), pleasing the material-sensual body in order to entice the tondi to stay in the human body, eating foods full of potency and nutrition, and engaging in the acts of studying or learning. Toba Bataks who are particularly strong in their Christian beliefs told me that the tondi can be strengthened by doing good works or praying.

In general, I was told that Batak adults' tondis are satisfyingly embedded in them, leaving temporarily only when the person dreams or becomes ill.[8] This strong connection of spirit and material selves is not just a concern of the individual; the family and community is concerned as well, because hearty tondis create a strong society. Visiting Westerners often note that the Toba Bataks commonly shout out the traditional greeting, "HORAS!" to whomever they pass along the roads. I was told that this word roughly translates as "hard" or "firm," and is an encouragement (perhaps even a demand) that one's tondi stay strong.

When people spoke to me of the tondi (which was not a common occurrence), it was with the knowledge that it *was* them: that it was a part of their "self." Nevertheless, all spoke of the tondi's needs and urges as being somehow removed. The tondi, as I understood it, was both part of the human—a person felt the hunger or the desire in their sensual body—but also *not* a part of it. Once, when Partoho's carving business was not doing well, he told me that his tondi was craving chicken. Ito bought one (an unusual expense for the family), prepared it using an elaborate traditional recipe, and served it just to him at dinner that night. The rest of the family ate rice, vegetables, and fish as he worked methodically through the entire dish, sharing none (in a culture where sharing is essential and common), apparently aware that their well-being depended on his focused act to satisfy his tondi. In essence, the Bataks' acknowledgment of the tondi is their acceptance of a kind of *segmented* self: a self that is part material body (the character or personality), and part spiritual entity (the tondi).

BATAK NOTION OF THE GROUP (COLLECTIVE SELF)

But the Bataks' notion of self is not simply bipartite. There is additionally a sense of self that is part of a collectivity. For the Bataks, the individual is always part of a group: family, peer group, profession, clan, ethnicity, and nation. As we will see, many authors have noted that Bataks often consider themselves as members of the society *before* they see themselves as individuals.

To fully appreciate this, we must realize that for the Batak, as for many other Indonesian groups, "tradition" (*adat*) is paramount. The moral and legal code handed down by the ancestors, called *adat,* outlines the appropriate behavior for *everything* from the sale of land to proper behavior toward elders. Adat is sacred, and the ways to enact it properly are taught from childhood.[9] Everyone who wants a contented tondi and blessings from the ancestors adheres to constraints of the adat, and everyone identifies with it personally. To reject the adat rules or the code is to divorce oneself from the group and to risk supernatural sanctions (Ross 1962:5).

Arne Bendtz (1986:26), a scholar of Batak culture, noted that a principle concept for the Bataks is that humans are esteemed beings endowed with the rights to respect and goodwill of each other, of nature, of supra-human powers, and of the supreme deity. To balance this individualism, Bendtz maintains that the individual "does not have a personal life apart from the collective life of the clan . . . loyalty to the community is therefore absolute" (ibid). A Batak *is* the collective, and so the love of the community is love of self; they are not separable. One's actions are guided by the community's laws and regulations, and one supports them as an expression of "self." Furthermore, one's sense of self is inextricably bound to one's family, particularly the patriline clan known as the *marga.*

The Bataks' marga society consists of three conceptual groups: (1) those who share your clan name (*dongan sabutuha,* translated roughly as "womb sharers," with whom marriage is impossible because it is considered incestuous); (2) those to whom your clan provides daughters as wives (*boru*), and who are considered to be slightly inferior socially; and (3) those from whom your clan accepts daughters as wives (*hulahula*), and who are considered to be socially superior.[10] These relationships are eternal, and cut across geographic distance and socioeconomic class; one may never marry dongan sabutuha, no matter how distant the actual ancestral connection is; one may always expect a favor from the boru; and one must always respect the hulahula.

The Bataks call this vital social arrangement *Dalihan na Tolu* ('the Three Hearth-stones," referring to the fact that three stones are necessary to hold up the pot in the kitchen firepit), and it is kept very much alive in everyday life. For example, Partoho was obligated to teach a distant cousin of his wife how to carve, despite the fact that the young man had very little real interest and even less talent. The erstwhile student chipped Partoho's best carving knives and wasted wood, but the teacher had to remain calm and respectful because the cousin was a member of his hulahula.[11]

In the village or town, everyone knows their marga relationship with everyone else, but when a Batak individual goes beyond the homeland, the situation can become complex. Because two Batak strangers must clarify their relationship before they can engage socially, the first question they ask of each other is *Margana aha do hamu?* ('What's your marga name?"). Once the name is known, they will know whether they will deal with the new acquaintance as a "brother," a social inferior, or someone to whom due deference must be shown.[12] Despite the fact that Bataks might want to portray themselves as unique individuals, and despite anything their tondi might urge them to do, the responsibility of a self as a member of the marga collective takes precedence; one must always act in accordance with the appropriate behaviors set out in the adat rules.

To make matters of identity even more complicated, Bataks, like many other Indonesians, tend to perceive others in their social world as divided into two different kinds of "we." In the Indonesian language, there are two words for *we*: *kita* and *kami* (in Toba Batak, the terms are *hita* and *hami*). Kita/ hita is the form that includes all (self and all others), and is sometimes referred to as the "collective we" or "we-inclusive." This is the term one would use to say, "In the end, we all must die." The term kami/hami expresses the *we* that assumes there is some Other that is excluded. What is interesting about the kami/hami grammatical formation is that it constructs the notion of *we* as a single entity, precisely because it is distinguished from *others*. The use of this construction requires that the speaker suppress the notion of a solitary self. As the Indonesian psychologist and philosopher Fuad Hassan says,

> It is essential for each individual sharing the *kami*-world to reduce his individuality and maintain a maximum solidarity with the other constituents in it. This is necessary for the sake of positioning *kami* against those outside it. The strength or quality of the feelings of solidarity among individuals constituting a *kami*-mode of togetherness depends very much on the readiness of each individual to inhibit or reduce his subjectivity. (1975:24)

In this way, the "self" is no longer the individual person, but rather the particular group as defined in opposition to all outsiders.

The nuclear family is the primary collective, and it is not uncommon to hear individuals of a family present their own personal opinions or observations by using the pronoun kami/hami (collective *we*) rather than the more accurate *saya* (meaning *I*). In most of my chats with Partoho and Ito, they used the term kami/hami, whether they were saying "I [along with my group] already ate," or "We [the family] are strong in our religious beliefs." This notion of a collective we/I emerged most clearly for me when I tried to gather information by means of a written questionnaire: I provided exactly enough forms for each family member to complete, and upon retrieving the forms, would get the same number returned . . . and these would contain precisely the same responses, carefully written out separately by each parent and each child.

FINDING BALANCE (THREE SELVES JOINED)

How can a Batak individual manage to get through a day if all these "selves" are in constant competition? Many Bataks clearly give little thought to this issue: instead, they try to satisfy their bodily cravings and spiritual needs the best they can, and follow the habits of cultural tradition in doing so. Conflicts of self usually arise only for those people who seek change in their lives, or who choose to behave in ways not ordinarily sanctioned by the traditional culture.

One of my Batak friends, a man of great exuberances and intense melancholies, told me that his true desire in life had been to write novels and short stories. As a youth, he completed several such stories for publication, and had begun sketching out a novel. I asked him what happened to his dream. He replied that his passion to write (the purview of the tondi) was thwarted by his fear of correction and rejection (feelings that are the purview of his more practical personality). This situation had created a huge conflict inside him, something that manifested itself as aimlessness and an urge to gamble. He left all his plans behind when he married and had his first child, since his most pressing obligations were now to his family. He told me that the "*stres*" (Indonesian for the English loanword *stress*) of trying to balance his desires, fears, and obligations to family and tradition were almost too much to take. Some Bataks leave the homeland to escape these pressures, but he decided to raise a family while he was still young. "Later," he said, "when I am old, maybe my fears will go away and let me feed my tondi." When I encountered him again several years later, he had not yet started to write his stories, but had managed to make a small fortune on a winning lottery ticket.

CONCLUSIONS

Are we now better able to answer the question "Who is 'me'?" Do we have, in the West, single solitary selves, inalienable from the physical body of our persons?[13] Or are we more like the Bataks, who believe that the self is segmented, separable, and situated in different particular social contexts?[14] Are you simply "me," or do you experience your self as one that always knows when it is a child, when a sibling, a friend, a stranger—whether it is motivated by its cravings or its obligations? Does it matter if that self is abroad, at home, or in a dream? The more you think about examples from your own life, the more you will understand the complexity of the simple question posed at the start.

In this chapter, you have been introduced to aspects of the Toba Bataks' perceptions of the sense of self as a complex amalgam of three intertwined parts, a kind of social braid: the personal character, the integrated spiritual entity, and the individual-as-collective. In addition, you have seen how none of the three takes necessary preference over the others, and none is fully in control of the others. While the scenarios presented here may imply that the three parts are constantly synchronized, this is not true. The complex interactions they share are not precisely defined nor easily constructed, and many Bataks find that their lives unfold as a constant struggle to find balance between them. They find, as many of us do in the West, that the working of one part of the self is always contingent on the interactions and contexts of the other parts.

Perhaps because Toba Bataks are attentive to the different parts of the self, they are able to face the adversities of life through a creative ability to draw on the strengths of each one of the parts (the personality/character, the spiritual tondi, the adat-bound collective), and in doing so both maintain the integration of them in the pursuit of a successful and long life. In thinking about the Toba Bataks' complex notion of self as presented here, we realize that perhaps it is not all that different from our own. An important difference may be their conscientious alertness to keep the needs of themselves always in balance with that of their social group, an alertness we in the West might learn to better develop.

NOTES

1. Totemism was for many years in the early twentieth century a foundational trope in the field, quickly losing ground when scholars such as Goldenweiser (1910) began to show the limits of the term's use; see also Levi-Strauss (1963).

2. Austronesian is a language family that stretches from the island of Oceania to the east as far west as Madagascar, centering around the Malay peninsula and the archipelagos of Indonesia and Philippines (Bellwood 1997:3).

3. This is term that defies precise translation into English. Stevens and Schmidgall-Tellings, in their recent Indonesian-English dictionary, gloss the word as "1. Appearance, look. 2. nature, innate character, disposition" (2004); Echols and Shadily (1989) add to this the definition "identifying feature," while E. Pino and T. Wittermanns (1955) gloss the word as "character, nature; quality, mark, feature."

4. Niessen 1985:121, Parkin 1978:145, Pedersen 1970:25, Sibeth 1991:66, Sinaga 1981:103, Tobing 1994:97.

5. Adams (1993:57) describes a similar kind of spirit/soul notion among the Sa'dan Toraja that is referred to as sumanga'.

6. It is important to note that not all Bataks agree about how to interpret the nature of the tondi: Tobing (1994:107), says the tondi is, in fact, God in man.

7. The Bataks with whom I interacted did not seem to see a conflict in this explanation of an individual's future with that of the Christian religion that avers that a person's life is not preordained. Both Sinaga (1981) and Parkin (1978) discuss this syncretic or accommodating nature of Toba Batak Christianity in great detail.

8. Adams (1993:58) describes the Sa'dan Toraja's similar belief in bombo, the spirit essence of people who are "soon-to-die," which wander away from the corporal self.

9. Similarly, Ross says, "The *adat* is, among other things, a codification of Batak social order. . . . It tells him how he is to behave toward others and what behavior to expect on the part of others toward him. The social order is an important aspect of the environment from which the individual abstracts his sense of ego identity in the course of his life experiences . . ." (1962:32), continuing on to say, "Instead of being based on the substance of the relationship with others, the individual's security is bound up in the social structure, and since *adat* equals structure, the *adat* must be defended and maintained as a vital part of the individual's sense of identity" (ibid).

10. See S. A. Niessen 1985 and J. C. Vergouwen 1964 for more information on Batak *margas*.

11. This story is told in more detail in Causey 2003:106.

12. George Sherman notes that the common Batak saying, "Revere wife-givers; request earnestly from wife-receivers," is not usually actualized outside the homeland, but nevertheless notes that knowing one's *marga* relationship with another makes it easy to engage socially (1990:94).

13. If so, then why has "identity theft" become so much more prevalent with improved computer technologies and the advent of the Internet? Why do people who engage in role-playing computer games create different identities or "avatars" for themselves?

14. The discipline Cultural Studies uses the phrases "situated subjectivity," "situated subject position," and "subjectivization" for the notion that any particular self in the world is partly defined (or "constructed") by the discourses in which it participates within the social and environmental contexts that surrounds it. See for example, Foucault 2002 (1973).

3

Poverty and Merit:
Mobile Persons in Laos
Holly High

When I conducted sixteen months of fieldwork in a poor, rural village in
Laos, I was required to obtain official permission from the central government. Before fieldwork began I spent more than a year negotiating this with
administrators in Vientiane, and I was resident there for much of that time.
When I finally received permission, it came in the form of a stamped and
signed letter. I was then free to move on to my fieldsite: the letter did not
stipulate where this would be, but I chose the southern reaches of the Mekong River, near the border with Cambodia and Thailand. The letter carried enough authority to allow me to pass from the national level of bureaucracy through the provincial level to the district level with relative ease. At
the district level, however, the letter lost some of its force. In the capital of
Munlapamook district I found that I had to negotiate afresh with the district authorities for permission to proceed to an outlying village. This took
two weeks. During this time, I stayed in the care of the staff of the district
education office. These two weeks were marked by a series of brief meetings
with district leaders concerning my research plans, and long, directionless
days filled with casual conversations with junior office staff. The office squatted in a muddy field of overgrown grass on which cows grazed, their bells
clanging. The office had no electricity and was too hot for comfort, so staff
gathered on a wide bench under an old tree outside for long streams of conversation, banter, and debate. After my first formal but uninformative five-
minute-long meeting with the office head, I was invited over to the bench.
"Oh you're beautiful," a chorus immediately began. Peng, a female staffer,
was held up for comparison. "Hold your arm against hers," a man insisted,
so we could compare the color of our skins. "Oh you are very black," the
man told Peng. Peng removed her arm very quickly. "I'm not beautiful!" she
exclaimed, smiling; "I am so black!"
    "Black is not beautiful," the man told me.
    "Holly, what about him?" Peng motioned toward the man, "Would you
take him as a boyfriend? He's not beautiful. He's very black." The group
laughed at Peng's rejoinder. "Not beautiful, not beautiful," they chorused.

I marveled at their carefree banter about such topics—race, beauty, love. These topics were held in such reverence in the cultural milieu of urban Australia, from which I had come. I felt a jolt of dissonance when this banter began: I had expected to discuss my research or perhaps the weather, but instead I found that it was my physical characteristics that were the topic of preferred conversation. In contrast to the office staffs' relaxed and playful mood, I was immediately awkward. I felt uncomfortable in my own skin as I realized, suddenly, that my body did not seem to mean to others what it meant for me. Those words, *white* and *black*, denoted *race* for me, and the topic of race had long since been dropped from everyday polite conversation in Australia. Educated, urban Australia no longer talked openly about difference in terms of "black" or "white." There, it is considered reasonably polite to ask "what nationality are you?" but certainly not "what race are you?" Difference is elaborated on in terms of "cultural" difference: there has been a proliferation of "multicultural" festivals and fairs, where food and dance form the acceptable and required modes of expressing difference, each national culture displayed in its distinct, cordoned-off stalls and performances. Race, however, is unmentionable. The very term—along with the words *white* and *black*—now evokes a visceral embarrassment, and the use of such words has been "carefully suppressed among modern, cosmopolitan citizens" (Cowlishaw 2004:13). In this milieu it would be uncouth in the extreme, racist even, to suggest that white was beautiful, and black not. In one of the most famous statements against racism, Martin Luther King expressed his dream that people "not be judged by the color of their skin but by the content of their character." In Dr. King's statement, there is a strong correlation between race and body—race is associated with the physical nature one is granted at birth, and over which one is thought to be effectively powerless. In this view, race is only skin deep, an accident of birth, not an indicator of a person's worth. Race, then, is bodily, natural, and not a useful indicator of achievement. The banter at the office confronted these sensibilities. The staff bluntly held that white skin was beautiful, black was not, and that such matters, far from unmentionable, were the subject of comparison, comment, and ridicule.

Peng was assigned as my friend and companion for my stay in the district capital, and shared my lodgings with me. That night in our rooms, she was happily rummaging through my possessions, trying on my clothes and cosmetics with an absorbed but lighthearted curiosity. My collection of sunscreens, moisturizers, and skin care products evoked particular interest. "What is this cream for?" she asked of each one, before applying a little. "For my eyes," "to make my skin soft," and "to stop the sun from burning me," I replied to her queries.

"Oh," came Peng's satisfied reply. "This is why your skin is so white and beautiful. You can afford to buy all of these creams and stay inside all day. You have money."

"My skin is white because my parents' skin is white," I replied. I was taken aback at the implication that my skin was the result of manufacture rather than nature. I felt a surprising surge of resentment at the realization that what I had taken to be bodily and given, my natural "self," was being perceived here as the result of deliberate achievement and manipulation.

"You wait until you have lived in Laos for one year," said Peng, smirking. "You will be as black as me. Maybe more black, because you are going out to live in the countryside with the very poor people. If you harvest rice, you will be black."

Peng's use of *black* and *white* here diverged from my own. Both Lao and Australian understandings of skin admit the notion that pigmentation can change with exposure to the sun and elements. And both also admit that the range of pigmentation that can be achieved by different people is strongly influenced by inherited characteristics. But there the similarities end. *Black* and *white* in Australia principally denote concepts of race, viewed as immutable, natural, and ascribed at birth. In Peng's usage, whiteness and blackness were variables, open to manipulation. And the key method of manipulation was wealth. Thus the color of skin was a particularly good indicator of relative wealth and current fortunes of the skin's inhabitant, and was subject to much comment and discussion.

Later, when I had established myself in a poor rural village to conduct long-term fieldwork, I observed that discussions of skin pigmentation in relation to relative wealth were common. For instance, Lot, a friend I made in my eventual fieldsite, echoed Peng's sentiment. She said:

Rural people are not beautiful: they are in the weather all the time, they come back black. People in the city, they are white, they are beautiful. They can look after their bodies, they have powder and lipstick and creams to wear. There's no shortage of things to buy to make yourself beautiful. All those things on Thai TV[1]—things to make your skin white and your hair black. Those people on Thai TV are beautiful. They have noses like yours—foreign noses. They all get operations on their noses to look like that. Those people have money.

Peng and Lot understood white skin as emerging from moneyed, urban lifestyles. Black skin, in contrast, was associated with poverty and rural lifestyles. The work of transplanting and harvesting rice is often referred to, and associated with causing black skin. Rural women comment on the lack of ability to afford or to find access to cosmetics such as effective whitening creams, moisturizers, and hair tonics to combat the effects of exposure to weather. The rural woman's gait—barefooted or in flip-flops, feet splayed and strides long and fast—is noticeably distinct from the urban middle-class woman's gait—hobbled and muted in ungainly platform or heeled shoes. Rural women's feet become flattened and hard against the soil of their rice paddies. Rural hands become rough and strong, adept with machete and hoe. Rural women's mouths are stained red with betel nut, and their teeth are stained black. Rural impoverished life writes itself onto the physical being of these women. They are, in Bourdieu's term, "branded" (Bourdieu 1984:178). Furthermore, exposure to illness is thought to leave its mark on poor bodies. Fevers, malaises, and maladies often go without a firm diagnosis and may receive only rudimentary treatment. When I brought a Western magazine to the rural village where I eventually worked, I asked one woman if she thought the pictures of the models were beautiful. "Of course they are beautiful," she said. "They have never been injured or had a fever; never." Such a categorical statement is, of course, unlikely to be accurate, but it does highlight the perception that this woman held of poverty as very much a physical experience that leaves traces on the body, especially ones that detract from beauty.

Rural impoverished women experience their poverty, among other things, as a physical state, as a particular body. As one rural woman commented:

> Rural people are small, thin, dark, not beautiful. In the city, they are robust, white . . . they have soap and other things to look after themselves. The little children have white shirts and shoes for school. Here the children have no shoes, they are dirty.

Wealth, on the other hand, is explicitly thought to produce beauty. The association of beauty with wealth and bounty pervades rural discourse. A bumper rice crop is described as *ngaam* (beautiful). Fields known to be fertile are described as ngaam. Hardy and fruitful vegetable strains are ngaam. This wide use of the term ngaam to describe not only beauty but bounty reinforces the aesthetics of wealth: bounty is beautiful, and poverty is not. The experience of poverty, then, is the experience of lacking beauty. Meew, sitting in the shade of her rural homestead, said, "I want beautiful things. But I don't see beauty here."

It should come as no surprise, then, that aspirations and wealth are often directed toward aesthetics and beauty, especially of the body. Small luxurious items crowd the shelves of regional stores, urban markets, and the baskets of traveling vendors—skin whitening creams, nail polish, lipstick, and powder. At 1,000 to 15,000 kip (0.1–1.5 USD) each, these miniature items offer a popular choice for the expenditure of small sums of disposable income. More expensive items, such as quality silk *sin* (Lao skirts), denim skirts and jackets, and baseball caps, are also admired. When a young woman in a nearby market town committed suicide, rumor had it that she had been driven to despair when she was unable to obtain one of the new caps that had appeared in the markets. This rumor struck resonances with the experience of poverty as frustrated desire for personal adornments and transformations.

Gold jewelry—either real or *falang* (foreign, fake)—is a coveted investment for larger sums of money. A young rural woman, Deeng, described her aspirations to me in these terms: "I want to be covered in gold—gold on every part of my body, my throat, my ears, my arms, my waist, in my hair. I like it so much." While its resale value is an important factor in the desire for gold, so is its social, cosmetic value. Deeng continued:

> If I have lots of money, lots of gold, I will have a boyfriend, and friends. Holly, if you were Lao, and poor like me, you would be alone like me too. Lao people don't like people who are poor. If you don't have money, you don't have friends, and you don't have boyfriends.

Deeng's comments confirm the intimate link between body, poverty, and social relations. Deeng's poverty was experienced as a physical shame, associated with a sense of social exclusion. At the approach of the village festival, Deeng mused: "The festival will be fun, won't it? But I won't dance. I don't have anything to wear, I don't have a *sin* (skirt) or a beautiful shirt. I don't have any gold. I'm too shy to go." The experience of poverty is a very personal one. It is an experience of shame in one's appearance and limited means, mingled with a desire for the transformation of one's physical and social status. Deeng, in fact, did not attend this festival. Instead, she traveled to a location where she could take up paid employment. When I saw her again several months later, I noted the small but important transformations that she had effected: she owned a brand-name jacket, platform shoes, and gold earrings. Her efforts at self-transformation through labor and consumption were indicators of the malleability that she perceived in her selfhood.

Houses are also indicative of this malleability in Lao notions of the self. In Laos, a house is the largest investment made by most rural residents, and is the center of most people's aspirations. Saving for house construction takes years, and the future home owner often accumulates materials such as timber and iron in small units whenever cash or items become available. If you ask a rural Lao person if his or her home is finished, she will in all likelihood answer *boor leew* ("not yet"). Most people experience their houses as continually unfinished projects, with more improvements and additions constantly planned. These desires may seem to contradict the aspirations for pale skin, gold, and clothing explored above, as they are somewhat more akin to familiar notions of practical or sensible investments. However, what all these aspirations have in common is their stubbornly personal nature, as they represent a constant project of self-improvement. Green has noted a similar emphasis on building a personal house in Tanzania. Green links the desire for a house to a notion of "personal development" based on "recognition of the potentiality of individual agency in bringing about social transformation" (2000:68). Green points out that such a personal, agency-focused view of development stands at odds with state development policies and the "participatory" community development interventions of foreign NGOs and donors, which draw on assumptions about "'traditional' collectivist values of rural African communities" (2000:81). The disparity, as Green has noted, is between the intensely personal and the resolutely generalizing.

Skin is likewise intensely personal. Rather than emphasizing the immutable characteristics of skin, everyday Lao usages of blackness and whiteness emphasize the capacity for transformation of the self. As the months of my fieldwork passed, my own body changed and I become used to the way conversations in the field would gravitate to take note of these changes. The director from the district education office shook his head when he saw me after six months, saying, "You are so black. You are not beautiful anymore." Small changes in skin color often escape notice (or at least comment, especially negative comment) in Australia but they do not in Laos, for these are the bodily indicators that Lao people read to gauge the current fortunes of an individual as he or she moves either upward or downward in the "cosmic hierarchy." In this milieu, poverty is intensely personal, to the point of being "branded" onto the bodily person. But this "branding" is viewed as mutable: skins are thought to be open to manipulation and are eminently readable indicators of a person's current fortune. This reflects a widely held view that social status, too, is open to manipulation through personal effort. White skin and wealth alike are held to be the result of achievement rather than ascription. To understand this agentive notion of wealth and poverty, it is worth tracing out more clearly how these have been understood in relation to the everyday practice of Lao Theravada Buddhism.

Bun is a central concept in everyday rural Lao Buddhist belief and practice. Translated as "merit," it refers to the benefits that accrue to individuals through their performance of good deeds. Buddhism as a daily belief system exhorts people to "Be merit mobile!" (Kirsch 1977:247). Hanks (see chapter 7) has described "the cosmic hierarchy" (1962:1248) where people find themselves enmeshed in a highly stratified social order. Yet "only the stations are fixed, while the metamorphosing individual beings rise and fall in the hierarchy" (1962:1248). One indicator of the current position of an individual on the hierarchy of relative suffering is wealth: wealth is indicative of past virtue, in this life or in past lives. Hanks notes that the notion of the meritorious poor of Christendom is noticeably missing: Buddhist tales of great merit tell of princes who give away their kingdoms, rather than beggars who gave their last coin (ibid.). In this conception of suffering, poverty is not valued and the poor are not held as particularly virtuous. Buddhism encourages people to endeavor to escape poverty and improve their circumstances more generally by accruing further merit.

In everyday practice in rural Laos, Buddhism was thought to teach that poor people can transform their status through hard work and the accumulation of merit. One elderly man provided a succinct account: "Buddhism tells us to work hard and accumulate wealth. It tells us to give part to monks who observe the precepts, and to give part to the poor. It valorizes diligence and ability to earn money." For the laity, one of the most effective ways of accumulating merit is through religious offerings. This can take the form of daily offering of food to the monks, major gifts of robes or other useful items during festivals, or grand donations to sponsor temple buildings or other decorative structures. Much like Lao homes, Lao temples are in a seemingly constant state of construction and improvement as donations and subscriptions are raised, new structures planned, and old structures repaired. Spiro (1966) and Moerman (1966) suggest that such religious donation is squarely aimed at generating future wealth. In a virtuous circle, then, wealth can beget wealth through the mechanism of merit. Yoneo Ishii suggested that monks here serve as "fields of merit," analogous to a rice field, where religious donations can be implanted with the expectation of future harvest (1986:13–20). Large donations are rarely anonymous: the names of major donors are often inscribed on signs in the temple grounds and read out at festivals and meetings. It is wealth that enables major donations, so in this sense wealth becomes a tangible and very public sign of moral virtue.

In the rural village where I worked, however, residents recognize that such an avaricious approach to donation is fraught with ambiguities. When discussing this topic, a young man told me the following story:

> A woman went to donate at a temple. After she made her donations, she said to the monk, "Give me merit. I want my merit. I'm not leaving until you give me merit"—the woman wanted an item that would be merit, something she could take back home with her.
>
> Of course the monk had nothing to give her, as we all know that merit is not an object and cannot be bought or given. But the woman would not be dissuaded. She demanded merit. She would not leave until the monk gave her something. So the monk turned his back on her and furtively picked his nose, and made a small wad of snot. Turning back to the woman, he presented her with the wad.
>
> The woman was satisfied at last, and turned for home. She was afraid to put the merit in her boat, lest it be lost. So, she placed it in her mouth. "How salty the monk's merit is! How delicious!" she exclaimed.

Those listening to this story started to laugh at this moment. Their laughter seems to have arisen from an ironic recognition of the everyday tension in merit-making: many people report that when they make religious donations, they do so with the hope that their act will bring them wealth and other positive outcomes, in this and the next life. Yet, at the same time, there is a recognition that official doctrine teaches that merit is not an object that can be "bought" with religious donations. In the story above, it is clear that grasping after merit is still grasping, and it is not virtuous: the woman appeared greedy and thus ridiculous. While the benefits of religious donation are recognized and desired, there is a concurrent recognition that in official doctrine, "Craving destroys the merit of any action and so conformity to the *dhammic* code for the sake of gain is self-defeating" (Sizemore and Swearer 1990:4). The storyteller, Cit, concluded this story by assuring me that in order to attain wealth it was necessary to work hard and be clever. Thus, while merit is seen as a factor in creating wealth, both wealth and merit are augmented by efforts of the individual.

I asked a young woman, a rice farmer with relatively little income but who had a sufficient supply of rice, if lack of merit could be a cause of poverty. Her reply was, "That's what the old people say." She herself did not discount this view, but her own discussions of poverty centered on tangible factors, such as few or poor fields, and laziness. It is common in rural Laos, even among the poor themselves, to depict the poor as lazy or stupid. One man said, "Poor people don't work when the rain falls. They just eat and sleep. People who 'have' [*mii*] work continuously." Another commented, "Poor people are lazy and don't like to work. They are not honest, and they do not follow the precepts of Buddhism." One farmer expressed impatience with my sympathy for the poor, explaining that his poorer neighbors didn't plant all their fields, did not try hard enough to find money, and used it frivolously when they had it. Poor people were routinely described as incompetent at farming rice, and too stupid to improve their lives.

This view of individuals as responsible for the circumstances in which they find themselves has a startlingly wide application. Illnesses were conceived often in terms of careless actions. When I fell ill with a fever, the people who came to visit me made polite conversation by speculating on what it was that I personally had done to create the illness. It was suggested that the fried bananas I ate in the market the day before had caused it. "Don't eat just anything!" one admonished. Other suggestions were that I had gotten too much sun, that I had not eaten enough rice, and that I had walked around too much. My own theories were that I had caught a virus from the five-year-old who lived in the same house as me, as he too was sick, or that my immune system was simply not used to the environment that I was being exposed to. Abstract ideas about germs, viruses, and immune systems failed to gain traction with my Lao interlocutors, however. They preferred to speculate on specific examples of my characteristics, activities, and decisions as the source of the illness. Likewise, in discussing poverty it was often the characteristics and past actions of the person involved that were viewed as decisive in their fortunes.

These dispositional explanations of poverty were discomforting for an Australian more accustomed to hearing explanations that assiduously avoid "blaming the victim." However, dispositional explanations also maintain the hope that people will be able to improve their own lot. In popular dis-

cussions of wealth and poverty in Laos, it is maintained that hard work, diligence, and intelligence can change one's fortunes from poverty to wealth,
and this resonates with the Buddhist doctrine "Work out your own salvation with diligence" (Moerman 1966:137). Thus, poverty may be an indicator
of poor merit and a flawed personality, but both merit and personal disposition are held to be open to improvement if one makes personal efforts to
change things.

While these dispositional explanations posit a universe of "just deserts,"
they coexist with circumstantial explanations. The experience of being able
to create merit is simultaneously the experience of carrying residual merit
from previous lives and actions. While this accumulated merit is conceptu-
alized as resulting from past personal actions, it is experienced largely as
part of the arbitrary context in which people must operate. Similarly, residents of my fieldsite complained about many circumstances beyond their
control that were felt to cause poverty: lack of credit, a poor exchange rate,
difficulty in accessing markets, no roads, no electricity, and natural disas-
ters. Persons born to poor families pointed to a lack of fields, or poor fields,
or no money to fund education or migration to find work. While such factors
might be recognized abstractly as resulting from one's previous actions mediated through merit, in daily life they were experienced as circumstances
beyond one's control.

Yet, even in discussing their struggle with such circumstances beyond
their control, the emphasis on personal effort was striking. One man explained to me his efforts to reduce his own poverty. He and his wife had
spent the previous week boiling alcohol produced from their rice crop. Each
morning they had risen at 4 AM to stoke fires and drain clear distilled liquid. The following week they had used more of their rice crop to produce
rice noodles. This involved arduous physical labor in grinding the rice on
a heavy hand-turned stone mill, boiling the mixture over hot fires, sun-
drying it into flat sheets, and then slicing these into strings. The couple then
spent a day traveling up river, stopping at each village to sell the dried noodles and rice whiskey. Before they left, the husband said that he hoped to
raise 500,000 kip (50 USD). On their return, he reported that they had raised
only 200,000. They had sold almost all their produce, but people had mostly
bought it on credit. "The people here have no money: it is hard to find money.
Even the people on the mainland who open shops and become traders don't
really have money: they are all in debt to the city traders. It is so hard to
find money here," he explained. And it was not just that money was hard
to find: it was also all too easy to spend, as expenses continually arose. In
particular, he noted the onerous cost of paying for school. These costs were
recurring, and he summed up the situation by stating *haa ngern bor than say*
(I make money but not before I spend it). Personal effort and diligence—
including the willingness to engage in repetitive, heavy physical labor—

mingled with an acknowledgment that even such diligence had only the limited possibility of delivering wealth, due to wider economic and state-driven contexts.

The theme recurs again and again—in personal poverty-reduction efforts, in ideas about skin color, in improving one's store of Buddhist merit, health, social status, and wealth—with all of these, the primary response is manipulation through personal effort. Poverty is perceived in Laos as emerging from both circumstantial and dispositional factors. Circumstantial factors are those that are beyond the control of the individual (the circumstances in which people find themselves), while dispositional features are the province of the individual (such as their characteristics, aptitudes, and skills). This mix of circumstantial and dispositional factors echoes the "social order" identified by Hanks (chapter 7), in which people find themselves inserted into a "cosmic hierarchy" of fixed stations but nonetheless perceive of their position in this hierarchy as open to change and manipulation, depending on circumstances and personal effort. Thus, despite the seemingly intransigent circumstantial factors that perpetuate poverty in Laos, the experience of this poverty is one of contingency, causing people to understand their status, and indeed their very bodily person, as malleable.

NOTE

1. Thai television is easily accessible and popular in Laos. The two countries share a long border (mostly along the Mekong River), the languages are very similar, and there are overlaps of religion and aesthetics as well. While domestic Lao television channels exist, they are unpopular in comparison to Thai broadcasts. It is worth noting that Chinese, Vietnamese, and Korean programs are increasingly popular as well, many of them dubbed in Thai.

4

A Question of Identity: Different Ways of Being Malay and Muslim in Malaysia

Judith Nagata

For more than two millennia, Island Southeast Asia, which is connected as much by sea as by land, has been open to migration and trade across and beyond the region. It has shared connections with China, South Asia, the Near East and, more recently, Europe. The original populations were sparse and geographically mobile, augmented by itinerant merchants and bearers of new religions, many of whom settled and intermarried locally. Contacts with outside cultures, openness to immigration, and social fluidity have been features of this part of Southeast Asia almost until the present, when the emergence of colonial and later, independent national states began to limit these flows.

During the first millennium, the region was in continuous contact with South Asia. The connections facilitated trade, migration, and early forms of Hindu-Buddhist religion, some of whose elements survive today. Many immigrant Indian merchants married locally, and several Hindu-Buddhist kingdoms were founded, including Srivijaya (in present-day Sumatra), whose leaders presided over an expanded political and economic domain. Traders arrived from different parts of India, speaking various languages of the sub-continent: language labels then often became social identity labels (Tamils, Bengalis, Gujeratis, Parsees). From the seventh century CE, the common trading language of this maritime area was Malay (Andaya 2001; 2008), whose vocabulary borrows heavily from Sanskrit and other Indian languages. That many of these loanwords concern trade, social, ceremonial, royal, and religious life, suggests the major domains of contact and influence: to this day, the Malay term for *religion* is an Indian word, *agama* (even for Islam) while modern Malaysian politicians use Indian honorifics such as the title, *Sri*.

As Malay became the commercial lingua franca in ports around South and Southeast Asia, its speakers became known as Malays. Early records, however, reveal that Malay was just an international working language. Malay speakers hailed from a wide area of disparate communities who had their own local languages and secondary identities (Andaya 2001; 2008). Being "Malay" had very little to do with what today are labeled "ethnicity," "race," or a "people." Thus, a trader born on the island of Bawean (off Java's east coast), whose family spoke Boyanese, might have had Buginese and Iban trading partners. He might have settled and married in the kingdom of Johore (in the southern part of modern Malaysia), where he regularly did business with Tamil Indians, and he would typically use Malay to speak to all these varied individuals. Although outsiders would have seen him as Malay, when family and professional solidarity required, this same trader could also select other identities such as Bugis or Baweanese. Likewise, a Malabari Indian merchant might have settled and married a woman from an Acehnese community in North Sumatra, and might have used the Malay lingua franca for business; still, he could have identified himself by any of these other labels, depending on expedience. To represent Malays as a "people" on the strength of a common language alone is to ignore these complexities. The practice of adjusting identity situationally, according to family roots, business needs, place of birth, or origin, is in fact something that most people do everywhere, not just in Southeast Asia, usually unconsciously and without intent to deceive. Most people have a repertoire of different roles or identities appropriate to different reference groups or significant others, from Malays to "hyphenated" Americans. Limits to this fluidity were typically imposed by the rules of national states, and happened when European colonists and subsequently independent nations (such as Indonesia and Malaysia) created boundaries to migration, and substituted their own principles for classifying and administering their populations as ethnic, racial, or religious groups.

In the twelfth and thirteenth centuries, Muslim merchants began to arrive from Arabia and Yemen. Some of the newcomers had already established businesses and families en route, in Indian ports where they had lived for several generations. The merchants were multilingual and multicultural, having roots both in South Asia and Arabia. On their arrival to Southeast Asia, they repeated the processes followed by their Indian antecedents: they founded new families and, as many merchants were polygynous, they often had wives and families in different ports. Abdullah Munshi, a nineteenth-century colonial translator in Malacca (now Malaysia), wrote an autobiography in which he chronicles his descent from a Yemeni Arab who migrated to India and married a Tamil (Hill, trans: 1970:24). This man's son thereafter moved to Malacca via Aceh, where he married a woman with a Malay-Indian father and Malay mother, Abdullah's parents. Abdullah himself was fluent in several languages, including Tamil, Arabic, Malay, and English, and colonial authorities referred to him as a "Native Malayan scholar" (ibid).

GEOGRAPHICAL MOBILITY AND KINSHIP

Not all migration was long distance or by sea. Shifting cultivators were accustomed to moving in search of new land, which was abundant in this region. There were few political barriers to migration. Like the maritime traders, people frequently pulled up roots, settling in or founding communities elsewhere. Mobility was made possible by the fact that many Southeast Asian kinship boundaries are vaguely defined, fading out on both maternal and paternal sides from close to distant, "like the smell of a mango tree" (*bau bau bacang*). Beyond the immediate family, Malay kinship is not based on biology or blood and there are no group surnames: everyone is either "son of" or "daughter of" their father, and genealogies rarely go further. Kinship terms are used strategically for those with whom there is a need to cooperate or have a relationship. Kinship can be created by fiction, adoption, or marriage, including with foreigners and immigrants, where physical traits seem not to be an issue. In Malay society, nonbiological fictive kin are plentiful: "aunties" and "uncles," "older siblings," "younger siblings," "cousins," "grandparents," and gender, relative age, and personal closeness to the speaker determine modes of address. This writer is "auntie" or "older sister" to numerous younger friends or children of friends in Malaysia. Whatever one's own self-perception of youthfulness, it is the speaker who chooses the term of address, revealing their own perception of age difference and the relationship. Promotion to "grandparent" status may be less a measure of gray hair than of deference: even youthful teachers can be addressed by the grandparental term *tok guru* ("grandfather teacher") as a form of exaggerated respect. If I am addressed as "grandmother," is this a reflection of anticipated exam results or affection? One can also signal rejection of biological kinship by changing terms of address. For instance, an upwardly mobile couple who migrated from the village (*kampung*) to Kuala Lumpur invited along a poorer country cousin as a live-in helper, who was initially introduced as a "younger sister" (*adek*). A few months later, she was referred to as a "maid" (*orang gaji*), a denial of kinship ("she is too poor to be our sister"). Malay kinship, then, is a symbolic way of expressing social closeness or distance, and of adjusting to changes of status.

In Malay society, women generally enjoy relative freedom of movement for economic and petty trading activities. East coast Malay Muslim women are accustomed to leaving their families for days on end to trade cloth, crafts, and special foods up and down the coast in local markets, where they are famous for their brazen promotion of their wares and for telling bold jokes in public, to men and women alike. In their absence from home, there are always plenty of sisters and aunties to take over domestic needs, even through temporarily adopting children from other households. One woman active in small business told me that she had "too many [sixteen] children" to pursue her trading, so she decided to place three of them with a sister who only had two. Passing children around between households to balance resources is not uncommon, and Malay families sometimes adopted unwanted/orphan Chinese girls, who were then raised socially and culturally as fully accepted Malay Muslims (anak angkat). For centuries, such flexible family arrangements have enabled immigrant or foreign spouses to merge into Malay life.

RELIGIOUS IDENTITY: CONVERSION AS A SOCIAL PROCESS

The first arrival of Islam in Southeast Asia was gradual, borne not by the sword, but peacefully, by merchants, scholars, teachers, and Sufi mystics. Their influence was strongest in what are today Indonesia, Malaysia, and the southern Philippines. From the sixteenth to twentieth centuries, scholar/ gurus founded rural schools, spreading Islam and literacy to villagers of all ages. Even today, a number of Malay residential religious schools accommodate pupils of all generations; besides educating the youth, they may serve as homes for the aged, allowing the "grandparents" to tend to the kitchen, gardens, and supervision of the young students. Some schools were run by Sufis, known for their mysticism and meditation. Each residential religious school community was presided over by its own sheikh, who was simultaneously "father" or "grandfather" and leader, blending kinship and respect. Like merchants, religious teachers were often polygynous, marrying wives from different regions, thereby enlarging their social networks and influence; some teachers in Kedah, north Malaysia, had wives from Thailand, Sumatra, and Java. Bonding among students in schools, and later universities, has long provided pathways for spreading new ideas and influencing others (a principle exploited by missionaries of all faiths). Incorporation into the wider Muslim community (umma) brought Malays into a world civilization and economy. Intermarriage between Malays and Arab immigrants created families whose offspring were Malay, but who sometimes claimed Arab identity for the higher religious status and the prestige of connections with the Holy Land.

Merchant communities were the main circuit for the diffusion of Islam in Southeast Asia and for new opportunities for trade with Arabs and Indians overseas. Muslims were skillful in diplomacy, effecting political alliances with local rulers and managing commercial law and disputes, all enhancing Islam's appeal across the region (Federspiel 2007). Not wishing to lose their own markets and taxes, the region's rulers became Muslims, transforming themselves from rajahs into sultans, although retaining much of their Indic royal ceremonial. Emulating their leaders and role models and joining public Muslim rituals became as necessary to the careers of ambitious commoners as religious knowledge. Initially, the economic and social rewards for being Muslim took precedence over mastery of doctrine. In the

Malay world, conversion was as much a matter of social and group conformity as of theology, which followed later (cf. Bulliet 1990). Lacking a word for *conversion*, "becoming Muslim" (*masuk Islam*) in the local context was popularly equated with "becoming Malay" (*masuk Melayu*).

The Islamization of Malay culture did not erase all Indian traditions. Symbols of kingship, including the royal yellow umbrella and wedding rituals (notably the presentation of the bridal couple as "king and queen for a day"; *rajah dan rani sehari*—Sanskrit terms) sitting on a throne and dais (*bersanding*), garlanded with rose petals, henna, saffron, and incense, as well as many rituals of the spirits of the sea, and veneration of tombs of holy men, have all survived as reminders of a pre-Islamic era. Rather than being displaced, these were relabeled as "custom" (*adat*) and tolerated alongside the Muslim *agama* (religion), like Christian pagan adat at Easter and Christmas.

MALAY MULTICULTURAL SOCIETY: FROM COLONIAL TO MODERN STATE

By the nineteenth century, being Muslim was generally accepted as part of being Malay. All the rulers and most subjects of the Malay peninsular states professed Islam and, under British colonial rule, Malays were placed under "Mohammedan" law, while new immigrants continued to *masuk Melayu* by becoming Muslim. At the time, the convert only had to adopt a Muslim name and to be able to recite the Shahadah (the first verses of the Qu'ran), leaving religious studies to follow.

Colonial administration of the Malay peninsula was based on three "races" or "communal groups": Malays, Indians, and Chinese. This was the foundation of most political rights and privileges in postcolonial Malaya, which in 1963 became Malaysia (Roff 1967; Nagata 1979). Until 1931, censuses recognized Buginese, Bataks, Boyanese, Acehnese, "Manilamen," Singhalese, and Arabs as separate identities (Low 1972:125–126; Nagata 1974; 1979), but by independence in 1957 these had disappeared from the census: they were compressed into a generic "Malay" category, although the other identities were not lost in social memory.

In 1957, Malaya became independent and, in 1963, added parts of Borneo to form Malaysia. According to the 1957 national constitution, a Malay is defined as one who habitually speaks Malay, practices Malay custom (adat), and is a Muslim. This is not a genealogical but a cultural profile, which technically could be adopted by anyone, including foreigners. Some Malays today wish to go further and distinguish "pure" or "real" Malays (*Melayu jati/ asli*) in a sea of "immigrants" (*pendatang*), despite the known mixed origins of almost everyone. In 1973, a new economic policy entitled Malays to gain important political and economic advantages, including entrance into cer-

tain white-collar occupations and special government and education quo-
tas not offered to other Malaysians, which enhanced the appeal of the Malay option. Although many "mixed" immigrant Muslim families, especially
in Penang, technically fulfill the constitutional requirements of Malayness,
and hence are eligible for privileges, the following episodes, recorded in
Penang in the 1970s and 1980s, reveal how in everyday life, "mixed" immigrant Muslim families still play the identity field, without losing a foothold
in the Malay community.

WHO IS A MALAY TODAY? EVERYDAY LIFE IN
MODERN MALAYSIA

In modern Penang, Muslim Indians (locally called Klings) and "Arabs" typically have distinct business networks, in which languages such as Tamil,
Gujerati, and Arabic are spoken, although Malay is the national language.
Muslim Indians and "Arabs" are noted for frugality, for hard bargaining
and deal-making, for training their children in business at an early age, and
for their success in manipulating economic institutions such as chambers
of commerce, the Penang religious council, and political parties. By contrast, Penang Malays consider excessive haggling indelicate (tak elok), and
those with small businesses, such as satay stalls and coffee shops, take pleasure in offering treats to their kin, friends, and neighbors (layan pelanggan),
where the maintenance of social relations overrides the profit motive. When
there are profits, Malays enjoy small personal luxuries, investing in hospitality before business. The Penang Arab community still maintains business
connections between Malaysia, Indonesia, India, and the Near East, even
as many prominent local Arabs serve as members of the Malay Chamber
of Commerce, and draw on grants to restore their properties under Malay
heritage programs. While other Muslims in Malaysia regard Arabs with a
mixture of respect for their presumed religious knowledge and links with
the Holy Land, they frequently comment negatively on the global image of
Arab wealth and power. For the Penang Arab community, these comments
are constant reminders of their immigrant origins.

Since few Penang Malays are truly "pure Malays" (Melayu jati), it is in
their daily lives and conversations that their other identities are revealed.
A speaker may attribute the wealth and success of a colleague to excessive
greed, and may point out that the other worker does not always give correct weights in sales, or might claim that the colleague has unfair access to
the Malay Chamber of Commerce, "where they are all Klings or Arabs,"
while "we ordinary Malays [kita orang Melay biasa]" cannot compete. In reverse, those same (Kling or Arab) members of the Malay Chamber of Commerce, when impatient with kampung dwellers foot-dragging over proposed
improvements, will castigate the residents as "backward or underdeveloped

[*kurang maju*] Malays." Yet when the Chamber requests a government loan for those same developments, their members suddenly become monolithically Malay. That individuals who live their private lives as Tamil-speaking Indians or as Arabs, yet affiliate with the Malay Chamber, shows that situational identity is institutionalized. For several years, the head of the Malay Chamber of Commerce rotated between prominent Indians and Arab families, and although Malays generally tend to respect Arabs, in disputes they are quick to accuse them of being "proud and self-interested" (*orang Arab yang sombong dan ikut kepentingan sendiri*). Not all ethnic labels entail negative stereotypes. Some ('pure") Malays are self-deprecating about their own business skills, and one member of the Malay Petty Traders' Association regretted aloud that "we Malays always quarrel [*biasa gadoh sau sama lain*] among ourselves and seem unable to co-operate like 'the other groups.'"

Where conflicts occur in personal relations, parties may increase social distance by asserting a different identity. When an employer usually thought of as Malay needs to exert discipline, he may for the occasion assert his Arab status as he castigates his "lazy Malay" servant: "We Arabs are not lazy like Malays." Or a Malay employer might note that her housemaid, whose cleanliness is in question, "is really a Kling . . . not like us Malays." Occasionally, an individual may alternately denigrate both sides of a mixed identity. One young man, the son of a Tamil-speaking father and a Malay mother living in a Malay kampung, complained about the trick a Kling goldsmith used in cutting the weight of a wedding ring he was purchasing. The same young man was later heard criticizing Malay neighbors whom he claimed take advantage of secure government jobs (*makan gaji*) without having to struggle for a living like hardworking (*rajin*) Indians.

Within the realm of the family, some individuals manipulate cultural practices and the finer points of religion versus adat as symbols of shared or different identity, as needed. When Arabs wish to assert their religious superiority and purity, they conspicuously refuse to follow the Malay bersanding marriage rituals, on the principle that these are not Islamic, for in Islamic marriages incense and flowers have no place. Some Arab families, however, do follow bersanding. When questioned, they claim that it is just a custom that does not interfere with true Islam, and that "we too are like Malays now" (*sekarang saperti orang melayu juga*). But Arabs who do not practice wedding adat may still want to be recognized as Malays, in the chamber of commerce or Penang religious council, explaining that they are merely setting an example by following the pure, original form of Islam.

Arab prestige is not only associated with religious correctness but also with illustrious family genealogies that are displayed on the walls of homes. Some even reside in named Arab kampungs. Unlike Malays, Arabs are patrilineal and patriarchal, have distinctive surnames (e.g., Alatas), and many bear religiously prestigious hereditary titles (*Syed* for men and *Sharifah* for women), indicating descent from the Prophet Mohammed. When I discovered that a woman I knew, then married to a poor trishaw driver, was related to a prominent Syed family, I asked her why she was not using her title, to which she responded that she is "too poor to be a Sharifah." Arab surnames and titles that may be traced back to Arabia are crucial to family identity and prestige, but this has not prevented many intermarriages with local Malays and even Chinese. Most Arab families have long intermarried with non-Arabs without loss of status. In at least two Arab families in Penang, several successive generations of males have married women from wealthy Chinese families, with the result that an Arab might have a Chinese father-, brother- and son-in-law as business partners. Despite the fact that members of the family are biologically more Chinese than Arab, the Arabic patrilineal name, titles, and prestige remain intact, and race is not an issue.

With each generation, the advantages of being Malay in what is now a Malay national state have led more Indians and Arabs to join a Malay political party and to request Malay IC (identity) cards to clarify their public, if not private, identity. That ethnic boundaries are not so tidy is evident even among Malay national elites. Five of the first Malaysian prime ministers had non-Malay ancestors, who were ether Thai, Buginese, Turkish, Indian, or Bedouin. And several Malay sultans have Chinese, Thai, Japanese, Eurasian and European antecedents. While these facts are publicly known, they are only mentioned when there are negative political points to be scored. Thus one unpopular "Indian" (Kling) prime minister was vilified as "Mahathir the Maharajah," while Abdullah Badawi (the Bedouin) was respected for his family's Middle Eastern religious connections.

SHIFTING RELIGIOUS IDENTITIES SINCE THE 1980S

One generation after Malaysian independence, a major shift in Malay identity became apparent. The late 1960s saw a second Islamic resurgence emerging, and the arrival of new religious ideas and immigrants to Muslim Southeast Asia. The revival emphasized Malays' membership in the global Islamic community (*umma*) beyond their ethnicity, and they became linked to events in Arabia, Iran, and Afghanistan. Malays now thought of themselves as Muslims first. Most of the Malay leaders were young, and the youth were the first to follow this "call to the faith" (*dakwah*) movement, whose ideas spread rapidly among school and university students, along the timeworn conversion paths of personal, peer, kin, and friendship networks. The visible signs of dakwah include a shift to more Arabic styles of dress: long robe, white skullcap and beard for men, while women substitute a more voluminous, body-obscuring dress (*baju kurung*) for the traditional *sarung,* adding a fuller head covering (*tudung),* leaving just the face visible). In matters of dress, Malay women often display remarkable creativity, managing to be religiously correct and "groovy," too, in the English of local fashion magazines). Malay Muslim women generally stand out from their Middle Eastern cousins in their ability to make the most of richly colored local batiks and silks, inventing stylish ways of draping their headscarf, and adding personal touches of jewelry, high-heeled shoes, fashionable umbrella, and parasol. In this they are aided by an active local fashion (*fesyen*) industry, promoted by alluring magazine features. This is the now standard modern Malay female style in rural and urban areas, a new ethnic costume with Islamic characteristics. Some women claim to find this form of dress liberating, as it relieves them from the body-image tyranny of modern international fashion, while still allowing individual expression.

Initially, under pressure to become more visibly Muslim, each Malaysian woman faces a personal decision: how and when to cover her head and shed jeans and tee-shirt or tight sarong for baju kurung. University dormitory life allows women to share their thoughts on these matters with each other, as well. As a way of "self-testing" (*pecubaan sendiri*), some girls vow (*niat*) to wear a veil if they pass their exams; more frivolously, her vow may be contingent upon being noticed by a boy. Covering one's head with the tudung is invariably the first and most important symbol; girls at this first stage may enter a swimming pool in a long wetsuit and a towel on her head as a "veil." Having made the first step, wearers realize that Muslim dress conveys expectations of piety to others, creating anxiety about giving up movies or eating in non-*halal* fast-food places. To backslide is to lose face. Once these young women embark on experiments with their new religious images, girls act as vigilantes over each other's food and dress habits. They take care not to be seen outside during prayer times, accompany one another to prayer, carry prayer robes in their briefcases, and in sisterly style, push stray strands of hair inside a friend's veil after ablutions. Thus evolves a whole new lifestyle of insider rituals, which reduce the possibilities of eating or socializing with non-Muslims and with even non-dakwah Malays.

Within their families, newly veiled girls and bearded, robed males often encounter opposition from their parents, who remain clad as traditional Malays. Zealous daughters chide their bareheaded mothers for "not being sufficiently Islamic" and are reprimanded in turn for lack of respect to their seniors. One frustrated woman I knew told her dakwah granddaughter that the grandmother would "not go to hell for not wearing a tudung." Young Malaysian Muslims ready for marriage are now asking their parents to find them suitably religious spouses, and to bypass "non-Islamic" adat wedding rituals, a blow to large family gatherings and feasts. One mother claimed to feel like a hen who had hatched a duck egg when her daughter who had left Malaysia for university overseas wearing jeans, had returned in a robe and tudung. Parents fear, too, that outsiders see their dakwah offspring as "fanatical and narrow-minded" (*fanatik dan berfikiran sempit*) and that this renders them unable to get government jobs. But another mother I knew confided that she preferred her children to be with a Muslim group than with gangs or doing drugs.

A more extreme expression of Malays-as-Muslims-first was the reform Darul Arqam movement (founded in 1968 and banned in 1994), which espoused that the value of religious unity transcends (Malay) ethnicity. Arqam members of both genders were mostly young Malay graduates of local and foreign universities, noted for their technological and business skills and their success in selling commune-produced crafts and products across Malaysia and Indonesia. In Arqam communes, everyone was family, "brothers and sisters" in Islam; Malay relations were expressed in Arabic terms. Their missionary strategy drew on old conversion patterns, of recruitment by marriage, especially of female converts outside Malaysia, who became second or third wives to missionaries. Families were patriarchal and often polygynous, and all women wore full *purdah* (long black robes, full face veil, gloves, and socks). The sight of a gloved woman managing a computer or camera in tropical heat was common. Some of Arqam's own promotional magazines illustrated how professional jobs, such as nursing, could be performed by women in purdah: the movement aimed to show that Islamic attire is not anti-modern.

Sixty percent of Arqam's recruits were women, whose apparent subservience to males was a mystery even to Malay feminists. From their own statements, they showed no evidence of coercion: "It is a privilege to serve Islam . . . as a right-minded and disciplined example to society . . . for the sake of Allah. . . ." But they also calculated the benefits. Some joined to follow men they admired, and since "dating" in a Western sense was impossible (it was considered "un-Islamic"), it was a fast-track to a marriage, even if one were to be a second or third wife. The women were also swift to justify the advantages of multiple wife arrangements. Co-wives could rotate jobs outside the home with domestic duties of marketing, cooking, and child-minding, such that there was always one wife at home. One could thus "have it all" without the need for a servant. Co-wives called each other by older/younger sister terms in Arabic, and their children collectively called them all *umi*, Arabic for mother. Where women had jobs in other communities, co-wives lived separately, and the husband was expected to rotate and treat each of them equally, even to ensure they had the same number of children. For Arqam women, this lifestyle meant freedom to enjoy both a profession and the security of a religious community. Their attire, intimidating to outsiders, was a protective barrier, liberating them from the fashion and consumer tyranny of the "moral stone age [where] the miniskirt is of the dark age." In addition, their clothes constituted a statement of their chosen identity. However, Arqam communities were rife with covert sexual tension. Single men can only imagine the looks of women they cannot see; curious men would ask other women (including this writer) to observe women in quarters forbidden to unrelated males, in order to determine whether

"Aishah is pretty" without her veil. Behind the scenes, women, well aware of this interest, would let down their hair, make sweet snacks, and joke, "if only the men could see us now!"

Life was not necessarily austere in Arqam communities. Bonding and evangelism were promoted by group chanting (*dzikr*) and music, a reminder of older Sufi practices. To this end, groups of men and boys would regularly perform in Malaysia and overseas with their haunting chants, entertaining Muslims and others in public places. Non-Muslims, audiences, were entranced by the music, and eventually the original *Nada Murni* ('noble rhythm") troupe mutated into best-selling commercial pop groups (Sufi pop). Arqam was eventually banned by the Malaysian government for fear that its devaluation of ethnic nationalism threatened the Malaysian state.

Malayness today is defined almost exclusively by Islam (but not all in the Arqam lifestyle). The religious (*Shari'ah*) courts intrude deeply into daily life. In fact, Malays have no freedom of religious choice, since to be Malay, by definition, is now to be Muslim. But what happens today if a Malay converts to another religion? By constitutional definition, a non-Muslim Malay is an anomaly, a nonperson without an ethnic identity. Rejecting Islam is also a sin of apostasy, with severe penalties under Shari'ah law. One Malay woman, Lina Joy, who publicly declared herself Christian, was forced to surrender her identity card and passport, and with them, her Malay identity. She was threatened by the religious courts and was unable to live a social life in any Malaysian Muslim community, and eventually fled to Singapore. At the time of this writing, her case is still the unresolved subject of acrimonious political, religious, civil, and human rights debates in Malaysia. Notwithstanding the historical record of Malay Hindu-Buddhists, in today's Malaysia, it is impossible to be a non-Muslim Malay. Expressions of Malayness and its relationship to religion have changed constantly over the centuries, and this may not be the end of the saga.

PART TWO

Family, Households, and Livelihoods

The flexibility, stability, and shape of Southeast Asian social structures have been dominant themes in the anthropological study of the region at various points. While anthropologists today do not devote as much time to the study of social structure and kinship as they once did, understanding these aspects of social life is still essential to understanding how people of Southeast Asia relate to each other—because those people use these structures and roles to figure out their rights, duties, and obligations to one another.

Southeast Asian social structures have often been described as loosely structured (Embree 1950). Up until the mid-twentieth century, scholarly research on social structure had been dominated by the study of lineage societies. The ethnographic example of Southeast Asia opened up a new perspective, a different possibility, for examining social structure. Loosely structured societies are marked by dyadic relationships, relationships between two people. We have already seen in chapter 1 (Aragon) that personal pronouns are not stable for a person (in contrast to English, in which "you" are always you), but in fact shift depending on who "you" are interacting with. Likewise, in many Southeast Asian languages, personal pronouns shift, depending on whether one is speaking to someone older or younger, more prestigious or less prestigious. This is an expression of dyadic relationships.

The term *loosely structured* implies a lack of structure, and many anthropologists who have worked in Southeast Asia have found this unsatisfying. There is structure—people interact in patterned ways and act to keep these types of relationships in place. But it is clear that some existing structures are so unlike the classical analytical units of kinship based on African models that they are not evident to observers. This issue has been addressed frequently in anthropological literature about Southeast Asian societies.

In "Merit and Power in the Thai Social Order" (chapter 7), Lucien M. Hanks, Jr. demonstrates the importance to Thai social structure of the entourage, a kind of patron–client relationship. These are based on dyadic hierarchy—a series of relationships that are not equal, in which each person in the relationship is subordinate or superior to the other. Entourages are structured around a person of power, whose charisma is based on concepts of "soul stuff" or "prowess" (Wolters 1999), a kind of personal efficacy. This, too, is a key concept throughout much of Southeast Asia. We will see in Part III on "Crafting the Nation-State" how this concept is implicated in political systems.

A common kinship form in Southeast Asia is cognatic (Murdock 1960), meaning that kinship is reckoned through all descent relationships—that is, through both the mother and the father. Cognatic kinship systems are marked by small domestic households, often owning property together (corporate); and all of the kinspeople on both the mother's and the father's side are called the kindred. This form will be quite familiar to many readers of this book—it is the kinship type practiced in the United States. We can visualize these as kinship circles that surround each person (Eggan 1960). The Hanunóo discussed in chapter 5 (Conklin) have this type of kinship. There are advantages to this system—in particular, it supports mobility and flexibility because each person can call on a wide range of kin for support and access to resources; and wherever one goes, there are likely to be kin. It is also a kinship system that made sense within the cultural logic of Southeast Asian history, in which populations moved around in response to war or disaster or new access to resources. This is also the foundation of other features of Southeast Asia noted by observers over time: the flexibility of marriage and frequency of adoption. But this kind of kinship has implications for political power, as Anthony Reid (1988) pointed out in his discussion of common phenomena that unite Southeast Asia. Succession and inheritance are unclear in a cognatic system. Therefore, considerable competition exists for power and social influence. People show this by demonstrating their personal power and attracting followers; the costs of the need for ongoing demonstration of one's prowess, of one's prestige, are illustrated by the story of the Thai "Rocky" as told by Pattana Kitiarsa (chapter 15). Personal power is the basis of the patron–client entourage in Hanks's discussion. For the Thai and other Buddhist peoples of mainland Southeast Asia, the power of the patron of an entourage is rooted in concepts of merit and virtue, both earned and kept by individuals. Merit has already been discussed by High (chapter 3), and is further discussed by Darlington (chapter 11). An individual's power can also be rooted in Brahmanic concepts of sacred power *saksit*.

Nevertheless, it can be argued that the cognatic kinship system is not sufficient to understand Southeast Asian people's social organization. Certain cultures with cognatic kinship also conceptualize identities in terms of houses. The idea of "house societies" originated with Claude Lévi-Strauss and has since been applied (with adjustments) to Southeast Asia by various anthropologists, particularly those working in the islands. Levi-Strauss defined the house as "a corporate body holding an estate made up of both material and immaterial wealth, which perpetuates itself through the transmission of its name, its goods and its titles down a real or imaginary line, considered legitimate as long as this continuity can express itself in the language of kinship or affinity and, most often, of both" (Lévi-Strauss 1983:174). The key elements are, therefore, the ideal of continuity, the passing down of some form of valued property; and the use of the language of kinship (Waterson 1995:49–50). As Roxanna Waterson notes, across island Southeast Asia, we find shared themes in how people talk about houses and relate to them: there is a common tendency for the house to serve as a key social unit and for house idioms to be used to express ideas about kinship. Whether or not the house is occupied, it is frequently an important ritual site, an ancestral origin place, named, and sometimes replete with ritual titles. In a number of island Southeast Asian societies, those affiliated with the ancestral house may be buried in or near the house, ancestral heirlooms may be stored in these houses, and founding ancestors may be symbolically (or literally) present in the house (Waterson 1995:54).

For example, the Sa'dan Toraja (see chapter 14, by Kathleen Adams) can be considered a house society. The Toraja ancestral houses, known as *tongkonan*, are central to how people conceptualize their identities. Each Toraja individual is affiliated with a number of named ancestral houses, some more prestigious than others. One's affiliations with these houses are acquired through both parents and will endure as long as one maintains ritual obligations to the houses (for instance, by contributing to house consecration rituals). So strong is the association with these ancestral houses that Torajas meeting for the first time far from the homeland may inquire as to each other's house affiliations. For instance, when Kathleen Adams first encountered a Toraja graduate student studying in Chicago and he learned of her "adoption" into a Toraja family, he immediately inquired as to her adoptive family's house affiliations. Upon discovering a shared ancestral house, he declared a kinship tie, established that he was younger than Adams, and playfully reminded her of her social responsibilities toward him as her "younger family member."

Although different from the Toraja, the Hanunóo also appear to have some of the features of a house society. They live in single-family dwellings in nuclear families; this is the only corporate group. A groom goes to live in his wife's village (and thus the society is matrilocal). Villages are not as important; they shift and people come and go over time, and so are not permanent. Kin groups are not named permanent groups, but people inherit from the people of their household. As we see in Conklin, the grandparents name the child—a marker of family continuity.

Cognatic descent is not the only kind of kinship in Southeast Asia. The predominant form in Vietnam is the patrilineage. There, patrilineality is modeled on Chinese kinship, likely the result of a thousand years of Chinese colonization from 111 BC to 938 AD (Vietnam was incorporated into the Chinese state long before much of the territory that is now China was). Even after independence, Chinese models of social structure and governance remained as an ideal in Vietnamese society. Vietnamese patrilineages are formally much like Chinese patrilineages, supported by Confucian ideals of order through ancestor worship as well as age and gender hierarchies. Patrilineages are the main form of extra-household organization in villages, and are often managed by a council of the elders of the patrilineages in the village. Much of social life revolves around ancestor worship and the maintenance of ancestral shrines or communal houses. Nevertheless, we cannot understand Vietnam as simply a miniature version of China. One distinct feature of Vietnamese society is the perception that, as in much of Southeast Asia, there is a high degree of gender equality and women often carved out spaces of authority for themselves in village life (Nhung 2008). Regardless of the role of women, patrilineages are indeed significant to people in everyday life in Vietnam, designating their primary identification and placing people in social space in regard to each other.

Patrilineages are important elsewhere in Southeast Asia as well. The highlands people of mainland Southeast Asia are largely patrilineal (see Hjorleifur Jonsson, chapter 8, and Chris Lyttleton, chapter 21). Yet we should not assume that all patrilineages function in the same way. The Lisu, for instance, identified themselves as patrilineal and patrilineages were ideologically favored; however, when political and economic conditions permitted, they appeared to be more cognatic than patrilineal (Gillogly, chapter 6). This sort of oscillatory shift between kinship forms is not unusual; Edmund Leach demonstrated that this shifting social structure was inherent to Kachin social and political organization (Leach 1965). We also find patrilineality more often among the elite of a centralized state. In Thailand, patrilineality is the predominant form among the urban well-to-do and aristocracy, as well as the Sino-Thai; while matrilineality exists alongside the state-validated patrilineality in the north and northeast (see Walker 2006 for a new view on this dual orientation).

Matrilineages also exist in Southeast Asia. Societies in which matrilineages predominate have captivated many outside observers. Classic examples include the Minangkabau in western Sumatra, Indonesia; and the Musuo on the northern reaches of the Southeast Asian cultural region (in far southwestern China). With the predominantly Muslim Minangkabau, one "belongs" to the group of one's mother; rights to land and wealth are passed down through the female line. Although migration has eroded Minangkabau's residence patterns, traditionally sons resided in their mother's household, even after marriage. In essence, husbands were more akin to guests in their wives' homes, and their key role as adults was not in their wives' homes but in their sisters' households (Blackwood 2000). For centuries, Minangkabau males have partaken in a rite of passage known as *merantau*, which removed young men from their communities for long periods of time; young men would leave to seek experience, work, and wisdom away from the homeland, with the expectation of eventual return. Similarly, among the Musuo, households are matrifocal; there is no marriage among commoners; and men were often away on prolonged absences for long-distance trade or living as monks in Buddhist monasteries (McKhann 1998). Another form of matrilineality is found in northern Thailand. Land there is passed on from mother to daughter, although management of farms is under the control of husbands; women also carry out ritual through trances to negotiate the welfare of the household with the matrilineal ancestors, who punish young people for social transgressions (Cohen 1984); and these matrilocal descent groups are also politically significant (Bowie 2008). It was, in fact, his observance of matrilineal relationships that led Jack Potter (1976) to argue that the model of "loosely structured societies" was wrong. In not recognizing the structures that were there, earlier observers had concluded that there was no structure.

Finally, age and gender are two key features that interact with kinship systems to structure social relations. Most languages of Southeast Asia draw distinctions on the basis of age, particularly to contrast the older and the younger (as Aragon notes in chapter 1). In the languages of many island societies, pronouns for the third-person singular are not marked by gender or age so that, unlike in English, it is impossible to know if the speaker is talking about a male or a female. In most mainland languages, gender is also potentially recognized. For instance, your siblings are marked as older or younger than you and while it is not always necessary to signal gender, a word indicating gender can be added to the terms for sibling. In addition, a Thai person needs to know whether a parent's brother or sister is older or younger than the parent in order to address them. Relative age is also marked through patterns of naming in societies influenced by Chinese culture, as among the Lisu (chapter 6).

We would be remiss not to note that modernity has added new wrinkles and brought some changes to family systems in Southeast Asia. Urban life, commodification, and cash-based economies now color the family and social structure patterns that earlier generations of scholars chronicled. In some cases, these dynamics have led to an efflorescence or exaggeration of older patterns. For instance, amongst the Toraja of Indonesia (Adams, chapter 14), a "house society," decades of out-migration for work in mining, timber, and other fields, and employment in the tourism sector have meant that many Toraja have invested some of their new wealth in "traditional" places. Over the past few decades, Toraja ancestral house-based rituals and funerals have become dramatically inflated. Those without the means to keep up with the often inflated expectations for ancestral house and funeral contributions find themselves with limited options: debt, shame, or opting out. Some members of the younger generation migrate to distant cities and relinquish their involvement in the rituals of all but a select few ancestral houses. Others marry non-Toraja spouses, a strategy that minimizes the number of ancestral houses to which one is tethered. Jonsson, writing about the Mien, has also found that household form has been responsive to the regional political economy (2001; see also chapter 8). In other parts of Southeast Asia, life in urban settings where a younger generation has access to salaried jobs has eroded parental authority to enforce kin-based expectations. For instance, Tania Murray Li's research chronicled what could be termed the "nuclearization" of Chinese and Malay families in Singapore. She is careful to stress, however, that the monetization of social relations in Singapore has "revised and restructured, but not eradicated in any uniform, pre-determined way" Chinese and Malay families (Li 1989:157, cited in King and Wilder 2003:299). In a sense, we can say that as in the past, new influences and opportunities now play on older Southeast Asian patterns.

5

Maling, a Hanunóo Girl from the Philippines

Harold C. Conklin

Just before dawn, one day in late September 1953, seven-year-old Maling tiptoed to the edge of my sleeping mat to wake me with a short but sad announcement: *"namatay yi kanmi 'ari'"* (our younger brother is dead). Still an infant, Gawid had succumbed to an unknown malady during the night. On his death, the Mt. Yagaw Hanunóo family with whom I had been residing in the small hamlet of Parina for almost a year immediately arranged for his burial and began the observance of a five day religious restriction on agricultural work, bathing, and travel. To understand how Maling interpreted this turn of events as she waited for me to get up and help with the preparations, it is necessary to know the part she had played in the activities connected with Gawid's birth eighteen days earlier.

For that occasion, Maling's father, Panday, had rethatched a small, dilapidated annex to the family house and had built a sturdy rail fence around its wooden piles and storm props to keep the foraging pigs away from the space under the bamboo slat floor. Although the period of pregnancy had not been marked by any of the anomalies recognized by the Hanunóo, the customary magical precautions such as refraining from unnecessary binding, tying, or planting activities had been strictly observed for the preceding week by both Panday and his wife, Sukub. On the day before the birth, after a brief final weeding of the maturing rice crop in her steep jungle clearing, Sukub harvested enough bananas for the next two days and returned to Parina to spend most of the afternoon and evening in her rattan hammock-swing.

Maling came to tell me of these things and of how she had helped mend an old buri [eds: fan palm fiber] mat which her father had set up as a screen to shut off the annex from the rest of the house. Her older sister, Hanap, was responsible for most of the family cooking and during this period often relieved Sukub in caring for two-year-old Iyang. Thus, Maling was relatively

From "Maling, a Hanunóo Girl from the Philippines," in *In the Company of Man: Twenty Portraits by Anthropologists*, edited by Joseph B. Casagrande (New York: Harper & Co., 1960), 101–118.

free to visit the other four households in our small settlement and occasionally to discuss her views on daily events with me. While I made more systematic attempts to elicit adult interpretations of such events, Maling often volunteered crucial details which her elders deemed either too obvious or too intimate to be mentioned. It was partly for this reason and partly because of her cheerful disposition and youthful enthusiasm that I was immediately drawn to her. Despite her childish exuberance, Maling was an obedient and respectful child, capable of almost infinite patience and concentration if necessary. She was one of those children who felt equally at ease whether sitting for an hour quietly watching her grandfather carve intricate sigmoid curves into a bolo [eds: machete] handle or publicly—though jokingly—chiding and poking him for ending a humorous tale with an excessively lewd remark. Her poise with both children and adults in quite varied situations (including even an ethnographer's presence), was a fortunate circumstance for which I became increasingly appreciative.

Early the next morning when I entered the refurbished room that served as the birth chamber, Maling and her two sisters were standing with their backs against the palm-leaf thatch on the side opposite the door, with their eyes glued on the scene directly in front of them. Panday had girth-hitched his loincloth around a low beam at a point only a foot above Maling's head. Sukub, who was facing her daughters in a kneeling position, had wrapped the loose ends of this white cotton fabric securely around her wrists and was pulling—almost hanging—on the taut webbing that stretched from her raised hands to the beam. Sitting on the same floor mat and just behind her, Panday was helping his wife through the first stages of labor by massaging her abdomen and applying arm pressure. No elaborate preparations had been made for the occasion. The usual commonplace objects were left in the room. In the corner beyond the couple were two buri rice sacks, some odd bits of clothing, and a blanket. Winnowing trays, coconut shell dishes, a pitch candle, two bundles of bark and roots used in making incense, and various medicinal herbs filled the remaining corners. Except for a blood-red scarf wrapped tightly around her waist and the broad rattan pocket belt at her side, Sukub was dressed as she had been the day before—in a short homespun sarong with three loose, plaited waist bands and numerous bead necklaces.

The three sisters were dressed like their mother in miniature, except for the addition of loose cotton blouses. Several medicinal charms and an old Spanish silver coin dangled from Maling's beaded necklace. In her tiny sensitive face one could easily read the signs of intense observation. Below a faintly wrinkled brow, her large, somber eyes remained motionless. She had almost succeeded in keeping most of her slightly tousled, shoulder-length hair back from her face with a tight-fitting beaded fillet. One stray lock, however, escaped the encirclement of this headband and fell in a wisp over her smooth brown cheek.

A few minutes after I had sat down next to Iyang, Panday asked Hanap to start heating some rice gruel in the next room. Maling prepared a betel quid for her mother, at the latter's request, and helped Hanap pour some water from a bamboo tube into an earthen cooking pot. By the time Maling returned, her mother had already uttered the first in a series of long, piercing cries, "Udu-u-u-u-u-y, 'udu-u-u-u-u-y, . . . ," which signaled to the settlement at large as well as to those in the room, that the second stage of labor was about to begin.

During the next hour, Maling continued watching every detail intently, often drawing my attention to particular points that differed from the way Iyang had been born in Alyun two years before. "Then," she explained, "Mother's contractions were delayed much longer. And she had to tug on a rough abacá cord instead of a homespun loincloth because Father's was being washed."

A little while later, Maling told me confidently that this looked as if it would be a normal delivery, pointedly adding that her grand-uncle had been a breech baby and still had the name Su'i (Legs First) to prove it.

From the beginning, it was obvious that the family wanted a boy. Maling had told me how she envied her girl cousins who had younger brothers to take care of, and how her father would like to have at least one son who, as he grew older, could help with house construction and the felling of larger trees during the annual forest clearance. Even Sukub had once mentioned that she and a mother of three sons (but no daughters) had exchanged waist bands several months earlier to "switch their luck." More recently, Maling had confided to me that she was afraid her Aunt Agum was correct in saying that Sukub's buttocks seemed to be getting flatter—a sure sign that the unborn child was a girl. Consequently, right up to the time the baby was born, considerable anxiety over the sex of the expected offspring was combined with the usual concern about the condition of the mother.

It was a boy, and Maling had the pleasure of announcing the fact to three of her cousins who had gathered outside on the veranda. In a matter of seconds the word reached the rest of the hamlet and attention shifted abruptly from the untouched neonate in front of Sukub to Sukub herself. From previous questioning, I knew that no one would move the baby until the afterbirth was expelled, no matter how long this might take.

During the first hour, Sukub was given all of the comforting treatment customarily provided to induce a rapid expulsion of the afterbirth and to prevent any of the numerous kinds of relapse distinguished by the Hanunóo. Hot, liquid infusions were rubbed over her limbs which were then bathed in sweet pitch incense. She perspired heavily as the room filled with the fragrant smoke. Maling was asked to knot the ends of the loincloth so that Sukub could rest her elbows in the resulting loop.

Never leaving his wife's side, Panday efficiently supervised all of these activities, now in a soft voice asking Hanap or Maling to prepare a betel quid for their mother, now adjusting Sukub's waist band or wiping her forehead with an old shirt, and always checking to see that the requisite magical procedures designed to hasten this last stage of labor were properly carried out. Under his direction, Maling helped Hanap untie everything in the house that either of her parents had lashed, woven, or spliced together in the last few months so that the afterbirth would come "undone" likewise.

Hanap fed her mother some hot rice gruel and kept the fire going while Iyang and two of her cousins spun areca nut tops on a nearby winnowing tray. Periodically, Maling added hot embers to the shell bowl in which fresh scented herbs had been mixed and passed the vessel around her mother several times.

Still, there were no results, even after Sukub's older sister, Ampan, arrived from the settlement across the Silsig valley with additional rice gruel and a new supply of pitch. As the delay extended into the second hour, Sukub became noticeably weaker and even Iyang, who had become extraordinarily quiet—saying she no longer wanted to play outside—began to reflect the urgency of this situation for the entire family.

During the next few minutes, Panday, Hanap, and Ampan conferred hastily on the most effective steps to be taken to help free the afterbirth. Maling had witnessed several such discussions under similar circumstances during the last few years, but this was different. Previously, she had listened to older relatives talk about events which did not concern her directly. Now, however, she found herself involved in almost every activity mentioned.

She had been with her father, for example, when he had planted sweet potato vines three weeks past, and was the only other person present who knew exactly which area in the family clearing he had "seeded." Furthermore, in regard to this particular incident, it was agreed unanimously that Panday should not have planted any new crops so near the end of his wife's pregnancy and that the vines would have to be uprooted. Knowing that Panday could not leave Sukub at this time, Maling offered to take Hanap to the sweet potato patch where both of them could perform this mechanical act of sympathetic magic in hopes of easing the passage of the placenta.

The two girls left almost immediately, stopping on the veranda just long enough to pick up two empty bamboo water tubes to be filled on their way back from the field. I decided to go with them, leaving Panday and his sister-in-law considering other possible sources of Sukub's difficulty. The baby remained untouched, and for the moment, unthought of.

Hanap, followed by her equally slight and even more diminutive younger sister, led the way down the six hundred yards of mountain trail connecting Parina with Panday's clearing. As usual for this time of year, the steep, narrow path was muddy and slippery and, at several points where it led around the brim of a forty-foot ravine, even dangerous. Because of their daily trips to fetch water, however, the girls knew every inch of the route intimately. Where recent heavy rains had loosened rocks and made the footing precarious, Maling turned to warn me, adding at one point how only two nights before she had nearly tripped on a wild yam vine that had grown across the trail. Along the way we passed familiar stretches of bamboo forest and second-growth jungle, through two stands of coconut and other fruit trees, and across a small stream where the girls left their heavy containers.

Once in the field, Maling took us straight to the vines Panday had planted, and the girls began pulling them up. As soon as this task was done Hanap hastened back to Parina to inform the others.

Maling and I paused at the stream to talk briefly with one of her young cousins who had stopped there to prepare a betel chew. Before he went on his way Maling asked him to cut some coconuts for us from a nearby tree which belonged to her family. He appeared happy to do this, and while he was detaching nuts from the crown of the nearest palm she emphasized how useful it is to have a young man in the family who can climb such trees. By the time she had filled her water tube from a stream-side spring, her cousin had opened three of the felled fruits for our immediate consumption, and was husking two other coconuts to make it easier for me to carry them back to Parina. Having had nothing to eat since early morning, we were greatly refreshed by this common midafternoon snack.

After our pause at the stream, Maling and I continued the trip back alone, and although it was a difficult climb most of the way, she kept up a lively conversation about the things she noticed along the trail. On numerous other occasions Parina children had amazed me with their precise knowledge of the plant environment. This was no exception. Before we reached Parina Maling had drawn my attention to five separate clumps of productive perennial crops—ranging from bananas to betel palms—each of which had been planted by her grandfather or by one of his sons, and she had shown me two wild herbs used for making *panrunas,* a medicinal preparation which, when accompanied by appropriate rituals, is believed to be a permanent oral contraceptive.

"They say," noted Maling, "that's the reason why Father doesn't have any younger sisters or brothers. Grandmother took the *panrunas* treatment soon after he was born because his had been such a difficult delivery."

"Do you know," I asked, "what other ingredients are needed to make *panrunas?*"

"I'm not sure," she replied, "but I think *tunawtunaw* weed is one. Hanap says parts of seven different plants are needed; she probably knows what the others are."

In the course of many similar conversations, Maling had demonstrated an astonishing maturity of interests and experience, richly illustrating the way in which a Hanunóo child, without formal instruction, acquires an increasingly detailed acquaintance—direct or vicarious—with all sectors of the local adult world. Geographically, this is a small universe, limited often to an area within ten kilometers of one's birthplace. (Maling had only once been farther than a half-hour's walk from Parina.) But this small orbit comprehends a comparatively vast realm of knowledge in all provinces of which any member of the society is expected to be at home. In this setting, Maling's parents never thought it particularly precocious that on some occasions she should be as interested in contraceptives as in learning to spin cotton or take care of her younger sister. Nevertheless, I was constantly impressed with her independent thinking and utter frankness which seemed to recognize no boundaries, except of degree, between child and adult knowledge. Her status as a child neither prevented her from occasionally accepting some of the responsibilities of her elders nor blocked her intuitive analysis of their adult roles.

As we approached the edge of our settlement, Maling suggested we pick an armload of the soft, leafy heads of the aromatic *'alībun* shrub, explaining that not only could we use some of them to wipe the mud from our feet, but that her mother would appreciate having a few in the room because of their fragrance.

After hanging her filled miniature water cylinder on the veranda rack, Maling lifted the screen matting and quietly entered the room where her father, sisters, and aunt were watching Sukub and talking in very low tones. Maling sat quietly looking around the tiny room. Sukub and Panday had both undone their hair knots, and someone, probably Panday, had hung half a dozen untied lashings, unwound arrow bindings, and the like, over a low crossbeam. While we had been gone, many efforts had been made to recall and remedy any recent act by Maling's parents that might be the root of the trouble. Hanap leaned over to tell Maling that at Panday's behest, Aunt Agum had gone to a nearby banana grove to pull up the first and last of thirty banana sets which Sukub had planted in August. This had seemed to please Sukub, but the afterbirth still had not appeared.

Ampan remained attentively at Sukub's side while Panday looked once more through his betel bag, and Maling joined in the search for nooses, slip knots, balls of wound yarn, pegs, and other bound, joined, or fastened objects that might have been overlooked. The muffled voices from the adjoining houses and the occasional gusts of wind up from the Silsig valley only served to underscore the gravity of the quiet but intensive search inside. Maling broke the long silence by inquiring if anyone had undone the leash of the new wooden turtle that Panday had carved for Iyang. No one had, and it was agreed that perhaps this was the knot which was causing the delay.

Maling went into action swiftly, but calmly. By gentle questioning she learned from Iyang that she and her cousins had been playing with the toy turtle earlier in the day. Since their own house had already been thoroughly searched, Maling decided to check in the adjoining house where her cousins were still romping about. Her hunch was right; the toy was returned, and the leash carefully untied, completely unknotted, and thrown over the beam along with the other lines and cords. All eyes again turned to Sukub. After a few more minutes of anxious waiting, and much to everyone's relief, she indicated that the final contractions had begun.

With the expulsion of the afterbirth, the tension relaxed and things moved quickly. [. . .] Panday cut the tip of an old arrow shaft into a long tapering blade and quickly fashioned one of Maling's empty water-carrying tubes into a small bucket-like vessel to hold the umbilicus and placenta. Maling joined me in the background and, knowing that this was the first time I had observed such a ritual, eagerly explained to me all that she knew about the procedure.

"See," she said, "we can't use an iron blade to cut the cord. Even an arrow shaft is dangerous if the poisoned tip has not first been removed because then the child would grow up to be easily angered. He might even fight his parents, and seriously injure them."

Finally, nine hours after Gawid's birth, and after both the bamboo container and reed knife were prepared, Panday placed the baby on its back and proceeded to tie the umbilicus close to the infant's belly with a piece of homespun yarn. Yuktung, who had been called in from his house, then took Panday's place and with a sawing motion, severed the cord just above the cotton binding with very deliberate short strokes. In rapid succession, he then touched the moist blade tip to the baby's lips, waved the shaft in a zigzag pattern over its head, and uttered a barely audible magical formula to insure rapid healing. As he stuck the shaft in the roof thatch, Maling leaned back to tell me that in a few days her father would shoot it into a tree so that her brother would be a good shot with a bow.

Sukub now handed the afterbirth to Panday who placed it in the bamboo container, filled the tube with earth, and then went off into the forest where, Maling said, he would hang it from a high limb out of reach of large animals. The bamboo floor in front of Sukub was cleared and spread with an unused homespun cloth on which the infant was placed for bathing. While this was Sukub's responsibility, Hanap and Maling helped by heating water and bringing it to their mother's side in large coconut shell bowls. Soon Sukub was holding her young son in a cotton wrap and discussing the events of the past day with her children. Hanap began to winnow rice for the evening meal, Iyang cried for her plaything, and the household gradually settled down to a more normal schedule. When I left, Maling and her mother were still talking about the knot around the turtle's neck.

For the next few weeks Maling was an enthusiastic observer and participant in the care of Parina's youngest resident. Within this settlement of independent nuclear families residing in two lines of veranda-linked dwellings, she served as the chief disseminator of news about the infant's progress. She spent some time in each of these households almost every day, ostensibly to borrow a shellful of salt or a needle, or to check on the identity of an unfamiliar visitor for the folks at home. On these small errands as well as during her casual visits, she could not resist the opportunity to talk about her brother. Her little cousins would sometimes go back with Maling to examine for themselves the various items of behavior and appearance which she had reported. First it was his feeding habits that drew their attention. Then his somewhat flattened head (which Aunt Agum assured Maling would grow "round again" in a few months), then his manual skills, and so on.

One day Maling was sent by her parents to see if the door had been finished on a nearby rice granary which was being built for the family by one of her uncles. She said she wasn't going to be gone long and wondered if I wouldn't walk along with her. [. . .] Maling seemed to be in a talkative mood.

"Mother went down to the stream to bathe today," she began, "and left the baby all alone with Hanap. We were awfully worried that something might happen, but nothing did. He is six days old, and he doesn't have a name yet. Our grandparents are coming up here in a day or two and I suppose we will decide on a name then."

"What do you think would be a good name for your brother?" I queried.

"There are a lot of names that are good for boys, but some we don't like because they sound too much like those used by the lowland Christians. Others we can't use because they belonged to relatives who have been dead only a few years. I think the best name would be the one Father has suggested, Gawid. My great-great-grandfather's name was Gawid. See that peak beyond Alyun? I've never been there, but they say that's where old Gawid once shot two deer with the same arrow. When my brother gets Grandfather Andung to prepare some hunting medicine for him, he should be a good hunter too.

"You know, we used to have a brother, who was several years younger than Hanap, but he died of a sudden illness two rice harvests ago. It was really too bad. He was just learning how to trap and shoot. If he had lived we would now have fish and game to eat with our rice or bananas almost every day. And there are so many things he could have helped Father do. He could have operated the bellows while Father worked at the forge, and he could have built this granary. As it is now, Father will have to forge two bolo blades to repay my uncle for this job. [. . .] It just isn't the same as having one's own son for a helper.

"With Mother it is different. Hanap already can do most household chores including cooking, and she is pretty good at spinning and weaving baskets. I haven't learned to do all these things yet, but by the time Hanap gets married, I'll be able to take her place."

Our conversation was interrupted at this point by Hanap's call for Maling to go with her to fetch water. As we walked down to the main settlement clearing, Maling asked if girls in America also carry water like the Hanunóo, and whether their brothers ever helped them. Before I had time to answer she had joined Hanap and two other Parina girls on their way to the spring.

The infant's ears were pierced the following day and, not unimpressed by Maling's (and her father's) enthusiasm, the family decided to name him Gawid. Sukub was now able to gather firewood, cook, harvest bananas and beans, and work in the family fields—never, however, without Gawid slung at her side, or in Hanap's care.

During the second week, Maling helped her mother tie small circlets of red and white beads around Gawid's wrists and legs, and a tiny medicinal amulet about his neck. He was now well on his way to becoming accepted as a full-fledged member of the community and Parinans stopped calling him "the infant" as they began to use his proper name.

Parina children were already including Gawid in their play activities, such as the mock feast they held one afternoon behind Panday's house. Sukub whispered to me that they had been dining on twig and turmeric stalk stew and a main dish of ashes for almost half an hour, as I followed her quietly to observe them from a natural blind. Iyang, Maling, their cousin Biru (Yuktung's son), and four other three-to-eight-year-olds had set out a row of banana leaf trays on which these foods had been placed. Mimicking their elders, they were exclaiming loudly about the quality of the meal and shouting for the men to fill up their shell bowls with more "stew." Maling and the gourmandizing tots demanded better service from Gawid and other males not actually present almost as often as they did of Biru and his older brother. This most entertaining make-believe meal ended in a round of laughter on all sides as Gawid himself betrayed our presence by beginning to cry.

Though no one would say so, it was obvious that there would be an abundant rice harvest. Maling evidently knew this should not be stated directly, but at the same time she found it difficult to ignore. Once, for example, she suggested that I visit "her" field in order to gather some cucumbers which were now ripe. "And," she added, "one of the two kinds of rice Father gave me is almost ready to be cut."

Maling was still too young, of course, to do much agricultural work of her own, but she took immense pride in the fact that she possessed some seed of her own which had actually been planted in a full-sized hillside clearing instead of only in a play garden such as the one she had helped Iyang make in their Parina houseyard.

That afternoon I accompanied Sukub and Maling on a brief cucumber-picking visit to their fields, during which I saw for myself that the rats and grubs had not done nearly so much damage as local farmers would have led one to think. In a few months there would be plenty of rice for a large community-wide feast.

Recalling that the last feast her family had sponsored was for the disinterment of her deceased brother's bones, Maling proposed that this year they should hold a post-harvest rite to celebrate Gawid's birth. On the way back, she composed, in the form of a familiar children's chant, a number of extemporaneous verses addressed to Gawid, informing him of the preparations which would soon be undertaken in his honor, how much rice his different kinsmen would contribute, how many people would participate, and how many pigs would be slaughtered:

'Anung 'ari'ari'an	Oh little brother
kang di waydi sabīhan	I must say again
dūru ti 'gdulud 'aban	That more than fifty
balaw lāmang kalim'an	will attend,
kay pāsung dūru hanggan	And that our feast will
kay bābuy 'imaw diman!	never end!

In a few words set to a very simple melody she expressed the spirit with which the whole family looked forward to the harvest season.

During the third week after his birth, however, Gawid caught a slight head cold which was evidently accompanied by complications other than those observed by his parents. Two days later, on the seventeenth night of his short life, he died quite unexpectedly—while the rest of the family was asleep.

Maling had seen death before. She knew only too well what would happen that morning when she woke me with the sad news. Her father would cut a digging stick and sufficient bamboo poles for the grave mats, while her mother would wash the baby and wrap it in cotton cloth and beads. Hanap would help her mother tie the corpse and carry it out through a hole in the wall on the eastern side of the room in which he died, while Maling herself would assemble some of the usual grave goods, including a small cooking pot, some rice, water, and vegetables in separate shell dishes, and a small betel basket with all essential ingredients—nuts, leaves, lime, and tobacco. Iyang would cry. Many rituals would be performed at the grave and the family would not be able to leave the settlement, even to visit their ripening grain fields for five days, lest all types of misfortune descend upon the already grief-stricken household.

However, there were no tears. While this was a very sad moment for a seven-year-old, Maling was well prepared to accept such events realistically. Her voice reflected sincere disappointment, but, with characteristic optimism, she added that perhaps her mother's next baby would also be a son. As we went to join the other members of her family, she said succinctly, "mahal māna ti magkabalākih" (it would be nice to have the same number of both boy and girl children).

This, then, was Maling as I knew her in 1953. Four years later, in the summer of 1957, I returned to the small Yagaw hamlet where she and her family were living. The Maling who greeted me in the houseyard had the same thoughtful eyes and modest smile but she stood at least a head taller than when I had last seen her. Her black hair, still held in place by a beaded band, now fell gracefully down her back to the top folds of her sarong. Her very short blouse was beginning to flare out slightly in front, and she had tightened her corsetlike rattan pocket belt about her otherwise bare midriff in an obvious attempt to accentuate her fast developing wasp-waisted ("ant-waisted" in Hanunóo) figure. And straddled on her now shapely hips was a new member of the family.

This particular pose was to become a familiar one. From early morning until shortly after the evening meal, Maling's time was almost entirely taken up in caring for her younger siblings. She was unassisted by Hanap, who had graduated from this type of surrogate motherhood several years before, and who, in fact after a long series of courtships, was about to leave the immediate family circle to establish one of her own. Iyang of course was still too young to be entrusted with such baby-tending duties. And Sukub, except for the feeding and bathing of the youngest child, devoted most of her time to food-getting activities and heavy household chores.

Maling's two young charges were both boys. In 1954, within a year after the death of Gawid, Panday happily took a year-old orphaned baby (and distant cousin) as a foster son. Sukub nursed the infant whose name was Bilug, and Maling soon had the task of caring for him most of the time. When Bilug's mother's bones were ritually exhumed the following dry season, Maling proudly carried him at her side to the grave site several kilometers away. Then, in 1956, Sukub gave birth to a son of her own, Tabul, who immediately became the focus of the whole family's attention. After the first few months, and except for nursing and bathing, Tabul became Maling's main responsibility.

The constant care of two small children in a Hanunóo hamlet is by no means an uneventful or easy task. There are goats, pigs, chickens, cows, dogs, monkeys, and occasionally millipedes, lizards, snakes, and insects for them to watch, play with, or be harmed by. Flat areas being nonexistent on the eastern slopes of Mt. Yagaw, the houseyard itself is usually a steep incline down which a child may slide, tumble, or slip; and the fact that the raised verandas are frequently unrailed does not lessen the danger of falling. When one notes further that favorite playthings, even for a two-year-old, include such weapons as keen-edged meat knives and fire-hardened bamboo pokers, it is rather remarkable that Maling showed practically no outward signs of fatigue, impatience, or discontent with her lot. On the other hand, she seemed quite indifferent to the fact that her mother was again pregnant. And once I heard her say that when she got married she really wouldn't care if she didn't have any children at all!

Though her former enthusiasm for baby boys had waned, at least temporarily, her interest in older ones was rapidly taking its place. Soon she would become a full-fledged, marriageable young maiden, a status which is the acme of female social existence among the Hanunóo. With this change would come many new privileges and opportunities. Maling, as Hanap before her, would hand over what child-care duties remained to her younger sister Iyang, set up living quarters in an adjacent but separate pile dwelling, and, for several—perhaps five or six—years, lead a relatively independent life dominated by the direct but intricate local patterns of courtship ending in pregnancy, or marriage, or both.

Maling was well along in preparing herself for the new role she would be playing. In addition to dressing in a more meticulous manner, she had begun to oil her hair regularly, to trim her eyebrows, and to bind her wrists and ankles with fine red beads. Hanap had given her several decorative tortoise shell combs and a round mirror small enough to be carried in her pocket belt. Whenever her father went to Alyun, she would ask him to dig fresh vetiver roots for her to use as a sachet to keep with her sleeping blanket and extra clothes. Many of these practices she had started years before, but refinements in them had been added more recently by virtue of close observation of Hanap's behavior.

She had also begun to acquire many of the domestic skills that Hanunóo women are expected to learn. During the late morning hours when the children were napping, and by the light of a pitch candle after they had fallen asleep exhausted from a busy day at play, Maling could often be seen weaving a small betel basket, spinning cotton, or repairing a torn blouse. In this way, during the past four years, Maling had found time to learn many of the steps of basket and mat weaving, of producing homespun yarn, and of cooking native dishes. She still was not skilled in tailoring and embroidery, nor could she yet set up a cloth loom by herself.

Maling had learned to conduct herself in a more reserved manner in public, to initiate conversation with male guests only when asking for betel leaf or areca nut, and to communicate simple messages effectively with a minimum of facial gesture. All phases of betel exchange etiquette, which I had first seen her practice with mock chews or red sugar cane four years before, were now perfected. She had become quite versatile with the bamboo jew's-harp and had already learned the rudiments of nose flute playing from her mother and Aunt Agum.

To go with these instrumental skills, however, Maling knew she would need to build up as large a repertoire as possible of chanted verses which form the basis for most serenading and courting activities. While, like all Hanunóo children, she could already sing some 'ambāhan songs, she also knew that to memorize enough appropriate verses to participate successfully in extended repartee, it would be very helpful if she could record new lyrics solicited from her close relatives in some semipermanent form. Hence, about the time I arrived, she was attempting to learn the Hanunóo syllabary.

Inasmuch as Maling's newly acquired reticence in talking openly with men outside the immediate family did not extend to me, I was able to observe and discuss with her at great length the details of these various preparations. The manner in which she learned to read and write, for example, afforded an intimate picture of how she managed to acquire this bit of useful but specialized knowledge without any formalized course or tutor.

From previous visits to the Hanunóo, I knew that their Indic-derived syllabary of forty-eight characters functioned primarily as a vehicle of amorous and often poetic communication, and not as a means of historical, religious, or legal documentation. There are, in fact, no permanent records in this script, the component symbols of which are scratched into the hard but perishable outer surface of bamboo with a sharp steel knife. But what of the actual process of learning how to use this script which is never arranged in an "alphabetic" order or formally taught?

One morning after she had shaped toy animals from a half cylinder of green banana sheathing for Tabul and Bilug, Maling grasped the tip of her small knife blade between her thumb and forefinger and began pushing it across one of the flooring slats with her other hand so that a series of lightly engraved marks were produced. In reply to my asking her what she was doing, Maling said, "Nothing, just scribbling," and left quickly to stop Tabul from twisting the tail off Bilug's "carabao" [water buffalo]. She had seemed a bit embarrassed by my question, so I did not press the matter at that time. But later, when I had a chance to examine her "scribbling," I found half a dozen clearly inscribed syllabic characters among what apparently were a good many false starts and scratch-out erasures. That night she admitted that she didn't know what all the characters she had written stood for; she had simply copied them from her mother's tobacco tube. Yet she seemed quite interested in learning and said she would get Hanap to read some of the 'ambāhan their father had written on their lime containers so that she could memorize the words and compare them with characters.

A few weeks later, while her mother was bathing Tabul, Maling came to where I was typing and began to inscribe something along the edge of my large bamboo desk. From the halting way she was singing to herself, it was obvious that she was trying to write down the words:

kang ma-nuk sa bid-la-wan	My dear bidlawan bird,
nu ka-'in-da ma-'u-ran	In a storm like this
pī-san dap ti hu-ru-nan	We are perched together,
nu may . . .	But when . . .

Assuming that she had now learned to use some of the characters adequately, I gave her a simple "dictation test" covering the whole range of syllable types. After every word I paused while Maling inscribed the characters deliberately or told me she didn't yet know them. At the end, she had written eighteen characters correctly. These represented syllables of high frequency in simple conversation and children's 'ambāhan, and included those symbols necessary to sign her own name.

At six- to eight-week intervals thereafter I made additional checks to note Maling's progress. Each time she had learned seven or eight new characters, until she had mastered all but those representing the five or six rarest syllable types in the language. By that time she had become quite skilled in rapid transcription, and could and did read almost any verse she could find. Inside of six months, and without giving up any of her family duties she had all but completed the technical training she would need to record and read innumerable songs and letters for the rest of her life. No one person had provided her with more than a fraction of the reading materials she had studied, although Hanap, who at this stage spent a good many leisure hours practicing 'ambahan, was most frequently consulted.

Although Maling's ability to read and write will probably prove to be very useful, it will not introduce her to any worlds beyond that which she can see from Mt. Yagaw. She has remained close to home all her life and with Hanunóo marriage residence rules as they stand, her future husband will undoubtedly help her set up a new household in Parina or in whatever nearby hamlet her parents are living at the time. He will probably be a distant cousin from one of the other Hanunóo regions near Mt. Yagaw. Several young men of this description have already begun to visit Parina rather frequently. Ostensibly these visits are for medicines or bolo handles, but no one in Parina is deceived.

6

Marriage and Opium in a Lisu Village in Northern Thailand

Kathleen Gillogly

Alema (Second Daughter) walked into the community center building of Revealed River Village one brightly hot December afternoon as I sat at a hand-planed desk writing field notes. She slumped onto the hard bench across from me and leaned across the desk between us. She told me she envied me for being *issara* (the Thai word for "free") and then announced to me: "My mother says I have to marry a boy with land, one outside of the village. I can't marry my sweetheart because he has no land here." Alema was about seventeen years old; I was a thirty-something American divorced woman being consulted about marriage by an upland minority "girl." This interaction opened up a whole new perspective for me on how the end of the opium economy in northern Thailand had affected marriage, which is a key element in the reproduction of social structure.

Cultures exist through the people who live in them; people "carry" culture; it does not exist on its own. Therefore, we need to consider how this comes about. How do people become members of their own culture? An obvious answer is that children are enculturated or socialized through being raised by adults in their own culture—the language they learn, the social relationships they develop, the rituals they participate in, the work they learn to do—all teach children what is expected of them in their own culture. The culmination of this is, in many societies, marriage. Marriage marks a child's entry into adulthood, a fact that is apparent in many mainland Southeast Asian languages' marker of people as "girl" or "boy" for those who have not yet been married, regardless of age, and "woman" or "man" for those who are married. The wife and husband take on adult roles and responsibilities and will, as their parents before them, raise the next generation.

That is, marriage is about social as well as biological reproduction. Marriage gives the children born of that marriage a social identity. Intergenerational wealth transfer from the parents' household to the bride and groom is a core function of marriage as well, because access to economic resources is through the household. But cultures and societies do not just reproduce themselves, they also transform. The Lisu were an ideal people to study because of the profound changes that were taking place in their economic system. Concomitant were changes in the systems of kinship and marriage. My goal was to look at how social structure transforms in the face of dramatic economic change. In particular, I looked at how people strategized to achieve culturally constructed goals in the face of the end of the "opium economy," and in their attempts to reproduce their ideal social structure brought about its transformation.

BACKGROUND

The Lisu are an ethnolinguistic group living throughout northern Thailand, northern Burma, and in southwest China near Tibet. In the early nineteenth century, conflict between local people and the Chinese Empire brought about ethnic-based unrest that disrupted the regional overland trade routes that were the lifeblood of survival for people living in this region. The increasing dominance of Western colonialism in East Asia destabilized the region as trade was refocused to sea ports and to Western goods. Onto this unsettled stage came opium. Opium was an excellent cash crop, well suited to the ecological conditions of the region, and easily marketable. This crop enabled a new adaptation to a relatively stable agricultural economy. It transformed the agricultural strategies of Lisu and many other upland peoples, such as the Hmong, Mien, Lahu, and Akha. This opium economy is correlated with significant migration southward as far as Thailand starting in the late nineteenth century. When anthropologists and other observers studied upland minority peoples of Southeast Asia, they were looking at people who were opium growers. This particular historically constituted ecosystem had a profound effect on Lisu social structure.

THE AGROECOSYSTEM OF THE LISU

Lisu life must be understood in the context of the physical environment in which the people lived. The Lisu, like many other people who live in the mountains of Southeast Asia, practiced a form of farming called swiddening or shifting cultivation. Swiddening uses little in the way of tools or capital inputs. Nutrient inputs come from the forest itself.

Household heads selected fields on the basis of soil and vegetation qualities as well as the direction of slope, to ensure sufficient sunlight and rainfall. At the end of the dry cool winter, in March, Lisu families cut down the trees and brush and left it to dry through the hot season in April. The head of the household made offerings to local spirits of the land, stream, and forest to placate offended spirits who affected the productivity of the field (Durrenberger 1989). Burning and then planting occurred in April. Often, village elders regulated the burning of the swidden fields to ensure that winds did not cause uncontrolled fires (see, for example, Condominas 1977).

While swiddening sounds destructive, it is in fact an ecologically sustainable method of farming (Rambo 1983; 1984), as long as population density remains low to avoid overuse of thin mountain soils. Organic matter breaks down quickly in the heat and moisture of the tropics; the heavy rains quickly leach nutrients away from the top soil, making it unavailable for crops; soil is easily washed away on mountain slopes. Trees bring those nutrients back up into their trunks, branches, and leaves. Cutting and burning the trees release the nutrients in the ash, thus fertilizing the fields. The fire also destroys weed plants and seeds, with the result that the crops planted in the ash-fertilized field do not have to compete with weeds for a year or two; in fact, after two to three years when weeding became too much work for the women, the field is abandoned to grow back into forest. This is a very long fallow system; fields were reused every twenty years or so. The mountain minority peoples who practice swiddening are often labeled "nomadic" because they moved on a regular basis to find forested areas suitable for swiddening. Lisu, Hmong, and other opium growers tended not to return to a site—and have been labeled "pioneer" swiddeners. Before the late 1970s, a village rarely existed for more than ten years (Dessaint 1972). This subsistence-oriented agricultural system generally did not produce a surplus. Similarly, land was claimed by labor, not owned. While people maintained rights of first refusal over land they had once cropped, they did not own it; land could not be accumulated or inherited. Technology was simple (digging sticks, hoes, machetes; seed stock locally propagated), within the reach of all, and the main input to agriculture was labor. Households owned the labor and the crops produced. No one was dependent on anyone else to get access to the means of production—land—to feed themselves and their family. This was an egalitarian social system. As Lisu repeatedly told me, *"You work, you eat; you don't work, you don't eat."* For young people, this system was highly significant. Their energy and their ability to labor meant that all they really needed to make a start for themselves in life was a machete, willingness, a spouse, and an open piece of land—and there was plenty of land.

The profound egalitarianism of this system was heightened by the planting of opium poppy. Opium had been introduced as a cash crop to northern mainland Southeast Asia by the 1820s. While the opium trade was once widely believed to have been forced on the Chinese people, in fact peasant and tribal farmers in the far southwest of China had embraced this profitable crop well before the First Opium War (1832–1849) (Bello 2005; Zheng 2005). Opium was the perfect cash crop for independent small-scale farmers because the poppy could grow in marginal environments; opium was storable, and lightweight; and there was always a market for the product.

Opium gave people movable wealth, providing a small but reliable income for upland farmers. It allowed people to weather periods of scarcity. Lisu could save the opium or save the profits from opium as silver—silver made into heavy necklaces or decorative bullet-shaped pendants sewn on the clothing of young people and displayed at New Year. Opium brought economic wealth and stability to Lisu families by tying them into regional and global markets.

This new source of wealth and economic stability had consequences for Lisu populations and their marriage practices. The main form of display of wealth for Lisu is payment of bridewealth, in which a groom's family pays a substantial amount of valuables to the bride's family to claim her productive labor and the children she will bear in the marriage. Bridewealth serves as a marker of their own status, and establishes an alliance with their in-laws, the bride's family. Wealth display also occurs in the marriage feasts. Historically, with access to greater (relative) wealth from opium, earlier marriage became possible because it was easier to accrue the bridewealth silver. As a result of the introduction of opium as a cash crop, there appears to have been a population increase (earlier marriage led to more babies; a better subsistence base meant greater likelihood of children reaching adulthood). This appears to have fueled the significant population movement of Lisu and related groups southward from Yunnan (China) into Burma and Thailand by the late nineteenth and early twentieth centuries (Gillogly 2006:115–17)

In practical, everyday terms, opium funded the autonomy of individual households. The cost of bridewealth might otherwise have meant that boys were completely dependent on their parents to fund their marriages. But young people started their own fields to help fund their own marriages. In some cases, girls helped their boyfriends accumulate the silver needed for the boys to pay for the girl's bridewealth. After marriage, young couples were not dependent on their parents for land or capital. All a young couple needed to do was to open a new field, planting rice and corn as food crops and opium as a cash crop, to become a free and autonomous household (usually within two or three years after marriage; they lived with parents until then). Even young families with several small children (consumers) and only two working adults (producers)—usually the poorer type of household—compensated by hiring laborers from neighboring ethnic groups to weed opium fields. Young couples also supplemented their household livelihood by using the forest: they kept livestock that grazed in the forest; they hunted wild pig and birds; and women collected firewood and vegetables. As a result, young couples were able to become independent from their parents very quickly after marriage. These factors counteracted the relations of debt and dependency that might otherwise have existed between a young couple and their parents. We can see this in that lineages did not reside together.[1] In the days of the opium economy, when villages broke up and people migrated in search of better land, young couples were as likely to go with the bride's parents as with the groom's, or to go with a group of siblings (especially sisters) and cousins, or an aunt and uncle, or even an ally or patron rather than their lineal kin. Young couples were independent of lineage kinship obligations.

TRANSFORMATIONS IN THE AGRICULTURAL ECOSYSTEM

Land

This egalitarianism and freedom from lineage kinship obligations had become rare by the end of the twentieth century. When Alema told me she had to marry a boy with land, she was strategizing in the face of a radical change in the fundamental system of the household economy. That change was the result of the end of the opium economy and the extension of Thai state control over the mountain lands on which Lisu lived. Alema's predicament encapsulated the fundamental changes in the agricultural economy of Lisu in northern Thailand: land had become scarce, labor was now cheap, land and other valuables (capital) had to be inherited. Permanent status and class differences among Lisu households were emerging. No longer was it possible for Alema to marry and create a home and household with her husband through their own labor on open lands. She had to find a boy with land or other forms of wealth, which meant she had to find a boy whose family owned land that he could inherit.

As it grew and consolidated, the Thai state increased its control of territory within the boundaries of Thailand (boundaries that were created under the forces of colonialism), in part through forestry law (see Vandergeest and Peluso 1995; Thongchai 1994). As a result, land had become a scarce commodity by the early 1990s. Under Thai state control, all "unoccupied" land was declared to belong to the state unless legal ownership could be proven. Most farmers, and especially upland minority farmers, did not have that kind of paperwork and so lost the right to legally cultivate land. More recently, all mountain lands with a slope of over thirty degrees were decreed class 1A watershed land on which there was to be no human settlement, farming, timbering, or even collection of branches and plants in the forest. Land ownership was also constrained by the fact that few ethnic minority people had "blue cards" giving them legal residence in Thailand; fewer still had outright citizenship. Legal status therefore became a key factor in the choices a girl and her family could make about marriage.

In fact, Lisu and other upland minority peoples found ways to stay on mountain land—where else was there to go? But they were put in a position of dependency vis-à-vis government officials who now had the right to forcibly resettle them, or to tell them what they could and could not plant. In parts of northern Thailand, it was possible to buy land (illegally, but this was rarely an impediment where bribes were accepted). Those with ready capital bought land in many different parts of northern Thailand as security in the face of shifting development plans and policy.

Cropping

Changes in the cropping system put further pressure on this economic system. Opium had supported a relatively large population in the mountains by opening a new econiche that brought in resources through involvement in global markets. The ecological system could not produce enough rice and corn to fill subsistence needs. Opium had been a subsistence-oriented cash crop; its profits were used first and foremost to buy rice and a few other necessities. Rice crops were more heavily dependent on nutrients in the soil and had to be rotated out more frequently. With the enclosure of land in the mountains (and alienation of land by timber companies or lowland migrants), there was not enough land to grow rice because farmers could not rotate their fields. This occurred contemporaneously with the interdiction of opium. Thus, Lisu farmers desperately and anxiously sought new crops that had a stable and profitable market. These new cash crops—potatoes, strawberries, barley, and others—required capital inputs of pesticides and fertilizers, and the seeds had to be bought. Crops became far more expensive to produce; the means of production were not open to everyone due to the land and capital investments needed, as well as due to the specific kind of labor requirements these new crops entailed.

The end of the opium economy and the closing of the forests engendered greater risks and insecurities for Lisu households, straining the management of household production. The demographic cycle of Lisu households was altered, as were inter-household relations.

BRIDEWEALTH AND MARRIAGE

Lisu celebrate the Chinese lunar New Year. This holiday and the Little New Year that follows a month later were key not only in the ritual cycle, but in the marriage cycle as well. In the course of the celebrations, young people would find partners or wrap up their own progress toward getting married. During my second year in the village, I sat up with the elder men overlooking the circle dances of the young people. The unmarried girls, dressed in all of their family's silver and wearing decorated flat turbans, "tails" made of piping (strands of rolled colored cloth), and embroidered gaiters, danced in a circle around the New Year tree and musicians. Young men slipped into the circle next to the girls they were interested in. All of this was fondly observed by the older men and women, who praised the girls' beauty, suggested which girls ought to be getting married, and discussed the harvest that had just been completed. But this year, the elders were pessimistic. "Look at all the girls, and there's no boys," they worried. "We have too many girls." They discussed economic hard times and the fact that marriages were rare because there were few boys. And, in fact, in my nearly three years in these villages, I saw only four marriages. This inability to get married was seen as a social problem by young and old alike, and had given rise to much social dislocation as young men and women tried to find their place in a world that had closed certain paths to them.

One of the significant changes in household formation in Revealed River Village was the increase in the age at first marriage. I found that young women who married in Revealed River and its cluster villages were in their early to mid-twenties. This phenomenon is often thought to be related to "modernization," particularly because of the education of women (Caldwell 1976:142; Ezra 2003), but this was not the case in Revealed River. Rather, it was part of a more general trend among the Lisu, rooted in recent constraints on household resources, and was experienced by young people as a lack of opportunity to get married.

There was also a frightening increase in the numbers of suicides among unmarried girls in their twenties. The economic dislocation of the new agricultural system had had profoundly negative impacts on girls and young women who were not married by their early twenties; ashamed, many ran off to the lowlands to work (usually ending up in some form of the sex trade) or committed suicide (Hutheesing 1990:153–6, 168–171; Hutheesing personal correspondence, March 1994). An incident of a Lisu girl who threatened suicide by jumping from a telecommunications tower because her suitor was too poor to pay bridewealth was widely reported in the international media (Reuters 1998).

The mechanism at work here was the inflation of bridewealth in the opium days; this was not, however, matched by deflation with the end of the opium economy. To accept lower bridewealth meant shame not only for the parents of the bride, but also for the bride herself and for her children (Hutheesing 1990:113). This was based on the Lisu concept of *myi-do*, glossed as repute but also implying face, honor, respect, and reputation. Myi-do was a major motivating factor in Lisu strategies; it was tied to the profound egalitarianism of Lisu households in the days of the opium economy, when households demonstrated their repute through showing their productivity in the silver displayed on young people at the New Year and the household's ability to get their young people married.

As a result of the interdiction of opium and swiddening, Lisu households experienced severe economic constraints. One way that families dealt with lack of resources was to wait for better years to marry off their children. Household heads (both fathers and mothers) treated this as a short-term, temporary constraint and tried to reorient their daughter's marriage goals—encouraging them to not stay here, close to their mother and sisters, but to go elsewhere, where there might be opportunity to have land to work. "We are poor. When will we be allowed to grow opium again?" I was queried countless times. Hopes that policy would change were not irrational, given the past history of periodic government policy alterations in light of shifting international policy, trends in development, and state bureaucratic politics. People were waiting—for land to help their children establish viable households and for the cash to pay bridewealth and establish household repute, capital to set up new enterprises—and as a result, marriage was delayed.

Marriage payments had become a barrier to marriage. Households faced the practical problem of accumulating bridewealth when there was less surplus from agriculture and greater need for investments in economic activities to replace opium. These changes in the context of shifting political and economic conditions transformed the resources available to households and were experienced as constraining household wealth and repute. These shifts were not perceived as a permanent destruction of what was considered essential—establishing children in marriage, maintaining autonomy, and displaying repute. The strategies were oriented toward fulfilling these same goals in the face of new conditions. Accordingly, Lisu parents were able to use a range of strategies for bringing about marriage. One was attempting to direct whom their daughters married (and with a good brideprice, they would be able to afford a bride for their own son). Another strategy was to revive forms of marriage that had existed before the glories of the opium economy. One form of marriage, full of repute, was cross-cousin[2] marriage. I was told that this was a favored form but was rarely practiced; this apparently was true in the recent past as well (Durrenberger 1971:16). Despite the rarity, one of the few marriages I witnessed was indeed such a marriage. It brought repute without huge expense because the groom's family paid merely what had been received for the bride's mother thirty years previously. Another strategy was to have much less elaborate marriage feasts. There were some other, less expensive but less "repute-full" forms of marriage as well—but these left the families involved talking as if the marriage were a mere engagement (even years after children from the marriage were teenagers).

One important strategy previously used by poor boys to marry no longer existed: bride service. In the opium economy, this form was appealing to household heads as it was a way to recruit labor into their households; rather than losing a daughter, the household gained a son. Post-marital residence had been negotiable. Although patrilineal and patrilocal in ideology, in practice the terms of brideservice were negotiated in relation to the amount of bridewealth paid at the time of the marriage. Patrilineality was the stated ideal, with a recognized and common exception based on the conflicting principle of uxorilocal[3] post-marital residence for a period of three years (one year in Revealed River in the 1990s). After completion of bride service, the couple had been more likely to remain with the bride's family; in such ways, allegiance groups were formed. Bride service and uxorilocality had once been more common than patrilocality (Dessaint and Dessaint 1992:163; Durrenberger 1971:17–18; Durrenberger 1976; Hutheesing 1990:124, 196). In fact, the most common co-residents in a village were a group of sisters and their husbands, or a powerful man and his allies' families.

But uxorilocality was very rare where I worked in the 1990s. This is why Alema and other girls had been told by their mothers that they had to marry out.

One to two generations previously, it would have taken a Lisu one year to acquire the brideprice, but by the 1980s it would have taken more than two years to acquire brideprice *even if they could have grown opium poppies* (Hutheesing 1990:178). Young men had become far more dependent on their parents for bridewealth and for land to cultivate after marriage, making young men more subject to their parents' authority. Similarly, young women were constrained because their opportunities for marriage were subject to social judgment of them as good workers; to defy one's parents was to gain a reputation as poor marriage material. Thus globalization in the form of the global drug war had led to increased parental power and the power of the patrilineage in these Lisu villages.

In addition, the perception of decreased availability of wealth must be put in perspective by two factors: decreased value of labor as a source of household wealth and repute, and increased demands on the use of household wealth for investment in making a living. In the opium economy, labor had been the source of wealth; households competed to have the newly married couple reside with them because the couple's labor was valued. With the end of the opium economy, the means by which households gained wealth was no longer through expansion of production but through capital investment—in trucks, land, fertilizer, pesticides, or education. Each year, households had to strategize the means to subsistence, and bringing another producer into the household was a lower immediate priority. In particular, the labor of girls and young women was not as valuable as it had once been.

CONCLUSION

When land was open access and households could always grow enough opium to buy the rice they needed if they were not self-sufficient, the limiting factor in the economic system was household labor. Productive labor was organized by households, and thus by the kinship system. Recruitment of labor occurred through marriage, and so households competed to get young people married early and to get the newlyweds to live with them. In addition, young couples could very quickly repay their "debt" to those who had paid the bridewealth that allowed them to get married; they went on to establish "repute-full" autonomous households.

This avenue to repute was now largely gone. Productive labor of young women was not the key to household wealth. Rather, households focused on maintaining their patrilineal land and allocating scarce resources to trucks, motorbikes, education, new cash crops, and chemical inputs (fertilizer, pesticide) for those crops. Without wealth to pay bridewealth, marriage occurred later; young women sought young men who would be able to bring them into the boys' patrilineage and use their land. And so, young Lisu women lost their repute. Marriage was a key node, the locus at which these changes were worked out. The mechanism by which social structure was transformed was in marriage strategies.

Over time, Alema was under pressure to go to work in a lowland town. Her father's sister lived in a tourist town; Alema had told me before that this family was "rich" because they did not have to work in the fields and, in fact, did not even have agricultural land. But Alema resisted her father's request. Her middle-class Thai teachers at the government boarding school of "hill tribe" children had warned her that working in town was a sure path to sex work. When I left the village, she had told her father she would not go. But as opportunities for marriage looked progressively bleaker, making some kind of contribution to her father's household through work in the lowlands looked all the more appealing. She would make her own choice, but it would be within the structural constraints of political and economic life in northern Thailand.

NOTES

1. Lineages are a form of kinship in which people get their social identity from one side of the family—the father's in a patrilineal society and the mother's in a matrilineal society. The Lisu were patrilineal in ideology, meaning that their ideal strategies were based on patrilineal relationships. However, in the height of the opium economy, patrilineal relationships were not primary in people's choices.

2. Cross-cousin marriage is marriage to the son or daughter of a parent's opposite sex sibling. For instance, a favored marriage for Lisu was for a boy to marry his mother's brother's daughter; or a girl to marry her father's sister's son. While marriage is among first cousins is largely frowned upon in the United States today, marriage to a cousin has been allowed and favored in many times and places—witness the marriages of European royalty.

3. Uxorilocal residence is when the young couple live with the bride's father and mother. This is in contrast to patrilocal residence, the ideal form of post-marital residence, where the bride and groom live with the groom's family.

7

Merit and Power in the Thai Social Order

Lucien M. Hanks, Jr.

THE COSMIC ORDER

As good Buddhists, the Thai perceive that all living beings stand in a hierarchy of varying ability to make actions effective and of varying degrees of freedom from suffering. As actions become more effective, beings suffer less; the two vary together; such is the nature of existence. Above man in shimmering space stand the angels and gods who, with a single word, can stop the course of rivers. Man, however, must dig and delve to turn a rivulet, feeble efforts that may be wrecked in a moment by a sudden freshet. But man's effectiveness in action and freedom from suffering exceed those of the animals standing beneath him on the hierarchy. Animals share with man a corporeal existence limited to the surface of the earth, but man is somewhat more able to cope with rain and cold. While animals wander in search of food, man has learned to produce and store his, at least until the next harvest.

This hierarchy depends on a composite quality called "merit" (*bun*) or "virtue" (*khwaamdii*), or one may also speak of a graded series of penalties (*baap*). Yet in translation these words fail to convey the particular Thai emphasis. Like a dog snarling to keep his bone, a lower being is more covetous than a higher one who would generously give away his last bowl of rice. The emphasis lies in selflessness. Instead of using his effectiveness in action to tend his own wants, the selfless farmer, feeling compassionate toward creatures of greater suffering, feeds his buffalo before turning to his own meal. Compassion, however, cannot work unaided by understanding; the powerful angel in the forest allows many lost and weary travelers to pass unaided, for he chooses to help only the worthy ones who will be strengthened in virtue, knowing that the evil will continue their evil deeds.

In English, "merit" implies a fixed characteristic, but the Thai equivalent sees a person always gaining or losing merit. Even a humble ox can do good, be it only by drawing faithfully his master's cart. Of course, by dint of his greater merit, an angel is freer to help and also to harm than this ox. There are no fallen angels in the Thai cosmos. When sins cause the fall of Satan and Lucifer, they metamorphose for their next existence into creatures lower in the hierarchy with less effective action and greater suffering. The loathsome demons of the Thai cosmos are only powerful beings who inflict suffering on the sinful with as much justice as the angels who bring good.

Such is the nature of the cosmic hierarchy where effectiveness in action and freedom from suffering vary with the degree of merit, yet no being is fixed to any special position. Only the stations are fixed, while the metamorphosing individual beings rise and fall in the hierarchy. In accordance with past merit, one being may be born a snake to crawl helplessly in darkness while another may be born an angel free to move unhampered by matter. After death their positions might be reversed.

MANKIND

The same laws apply in the human social order which is but a segment of the cosmic hierarchy. Because of his greater merit, a rich man is more effective than a poor man and freer from suffering. He commands his chauffeur to drive him to the government office, while the peasant must tramp through the mud to his rice field. His dependent kinsmen and servants outnumber the peasant's small household. To this larger group the rich man gives more generously of his greater wealth; he must resist temptation to be miserly; even his servants receive better care than the peasant's children in their thatched hut. The rich man marries off his children with more elaborate ceremony and offers more alms at the temple. Contrary to the Christian gospel, a poor widow, giving her all to the priest, remains less blessed than the rich man; both have performed meritorious acts, but the Thai observe that the effectiveness of ten thousand baht far outweighs the widow's battered coin.

As with the cosmic hierarchy, the Thai social order roots individuals in no permanent rank. To be sure, depending on merit accumulated from past existences, one is born to the advantages or disadvantages of a given social position, but one need not remain a peasant until the end of his days. Peasants have become ministers of state, just as powerful kings have become slaves. Social life is a continuous process of changing station by earning and validating a higher one, or falling to a lower one. At any moment the lowest man may catapult himself to a position effectively superior to the king; he need only take the vows of a priest. As long as he submits to the discipline of selflessness required by the rules of the order, he may remain in this lofty position. On the other hand, there are limits to movement. Human beings have a lifespan of only a few decades, during which they must sleep, eat, and labor, always subject to corporeal limitations. Gaining in subsequent existences a higher form through virtuous conduct is the only route to overcome his suffering and gain greater effectiveness of action.

Let us examine the constitution of a group, so as to clarify the social process of rising and falling in the hierarchy. Here we translate merit-based effectiveness in action and freedom from suffering into daily living. Groups form only when a man has gathered resources and can distribute them as benefits to others. In the household one distributes to the members food, clothing, and shelter. Employers give opportunities for earning money, often food and shelter as well. A peasant may benefit his neighbor by lending a buffalo to help with the plowing. By accepting these benefits, one enters an explicit or tacit agreement to reciprocate with some service. A young man described going to Bangkok from the countryside and joining his father's younger brother and his wife:

> When I first went to live there, my aunt didn't have any children, but afterwards she did, but he's still only a little boy. Also, my aunt wanted me to take my uncle's place as the supervisor [of a small cutlery factory]. She has some land outside of Bangkok, and sometimes my aunt and uncle go on business to see this land, and I watch over the work instead of him. It seemed he really entrusted the work to me. I think that my uncle and aunt wanted me to live with them as their son until their death. That's why they always talked about giving me a house and a job. And after they had their own child, my aunt said she would entrust me to take care of him, and would give me a house and some land. And she said she would divide the land. She would entrust me to take care of her son until the end of my life. This is what my aunt said; but my uncle didn't say anything. (Phillips 1957)

By accepting the wages, food, housing, and the promise of becoming a factory manager, the young man obligated himself to supervise the factory, to care for his aunt and uncle in their old age, and to look after their son when they were dead. The aunt and uncle, by offering these benefits, established themselves as the superiors over the young man who became their client. They would never have made an offer of this importance to a nonkinsman, though nonkinsmen did work in the factory at lesser jobs. Such a transaction with its connotation of inequality is the indispensable condition for group existence.[1] Groups themselves are tiny hierarchies with a superior showering benefits on his nearest inferior, who in turn relays a portion to someone standing beneath him. Such a linear structure of groups does not mean that each member addresses himself exclusively to the person on a station immediately adjacent to him, though such an arrangement may be approximated in circumstances like a large government bureau. The leader must see that even the lowliest member is adequately cared for, yet the linear organization is evident. The peasant who feeds and shelters his children grants them attention in accordance with age, except for the often "spoiled" youngest. Among siblings, confidence and affection is most apt to develop between those of adjacent age, and the hierarchic compulsion becomes clearest when twins, born a few minutes apart, are carefully instructed to address each other as older or younger. The king standing among his ministers, though regarding them all as ministers, recognizes an implicit hierarchy based on wealth and size of group that each commands. Without hierarchy, order cannot reign, though the equality of husband and wife forms a startling exception to this rule.

The coherence of Thai society rests largely on the value of becoming a client of someone who has greater resources than one alone possesses; a person is ill-advised to try to fight one's own battles independently. Security grows with affiliation, and the crowning moment of happiness lies in the knowledge of dependable benefits distributed in turn to faithful inferiors. At the top stands the gracious king meeting with his courtly officials. Below them, with mounting uncertainties and smaller benefits to distribute, follow the ranks of deputies and assistants down to the clerks and sweepers. Some of the merchants and artisans may surpass the lower governmental positions in wealth and power, but in the paddy fields, existence becomes more isolated and precarious. At the bottom is the forest where some lone, uncouth hunter, deserted by his wife and children, stalks his prey. Because of unruly temper and undisciplined manner, he can find no one who will long reciprocate his undependable services. From top to bottom groups dwindle in size and stability. The organization is like the leaves, twigs, branches, and boughs of a great oak. One may trace a linear path from the heart of the tree outward to any leaf; each leaf, twig, and branch, standing at a unique distance from the heart, receives varying amounts of nourishment. In the frail twigs at the ends of the branches is found the greatest fragility, while the heart and adjoining boughs safely stand through many storms.

SOCIAL MOBILITY

Clearly, station in the hierarchy improves by amassing greater resources for distribution. In accordance with one's reputation for generosity and managerial skill in making benefits more enduring, one's group grows or withers. Thus to increase status, one may first, through personal diligence, accumulate resources for broader distribution. At the same time the system offers a second manner of rising, for a man of lower station often cannot hope to increase his resources independently: he may offer his services to another with resources greater than his own and redistribute the resulting benefits among his own following. A village headman can, perhaps through his own resources, hold his kinsmen, but to hold the entire village may require his rendering services to the circle headman (*kamnan*) and perhaps also to the district officer (*naaj amphoe*). The additional benefits received from these higher officers, for instance as work opportunities for his villagers, can be distributed by the headman to secure his position.

Among the Thai the relation endures only as long as it serves the convenience of both parties. A superior may terminate benefits, or an inferior may cease rendering services at his own discretion. A Thai freeman formerly sought out the advantages of rendering services, for the benefits increased his security. In contrast, the bottom ranks of feudal society, excepting the outlaws, were by and large the most tightly bound and least mobile. The absence of peasant revolts in Thai history demonstrates this difference, and freedom to contract anew helped reduce a master's tyranny.

To be sure, freedom to make and break liaisons to a superior was not always equally or immediately available, yet even slavery implied no fixed position. All slaves might regain their freedom by payment to their masters. In the case of prisoners of war and their children the price of redemption was fixed by law in 1805. Debt slaves might repay their obligations through labor and were always free to change masters by finding someone to pay off their debt in return for their services (Duplatre 1933). Free peasants might not in fact always have access to another superior, and the perils of isolation might outweigh considerable abuse by some local Caligula. Yet ultimately a freeman could always escape to the forest, and the excessively cruel master was always considered to be cutting the bough beneath his own feet.

Of course, freedom to contract anew did not obviate the use of force to sustain a liaison, and many a military expedition set out to punish a vassal who delayed in forwarding tribute. Yet here, the right to affiliate with another was not in question, rather the wisdom of attempting it. Indeed former affiliation with an enemy did not necessarily blight participation in a new alliance. Traitors as morally despicable figures are absent from this scene.

The history of 19th century Thailand contains many incidents that can only be understood in these terms. Cambodia and, for a brief period, the principality of Vientiane sent tribute both to Bangkok and to the rival Annamese power at Hue (Vella 1957:80, 95). [. . .]

One of the latest of these shifts was the return of Field Marshal Pibul Songkhram to the office of Prime Minister in 1948, even though he had earlier been accused of leading the Thai to defeat by his alliance with Japan during World War II.

Change of affiliation is not a privilege of aristocrats and statesmen but extends as a right to all people. The young man from the country who seemed to have secured a life-long contract with his aunt and uncle subsequently abandoned his benefactors (see above); he said simply:

"About my uncle's work, there was a controversy between my uncle and the person who bought the bronze knives. At my uncle's place there was less work; we didn't make as many knives as usual. So I returned [home to the country]." When asked why he returned, he replied: "Because . . . we had to work harder and make less money." (Phillips 1957)

Even between kinsmen the obligation endured only as long as it served the mutual interest.

Efforts to depict social classes in Thai society founder because of miscon-struing the nature of this social order, which resembles a military organiza-tion more than an occidental class-type society. Like an army, Thai society has a hierarchy of fixed ranks which determine occupation, but one moves freely from occupation to occupation up and down the hierarchy. The king might grant title to commoners as easily as a master could free his slaves. On suffering defeat, kings could become slaves with little to comfort them for having once held power. Neither noble nor commoner had to defend his new status against criticism, any more than a captain reminds his newly commissioned fellow captain that yesterday he was only a commander. A man rises because of merit and is accepted without regard for his humble origin. Indeed, a humble origin implies a considerable store of merit and might increase his prestige.[2]

What we designate as the individual or person is more restricted in Thai than in Western society. A Thai is a minister or a farmer only as long as he holds the station. When a farmer, he acts as a farmer, but when he receives his insignia of office, he discards his rustic ways. A man described his ser-vice as a priest under a very strict abbot who disciplined him on more than one occasion, and who made living in this particular temple unpleasant for the entire order. Later, when both had retired from the priesthood, the two became great friends. The raconteur with no trace of resentment explained that his friend, the former abbot, had then to act strictly but could under new circumstances be a very warm friend. Thus one emphasizes the sta-tion of the moment. People tend to speak of Mr. District Officer (*naaj amphoe*) rather than the more personal Mr. District Officer Suk. One prays for assis-tance to an impersonal Lord of the Place (*cao thii*) rather than to a certain sainted Francis or Michael. Formerly the king in raising a person to higher rank gave him also a new name in harmony with his title. His name from childhood was discarded, and on retirement he would be addressed only by the latest and presumably most honorific of several names.

By emphasis on status rather than person, the Thai equip themselves for mobility and transient position. To a greater extent than in the West, the in-signia transform the person. To a lesser degree do people speak slightingly of the "newly arrived" or seek flaws in the clothing that intends to make a gentleman. Thus the uniqueness of the person, his personal identity, sub-serves his position on the hierarchy.

A FEW RULES OF SOCIAL MOVEMENT

To describe adequately the Thai social scene requires a calculus of movements rather than an appeal to geometric concepts. As we have already seen, groups under a leader vary in size and stability; those rising in the hierarchy become larger and more stable. In turn, size and stability depend on the economic resource ready for distribution. Hence, a primary rule of social movement may be stated: As groups grow in resources, they grow larger and more stable. Conversely, as resources diminish, groups dwindle in size and stability.

Within a group the movements correspond very closely to this picture also. As the resources of a group increase, benefits accrue in greater measure to those standing near the leader and are distributed in diminishing amounts down the scale. Thus each group, like a comet, has its greatest solidarity at the head, while toward the tail greater instability occurs.

Similarly, in affiliating with a superior, the person with the larger and more stable group, hence greater resources for rendering services, receives a higher position within a group than persons with fewer resources to offer. Conversely, in terminating an affiliation with a group, those persons or groups with fewer resources and fewer benefits are more likely to seek to affiliate elsewhere.

From these variations in the resources necessary for affiliation at various points on the hierarchy, we may speak of a "price gradient" for affiliation. This means simply that the price of affiliation changes progressively as one rises in the hierarchy. Such a "price gradient" for affiliation may also be expected to vary for the areas of Thailand. Bangkok would have the highest, while the gradient would diminish as one moves from provincial capitals toward more isolated communities. [. . .]

THE FUNCTION OF POWER

[. . .] The hierarchy and the movements of people on [this scale] have been derived from the single function of merit. To be sure, merit has traditionally been the most important explanation of position in the hierarchy and degree of mobility, but moments of perfect justice in an orderly system are rare. Poets have described those fleeting moments where each benefit is faithfully reciprocated with diligent services under a benevolent monarch. More often the workings of justice are slow; faithful servants toil for ungrateful masters, and benevolent masters fail to discover their servants' deceit. Indeed, when misfortune strikes, Thai do not conclude immediately that they possess insufficient merit to attain their ends and then hurry bearing alms to a temple. Instead, each seeks first among his own resources to improve his lot, and to the extent that he succeeds, merit may or may not seem relevant.

To make the case clearer, we may ask, what enables the lowly hunter to turn brigand and live more comfortably, at least for a while, on the loot extracted by force? What permits a cruel and unjust tyrant to maintain himself, when the law of morality clearly says his reign must stop or, for that matter, never should have begun in the first place?

The Thai recognize a second factor operating in the social order in addition to merit. They speak of "power" (*khaeng, khaengraeng, 'amnaad*) with very much the same amoral implication as the English word. This power may be a personal characteristic, like indolence or energy. Some power arises from experience, some from special knowledge; a shrewd man can sell his buffalo at a better price by timing the sale with favorable astrological influences. Another may succeed in his endeavors or counter another's plan through power derived from amulets, and some persons are specially favored because they stand in the protective aegis of a guardian outside the social order of mankind.

In principle one may easily distinguish power from effectiveness. Though both aid the success of an undertaking, power may belong to anyone, while effectiveness derives only from merit. Because effectiveness of action stems from enduring moral principles that govern the cosmos, gains made on this basis outlast gains from amoral power. One may overcome a girl's reserve for a night or two with love magic, but an enduring marriage can only come from merit. In practice, effectiveness may be difficult to distinguish from power. Amulets, tattooed marks, verbal formulae, and a host of other devices enable the gambler to win, the boxer to beat his opponent, the soldier to win in battle, and the physician to cure a patient.[3] In addition, a considerable proportion of the population seeks to insure the outcome of critical undertakings through offerings to various spirits. [. . .]

As a rule, people infer the basis of success from a variety of surrounding circumstances. Few would disagree when a robber escapes with loot that he had special power. If the police arrested him the following week, this would clinch the argument. Judgment might be harder when someone discovers, say, a treasure of gold buried in the ruin of a long-abandoned temple. If the finder gave it to the priests at a going temple, this might persuade some that merit lay at the roots, but they would suspect power if he just lived high for a while. A sensible person would probably give some to the priests and live well too. Here judgment would have to wait to see whether his good fortune continued. The following case illustrates such a transformation:

> Naaj Chyyn moved into a country village with a clouded reputation and quickly proved his prowess with a sword. He had moved in order to avoid further conflict with his creditors and the police. Together with his wife and two children, he settled on rented land, built a thatched hut, and began to live the life of a farmer. People of the neighborhood treated him respectfully

so as not to encounter his wrath. One day a leading member of the locality asked him to accompany a group of local residents to attend a [nearby] festival. [. . .] He should protect them against robbers and thugs. So effective was his surveillance that the people asked him to accompany them on further outings, and he soon became an informal kind of constable for the village. Later, when a nearby temple was being built, the head priest and village headman invited him to manage the construction. He could control the hired workmen, settle quarrels, and keep them on the job. When the temple was finished, the head priest appointed him manager and guardian of the temple, for during fairs and on other occasions rowdies came disturbing the celebration. At feasts in private homes his neighbors gave Chyyn a place of honor, and he died a respected member of the community (a personal communication by Lauriston Sharp).

In addition to the many amulets that effectively protected him in his encounters, people concluded, he must have merit as well.

The uncertainty of power adds a special moment of flux to the scene. Social liaisons on this account become more brittle, and especially so near the top where the stakes are high. A government official, who has labored long to build his following, may find himself undercut by a rival at the moment he had expected to advance. Another who considered himself secure in office is asked without warning to resign in favor of a newcomer. Such demotions result in loss of benefits for followers who in turn must seek a new benefactor if they would hold their gains.[4] Of course, similar events with equally disturbing effects plague rural people too. Unpredictably a spouse disappears with someone recently moved into the neighborhood. A tenant of long standing is told one day that he may not till the land during the coming year.

People build in certain adaptations to this uncertainty. To each other everyone is outwardly polite, even light-hearted, but they are rarely frank. Because the other person is superior or inferior, he must be treated circumspectly, particularly if he is a stranger, for he may become the source of some advantage or disadvantage. Even those of long acquaintance may not be trusted implicitly, for they too may lead one to catastrophe. From this atmosphere arises the Thai proclivity to maximize the harmony and pleasantness of meeting others: it is well to avoid debates and best to keep the topic amusingly light. Because of unseen dangers, a leader ordinarily avoids giving benefits to strangers, and a potential member of a group must be introduced by a known person. Similarly, a liaison between superior and inferior once established needs continual validation, be it merely through the smile of a servant or the commendation of a master.

Uncertainties become moot problems when a young man is tying himself to a rising star. He must sort the evidence to determine whether his prospective patron's success is based on merit or power. The bold ones, perhaps spurred by special knowledge from their own esoteric sources of power, rush to share the ascent. The cautious delay, waiting for more certain evidence that time will yield. When a secure position seems to establish merit as the basis for success, and when one no longer risks anything to join him, perhaps then the star will decline. People then say that, having established the meritorious base, he has exceeded his merit. So, despite these judgments, one never knows. Saints may turn into criminals, and brigands into stalwart leaders of a community. Agility in changing allegiance at the proper moment is a valuable asset.

The player of this social scene must be continuously alert. As Sharp (1957) observed, one must look up and down the hierarchy to confirm one's position. The provincial governor must not only wear the extra bar of office that distinguishes him from his deputy but outshine him by riding in a better car to a more expensive restaurant where after a heartier meal he leaves a larger tip. To overlook the etiquette of one's station is a first step toward decline. And at the same time, the wary person must not forget an occasional glance to the side, to someone standing near one's station in another group. He is a potential rival for higher station, should be granted no quarter and expects none.

[Westerners] [. . .] wilt under the impermanence of [these] arrangements. The government official who personally smoothed an impasse has been transferred and cannot repeat his charity. The farmer who sold those fresh eggs last week has sold his whole flock of chickens and established a coffee shop. International agencies complain that their training programs and carefully organized projects may be negated by shifts of the cooperating Thai civil officials. Even more disconcerting to a Westerner, the ethics of loyalty and honor seem to be badly developed in the Thai scene. These values, as defined in the West, though, depend for implementation on a society of relatively fixed position. Enforcement of "honor" or "loyalty" depends on the expectation of incessant shaming by unavoidable associates. But in this shifting social scene, contracts and promises sincerely made are little better indicators of future action than casual statements.

MOMENTS OF STABILITY

We dare not leave this vista of kaleidoscopic impermanence without mentioning a few factors in stability. Certainly the merit-based hierarchy represents the fixed field on which action occurs. Though power blurs the clear edges of cosmic justice, one may think of justice lagging behind, like a court with a clogged calendar, in exacting punishments and awarding compensations. The stations on the hierarchy, too, are relatively fixed. While the particular priests in a temple change from year to year, as do the members of a government bureau or the artisans in a tinker's shop, the tasks at each of these stations remain roughly the same. In all sections of the hierarchy the general rules apply for the reciprocation of benefits and services.

Sex and age further define action and limit the range of mobility. Though men stand on the whole slightly above women and though both sexes share tasks flexibly, the man is expected to be "hard" (*khaeng*), since he must advance the group on the hierarchy. Women are "soft" (*auaun*), hence are less directly concerned with social advancement; they work to solidify the group. A child, though inducted early into the system of benefits and services, is considered too weak for the rules to apply with full vigor. Similarly, after a life-time of benefits and services, the aged reciprocate only if they are so inclined. The rules of reciprocation and the struggle for position focus particularly on the adult male until his nominal retirement.

In speaking of "rigor" in applying the rules, we are only affirming that the expectation of services in return for benefits varies between a meticulous accounting and the never-calculated, easy transactions of old friends. When a farmer exchanges uprooting labor[5] with his neighbors, all parties know the exact number of bundles that must be bound within the work day. When an older brother houses and feeds, clothes, and treats his younger brother, neither party in this liaison knows the services that are to be returned nor expects them within a particular time. As long as "love" (*khwaamrag*) and "respect" (*nabthyy*) dominate, neither partner reckons his efforts. Love and respect thus become stabilizing factors in liaisons, for then fewer are inclined to break the relationship. These qualities mark the relations especially of kinsmen, and kinship accordingly promotes more permanent liaisons. Yet, as we have already seen, the right to terminate a liaison is exercised among kinsmen as well as nonkinsmen. When convenient, parents leave their children with aunts and uncles; siblings take off on their own.[6] A wife departed with the cash, livestock, and tools of her jailed husband to join another man, but no one questioned her right to do so; people observed only that she loved her former husband for his property. Yet certainly "love" and "respect" slow the speed of breaking liaisons.

[. . .]

Before the 20th century, slow transportation limited the geographic area of mobility, and within a given area the special privileges and restrictions applying to nobles, commoners, and slaves further curtailed the easy range of movement. However, the abolition of slavery in 1872 lifted one barrier to social mobility. The demise of the royal harem in the second decade of the [previous] century together with the revolution of 1932 reduced the privileges of nobility to a smaller portion of the population and modified these privileges substantially. In these ways social mobility has been increasing [since the nineteenth century], to say nothing of the transportation which has multiplied geographic mobility. Yet important new restrictions are developing.

Education presents the single most important new barrier to movement, for without satisfying educational prerequisites for governmental posts, many lack access to advancement. Certain occupations, e.g., medicine and engineering, are developing relatively closed groups where admission requires special training. [. . .]

In these manners, new rules for moving in the social scene are developing. Yet the fundamental principles of merit and power still operate, and the new occupations are readily fitted to the hierarchy. Desire to rise and fear of falling remain the emphasis. Specialists trained abroad may or may not practice their specialties at home, but the letters of a foreign degree after one's name opens the way to higher station. As new occupations appear, people learn the skills in school or on the job, but [for the] Thai these [acquired] skills lie more peripherally in the ego; to the Thai they are more instrumental than personal, like carrying an umbrella on a rainy day or learning to row a boat. Concerned mainly with the advancement, the power, and ultimately the merit, they treat their skills as insignia for a higher rank.

NOTES

Originally published as "Merit and Power in the Thai Social Order," *American Anthropologist*, New Series 64 (6, December 1962):1247–1261. This work has been edited for length [ed.]

Field data were gathered in Bang Chan, Thailand, under the auspices of one of Cornell University's Thailand projects, between 1948 and 1957. I have drawn liberally from the field notes of Jane R. Hanks, Lauriston Sharp, Kamol Janlekha, Robert B. Textor, Herbert Phillips, Saovanee Sudsaneh, Aram Emuran, and Jadun Kongsa, whom I would thank for their insights. My work was supported by the U.S. Fulbright Foundation in Thailand, the Wenner-Gren Foundation for Anthropological Research, the American Philosophical Society, and the Social Research Council.

1. The relationship called *dyadic*, as described by Foster (1961), has interesting comparable features. It is associated in Thailand also with a cognatic kinship structure, takes place between individuals. The Thai version is asymmetrical, occurring only between persons of unequal status and, because the contract may involve one's subordinates, thereby knits groups rather than just pairs of people.

2. [. . .] Thai society differentiates social positions and gives them value; it does not restrict movement, as stratification implies, but rather establishes the rules for mobility.

3. R. B. Textor (1960) describes 118 supernatural objects, of which approximately half contribute to success in action.

4. Wilson (1959:37–38) mentions this kind of movement in politics: "Party labels are incidental. [. . .] Parties have never represented substantial social forces but only cliques and individuals within the top level of the ruling class." [. . .]

5. The labor of pulling up rice seedlings for transplantation to the rice fields [ed.]

6. For an example of an unsettled childhood see Prajuab (1958).

PART THREE

Crafting the Nation-State

Traditional states in Southeast Asia were substantially different in form from modern states. Little is known of the earliest states in the region, in part due to conditions that militate against the preservation of cultural materials made of organic matter. The earliest known state on mainland Southeast Asia was Funan, believed to have been established in the first century AD, and extending across the southern part of what are now Cambodia and Vietnam. Nevertheless, little is known of this kingdom beyond what can be derived from reports of early Chinese traders. This raises a key point about these ancient states—that trade was an essential element of their emergence. One of the best known of Southeast Asia's early states is the Khmer Empire of Angkor, which flourished from the ninth to the thirteenth centuries AD. Known today primarily for the magnificence of just one of its many temples, Angkor Wat, Angkor covered a vast portion of modern-day Cambodia, Vietnam, Laos, Thailand, and even stretched into Burma and Malaysia.

These early state sites reveal to us that by the time of the Khmer Empire, cultural—particularly religious—influence had come from India. The influence of Hinduism, and therefore presumably of India, is evident in much of the monumental architecture of early Southeast Asia. Angkor Wat was the sacred center of this vast and enduring (five-centuries-long) empire. The word *Angkor*, itself, comes from the Sanskrit word *nagara*, which is generally translated as "city" or "holy city" (Mannikka 1996; Higham 2001). The temple complex was laid out to actualize cosmological principles of Hinduism and, later, Buddhism. The design was a replication of world cosmology, a microcosm linking the heavens and the political power of kings. While the king might have been considered a *deva-raja*, a physical manifestation of a god, Mannikka argues that it was physical objects that carried the essence of the divine, a sacred power. In early Southeast Asian kingdoms, the possession of particular sacred objects often gave one the authority to rule. (The closest we have to this idea in Western lore is the tale of Excalibur's sword.) This is a persistent theme in the cultural logic of early Southeast Asian states (see the introduction to part 5 for further discussion of ideas surrounding sacred objects and divinely mandated leadership).

The role of early Indian priests and traders in the formation of Southeast Asian states has been widely debated, but ideas of power and the sacred were woven into local cultural frameworks. The element of a sacred center and divine objects continued in Southeast Asian statecraft for millennia. Stanley Tambiah has called this model the galactic polity. The state is envisioned as a mandala, with power lying in the center and diffusing outward. One might imagine this visually as a series of concentric, ever-widening circles, with state authority fading as the circles widen; a clear example of this form is at Borobodur, in Indonesia. In contrast to contemporary conceptions, then, these early states were porous. What mattered was the sacred center, not the borders (Tambiah 1977). Elements of this sacred center exist to this day in Thailand (the Temple of the Emerald Buddha, discussed in the introduction to Part 3), and perhaps even in Burma, where the ruling junta of Myanmar moved its capital from Yangon (Rangoon), a colonial port city, to Pyinma, a site nearly two hundred miles to the north. The reasons for this move were not clear, but it might have been for ritual or magical reasons (BBC Online 2005).

Nevertheless, this was not the only model of the state in pre-modern Southeast Asia. The Tai, who moved into mainland Southeast Asia in the eleventh–twelfth centuries AD, adopted the mandala model and its rituals for their kingdoms, but also based their kingdoms on the *mueang*. This term refers to different levels of political organization, from village, to local principality, and to the state, with the smaller incorporated into the larger while maintaining its identity. The protective spirits and chiefs or princes of the *mueang* similarly could be incorporated into the larger state as subordinate to the spirits or princes of the larger *mueang* (Condominas 1990), forming a sort of patron–client relationship. This was a remarkably flexible political structure that allowed Tai-speakers to rapidly expand political control after the twelfth century.

The Vietnamese state model, in contrast, was based upon Chinese state models of governance of Confucianism and merit bureaucracy. Here, the focus was on "right ordering," including seniority within and between patrilineages, and validation of rule through ancestry (ancestor worship), along with education and examinations. In tandem with "right ordering," knowledge of classic Confucian texts and the mastery of traditional skills conferred the authority for one to assume leadership positions in the bureaucracy. But at the same time, the unity/insularity of the village remained.

Across the landscape of northern Vietnam, villages are clustered together, surrounded by dense, wall-like growths of bamboo and trees; politically, the village manages itself and, as a unit, sends taxes to the central government. Is Vietnam Southeast Asian? Some have argued that Vietnam is essentially Chinese (fully incorporated into the Chinese polity long before many parts of modern China were) or at least that their historical political structures were clearly modeled on China (Woodside 2006); that it was not a pale imitation of China, but one variation on East Asian themes. On the other hand, as Taylor (1998) has pointed out, the Chinese-ness vs. the Southeast Asian-ness of Vietnam is not in itself a particularly enlightening topic to debate. It is probably more fruitful to think of Vietnam as frontier, a blend of Chinese cultural influences and models of rulership embodying uniquely Southeast Asian cultural constructions of spiritual power and social relationships. Regardless of how we categorize the Vietnamese state, the political history of Vietnam puts it on a very different cultural and economic path from the rest of Southeast Asia (Jamieson 1995).

Chinese influence was also significant in other parts of the region. Although it ebbed and flowed in tandem with political concerns at home, Chinese waterborne trade was historically very significant in many coastal cities, and overland trade between China and India and between China and northern mainland Southeast Asia also brought a significant flow of goods, people, and ideas into the region (Sun 2003).

Another type of early Southeast Asian state is found in important Malay maritime states such as the Sulu Sultanate. Based in a string of islands in what is today the southwest Philippines, the Sulu kingdom was an Islamic state that came into being in the fifteenth century and endured into the nineteenth century. Rooted in an early boat-dwelling way of life that centered on nomadic seafaring, and featured trading and slaving, the Sulu Sultanate was established with the arrival of Islam in the region. Scholars describe the Sulu Sultanate as a "segmentary state" comprised of subunits with their own leaders, and still more subunits within these divisions. Personal ties bound leaders of these smaller subsegments to those of larger ones. These sorts of relationships have been described in various ways, as akin to "patron–client" relationships, or alternatively in terms of the Philippine concept of *utang na loob*, which roughly translates as a kind of "moral debt" or "debt of the inner self" that binds people to benefactors in profound, emotional rather than legal ways. (See Nancy Smith-Hefner, chapter 12, for a fuller discussion of *utang na loob*).

By the 1500s, the allure of trade in this region drew Europeans, ultimately laying the foundations for the European colonization of Southeast Asia. Later, much of the colonization of Southeast Asia by Europeans entailed conquest or cooptations of indigenous systems of governance (with the notable exception of Thailand). But one Southeast Asian nation—Singapore—was essentially entirely born in this colonial period. In 1818, British trader and colonial administrator Sir Stamford Raffles persuaded the British East India Company to permit him to hunt for a trade base in the region. Ultimately, he settled his sights on an island off the southern tip of today's mainland Malaysia that was home to a small Malay fishing settlement and under the control of the Sultanate of Johor. By the mid-1800s, this had become a major trade entrepôt for the British, and the base of their operations in the Straits Settlements (Penang, Malacca, and Singapore). As Carl Trocki points out, in many ways Singapore can be seen "as much as the successor of the Malay *entrepôts* of the Straits as it was the brilliant innovation of Thomas Stamford Raffles" (Trocki 2006:2). The entrepôt was soon drawing Chinese, Indian, and Malay immigrants, leading some scholars of Southeast Asia to describe Singapore as a "plural society" wherein several distinct populations reside side by side, mixing but not combining—co-mingling only in the market. The idea of "plural society" was based on observations of Netherlands India (Dutch colonial Indonesia) and British-colonial Burma made by the colonial public servant and Burma scholar J. S. Furnivall (1956). In his classic writings, Furnivall cautioned that such plural societies were inherently unstable as they lacked common will and shared values. At the heart of the contribution by John Clammer (chapter 9) is this legacy of ethnic pluralism in Singapore. Clammer explores how it plays out in the lives of contemporary Singaporeans, and how the relatively young and Chinese-dominated Singaporean state attempts to shape its ethnically plural society, even as it builds overarching, nationalist sensibilities.

The challenges, strategies, and marginalizations presented by nation-building have been dominant themes in much of the anthropological writing about Southeast Asia. Colonialism transformed states, combining once-disparate regions into one territory and splitting others. Given the tremendous ethnic, cultural, and religious diversity in Southeast Asia, it is not surprising that colonial governments found it challenging to rule these territories. All of the nations of Southeast Asia came into independence after World War II (with the exception of Thailand, which had retained its autonomy). These relatively new nations have inherited similar nation-building challenges to those faced by the colonialists that proceeded them. Benedict Anderson, who is perhaps one of the world's most famous writers on the rise and spread of nationalism, has drawn much of the inspiration for his writings from his research in Indonesia, Thailand, and the Philippines (cf. Anderson 1991 [1983]). As he famously observed, the nation is essentially an "imagined community." A nation does not have the attributes of a face-to-face community wherein shared concerns are rooted in local history and local ties. Given the great number and diversity of citizens within a nation, nationalist sensibilities are not natural: they must be cultivated. Citizens must come to embrace an idea of belonging to a nation, of sharing a broader national fictive kinship with their fellow citizens. In this regard, the nation is an imagined community, based on the construction of shared cultural elements such as the establishment of a national language, national newspapers (which inculcate a sense of connection to events elsewhere in the nation), a uniform educational system, shared national holidays, national history museums, and among other things, the inculcation of nationalist ideologies (such as Indonesia's celebrated *Pancasila*—or "five pillars"—the official state ideology that includes democracy, monotheism, justice, etc.).

Two of the contributions to this section, by Hjorleifur Jonsson and Christina Schwenkel, address dimensions of Southeast Asian states' efforts to construct nationalist sensibilities. Jonsson (chapter 8) examines the ways in which upland minority peoples become active agents in the state's civilizing mission. It can be popular to think of "the state" as assimilating minority peoples in a Borg-like fashion ('Resistance is futile. You will be assimilated"), but this is by no means the full story. As Jonsson subtly shows, the Mien are concurrently objects of national development and repositories of quaint "custom." The Mien negotiate these state actions to tell their own story of themselves, participating in documentation of their tradition and creating new activities, such as sports competitions, in which they can demonstrate their participation in the project of nation-making. Similarly, war museums in Vietnam are meant to unify the nation as sites of national memory-making. As Shaun Malarney (chapter 18) shows in a later section of this volume, even memorializing the honorable war dead is a statement of a kind of meta-citizenship (certain dead are officially remembered and others are not) that simultaneously honors the deceased's sacrifice and models the good Vietnamese citizen for the living. Schwenkel's contribution (chapter 10) demonstrates that, for the younger generation, the museum resonates in different ways than anticipated by the state, for this generation is less interested in entering the galleries (wherein they would be given a visual lesson in nationalism), and is more interested in socializing with friends outside the museum or using these tourist sites to meet foreigners with whom they can practice their English.

We have dealt with Burma very little in this collection. Given political conditions in Burma, it is difficult to find accounts of everyday life there. But we would be remiss if we did not mention the very different form of crafting the nation-state in Burma. The Union of Burma formerly established its independence from the British Empire in 1948; on the eve of this independence, the new leader of the country, Aung San, and his cabinet were assassinated. The original constitution granted a degree of autonomy to the ethnic 'minority' peoples (in fact, Burma is one of the most ethnically diverse states of all Southeast Asia; ethnic Burmans comprise about 68 percent of the total population), but by 1962, the military had taken over the government of Burma and they abrogated the promised autonomy for ethnic minority territories. Burma has continued under various forms of military rule to this day, despite elections in 1988 won by Aung San Suu Kyi's National League for Democracy. Repeated brutal attacks on ethnic opposition groups (as well as on ethnic Burmans) have resulted in hundreds of thousands of refugees, both within Burma and to its neighbors. Gillogly did research in a Thai forestry project not far from the Burma border and frequently observed Shan refugees from Burma fleeing the latest military campaign there. Nicola Tannenbaum (2009) has recently written about Shan refugees from Burma in Thailand. Sue Darlington, author of chapter 11 in the next section, has worked closely with Karen refugees; changes in United States regulations in 2006 now allow Karen refugees to resettle in the United States. In short, the model of nation-building in Burma is by no means one of incorporation or imagined community.

8

Recording Tradition and Measuring Progress in the Ethnic Minority Highlands of Thailand

Hjorleifur Jonsson

It was clear that government interventions in highland farming had made local livelihood rather precarious by the time of my first fieldwork with the Mien people of Thailand in 1992–1994.[1] Shifting cultivation had been outlawed for decades, and the bulk of highland ethnic minority peoples had not been granted citizenship, the legal prerequisite for owning land. Occasionally whole settlements were evicted, and in some places people's fields were overtaken by lowland farmers with better connections to government officials. Sometimes I asked Mien people why they did not attempt to move across the border to Laos, where I assumed government intervention in farmer livelihood was limited. The most common answer to this query was that there was "no progress" there. *Progress* implied roads, markets, schools, health care, and the like, the local measure of modernity and well-being. To hear from older people that "progress" (Thai, *khwaam jaroen,* often used interchangeably with *kaan phatthana,* "development") made their livelihood difficulties bearable was puzzling. Older people who talked with me also made this contrast with life in the past, the 1960s of ethnographies I had read in preparation for my own fieldwork. This was another puzzle to me, possibly because at the time I still thought there were hill tribes, ethnic groups with distinct cultures, in which older people (at least) were nostalgic for the social and cultural frameworks of their pasts. But they were not nostalgic.

I was well versed in the earlier ethnography of the area and its peoples. I expected traditional shifting cultivators with specific forms of kinship and ritual that reinforced ethnic identities. My expectations did not include the successful insertion of the Thai ideology of modernity into the fabric of everyday life among the Mien, through schools, media (newspapers, radio, and television), and meetings. This ideology wed nation (Thai) and modernity (progress) partly through presenting the image of "unreformed" hill tribe peoples as a source of Thailand's problems. If I could not easily cling to notions of ethnic culture to account for local social life, should I anchor my findings to national politics and ideology instead?

But to think about Mien life today as merely a set of opposing orientations of "past/tribal" and "Thai/modern/state" is restrictive. There are multiple intertwinings of culture and politics, of the local and the national. To chase after these, I will relate some of my steps toward an understanding of Mien life, with a description of vignettes of Mien enactments of culture and identity in various settings.

DEMOCRACY AND KINSHIP

"They don't like to grow rice, so they look for work in towns and also abroad," said Dr. Chob Kacha-Ananda. He was an expert on the Mien at Thailand's Tribal Research Institute (TRI), an arm of the government's administration. In October 1992, Chob had kindly invited me to join his team on their trip to document a Mien wedding in the village of Rom Yen, near the town of Chiangkham in Phayao province. This seemed a good opportunity to visit some villages to find a fieldsite for my research. Rom Yen village is a five-hour drive from the city of Chiangmai, the administrative center of northern Thailand, where I was then based and where the TRI is located.

On our way to Rom Yen, we first went to the Mien village of Pangkha, where we spent the night. Chob told me that the Royal Forestry Department of the Thai government planned to evict six villages from the Pangkha region in the interest of forest protection, and that the villages had purportedly agreed to move. One of the six would most likely be allowed to stay, he added, since the king's mother (the Princess Mother, Mae Fa Luang) had donated a large school to the people there. According to Chob, this was the village of Pangphrik, where people "don't like to grow rice. . . ." The Pangphrik school was run by Thailand's Border Patrol Police (BPP). It was a remainder and reminder of a war of Thai military and mercenary forces (with American support) against the Communist Party of Thailand and its sympathizers. During the 1960s and 1970s, ethnic minority highlanders were viewed as holding uncertain political allegiance at best, and as communists at worst; active fighting lasted until 1982. A decade later, the BPP was still involved in instilling a sense of national belonging and indebtedness among Mien and Hmong ethnic minority peoples. Their mission was equally to guard the borders of nationhood and the physical terrain.

While Chob described the planned eviction of settlements as a matter of fact that was of little concern, he became quite animated when describing his vision for democracy in Mien villages. He said that there was much clan favoritism in traditional village life, as members of a single clan (lineage, kin group) could largely run the affairs of a village. Chob had suggested that the village committee have representatives from each of the clans present, and more than one representative if the clan had more than five households in the village. He advocated this scheme to the villagers, many of whom were to be evicted.

What Chob described as clan favoritism was, from his perspective, an undemocratic practice. His concern was to introduce his idealized model of democracy into the dynamics of Mien villages. In this imagery, a clan was the equivalent of an interest group seeking to monopolize resources, and Chob's democratic intervention consisted of a mechanism for making access to state resources proportionate to the presence and relative strength of each interest group, in order to distribute such resources more evenly. Thai national political trends thus facilitated a particular understanding of Mien political practices as favoritism, corrupt practices that were once common in Thai social life but were now, it was assumed, fast disappearing because of a wave of democratic reform. In other words, the modern democratic future presumably would erase the undemocratic past. Modernity would happen as a process of change from an undesirable condition to a desirable one.

Mien kinship is patrilineal, but while there are identifiable lineages these had not (in my experience) emerged as separate interest groups. Conventions about lineage exogamy and status rivalries among relatives made local politics more complex than mere interest groups. And contrary to the Thai anthropologist's understanding, there were at the time no public resources to compete over or monopolize highland villages. The envisioned changes were basically an attempt to align these local dynamics with the national structure of control. If successful, they might in fact establish what they were supposed to counter: kinship groups as separate political units.

The site for these intended reforms among the Mien was the locally elected village committee, an institution mandated by national law and created in Mien villages in line with the state's modernizing agenda for the countryside. A mobile development worker, a Thai man, had arrived in Rom Yen to oversee the elections. This and various other aspects of the modern state and nation linked Mien villages to larger social fields, assuming a binary opposition between tradition and modernity. But such terms had no fixed meaning. They shifted in relation to the ways in which people used these concepts in their lives.

LIGHTS, CAMERA, TRADITION!

The goal of the TRI ethnographers with whom I traveled to Rom Yen was to document a traditional wedding. It seems that while traditional practice had to be uprooted when it influenced what had come to be defined as politics, ceremonial practices that were labeled ethnic culture were to be recorded. These were some of the goals of government officials, whose task was equally to classify and document ethnically specific practices and to contribute to the national integration of peoples classified as ethnic minorities.

Current understandings of modernity (*than-samay*) and development-cum-progress (*kan phatthana, khwam jaroen*) in Thailand have recently produced a "national culture effect" that is expressed in the quest for manifestations of ethnically specific practices that are of the past. National engagements with modernity triggered a reactionary and nostalgic search for ways of the past and various celebratory expressions of tradition. In relation to ethnic minority rural populations in the northern highlands, this is a very recent occurrence. For decades, Thai authorities and Thai society at large had viewed "hill tribe customs" as something to be eliminated because they were not only considered an impediment to progress but also were a threat to the nation in their marked differences.

In contemporary Thailand, the work of tradition appeared to have two strands, which assumed and projected a fundamental difference between Thai and their Others. Thai and related peoples were in linear history, whereas the Others, particularly highland ethnic minorities, were considered of the past. This was manifest in the celebration and revival of Thai traditions as a collective, national heritage, and in the mapping of the past on non-Thai ethnic minorities, as manifest in museums, television documentaries, coffee-table books such as the *Encyclopedia of Ethnic Groups*, and the documentation of the traditional Mien wedding in Rom Yen. Images of the non-Thai Other served as a vehicle for the self-fashioning of a modern, Thai subject. That is, the work of culture, tradition, and identity facilitated the establishment of particular, ethnic, and national landscapes.

A Documentary

One example of this culture/identity work was characterized by a Thai television documentary about the Mien (Yao, as they are officially known) from early 1992. The narrator was dressed in expensive-looking, safari-style clothing when he arrived in his modern 4WD vehicle at a forest covered setting. He made a few introductory remarks about the ancient history of the Yao people and about their ancient Daoist ritual practices, and then the rest of the roughly half-hour documentary featured a staged *kwa-tang* (*guaax-dang*) ordination ritual with an occasional voiceover explaining the meaning of the action. These rituals were said to elevate the ordinands' status in the spirit world and the afterlife. Among the benefits were that each gained a number of spirit-helpers for whatever rituals they may conduct in the future. In themselves, the ordinations to ritual rank did not bring any material benefits in this life. They were expensive to hold, and in most cases people conducted them to improve the well-being of deceased parents or grandparents in the spirit world. Yet, the video's narration made it seem that every Mien family followed these customs, and gave the impression that the ritual was somehow a part of the package of being this particular kind of "traditional" people.

I viewed this video at the home of Le Tsan Kwe, a spirit medium and a well-known Mien man, in the village of Phale. He had been paid the equivalent of USD 400 for arranging and leading the performance, and later received a copy of the televised program. Thus at least some Mien people had participated in the forging of their Thai image as of the past, for good payment in this case.

A Wedding

Interpreted in this context, the exemplary Mien wedding that I saw in Rom Yen was squarely within the realm of state control and the national currents of Thai modernity, but it was simultaneously a local event that made particular Mien statements. The household had a spirit medium perform a ritual of appeasing the ancestors (*orn zouv*), which took place during preparations for the wedding ceremony. The ritual lasted for about four hours on the evening of October 13th, while household members and their relatives prepared for the guests. A group of men killed and cooked at least four adult pigs, and up against one wall were some fifty cases of soft drinks and bottled water that the groom's parents had purchased for the event. During the *orn zouv*, which honored the male household head's ancestors, the medium chanted from memory and from text. He drew the spirits in with the smoke from burning incense, blew into a hollowed-out buffalo horn, rattled his spirit-knife, and occasionally threw down divining sticks. Later he, along with the groom and the groom's father, offered spirit money to the ancestors. The spirit money consists of sheets of paper that are hammered (to make coins) or printed (to make bills) at the household for the occasion. It acquires value as it is burned and thus is considered transformed into the realm of spirits. The men kneeled down and held trays over their heads on which they burned the bills of spirit-money on a bed of corn. When the spirits had partaken of the offering, and had indicated their approval via the divining sticks, the medium sent them off. These exchanges with ancestor spirits brought honor and wealth into the spirit world and urged blessings and wealth (wealth is a manifestation of blessing) for the household. The more wealth a household has, the more it can oblige ancestors and other spirits.

The orn zouv ritual was only for the groom's household and lineage, the event's hosts. The bride's side would arrive the following day. On the morning of that day, a Mien band playing a double-reed oboe, drum, gong, and cymbals went out along the road to receive the guests and to bring them in the direction of the house. The host-side guests were already seated, males and females forming separate halves of a circle, and were being offered tea and cigarettes when the bride's group arrived at about 11 AM. There was much ceremonial bowing between the sides of the groom and the bride, hosts and guests. By 5 PM, the band led the guests, almost a hundred people, to the dinner tables. The number of guests was such that the meat from four adult pigs would not suffice, and the household rushed to buy a cow from a Thai villager to add to the food, which cost them about Thai Baht 7,000 (USD 280). The scale of the wedding was far beyond the means of an average household. As an elaborate affair, it was more representative of ideals and aspirations than of what such events should be like in Mien villages. In part, this was what made it appropriate for video documentation.

Behind the scenes at the formal presentations of the two kin groups—the couple to the guests, the householders to the ancestor spirits, and the Mien ethnic group to the video crew from the TRI—there was an ongoing practical joke in the kitchen involving each of the four pigs. Whoever entered the kitchen was asked to wield the knife to kill the pig, while several men held it steady on a bench, ready with a bowl to catch the blood. The knife they gave out was blunt and never pierced the pig's skin. After a few frustrated attempts, the joke's victim was let in on the fun, everyone laughed, and the pig was killed with a better knife and then prepared for the anxious hosts and their numerous guests. I did not see such joking at other weddings, but I mention it here because it shows that for Mien participants, "traditional" tribal ways are not reverent proceedings constrained by an idealized past.

The bride finally entered the groom's house at about 4 AM on October 15th. The hosts offered her and her kin group sticky rice to eat, a metaphoric reference to the lasting union of the couple and their families. At this point, the TRI team started video recording. Around breakfast time, the guests "washed the face" (nzaaux hmien) of the bride. She and her assistant went around the tables with a bowl of water and a washcloth, and the guests gave her some money, usually in the range of Baht 20–50 (USD .80–2.00). People did not literally wash the bride's face, or in many cases even touch the cloth. Rather, this was a formal and public way of declaring that the bride was honorable. After the assembled guests had lunch, the bride and groom went around the tables together with two assistants, offering people cigarettes, tea, and liquor. The guests again gave money, in the range of Baht 20–100 (USD .80–4.00). This exchange marked the honor of their union.

The video crew set up their gear again as the band led the groom and bride inside; there, the couple bowed in front of the altar to the ancestors. The bride and groom were barefoot and decked out in elaborate, embroidered Mien clothing. Each was accompanied by one assistant. Khru (Thai, "teacher") Khe Win, the Mien headmaster of the Pangkha school, gave a speech in Thai through a microphone, and spoke about marriage customs. Each tribe has its own special customs, he said, but weddings are most elaborate among the Mien, and he described some key elements. He then gave the microphone to another Mien man, who spoke in the Mien language. I did not yet understand the language and his words were lost on me. The band played its music, and yet another Mien man addressed the couple. They, particularly the groom, bowed in a very elaborate fashion in front of the altar to the ancestors, variously kneeling and standing up. Decked out in their finery, they made a good show, for the household as much as for the Tribal Research Institute, and the visitors appeared impressed.

CONTEXT

Two aspects of this event illustrate the contest over the meaning of Mien culture. The household-based ritual for the ancestors, coupled with a feast for the bride's lineage and other guests, constitutes one part of the equation. It established the honor of the couple and their new household and thus was part of the Mien discourse about weddings, households, honor, and feasting. The other side of this is the objectification of culture, via the medium of video, through the actions of the TRI staff. Outsiders' interest in Mien as a traditional people rested on their assumed distance from modernity. Mien people's engagements with their own traditions tended to fall outside this framework, except in the sense that they had taken to staging aspects of their traditions to suggest compatibility with national definitions of heritage as the property of ethnic groups.

In some respects, there was an urban, upper- and middle-class Thai fantasy that the countryside was a place of colorful ceremonies by contented farmers, people who "like to grow rice." This then led to disappointment over farmers' discontent or quest for more rewarding wage work. The notion was part of a national and global discourse on the coordinates of culture, space, identity, and work. The image that appeared, for instance, in a recent Thai cultural encyclopedia entry on Mien as an industrious people, was related to the politics of defining the relations between cities and the countryside. Discursive practices of both the nation and the state took place in the context of capitalist transformations that had significantly undermined the ability and willingness of rural people to sustain themselves from the proceeds of their farms. The cost of living, combined with marginal returns from farming, had made wage labor in towns and cities an increasing necessity for rural households. Those who were better off sometimes took a sizeable bank loan to finance the cost of a labor contract abroad (in Taiwan, Japan, Hong Kong, the Middle East, or the United States), while many others took low-paying jobs within Thailand. In the last decades, many hundreds of thousands of workers from neighboring Burma, Laos, Cambodia, and southern China entered an underground labor market in Thailand.

The urban middle class in Thailand shared many basic assumptions with Western-educated academics about education and democratic reform to create modern individuals, contemporary national communities, and a global order. The countryside was posited as modernity's antithesis: a place of contented peoples who were caught up in elaborate, traditional ceremonies and deep, articulated worldviews that united them as ethnic groups. In my next example, I will show how marginalized peoples such as Thailand's Mien played to such expectations in order to gain benevolent attention from outsiders.

PROSPECTING FOR COLLECTIVE IDENTITY

More significantly, Mien people formed an ethnic-group association that sought to articulate their identity in relation to culture and development. That is, Mien people appeared to seek to combine tradition and modernity as they fashioned themselves in relation to the nation. The dynamics appeared contradictory in the effort to emphasize the local and traditional Mien entanglements with aspects of state control and the regulation of identity and social life.

Just a few days after the wedding in Rom Yen, I was in the village of Pangkha for a meeting about Mien relations; as stated on the event's welcome-banner, the meeting's focus was on the "development and the preservation of culture." The main organizers took a broad view of culture and included issues of livelihood and ways of dealing with the government, along with the more commonly assumed ingredients of customs and traditional practices. The issues at the meeting ranged widely. Significantly, one of the speakers mentioned that according to Dr. Chob of the Tribal Research Institute, the Mien were the most progressive of the country's hill tribes; they were most advanced in *phatthana* (development) and *khwaam sa-at* (cleanliness). This formulation assumed the condition of "unmodernity" (tradition) as one of filth. The dynamics of modernity invited frequent measurements of progress. Development, progress, and cleanliness as markers of modernity and modernization were thus wielded locally as a sign of the achievements of Mien people as an ethnic group in the context of other ethnic minority highland peoples. It was somehow a good sign that the state's ethnographers found the villages of other ethnic groups filthier than those of the Mien. The statement at the Rom Yen wedding that Mien wedding customs were the most elaborate among all the hill tribes was a variation on this pattern.

A range of views on establishing an ethnic association was manifested at the initial meetings, including disapproval of the commoditization of culture. Privately, some younger people made negative comments about Le Tsan Kwe's staging of a kwa-tang ritual for the Thai television crew. My Mien acquaintances said that he had fallen seriously ill within months of staging the ritual and that there was a direct connection; people should not call on spirits in jest or for trivial purposes, as the spirits will strike back and cause them illness or death, as had happened to Le Tsan Kwe. "See!" Other critical voices variously assumed or questioned the previous framework of Mien relations with spirits. The range of voices presented three different perspectives. One was that of NGO activists who were keen to define culture as related to eco-wisdom and other matters of defending the rights to livelihood. Another was that of schoolteachers and other leaders who were most interested in the staging of culture and identity for a general audience. The third was that of farmers, both men and women, who saw younger people's immersion in Thai ways as a threat to the continuation of rural households and ritual practices. No one perspective clearly had the upper hand, and everyone who wished to had a say at the meeting.

Despite some voices of criticism, the shared concern of forming an organization around matters of identity and culture played into the hands of a particular segment of Mien social life, those best connected to outside agents such as the state and nongovernmental organizations. The effort served to mute a range of Mien agendas, particularly those assuming the primacy of households in social life. The Tribal Research Institute's documentation of the Mien wedding expressed the same redefinition of the parameters of social life. An expensive, household-based wedding was captured as representative of the ways of the ethnic group as a whole. In public view via a documentary video for the TRI's Tribal Museum, no local agendas were presented, simply the shared ways of traditional peoples.

The meeting in Pangkha established the Mien Association as an organization, an interest group, centering on matters of their identity and culture and the defense of their rights in the context of state control and various issues of development. As a vehicle for the identification of a marginalized people and with various implied links to national and international organizational and funding bodies, the Mien Association has many parallels within an increasingly global world of indigenous peoples. The association expresses a local response to modernity and modernization.

While the Mien Association was formed between late 1992 and early 1993, their first public event was not held until 2001, when a sports and culture festival brought together teams from seventeen out of two hundred Mien villages in Thailand to compete in soccer and other "modern" sports associated with Thai schools. For two evenings during the four days of the fair there was entertainment that combined traditional song and dance, history/heritage in the form of an old, handwritten and illustrated scroll that described Yao origins and their relation to Imperial Chinese society, and a combination of quiz shows and pop songs that emulated national television. The event shared elements with village and subdistrict festivals that I had seen in the early 1990s. For example, there was gender division between the organizing Village Committee (all men) and the Village Housewives' Group (all women) who cooked and served lunch for the participants. Both the Village Committee and the Housewives' Group were institutions that grew out of the state's modernization agenda for the countryside.

The sports events that were somewhat common in the early 1990s appropriated much national imagery, often featuring a speech by an invited politician, and always containing flag-raising and the singing of either the national anthem or a song honoring the Thai king. The fair in 2001 was an explicit celebration of Mien tradition and culture that contributed to the more widespread alignment of nation and modernity in the public sphere and blurred whatever boundaries there were between Mien realities and domains of the Thai state and nation.

Mien people's enactments of culture and identity at weddings and rituals for Thai video crews did not match the standard definition of political action. As distraction and potential entertainment to Thai viewers of television, traditional ethnic culture is the mimetic expression of an urban, national stereotype of modernity's opposite. Minority people's explicit politics or agitation had been suppressed as anti-national. Displays of tradition and identity provided an avenue for recognition and rights that would otherwise have been precluded in the national arena. Public Mien enactments of identity played to the national stereotype of happy and apolitical farming populations as they attempted to redefine the conditions of their everyday life. Mien organizers might have brought some benefits to their rural communities. But the separation of culture and identity from any questions of basic rights and livelihood might have also reinforced the national bias against the needs of minority farmers who "don't like to grow rice." There is, in some ways, a constant risk in treating culture as something distinct from the dynamics of everyday life.

NOTE

1. This chapter is based on my "Mien Alter-Natives in Thai Modernity" (2004). For more on Thailand's Mien, including sports festivals and political protest, see my *Mien Relations: Mountain People and State Control in Thailand* (2005). See also the video documentary *Mien Sports and Heritage, Thailand 2001,* which is accessible over the Internet on my homepage at Arizona State University. For a classical account of a Mien wedding in northern Thailand (a composite of many events from several observers), see Jane R. Hanks (1965).

9

Everyday Life and the Management of Cultural Complexity in Contemporary Singapore

John Clammer

URBAN LIFE IN SOUTHEAST ASIA

In this chapter I illuminate the ways in which Singaporeans negotiate complex social, cultural, and economic environments in their everyday lives. In this way, I illustrate how various Singaporeans confront the realities of life within a city that is co-terminal with the boundaries of the state. With the elimination of the last vestiges of the rural sector in the last few years, Singapore[1] is now a totally urbanized society entirely committed to what is sometimes termed the "modernist project," that is, of effectively bringing the whole of life under the regime of efficiency, technology, and managerialism. For these reasons, the study of Singapore society is not only of interest in the comparative ethnography of Southeast Asia, but is of much wider theoretical interest to scholars of urbanism, modernity, and social planning.

FOUR VIGNETTES AND A CODA

One good way to understand the nature of a society is through the daily lives of its inhabitants. In the pages that follow I offer brief descriptions of the lives of a group of Singapore's citizens, differentiated by ethnicity, class, and occupation. In this way, I aim to offer an informal cross section of this small but complex society. In particular, these stories feature the sometimes problematic and negotiated nature of the daily interactions between members of different cultural communities sharing the same political and physical space. The vignettes are based on the lives of real people whom I met in the course of twelve years of residence and fieldwork in Singapore, but with names changed to conceal their actual identities.

A SNAPSHOT OF A MIDDLE-CLASS CHINESE SINGAPOREAN'S LIFE

The first thing that Lim Kiat Chee notices as he climbs out of bed early each workday morning (which includes Saturdays) and pulls the curtains of the master bedroom of his three-bedroom HUDC maisonette (a townhouse or terrace house with a tiny downstairs garden for those inhabiting the ground floor) are the rows of high-rise apartment buildings visible in all directions from his upstairs window, each separated by grass and quite often containing playgrounds for their younger inhabitants. He considers himself lucky to live close to the street level in a maisonette rather than up to twenty-four stories in the sky, where he would have to face the daily confrontation with the often unreliable elevators. His three-bedroom unit was originally built as public housing for mid-income professionals like himself and has since been privatized. Lim Kiat Chee is a mid-level manager with Singapore Airlines and he bought the apartment with money accumulated in his compulsory Central Provident Fund account. This is the Singapore substitute for a pension scheme into which both employer and employee pay a percentage of their income monthly into a savings account held either as a retirement fund or for buying property and certain permitted investments. Now that the apartment is almost paid for, Lim says he is "happy with my home, my marriage—a love match and not one arranged through government sponsored 'love boat' cruises or relatives—and my statistically average number of children." His working wife, a former SIA flight attendant, now works for a travel agent in the city. Their two elementary-school-aged children both attend a nearby Christian school despite the fact that they are Buddhist (although the family rarely participates in formal religious practices other than attending funerals of elderly relatives).

As Lim Kiat Chee showers, he can hear the Filipino domestic worker bustling around downstairs preparing breakfast for the children. Like most middle-class Singaporean families, the Lims have a domestic employee, a Filipino woman not much younger than Mrs. Lim and actually better educated. "Aunty Maria" (as the children address the domestic worker) is a college graduate who gave up a career as a schoolteacher in the Philippines to earn twice as much income in Singapore. On her day off, Maria attends a downtown Catholic church and then gathers to picnic and catch up with many immigrant workers from the Philippines in the Botanic Gardens (Constable 2007; Yeoh, Huang, and Gonzalez 1999). On workdays, Maria takes the children to school, and does the daily marketing on her way home. Upon returning from the local fresh foods market with its cacophony of vegetable, fruit, fish, meat, tofu, and cooked-foods hawkers, Maria's daily routine entails doing the Lim family's housework. She cleans, washes, and irons, makes the beds, eats a simple lunch, and then collects the children from school before preparing dinner for the family.

Today, the senior Lims decide to go out together to one of the many nearby food stalls close to the market, where they can catch a quick breakfast of coffee, *mee siam* (a dish of spicy noodles), or *roti prata* (a kind of Indian bread dipped in a curry sauce). Following breakfast, Mr. Lim takes the subway that now runs out to the airport, and Mrs. Lim boards the air-conditioned bus downtown to her travel agency located in a large shopping center on Orchard Road, the main downtown thoroughfare. Despite the expensive costs of keeping a car in Singapore, where road taxes are deliberately prohibitively high to keep the car population low in such a small country, they do own a car. This they use mostly on weekends, for visits to their parents or for a day at the beach or zoo with the children.

The Lims speak a variety of languages in a typical week: they communicate entirely in English with their domestic worker, and primarily in English with their children. They speak Hokkien with Mr. Lim's parents and Cantonese with Mrs. Lim's parents. At work they speak either Mandarin or English, depending on the context. Fairly apolitical, they vote (they are legally required to do so)—but otherwise stay fairly far from politics. This they leave to the government (dominated since independence in 1965 by the People's Action Party), which they consider to be, if rather authoritarian, at least efficient and corruption free. On the whole, they consider themselves pretty well off—a nice family, a pleasant home, two good salaries, and a stable and secure living environment. Though their lives may be relatively uneventful, they are materially satisfying. In these respects, the Lims are fairly typical of middle-class Chinese Singaporeans. Although the Lims' income and middle-class culture separate them from working-class Chinese families in Singapore (with whom they share little except language), Chinese Singaporeans of all classes generally share a sense of common ethnicity as well as aspirations to better themselves and to participate actively in the Singaporean consumer culture (Tan 2008; Chua 2005; Kau, Tambyah, and Tan 2006).

BEING MALAY IN A CHINESE-DOMINATED SOCIETY

In one of the HDB rental high rises visible from the Lims' maisonette, lives Mrs. Katijah binte Ahmad, a Malay Muslim mother of five whose husband Jalil holds down a steady but low-paying job as the owner of one of the food stalls where the Lims often have breakfast. His stall sells *nasi goreng* (a fried rice dish) and *satay*. Business is a bit erratic and the competition is fierce from the surrounding stalls. The hours are also long: her husband normally starts cooking by 6 AM (breakfast time). Jalil enjoys a brief quiet period in the mid-morning before the lunch rush and again in the long, hot drowsy afternoons before dinnertime, when office workers and students start returning from schools and businesses. He has a fluctuating income and none at all during the Muslim religious holidays when he shuts the stall, or when he is sick, which he quite frequently is. He had a fairly wearying earlier life as a messenger boy for a large trading company, as a deck hand on ships sailing between Singapore and Indonesia, and as a cook in a Malay restaurant. In his youth Jalil even tried a spell in the Gulf as a construction worker, but found the work too heavy and the society unfriendly. In these uncertain conditions, it is necessary for both Jalil and Katijah to work to support their large family. Katijah works in a nearby factory making cardboard boxes and packaging materials. In the past, she worked in other neighborhood factories assembling circuit boards for electrical appliances. However, as Katijah grew older, she found her eyesight weakening and her fingers no longer dexterous enough for detailed microscopic work. Katijah also sews at home after her shifts, to earn extra money. When she has time and resources, she sometimes makes *kueh* or Malay style cakes of coconut to sell to her neighbors and to a nearly cake stall, to bring in a little extra pocket money. She will even help out at the food stall when not too tired.

With five children, Katijah and Jalil find there is not much income left after they have paid the rent on their three-bedroom HDB flat, paid utility bills, and bought food and clothes for their growing family. Time and energy are also in short supply. Katijah spends her limited leisure time visiting with friends. All her friends are Malay, even though she has Chinese and Indian neighbors because all HDB housing estates are ethnically mixed by government policy. She also visits the night markets on Muslim holidays, views an occasional Malay movie at a cinema, and watches Malay-oriented channels on television (broadcast from nearby Malaysia). Malay is really the only language Katijah knows well. Shopping is not a problem, since most of the market hawkers also know at least basic Malay. Malay is still the national language of Singapore (dating from the days when Singapore was still part of the colony of Malaya) and one of the four official ones—the others are English, Mandarin, and Tamil. Because of religious and diet barriers— she will never eat pork or non-*Halal* (foods prepared in religiously approved ways) dishes—she has little more than superficial interactions with members of other ethnic groups. Despite Katijah's linguistic barriers, her children's situation is very different. As Katijah said to me, "I am really proud of my children. They can all speak English and my elder boy has just received a place at the National University of Singapore." What she does not say, however, is that her son's slot is in the University's Malay Studies Department, and not in a "professional" school such as law or medicine. This is a common trend among Malay students, one that perpetuates the chronic underrepresentation of Malays in the professions (Clammer 1998; Li 1989).

Katijah's husband Jalil knows a smattering of Hokkien, Teochew, Cantonese, English, and even a little Tamil. These languages are necessary for serving the multiethnic clientele of his food stall. For her own generation, Katijah has little expectation of much social mobility. While she is largely accepting of this situation, she does comment that [I] "sometimes feel like a foreigner in my own country." Her feelings reflect a Singaporean reality: the Malays are a minority, comprising slightly under 15 percent of the total population. Once or twice Katijah and Jalil have discussed moving across the border to Malaysia, where Malays are the dominant group, but there are political and practical difficulties in doing so. In addition, the children are pretty well adapted to Singapore. Sometimes, though, hearing Mandarin spoken all around her, and the "Singlish" or distinctive Singaporean variety of English that she can recognize but not understand, Katijah wonders out loud what it might be like to live in a Muslim majority society where my lifestyle would be the norm and where people like my husband would have had greater educational opportunities. Katijah's eldest son has a government-sponsored university scholarship and she hopes his siblings will follow in his footsteps. Katijah also nurses hopes that the next generation of Singapore Malays will be truly equal citizens along with the Chinese and Indians with whom they share the same physical and political space.

SINGAPORE CITIZEN, CULTURALLY INDIAN

In fact, Katijah's second daughter Mariam is doing well at school, not least because of her energetic and warm homeroom teacher Mrs. Selvaratnam, whose life I turn to chronicle now. Mrs. Selvaratnam comes from a family who arrived in the 1920s from what was then Madras (now Chennai) in the southern Indian province of Tamil Nadu (Siddique and Purushotam 1984). She speaks extremely fluent English as well as her native Tamil, good Malay, and a smattering of Hokkien. Mrs. Selvaratnam's grandmother was brought over from India as the bride of her grandfather. At the time, her grandfather was a young single man working in a community that until the 1960s had a very imbalanced sex ratio. He thus did what was common at the time and sought a wife from his own natal village, a small farming community just south of Madras. Both these grandparents were from the Chettiar *jati*, a caste commonly associated with money lending. The grandfather rose to some prominence in the Tamil community, becoming a journalist and subsequently the editor of one of the Tamil-language newspapers. Their son, Mrs. Selvaratnam's father, went to what was then the University of Malaya in Singapore, to study English literature, at which a good number of Indians excelled and still do. Equipping himself with a working knowledge of Bengali, Hindi, and a little Gujarati, Mrs. Selvaratnam's father became first a journalist and then a teacher at his old university. He was a strong local follower of Mahatma Gandhi and took a keen interest in Indian politics. Eventually he married a woman whose family had settled in Singapore but was of Jaffna Tamil descent (the northern Tamil-dominated zone of what is now Sri Lanka). One of their children, Mrs. Selvaratnam, followed in her father's and grandfather's footsteps in attending the university, moving on to the Institute of Education, and then marrying a rising young Indian lawyer.

Mrs. Selvaratnam's family illustrates one of the significant patterns of how Indians fit into Singaporean patterns of social stratification. Whereas the Chinese profile can be visualized as a tall rectangle, with people of all socioeconomic statuses distributed more or less equally, the Malay profile is more like a pyramid with relatively few professionals and managerial workers at the top, but with a heavy distribution of working-class individuals and families at the bottom. The Indians, in contrast, have an hourglass-shaped profile with considerable concentration in lower-grade occupations such as cleaners and road sweepers and only a small middle class. But proportional to their representation in the population as a whole (6.4 percent), they have a large professional class of lawyers, doctors, teachers, journalists, artists, writers, and well-educated individuals (Arumugam 2002; Sandhu and Mani 1993).

The Selvaratnam family demonstrates this pattern very clearly. Even in India the family had been well off and, although not Brahmins, they are highly educated: both boys and girls are literate in Tamil and many of the boys in English as well. Although the family remains Hindu, many of the Singapore Tamil community are Christians. Entirely comfortable in English, Mrs. Selvaratnam and her family can negotiate Singapore life with ease. Educated and well traveled, politically astute, settled in Singapore but having cultural roots in south India, the Selvaratnam family is entirely cosmopolitan in public settings. Although they have Chinese, Malay, and European friends, at home the family largely observes certain Indian practices. They are vegetarians, and the females invariably wear either the sari or the northern Indian Punjabi pantsuit. For the Selvaratnams there is a fairly big divide between public and private lives. Although they would not entirely reject the idea of their children marrying non-Indians, Mr. and Mrs. Selvaratnam would much prefer that they wed other Indians of similar caste background rather than non-Indians or Christian Indians. But as one of their daughters has been dating a young European expatriate, they might have to confront the reality that caste and ethnic barriers have weakened considerably since their generation was their children's age.

AMBIGUOUS ETHNICITY IN A PLURAL SOCIETY

Also in Mrs. Selvaratnam's class is a young Eurasian boy, Philip Gomez. Not performing quite as well as Mariam in school, he faces a rather different set of daily cultural choices. First among these is his identity. Although by Singapore government classification he is categorized as Eurasian, in fact, both his parents are Asian—his father is Chinese, from the Peranakan or Baba subgroup. Many in this subgroup historically do not speak much Chinese, but rather speak a form of Malay that is dying out now (Clammer 1980; Chia 1980; Tan 1993). His mother is of Sri Lankan origin from an old community known as Dutch Burghers, a group who in the past intermarried with European settlers and planters in Ceylon. The term "Eurasian" itself is rather complex in Singapore and rarely refers to the children of mixed Asian–European marriages; such children are usually classified by the ethnicity of their father. Rather, Eurasian is a category encompassing a diverse array of peoples known as "Others" in the formal division of Singapore society into Chinese, Malays, Indians, and Others (CMIO). In Singapore, Eurasians are usually of mixed Asian descent. They have created a culture that contains a large percentage of Roman Catholics and is distinct in its hybridity. Philip Gomez's father has at least one Thai grandparent (Thai–Chinese intermarriages were quite common during the colonial period). He also has a Burmese great-grandmother. Often the Gomez family jokes (half-seriously) that they are actually "ideal Singaporeans—a little bit of just about everything somewhere in the family history." The problem is that in a society with a penchant for clear and unambiguous classifications, their identity is not well defined. The parents do not find this so problematic, but for Philip the situation is confusing and sometimes distressing. As all schools in Singapore are bilingual, he has to study a second language, but the question is, which language? On his identity card the box that says "Race" classifies him as Eurasian, but the one that says "Language" classifies him as one who speaks Hokkien, which he does not do, but which is his father's official language. His father does not really speak Hokkien fluently, either, as he actually speaks standard Malay, using the Peranakan dialect that is mixed with Hokkien, and English. Mr. Gomez runs a small fashion- and accessory shop in a medium-sized shopping center in one of the HDB estates. Many of the customers are Malay. Mrs. Gomez was a hairdresser when she married, and still helps out occasionally at a nearby hair salon. Although Mrs. Gomez retired from full-time work after Philip's and his sister Alice's births she kept all her hairdressing equipment and makes quite substantial pocket money doing the hair of neighbors and friends at home at bargain prices.

Although a Catholic (religion serves as an important bond in this diffused Eurasian community), Mrs. Gomez quietly practices birth control as she does not think they can afford more than two children. She is old enough to have kept her family size in line with the earlier government policy (now abandoned) of encouraging severe limitations on family size ("Boy or Girl, Two is Enough" used to be proclaimed from posters at bus shelters and was even projected in huge letters onto the blank end walls of HDB high-rise apartment blocks). In the 1980s, curtailment of family size was encouraged by way of tax breaks for those who conformed. Those who did not comply faced penalties such as lower priority status for admissions to elite schools for third and subsequent children. Mrs. Gomez is an active member of women's groups in the Catholic church in nearby Katong, an old seaside suburb now separated from the sea by new high rises on reclaimed land. She confides her worries about who her children will marry. Another Eurasian? A *nonya* (a Peranakan woman) for Philip? Or perhaps in Alice's case the ideal spouse might be an Australian or American. This sort of foreigner would be less likely to be concerned with the family lineage than with her daughter's attractiveness. In fact, this is the de facto choice for many Eurasians, not least because it carries the possibility of migration to nations where the intricate details of descent and ethnicity will not matter. Not surprisingly, many Eurasians, like many members of Singapore's once thriving Jewish community, have married out and moved to England or Australia. The west Australian city of Perth, only four hours by air from Singapore, is a particularly popular destination: it has become home to a large community of former Singaporeans, many of them Chinese, but with a substantial proportion of Eurasians and Jews.

And where can these single "Caucasians" (in Singapore parlance) who might end up marrying Singaporean women be found? Some might be drinking at a bar in one of Singapore's watering holes as many do on a regular basis since they have little real social life beyond their office, bank, or diplomatic jobs, other than the company of other educated foreign professional workers. Most likely he is one of the many "expats," the foreigners working for international companies in Singapore or for larger local companies too, some of which have attained the status of multinational corporations. Many of these now live in rented HDB flats in ordinary Singaporean neighborhoods, not in upscale air-conditioned apartments with huge balconies, multiple bathrooms, and bedrooms for the domestic workers as was once the case for foreign professionals.

ORDER AND CONTROL IN THE CITY-STATE

In everyday life in Singapore we see the intersection of two sets of forces. On the one hand there are the quite complex negotiations of everyday life: determining what language to speak, to whom and when; how to identify oneself; what to wear or to eat in what circumstances; and so forth. These negotiations are fueled by the complex multiethnic and multireligious nature of Singapore society and are intensified by its very small size and high level of urbanization. On the other hand, there are political forces that maintain this order. It is easy to imagine a society as socially and culturally complex as Singapore degenerating into chaos along ethnic or sectarian lines, yet this has not happened and there are no signs of this occurring in the future. There are, of course, internal factors in this order—a society of migrants with ancestral memories of poverty and political violence in their places of origin hardly wants to reproduce those same conditions in the new homeland. But politics has a great deal to do with it, too. At least one scholar has referred to Singapore in terms of "social engineering" (Wilson 1978). This refers to the constant tinkering with the social order, not only to retain the political domination of the PAP (the People's Action Party that has been the only party of government since independence), but equally to experiment constantly with means to maintain social order in a society that precisely because of its diverse origins and internal complexity has no common value system except self-interest (Yao 2007; George 2008). Indeed, in 1988 the then prime minister, Goh Chok Tong, attempted to introduce a "National Ideology" based on the idea of "Asian Values" in an attempt to create just such a value system (Clammer 1993).

By comparison with life in many other Southeast Asian societies, everyday life in Singapore is comfortable—safe, clean, and with all the amenities for shopping, eating well, sports, recreation, and, increasingly, the arts. Responding to the frequent criticisms that since its independence Singapore has been a "cultural desert," the government has put tremendous energy into developing a good (if not yet world class) symphony orchestra, hosting a major annual arts festival, and, among other efforts, building a new dedicated concert hall–theatre on reclaimed land on the sea front.

The social and cultural complexity of Singapore has, however, manifested its own problems. These include the issue of social exclusion and poverty, which does exist in Singapore. These were problems that had been masked to a great extent by the language of multiethnicity, which posits colorful ethnic differences as the main differentiating factor between groups rather than actual socioeconomic inequalities between them (Clammer 1997; Kipp 1993). Underlying such social and cultural pluralism is the constant fear of ethnic or religious conflict, as has happened in so many other parts of Southeast Asia. The result is remarkable social harmony, but a political culture that some have locally called "soft authoritarianism." Managed elections are held, but there is effectively only one party to vote for; political opposition and criticism is repressed, and "deviance" in dress, behavior, religious or cultural views, and artistic expression is strongly discouraged, helped by pervasive media censorship and self-censorship (Gomez 2000).

But it is these paradoxes that make Singapore such an anthropologically interesting society to study. Singapore is a highly managed (and intensely urbanized) country built upon the foundations of colonialism, having a history of in-migration with none of its current communities being indigenous to the place except for some of the Malays, and with a fragile economic base that has no natural resources. Its uniqueness in Southeast Asia is as a tiny city-state. Yet Singapore shares, through its ethnic and religious composition, much of the cultural heritage of the rest of the region and beyond to China, India, Europe, and the Middle East. Its commitment to modernism and technology while it strives to preserve something at least of the fabric of that Asian heritage makes this tiny society an inexhaustible source of anthropological interest as it poses questions of broad theoretical interest for anthropology as a whole, and especially for the anthropology of modernity, of urbanism, and of multicultural societies.

NOTE

1. Singapore is 239.6 square miles in area and the main island on which the city is concentrated is 41.8 km (26 miles) east to west and 22.5 km (14 miles) north to south. With a population density of 4,263 per sq.km it has one of the highest population densities in the world. More than 75 percent of households in the country have Internet access.

10

Youth Culture and Fading Memories of War in Hanoi, Vietnam

Christina Schwenkel

I met Mai and her young college friends outside the Ho Chi Minh Mausoleum on a warm, fall Sunday morning in Hanoi in 1999. For many Vietnamese, a visit to the mausoleum is a meaningful, emotion-laden experience, and visitors typically stand in long lines that wind around the massive granite tomb waiting to pay their respects to their nation's founding father, also affectionately referred to as "Uncle Ho." It was 8:00 AM. I emerged from the mausoleum and found a shaded park bench on the pedestrian walk across from the eleventh-century One-Pillar Pagoda that also occupies the grounds. Mai and her friends approached me without delay. "Do you speak English?" they asked. I replied that I spoke Vietnamese. They laughed. "Have you already visited the mausoleum?" I queried. They laughed again. Mai spoke up in hesitant English: "We do not come here to visit Uncle Ho, but to meet Western tourists and improve our English-language skills."

This chapter addresses what appears to be a growing tension in Vietnamese society: the increasing historical distance and disconnect of Vietnam's youth (who constitute the majority of the population) from their country's history of socialist revolution and war with France and the United States to achieve national independence. I use the words "appears to be" to identify the widespread sentiment among government officials and other older people who experienced and survived the war that Vietnamese youth growing up in a time of peace and prosperity no longer understand nor recognize the immense sacrifices made to liberate and reunite the country. To be sure, Vietnamese youth, most of whom were born after war with the United States ended in 1975, have grown up in an era quite different from that of their parents and grandparents who participated in the revolution and the wars of resistance between 1945 and 1975. Yet it would be mistaken to think that young people who grew up in peacetime are wholly disconnected from the violence of the past. On the contrary, while they may not have experienced war directly, youth in Vietnam have also suffered its severe and enduring aftermaths.

Substantial socioeconomic shifts took place in Vietnam in 1986 when the government instituted a series of economic reforms called *doi moi*, which opened the country to global market forces and foreign capitalist investment. As standards of living began to improve and poverty rates dropped, Vietnam was hailed as a "little Asian tiger," despite the alarming disparities in wealth that appeared. New global technologies and commodities flooded the markets, allowing younger generations to familiarize themselves with international brands and consumer products that remained largely unknown or inaccessible to their elders. Such are the social and economic conditions under which many Vietnamese youth have come of age. A rising, vibrant youth culture, thought to uncritically and irresponsibly embrace the global market and its commodities, as well as the association of young people in the press with "social problems" (drugs, promiscuity, night clubbing, motorbike racing, etc), have instilled moral panic in older generations who feel the youth have forgotten their nation's history, its moral values, and its cultural identity.[1] But the story is more complex than this. We can see youth as embodying the values and ideologies of betterment and development that were central to the revolution, although they use capitalism as their tool to achieve similar goals of national progress, sovereignty, and prosperity.

THE ROLE OF THE PAST IN THE PRESENT

All nations have a national memory enshrined in official history as "the past." Yet collective memory of a nation is always selective in that it involves the public remembrance of certain events and experiences, and the active forgetfulness of others. In 1882, Ernest Renan made an important observation about the nation as a type of spiritual family united not by a common language, religion, or race, but by "a rich legacy of memories" of past triumphs, regrets and sacrifices (1990 [1882]:19). Memories of mutual suffering, in particular, form the bedrock of a nation and its collective history that is communicated through textbooks, national holidays, war monuments, and museums. On account of its selectivity, national history is neither unchanging nor uncontested, as external forces refute and rework its dominant narratives and messages conveyed. These narratives not only transmit particular historical truths, but also important cultural and moral principles upon which the nation is founded. Knowing one's national history, such as singing the words to the national anthem, is thus a performative act of identification that signifies inclusion and participation in a national community.

National history is didactic; it draws upon stories of the past to teach the populace (especially youth) the normative ethics and values needed to become upstanding citizens—disciplined, loyal, and productive members of society. In Vietnam, the state regularly invokes national memories of past wars to commemorate and keep the spirit of the revolution alive. With the aim of communicating the ideals of the revolution to postwar generations, the state has a vested interest in emphasizing triumphant achievements and acts of solidarity that helped to secure the nation's historical victories. Take, for example, museums, which are sites of pedagogical power in which the state produces moral and educated citizen-subjects through the management and discipline of history and memory (Bennett 1995). In an interview, the director of the Museum of the Vietnamese Revolution, in Hanoi, emphasized to me the critical role museums play in imparting revolutionary values such as sacrifice, valor, and gratitude: "It is important to know about history. This museum is about Vietnamese freedom, unification, and independence. If the young people do not learn about this past, they will not have a proper understanding of the present, and they will not be able to build and modernize our country for the future" (Schwenkel 2009:150). Knowledge of the past thus serves as an anchor in the present period of rapid socioeconomic change and a building block for future nation-building efforts.

Similarly, we can look at *postmemory,* knowledge and memory of past traumatic events that youth did not directly experience but are intimately and deeply connected to (Hirsch 1997). Family photographs, and the painful stories of loss that accompany them, have been central to the transmission of Holocaust memory to the children of survivors. As a tool of remembrance and self-representation, photography mediates between personal memory and public history; the stories told through images of everyday life that survived the Holocaust have contributed to (re)constituting both family histories and national memory (ibid). In Vietnam, postmemory among youth is similarly informed by photographs and oral histories of war. The young adults I interviewed in Hanoi—some of whom came from the capital city, others from poorer rural provinces to attend university, secure employment, or enroll in the military—grew up hearing songs and stories about the war and revolution from their parents and grandparents. Lien, a college student born in 1979 in the central province of Nghe An, recalled her strongest childhood memories:

> I remember playing ball games with friends during the day and listening to stories about the war at night from my grandparents. They always told me about the hardships they endured, and the difficult living conditions with little food. Both of my grandfathers fought against the French and my father is a veteran of the American War. My mother worked in a factory. When I was young she used to sing us love songs about waiting for a soldier to return from the battlefield. My grandmother worked to provide food for the soldiers. Even in the worst of times, she tried to remain optimistic. She told me many stories, but the one I remember most was about 1972, when the Americans dropped so many bombs on Vinh City that everything was destroyed. She went from one village to the next looking for safety and shelter, often hiding underground to escape the bombs.

The youth I interviewed did not grow up with collections of family photographs to illustrate life during the war years, as private ownership of cameras at that time was rare. Rather, as Lien's words show, the transfer of traumatic memory to postwar generations occurred primarily through personal recollection and oral testimony. Cameras were, however, present on the battlefield with photojournalists who in an official capacity produced a large repertoire of iconic images that today offer a detailed visual history. Like photography of the Vietnam War in the United States, these images have important postwar meaning and currency, and continue to circulate and shape national memory. In Vietnam, photographs from the war are considered an important means for reproducing and transmitting historical knowledge, and also for motivating and inspiring postwar youth. In an interview, a battlefield photographer who exhibited his work at the Military History Museum in Hanoi in 1999 emphasized to me the national and moral values conveyed through his images: "Photographs from the war carry meaning about the past . . . I want students who come to my exhibit to learn to hate war, but they should also learn about the brave deaths of those who sacrificed their lives. When they see these pictures, they will understand the need to continue the work to build and develop the country" (Schwenkel 2009:62). Photography is thus imagined to bridge the widening gaps between self-denying generations who experienced the trauma of revolution and war and pleasure-seeking generations born in the aftermath whose consumption activities seem to have displaced national values and history from contemporary society.

YOUTH CULTURE AND REAPPROPRIATION OF PUBLIC SPACES OF MEMORY

During my fieldwork, Vietnamese youth in Hanoi expressed little interest in visiting historical sites or institutions associated with the war, such as museums or the mausoleum discussed at the beginning of the chapter. All had visited such places at one time or another, mostly on group fieldtrips, and few were inspired to return. Many cited a lack of time, while others felt bored by what they saw as repetitive and noninteractive exhibits. Perhaps not surprisingly, respondents preferred to spend their limited free time with friends and family in parks, cafés, or newly built shopping malls. Phuc and Thang, two male students who came to Hanoi to study English at Hanoi University, explained:

> *Phuc:* We are very busy and don't have time to visit museums. When we do have free time, we usually go home and visit our families in the countryside. I went to the Ho Chi Minh Museum once and enjoyed it.

Thang (nodding): Nowadays we are more concerned with fashion than we are with the war.

Yet despite such generational distance from national history, the youth are not wholly detached from the war and its legacies. Phuc lamented: "If the United States had not invaded Vietnam, we would now be rich and strong like the rest of Asia." Thang agreed: "We wouldn't be so poor today." Signs of poverty, mass death, environmental devastation, and other enduring effects of the war are still visible on the landscape, from demining operations to national monuments and martyr cemeteries. In recent years, some of these sites have been transformed into international tourist attractions, reconfiguring postwar memoryscapes in new and decidedly capitalist ways. Young Vietnamese at times also journey to these public spaces, yet they do so to engage in leisure and recreational activities rather than to interact with and learn about history.

Anthropologists have shown how public spaces, such as parks and plazas, are socially produced, shaped, and experienced by diverse individuals and social groups. The aesthetic, historical, and cultural meanings of such sites are always dynamic, "changing continually in response to both personal action and broader sociopolitical forces" (Lowe 2000:33). In Vietnam, youth often engage in social activities and spatial practices that reflect new uses and meanings of public space. The stone monument on *Thanh Nien* [Youth] Street at Truc Bach Lake marks the site where militia forces shot down John McCain's A-4 Skyhawk in 1967 during a bombing mission over Hanoi. U.S. aerial bombardment commonly targeted the city, killing thousands of civilians and destroying a quarter of all living spaces (Thrift and Forbes 1985:294). For older Hanoians, the monument at Truc Bach Lake, though recalling a triumphant act, is also a painful reminder of catastrophic suffering and loss. Young couples, however, are drawn to the site because of its sweeping views of the lake. They sit closely together on park benches adjacent to the monument, not far from crowded restaurants, holding hands and sometimes embracing, demonstrating how postwar generations have reappropriated spaces of war and violence, and transformed them into romantic settings for social intimacy.

At the Cu Chi tunnels tourist park, an hour's drive from Ho Chi Minh City, a similar reappropriation of public space has taken place. Cu Chi, declared a national historic landmark by the state, attracts hundreds of international tourists each day who crawl through a maze of deep and narrow underground passageways built by guerrillas during the war. Vietnamese youth also travel to Cu Chi; however, the attraction for them lies not with the tunnels per se, but with the on-site recreational facilities that provide a respite from the bustle of urban life. Pool tables, food stands, and outdoor cafés are sites where youth gather to eat, drink, talk, relax, and make new

Figure 10.1. Hanoi youth posing on a war monument at Hoan Kiem Lake, 1999. Photograph by C. Schwenkel.

friends. Cu Chi is a site of entertainment as well as a site for love, especially on the weekends, when the area is converted into *café ôms*, or hug cafés, for young couples to spend time together privately. In a country with few places for lovers to be alone and where public affection is generally discouraged, hug cafés offer the privacy of an individual cubicle in the city, and in more peripheral areas such as Cu Chi, segregated nooks for lovers under the trees (Schwenkel 2006:18). Not unlike the lakeside setting of McCain's crash and capture in Hanoi, the battlegrounds of Cu Chi have also been recreated by youth in ways that appear to disregard state-intended meanings.

VIETNAMESE YOUTH: APATHETIC OR EXEMPLARY?

Anxieties about youth and their alienation from history, coupled with a perceived fixation on commodities (exemplified in Thang's comment about fashion being more important than the war) have been reinforced in the mass media through reports of gendered acts of conspicuous consumption (see also Leshkowich 2008). In the summer of 2007, for example, the Vietnamese press reported that women in Hanoi were frivolously spending an average of 500,000 Vietnamese *dong* (approximately $30) per month on brand name beauty products and services, while the average monthly salary of workers and civil servants hovered around 1,000,000 *dong* ($60). Moreover, youth have been increasingly identified in media and government discourse as presenting a moral and cultural problem for society; they have been associated with a growth in "foreign" capitalist practices thought to undermine "traditional" and revolutionary values, leading, for example, to an increase in drug use and premarital sex. Such claims of conspicuous consumption and hedonism, however, reveal more about growing disparities in wealth, privilege, and power under market reforms than point to a deliberate rejection of cultural norms. In fact, looking more closely, the reverse may also be true: youth are not necessarily more apathetic about national traditions and revolutionary history, but have embraced new global market opportunities to carry out their familial and national duties more effectively.

While young people may not be concerned with "boring old history," they are highly motivated to build and "modernize" the country, just as the museum director and war photographer had envisioned. In this way, youth are indeed following and embodying national ideals and principles as conveyed through stories of hardship and sacrifice in museums, photography, and family histories. When I asked a focus group of university students from the province of Viet Tri what they most desired for their futures, they expressed the hope of betterment for their families *and* for the nation: good jobs, enough to eat, and a reduction in the national poverty rate. The students also expressed a belief in education as key to social and economic progress, but not just any education would do in their view. One must choose a field with skills that can be applied to the global economy (thus, one student gave up Russian to study English). Competition to gain acceptance into universities and departments of trade, economics, banking, and finance is high. Wealthier students increasingly take advantage of new opportunities to study overseas or to enroll in expensive international MBA programs in Hanoi or Ho Chi Minh City. The role of the past seems almost inconsequential to these students' lives and their efforts to attain prosperity for their families and wider society.

THE STORY OF MAI

To provide a more detailed case study of the seemingly contradictory ways youth in Vietnam reject and yet reaffirm the traditions of national history, I return to Mai, who along with her friends at the Ho Chi Minh mausoleum visited this public space to connect not to a revolutionary past but to an anticipated global future. After I met Mai in fall 1999, we began to meet regularly and still maintain a friendship. I mention her story here because I have been witness to the dramatic changes in her life over the past decade and because she is a typical example of a young woman from Hanoi whose actions exemplify the messages and principles taught in history, though she rejects the form and style through which they are conveyed. For example, Mai refused to go to a museum with me. When I asked why, she laughed: "I don't like museums. It's always war history, war history. I'm fed up. I've heard enough. I'm more interested in the development of the economy, than in politics and war" (Schwenkel 2009:150).

Mai was born in 1980. When we met in 1999 she lived in a poor, three-generation household of five on the outskirts of Hanoi in a dark and dank two-room cement house with a detached cooking area and toilet. There was little income flowing into the family; her father was a retired factory worker, her mother unemployed, and her grandmother earned petty cash by selling candy and other snacks close to the main thoroughfare. When I asked Mai about her most vivid memories of childhood, she answered bluntly: "Hunger, illness, and a lack of money for medicine." Like most of her classmates, as a child Mai participated in Youth Pioneer activities, including collective charity and volunteer work for veterans and "heroic mothers" who had lost their families to the war. She went on to join the Communist Youth Union, a social organization (not political for her, she said) in which most of her friends took part. In interviews and conversations, Mai rarely discussed her family's poverty directly, though she consistently emphasized the need to study hard to improve their lives. As the eldest daughter, the burden fell upon Mai to secure a better future for her parents, younger brother, and grandmother. In this way, she exemplified "traditional" family values, such as filial piety exhibited through moral acts of obedience, love, respect, and care for one's parents and ancestors (Rydstrøm 2003). Mai went on to study English and international finance at Hanoi National University, earning two bachelor's degrees by the time she was twenty-two. In her free time she studied Chinese and hung out with friends at Truc Bach Lake, not far from the McCain historical marker. She enjoyed Korean pop stars, Chinese soap operas, and Hollywood Vietnam War films—"more realistic than Vietnamese ones," she told me.

Four years later, Mai's life had changed significantly. At twenty-six, with two degrees and a working knowledge of Chinese, Mai had secured a full-time job at a domestic commercial bank, earning a monthly salary of three million Vietnamese *dong* (approximately $180). On Saturdays she regularly worked overtime to earn an extra one million *dong*, for a total monthly income of approximately $250, roughly $3,000 per year, only slightly more than the country's per capita GDP of $2,700 (2007 estimate). In late 2007, it was even harder to find time to meet with Mai. In addition to her fifty-hour work week, she had enrolled in evening courses at the university, studying international banking so she could obtain a higher position at her bank. "I'll get promoted through my hard work and education, not from doing favors and socializing with the managers," she told me confidently, revealing a strong belief in a capitalist work ethic. Sunday was also a work day— she taught Vietnamese to foreigners to further supplement her salary. "Do you think they would be interested in home stays?" she asked, passing me a classified ad she had taken out in an English-language newspaper.

Mai had a reason to be concerned about her earnings: she had recently built a spacious four-story house for her family. In September 2006, she took out a loan—seen by many as a new and risky financial practice—and hired construction workers to demolish her previous residence and build the new structure quickly before the lunar new year. The house was bright and airy, with indoor plumbing and a kitchen, along with a private room or area for each family member. At the time of my visit, Mai's bedroom was outfitted with a TV, a DVD player, and a karaoke machine. The modest yet comfortable home cost Mai $6,250, which she paid for with a low-interest loan of 1 percent for bank employees. Her monthly mortgage came to one million *dong*, leaving another three million for family necessities. Her aged grandmother, who was lounging in the kitchen when I arrived, no longer went out to sell candy.

Mai is now twenty-eight and not yet married, which makes her "old," according to popular belief in Vietnam. She continues to attend classes and take care of her family, while also providing financial support for her younger brother's studies, perhaps one day overseas, she confides. Mai is continually working to improve her English, brush up on her Chinese, and read new books about the international banking industry. She is an example of how industrious young people in Vietnam have taken advantage of new opportunities not simply to spend and consume frivolously, but also to support their families and contribute to "modernizing" their country. I share Mai's story not as a success narrative about Vietnam's global market integration. Compared to members of an emerging urban middle class, Mai is relatively poor, and her ability to consume is fairly limited. But as she shut the door to her bedroom and turned up the karaoke, she reminded me of how postwar generations, although seemingly indifferent to the state and its project of national history, still tend to emulate its moral values and traditions, and embrace its vision of an ideal and progressive modernity, even though Mai still will not accompany me to the museum.

NOTE

1. The term *moral panic* refers to a widespread social response, engendered and sustained by the media, to a perceived threat to the social order that also risks subverting deeply held cultural values (Critcher 2003). For a discussion of moral panic and youth through the lens of fashion in Ho Chi Minh City, see Leshkowich (2008).

Acknowledgments. Research for this project was carried out over thirty-six months between 1999 and 2007. I thank my respondents in Hanoi for their ongoing participation (note that their names have been changed here to maintain anonymity). I also gratefully acknowledge the constructive feedback I received on this essay from the editors, Kathleen Gillogly and Kathleen Adams.

PART FOUR

World Religions in Everyday Life:
Buddhism, Islam, Hinduism, and Christianity

Southeast Asia is a land of tremendous religious diversity. In addition to its plethora of indigenous religious practices, all of the world religions can be found in Southeast Asia today. In some Southeast Asian nations, such as Singapore, the world's major religious traditions coexist. A walk through Singapore's central neighborhoods takes one past Hindu temples, gleaming silver-domed mosques, ornate Christian churches, and incense-scented Buddhist temples. In other Southeast Asian countries, one world religion predominates. But even then, one finds variations in the forms the world religion may take, and minority populations also practice other distinct religions. In still other nations, such as Vietnam, people adhere to a range of religious traditions, strategically using different traditions depending on the social context, or moving from one to another set of practices over the courses of their lives. And, finally, we find generational and class differences in the conception, interpretation, and practice of world religions, for example, in Indonesia and the Philippines.

This religious diversity is a reflection of Southeast Asia's strategic position as both a destination and a way station in world trade. As early traders passed through en route from south or East Asia, the ports of Southeast Asia provided places to rest and trade while vessels waited for the winds to shift to continue on in their voyages. These seafaring traders' prolonged visits presented opportunities for introducing their own religious beliefs and practices to their Southeast Asians hosts. In some cases, as with Islam, when it became known that Muslim traders preferred to berth and trade in Muslim port settlements, local leaders expediently declared themselves (and by extension, their communities) Muslim, and trade, religious education, and genuine conversion followed. In other cases, it was intermarriage with local women, or the teachings of traveling Sufi mystics that spread the faith. By the sixteenth century, when Europeans arrived, much of Southeast Asia had already been profoundly influenced by Hinduism, Buddhism, and Islam. Drawn by the riches of the Spice Islands (eastern Indonesia), as well as the desire to trade with China (either in East Asia or in the Philippines, where trade with Chinese shifted when China closed its doors to Europeans), European traders' interests brought nascent colonial interests. As elsewhere, Christian missionization was part and parcel of the rise of colonialism in Southeast Asia, adding yet another set of religions to the mix.

Southeast Asia's contemporary religious diversity also reflects population movement and migration. This tapestry of diversity is further complicated by the role of religion in both legitimizing state power and as a vehicle for resistance to dominant groups. Here we offer a very brief review of key themes in some of Southeast Asia's major religions, with the aim of enabling the reader to contextualize the chapters in this section.

Forms of Hinduism are practiced not only in Bali but also in Thai and Khmer royal ritual (Wales 1931), as well as in everyday life. Brahmanic ritual practices are seen in the ubiquitous spirit shrines found in these regions. But Brahmanism is a slippery category of worship in mainland Southeast Asia. Erik Davis has discussed the interplay between practices we call "Buddhism" and "Brahmanism" at sacred sites in Cambodia (Davis 2009). For instance, *saksit* is a Brahmanic type of power gained through contact with sacred objects or via instruction from teachers with esoteric knowledge. *Saksit* can be contrasted with the Buddhist power of merit (the first is amoral, the second moral), but the two are sometimes joined together in certain men of power (see Wong 2001 for a discussion of how these ideas are activated in musical performance).

Theravada Buddhism is the dominant religious form throughout the lowland states of Burma, Thailand, Laos, and Cambodia (as well as in Sri Lanka). While it was originally introduced from India, there has been much exchange of religious objects, texts, and personnel with Sri Lanka in recent years. Like Brahmanism, Buddhism was recruited to bolster state-building, evidenced by the many ancient temples in Southeast Asia that are Buddhist in conception. In modern times, state control of the hierarchy of Buddhist monks has been a means of building national unity. Despite its formal recognition of religious freedom, Thailand is, for most intents and purposes, a Buddhist country. Loyalty to the nation is taught in classrooms by the iconic three pillars of flag (country), king, and religion—often depicted by an image of the Buddha. The king is considered to be a Buddhist exemplar, and the Emerald Buddha housed in the royal temple of Wat Phra Kaew (the Temple of the Emerald Buddha) is symbolically tied to the well-being of the nation. Visitors to Wat Phra Kaew are expected to show levels of respect not required in other Buddhist temples such as refraining from photography, covering one's shoulders, and not wearing shorts. In the 1980s and 1990s, visitors were greeted by a display of tins of camera film removed from the cameras of those caught surreptitiously photographing the sacred relic, and a collection of appropriately modest clothing was kept at the entrance, available on loan to casually dressed visitors. This intertwining of state and Buddhism contributes to the (at times violent) resistance of Muslim Malays in Thailand's south to the Thai government; and the (at times) militaristic response to this resistance by Buddhist monks in the south, who take up arms to "protect Buddhism" (see Jerryson 2010).

The main texts in Theravada Buddhism are in an ancient language called Pali, said to be the language of the Buddha. Ordinary people generally do not understand the texts or the chants used in temple rituals themselves. This makes the role of monks particularly important; they are the locus of transmission of religious knowledge. In Thailand, monks are institutionally organized as the *sangha,* although monks (such as the forest, ecology, and development monks discussed by Sue Darlington in chapter 11) might remove themselves from this hierarchy. Monks who go against the generally quite conservative sangha might face punishment by the institutions of the sangha and the state. Darlington's contribution in this section discusses an example of resistance to the status quo through practices that are culturally meaningful and powerful; Phrakhru Pitak's sponsorship of tree ordinations as a means of protecting community forests is quite radical.

In everyday practice, Thai Buddhists focus on the consequences of rebirth: the idea that each person carries a karmic load created by sin (*bap,* sometimes transliterated as *baap*) and alleviated by accumulation of merit (*bun*) (discussed by Holly High in chapter 3, and Lucien M. Hanks, Jr. in chapter 7; in contrast, Sue Darlington, chapter 11, defines *bap* as demerit. This illustrates the difficulty of straightforward translation of concepts). Belief in reincarnation implies that people who had relations in a past life might reconnect in future lives, continuing to work out their difficulties again and again. This is a common theme in people's justification for actions and in their discourses about the things that befall them. On one occasion, Gillogly was sitting on a veranda when a giant cockroach started to crawl across her foot. As she moved to smash it, she was interrupted by the exclamation, "Stop! That could have been your mother in a previous life!" The implication was that she would commit a great sin, possibly matricide, in killing the insect. This idea of avoiding sin (and maximizing merit) is a fundamental concept that the forest and ecology monks draw on in helping villagers protect the forest.

The religious tradition of Vietnam is often referred to as the "triple religion," in which Confucianism, Daoism, and Mahayana Buddhism are intertwined. It is not a matter of being a member of one or the other tradition, as we might expect in the West. Rather, practitioners make use of different sets of cosmological systems and practices depending on social context and personal inclination. Walking along an urban street in Hanoi or Ho Chi Minh City, one sees ancestor temples, attended on feast days or for lineage business, and Buddhist temples, crowded with elderly women bowing and praying. Vietnamese friends told Gillogly that Buddhism is the religion of the elderly, who turn to it when they think of death. In addition, practices overlap with a range of practices for contact with saints and spiritual advisors (see Taylor 2008 for recent studies of religion in Vietnam).

Mahayana Buddhism dominates in Vietnam and is historically related to the form of Buddhism practiced in Tibet and China. The dominant schools of Buddhism in Vietnam are "Pure Land" and Zen. Individual practice, perhaps under a revered monk, focuses on meditation and the chanting of sutras with a goal of gaining protection by a Bodhisattva (one who is near enlightenment, such as the Goddess of Mercy, Quan Âm) or inner peace and a sense of right living. An internationally known Vietnamese Buddhist monk is Thích Nhất Hạnh, famed for his resistance to the war in Vietnam and his advocacy of mindfulness and Engaged Buddhism (Thích Nhất Hạnh 1987).

Daoism imbues everyday life in Vietnam, rather than being a formally institutionalized religion. Nir Avieli's chapter (chapter 17, Part 5) presents a vivid example of how Daoist cosmological concepts are threaded through even the mundane act of eating. Confucianism is congruent with Vietnamese practices of patrilineality (see Part 2 and Shaun Malarney's contribution, chapter 18). In the pre-colonial kingdoms of northern Vietnam, it was also a model of governance (see Part 3). Under French colonialism, many Vietnamese converted to Catholicism, a point mentioned again in Part 6 because of its political significance. In addition, several syncretic religions that united elements of French culture and Vietnamese spiritualism arose in the late colonial period. Among the most well known is Cao Dai, marked for its exuberant architecture (Hoskins 2010) and designation of French cultural figures as saints.

Islam is well represented in Southeast Asia. It is the official state religion in two nations, Brunei and Malaysia. Furthermore, Indonesia is the most populous Muslim country in the world; with more than 90 percent of its population identifying as Muslim. The southernmost region of the Philippines and southern Thailand are also home to Muslim communities.

We will not retrace the history of Islam's early arrival and spread in Southeast Asia, since Judith Nagata has chronicled that history in chapter 4. However, her point about the resurgence of commitment to Islam currently under way in Malaysia is worth reiterating. As Nagata observed, the late 1960s was a period in which new religious ideas about the meaning and significance of Muslim identity arrived in Southeast Asia, as did new Muslim immigrants. Beginning around 1970 and gathering momentum in subsequent decades, a growing number of Malays and Muslim Indonesians came to feel (and sought) greater connection to the global Islamic community (*umma*). Lowered travel costs and increased prosperity in the 1980s enabled more Southeast Asian Muslims to participate in the pilgrimage to Mecca (the *hajj*). Also, some Southeast Asian Muslims pursued higher education at universities in Egypt and other parts of the Muslim world, returning home with new understandings of other ways of being Muslim. In Malaysia, as Nagata notes, Malays were coming to regard themselves as Muslim first: religious identity was to supersede ethnic affiliation, linking Malay Muslims with events and discourses in Arabia and Iran. In both Indonesia and Malaysia, the "call to the faith" (*dakwah*) movement was enthusiastically embraced by many younger-generation Muslims, and spread in schools and universities.

In chapter 12, Nancy Smith-Hefner pursues the theme of the varied ramifications of Islamic resurgence for young central Javanese women in Indonesia. Originally published in the *Journal of Asian Studies* but revised for this volume, Smith-Hefner's chapter explores the growing popularity of veiling among young university women on Java. As she notes, the mothers of many of these young women did not veil themselves when they were younger, but rather sported Western-style dress or revealing (by today's reformist Muslim yardsticks) tightly wrapped *sarongs* and *kebayas* (a traditional Javanese styled top, often made of semi-transparent bold-colored lace). Smith-Hefner takes up the puzzle of why a new generation of Muslim women raised in a modernist era would find the veil appealing. Her exploration sheds much light on the multiple motivations, pleasures, paradoxes, and quandaries faced by young Muslim Indonesian women who opt to adopt the veil. In reading her chapter, we are reminded that religious symbols, like other symbols, do not carry monolithic meanings.

Christianity is also found in various Southeast Asian communities, and Roman Catholicism is the dominant faith in two countries, Timor Leste and the Philippines. In contrast to the ways in which Hinduism, Buddhism, and Islam spread to Southeast Asia via trade and informal contact with new religious ideas, the introduction of Catholicism to the Philippines was deliberately and zealously pursued by the Spanish. From the time that Magellan claimed the Philippines for the Spanish crown, the archipelago was envisioned as a "showcase of faith." When the Spanish conquistadores arrived in the southern Philippines, Islam had already penetrated parts of the region; as some scholars have suggested, this was a nation that may well have become predominantly Muslim if not for the early missionizing activities of the Spanish. Early Spanish conversion activities entailed mass baptisms and implementation of the resettlement policy (or *reducción* policy) they had used in the New World, whereby indigenous groups were forcibly relocated to villages centered around plazas and churches (thereby enabling tax collection from Christianized Filipinos) (Russell n.d.). Historian Vicente Rafael's (1988) extensive research reveals how much miscommunication was involved in these early stages of missionization, when indigenous conceptions were grafted onto Catholic practices. For instance, inhabitants received baptisms assuming they were curative rituals, unaware of the religious conversion implied by the rite.

In time, Christianity in the Philippines, as elsewhere in the world, was adapted to the local context. Among lowland Christian Filipinos, the pervasive cultural idea of *utang na loob* or profound debt of gratitude was extended to one's relationship to God. Christ's favors (*puhunan*) and his ultimate sacrifice at the cross are said to be so great as to be unrepayable. Faith and devotion are ways of acknowledging this profound debt. (For a longer discussion of the nuances of this concept vis-à-vis Christianity past and present, see Rafael 1988:123–130.)

More recently, new Catholic and Protestant charismatic movements have arisen. In her contribution to this section, Katharine Wiegele (chapter 13) discusses the allure of one such movement for the poorer classes in the Philippines. Her focus is on the Catholic evangelical movement known as El Shaddai, founded by Mariano Velarde ("Brother Mike") in the 1980s. Velarde's weekly open-air prayer and healing rallies draw millions of participants; impoverished Filipinos might commit 10 or more percent of their incomes to this church. As Wiegele illustrates, Velarde's tremendous appeal must be understood both in terms of the contemporary landscape of religion in the Philippines and traditions of religiosity. As she notes, El Shaddai healing rituals in Manila neighborhoods "merge local shamanic or folk traditions with ritual elements of Catholicism and charismatic Christianity, producing what some residents see as 'authentic healing power.'" In short, El Shaddai creates forms of religious experience that are quite distinct from the mainstream church. As this movement globalizes, it remains to be seen how it will ultimately fare vis-à-vis the mainstream Roman Catholic Church.

Religious tensions and conflict, of course, exist not only within the landscape of Christianity in Southeast Asia, but among the different religious traditions as well. Although there have been and continue to be periods of peaceful accommodation, recent years have witnessed heightened religious tensions in some regions. This is an underlying theme in Kathleen M. Adams's chapter (part 5, chapter 14), which addresses Christian–Muslim clashes in Indonesia (which has pockets of Christian minority communities because Dutch missionaries converted highland and outer island animists to Christianity). Similar religious- and ethnic-based tensions exist in southern Thailand, as has been mentioned. Likewise, the southern Mindanao area of the Philippines has been a site of ongoing interreligious conflicts. State policies, initiated by Ferdinand Marcos, to relocate Catholic populations to the Mindanao homeland of the Muslim minorities exacerbated the marginalization already experienced by these Muslim minority communities, giving rise to interreligious conflict and a succession movement that waxes and wanes in this southern region of the Philippines.

11

The Ordination of a Tree: The Buddhist Ecology Movement in Thailand

Susan M. Darlington

A Buddhist ecology movement, developing in Thailand and other Buddhist nations, addresses local and national problems of deforestation and ecological destruction. While this is only one aspect of the growing environmentalism in Thailand (Hirsch 1996), the Buddhists involved in this movement see their religion as critical for providing practical as well as moral guidelines for ecological conservation. This focuses on how Buddhists, especially monks, put their concepts of Buddhism and ecology into action, and the consequent reinterpretations of both sets of concepts that result from such behavior. As Buddhism is increasingly used to promote social activism such as conservation, its role in Thai society is also being implicitly challenged and reworked. While the exact changes that will occur are unknown, the Buddhist ecology movement's potential direction may be glimpsed by examining how rituals, particularly ordaining trees, promote the ecology movement, lending it economic, political, social, and moral force.

"Ecology monks" are those actively engaged in environmental and conservation activities who respond to the suffering which environment degradation causes. A major aim of Buddhism is to relieve suffering, the root causes of which are greed, ignorance, and hatred. The monks see the destruction of the forests, pollution of the air and water, and other environmental problems as ultimately caused by people acting through these evils, motivated by economic gain and the material benefits of development, industrialization, and consumerism. As monks, it is their duty to take action against these evils. Their actions bring them into the realm of political and economic debates, especially concerning the rapid development of the Thai economy and control of natural resources.

ECOLOGY MONKS

In Thailand, the self-proclaimed "ecology monks" (*phra nak anuraksa*) are at the core of the Buddhist ecology movement. Although some participate in the scholarly debate on the issue, their priorities lie in action to preserve vanishing forests, watersheds, and wildlife and mitigate the negative consequences of their disappearance on people's lives. To understand the current ecology movement in Thailand, and ultimately in other Buddhist nations, it is important to examine the effect of the practice of the ecology monks on religion in Thailand to see how they base their projects on Buddhism, reinterpreting and rearticulating religious concepts, the role of the Sangha (the order of Buddhist monks), and the function of Buddhist rituals in the process.

The number of monks involved in the ecology movement in Thailand, although small, has recently grown rapidly,[1] with the popularity of environmentalism currently sweeping Thailand. Given the respect the Sangha commands in Thai society, the potential for their ecological activism is high. This can be illustrated through the analysis of an ecology project conducted in 1991 in Nan Province, northern Thailand. This project, coordinated by a Buddhist monk, involved the creation and sanctification of a protected community forest through the ordination of the largest remaining tree in the forest. The tree ordination provides insight into how the ecology monks throughout Thailand are rethinking Buddhism and adapting Buddhist rituals to promote their cause. Their concern is as much to maintain the relevance of the religion in a rapidly changing world of industrialization and modernization as to create an environmental awareness among local people and the Thai nation as a whole.

Over the past century, the government has taken over many traditional activities of Thai village monks. While the temples remain the spiritual heart of villages, they only occasionally still house schools or serve as health care centers or community centers (Darlington 1990; Kingshill 1965; Tambiah 1970). To compensate and maintain close contact with the laity, many monks perform an increasing number of ritualistic ceremonies. The more active, visible, and, in many ways, controversial response has been to move toward socially engaged action. This first manifested itself in Thailand in the 1970s through the rise of the development monks (*phra nak phadthanaa*), who promote grassroots economic development throughout the country (Darlington 1990; Somboon 1987, 1988).

From the development monks emerged the ecology monks, who see their work as monks and Buddhists as promoting human responsibility toward the natural (and inherently social) environment. They stress an interpretation of the religion that emphasizes the Buddha's connection with nature and the interdependence of all things. While many of these monks work independently in their conservation programs, they are aware of the actions of other monks, share ideas, information, and experiences, and participate in regional and national training seminars. Through their preaching, educational programs, and conservation activities, ecology monks have influenced Thai society in the way Buddhism is viewed and, to some degree, practiced. They have raised the nation's consciousness regarding its environmental responsibilities as their activities have drawn significant attention and media coverage.

Ecology monks argue that it is their responsibility as monks and as Buddhists to become engaged in this manner. Buddhist ecologists (and socially engaged Buddhists in general; see Queen & King 1996; and Thai Inter-Religious Commission for Development & International Network of Engaged Buddhists 1990) stress their connection with the Buddha's ideas of nature, the origins of the religion, and the Buddha's admonitions to be concerned for relieving suffering in the world. Theirs is not a movement advocating a new form of Buddhism, they argue, but an effort to put the basic ideas of the religion in terms that meet the needs of the modern world. They see this movement as one of "radical conservatism,"[2] returning to the original teachings of the Buddha as applied to contemporary situations.

Some monks in Thailand have been concerned about the environment for some time, such as Phra Ajarn Pongsak Techadhammo in Chiang Mai (Suchira 1992; Renard n.d.) and Buddhadasa Bhikkhu in Surat Thani, but their actions and teachings had limited scope. In the 1990s, the Buddhist ecology movement coalesced into a conscious and somewhat coordinated institution. Its coherence and the increased cooperation and dialogue among monks from different regions of the country have drawn public attention to the movement and greater acceptance of its methods and the appropriateness of such actions by monks. This new approach to religion and monks in Thai society and the creative application of the ecology monks' philosophy to make Buddhist rituals tools of social action may change the concepts and practice of Thai Buddhism. One example is the work of Phrakhru Pitak Nanthakhun of Nan Province, the monk who coordinated the tree ordination examined here.

HISTORICAL BACKGROUND

Phrakhru Pitak's sponsorship of tree ordinations and other environmental actions came from his experience in a remote mountain village affected by deforestation and the promotion of cash crops and consumerism. In the mid-1970s, after over twenty-five years as a monk, Phrakhru Pitak became alarmed at the deforestation and damaged watersheds in the region around his home village due to extensive logging by large companies and clear-cutting by northern Thai farmers in order to plant maize as a cash crop. The villagers continually had to cut into the forest to grow maize as a source of income, and the maize itself caused significant erosion and damage to the soil, necessitating further clear-cutting for agricultural land. His district became the poorest and driest in the province, with the highest rate of adults migrating to find work in Bangkok. For years the monk preached about ecological conservation, stressing the interconnection between social and natural environments and humankind's responsibility toward each.

Despite Phrakhru Pitak's preaching, the destruction continued. The villagers came to him to make religious merit and listen to his sermons, then returned home to clear the land. The logging companies cut the forest and the villagers were either too afraid of retribution or too unorganized to oppose them. If they saw a connection between their actions, their increasing poverty, and the environmental crisis, they did nothing about it. In early 1990, Phrakhru Pitak visited Phrakhru Manas of Phayao Province, the monk credited with performing the first symbolic ordination of a tree to make people aware of environmental responsibility. In June 1990, Phrakhru Pitak moved beyond preaching an ecological message and sponsored a tree ordination in the community forest of his home village (see Darlington 2003b), and in July 1991 he performed a second one to sanctify the forest surrounding ten neighboring villages.

These ceremonies were only a small portion of the monk's projects, which included several months of working with and educating villagers about environmental issues, training young temporary novices about the natural environment, promoting economic alternatives to growing maize as a cash crop, and establishing protected community forests (see Darlington 2003b, Local Development Institute 1992; Saneh and Yos 1993). Phrakhru Pitak promoted self-reliant development projects, such as integrated agriculture emphasizing planting for subsistence rather than for sale, because merely protecting the forest by denying the villagers access to it would not be successful. Economic alternatives needed to be established to ensure villagers' cooperation in preserving the forest. Local committees were established to manage the forests, patrol the sanctified areas against incursion, and sponsor continued ecological activities to keep the commitment of the projects alive.

The tree ordination was the symbolic center of Phrakhru Pitak's conservation program. The discussions with the villagers leading up to the ordination and the conservation activities organized by them afterward were all motivated by the emotional and spiritual commitment created by the ceremony. Throughout the ceremony, Buddhist symbols were used to stress the religious connection to conservation, the villagers' interdependence with the forest, and the moral basis of the project.

THE TREE ORDINATION CEREMONY

Tree ordination ceremonies (*buat ton mai*) are performed by many participants in the Buddhist ecology movement in order to raise the awareness of the rate of environmental destruction in Thailand and to build a spiritual commitment among local people to conserving the forests and watersheds.

Some large-scale ordinations have been carried out for publicity and public sympathy to make the government see the environmental impact of some of its economic development plans. (This was the case in the southern province of Surat Thani in March 1991, when over fifty monks and lay people entered a national park to wrap monks' robes around all the large trees in a rainforest threatened by the construction of a dam [Pongpet 1991].) Most tree ordinations are aimed at local areas, and villagers, through their participation in these ceremonies, signify their acceptance of this adaptation of a Buddhist ritual to sanctify the forest and thereby protect it. The regulations the monks establish limit their use of the forest, forbidding cutting any trees or killing any wildlife within it.

In July 1991, I attended a tree ordination ceremony in Nan Province in northern Thailand sponsored by Phrakhru Pitak Nanthakhun. Although the tree ordination was the culmination of months of preparation and was one aspect of a larger conservation program, the actual ceremony involved only a day and a half of activities. Phrakhru Pitak invited over twenty monks from Nan and other northern provinces to assist in performing the ceremony. Recognizing the importance of gaining the support of the Sangha hierarchy and the local government for the project's success, Phrakhru Pitak consulted with and involved members of the province's Sangha organization, especially the senior-most monk in the subdistrict of the ten participating villages, the district officer, and other local bureaucrats.[3] Many local government officials and mid-level members of the Sangha hierarchy participated in the ceremony. Given the independent nature and potentially controversial aspects of the activities of most socially engaged monks, Phrakhru Pitak's attention to convincing the Sangha hierarchy and the government of the project's importance is significant for assuring its success. The night before the ceremony, representatives of Wildlife Fund Thailand (WFT; an affiliate of World Wildlife Fund) showed slides for the villagers. Their co-sponsorship of the project placed Phrakhru Pitak's work on a national stage and gave it further legitimacy. Not only is WFT one of the largest environmental NGOs in Thailand, it also has royal patronage.

The ordination ceremony began in the morning with a modification of a traditional ritual, *thaut phaa paa* (the giving of the forest robes). Usually, this ritual is performed by Thai lay people to donate robes, money, and other necessities to monks for religious merit. Since the 1980s, this ritual has been increasingly used across the nation to raise funds for local development projects; those contributing offerings to the monks gain merit, and the monks allow the money donated to be used for projects ranging from building or repairing a school to establishing a local credit union or village co-operative store. People's commitment to such projects is often stronger because of the religious connotations behind the funds. Phrakhru Pitak added a new twist to this ceremony. Several tree nurseries around the provincial capital and some wealthy patrons offered twelve thousand seedlings along with robes to the monks. Once the forest robes were ritually accepted by Phrakhru Pitak, he and the highest-ranking monk present accepted the seedlings, thus sanctifying them and conferring merit on the donors and the participants. A few of the seedlings were planted around the temple grounds and at the site of the tree ordination as part of the ceremony. Most were given to the villagers to reforest areas that had been denuded. These new trees were chosen carefully; they were species, such as fruit trees, that were profitable without having to be cut down. Having been sanctified and given by the monks further protected them as the villagers would see cutting them as a form of religious demerit (*baap*).

After planting the trees at the temple, all the participants climbed into trucks, vans, and buses to make the five-kilometer trip into the mountains to the tree chosen to be ordained. Over two hundred people accompanied the more than twenty monks to the site. A four-foot-tall Buddha image sat on a concrete stand at the base of the giant tree. Phrakhru Pitak commented that over twenty years earlier, when he walked from his village through the deep forest to school along this route, this tree was not unusual for its height. Now it clearly stood out as the tallest remaining tree. One could see for miles from it across a landscape dotted with near-vertical maize fields, visible because of the deforested hillsides.

In this ceremony, as in all tree ordinations, the monks did not claim to be fully ordaining the tree, as that status is reserved for humans only. The ceremony was used symbolically to remind people that nature should be treated as equal with humans, deserving of respect and vital for human as well as all life. The opportunity of the ordination was used to build spiritual commitment to preserving the forest and to teach in an active and creative way the value of conservation. The main emphasis of Phrakhru Pitak's sermon during the ritual was on the relationship between the Buddha and nature, and the interdependence between the conditions of the forest and the villagers' lives.

During the ritual, at the same point at which a new monk would be presented with his robes, two monks wrapped orange robes around the tree's trunk, marking its sanctification. A crowd of photographers from local and Bangkok newspapers and participating NGOs, one anthropologist, and two camera crews documented the quick act. The robes stood as a reminder that to harm or cut the tree—or any of the forest—was an act of demerit. While it was not unusual to find bodhi trees (the tree under which the Buddha achieved Enlightenment) wrapped with sacred cloth, in those cases the tree was already seen as holy; the cloth served more to honor the tree than to sanctify it. The innovation here was that the tree ordained was not already treated as sacred but was made so through the ritual.

As in most ordinations, the ritual included the sanctification of water in a monk's alms bowl. A small Buddha image was placed in the bowl and candle wax dripped into the water while the monks chanted. Traditionally, this holy water (*nam mon*) is sprinkled on the participants, conferring a blessing on them. This water is seen as ritually very powerful (Olson 1991). On this occasion, Phrakhru Pitak used the blessed water in an original manner. Each of the headmen from the ten villages drank some of the water in front of the large Buddha image to seal their pledge to protect the forest. This use of a sacred symbol to strengthen such an oath was another innovation that reinforced the notion of environmentalism as a moral action. It made the protection or destruction of the forest kammic action: protecting it would confer good merit (*bun*), destroying it would confer negative merit, the balance of which would ultimately affect one's rebirth or even quality of living in this life. Beyond that, it drew on the belief of the villagers in the magical powers of the holy water; while specific sanctions were not mentioned for failing to uphold the headmen's pledge, the implications were that breaking it would involve going against the power secured by the use of the water.

Perhaps the most telling aspect of the ceremony (the one which is open to the greatest variety of alternative interpretations) is the plaque that was nailed to the tree prior to the ordination. (See figure 11.1.) No formal mention of the sign was made during the ritual, nor was much discussion or fanfare made concerning its content or placement. Yet, it always draws the most attention and discussion from Thai who are introduced to it. The sign reads, in Thai, *tham laay paa khee tham laay chaat,* which can be translated, "To destroy the forest is to destroy life." The word *chaat* (life) is problematic, and can carry several meanings, all of which relate to the issue of conservation on various levels.[4] *Chaat* can mean life, birth (as in rebirth), or nation. The sentence could thus be read, "To destroy the forest is to destroy life, one's rebirth, or the nation."

The first meaning is the most straightforward from the point of view of environmentalists whose concerns do not necessarily involve either religious or nationalist connotations. Yet it also implies the Buddhist idea that one should respect and care for all life because any being could have been one's mother in a previous life. The second meaning, to destroy one's rebirth, invokes the concept of *karma.* It raises the idea that destroying the forest is an act of demerit and consequently has a negative influence on how one is reborn in one's next life. The third possibility, that of destroying the nation (meaning both territory and people; Reynolds 1977:274, 1994:442), is the most complex. It evokes nationalist feelings, linking the condition of the forest with that of the state. It draws upon the moral connection between nation (*chaat*), religion (*satsana*), and monarchy (*mahakeset*), the trinity of concepts that supposedly makes up Thailand's identity (Reynolds 1977, 1994). Even this meaning is double-edged. While it invokes the villagers' loyalty to the nation and the king in protecting the forest, it also calls upon the nation itself to uphold its moral responsibility to preserve the forest. Given the political undertones of the conservation issue, it is unlikely that this implicit meaning is present by mere coincidence.

Figure 11.1. Ordained tree in Nan Province, with sign: "To destroy the forest is to destroy life."

The use of the word *chaat* on the sign demonstrates the complexity and significance of the tree ordination. Concepts of religion are being reinterpreted to promote environmentalism at the same time the latter is linked through moral ties with local and national political and economic issues. Throughout the ordination, and the larger project of which it is part, Phrakhru Pitak extended his traditional role as spiritual and moral leader of lay villagers to embrace an activism that necessitates political involvement. The same kind of role enlargement is recreated in every project run by ecology monks, from tree ordinations and the establishment of sacred community forests to tree-planting ceremonies and exorcisms at sites threatened by ecological destruction.

THE MORALITY OF ENVIRONMENTALISM

Monks are not supposed to be concerned with worldly issues such as politics. At the same time, however, the ecology monks see environmental destruction as a crucial factor in what is their main concern—human suffering. They cannot avoid a certain degree of involvement in the former if they are to deal with the latter. They feel responsibility as monks to teach people environmental awareness and show them the path to relieving their suffering. The root causes of suffering are, in Buddhist philosophy, greed, ignorance, and hatred. As the destruction of the forest is caused by these evils (through people's selfish aims at economic gain or unconsidered use of natural resources to meet needs arising from poverty and overly rapid development), the monks see it as their duty to adapt traditional religious concepts and rituals to gain the villagers' acceptance and commitment to their ecological aims.

The destruction of the environment was not a significant issue in Thailand until the rapid industrialization of the country became a national priority after World War II (Sponsel and Natadecha 1988:305). Even then, it was not until the 1980s that nature conservation became a widespread concern. The adoption of the issue by the ecology monks beginning in the mid-1980s has raised the movement to a new level. It can no longer be seen simply as an economic or political debate between environmentalists and developers, but has now been placed on a moral plane. The monks are concerned with the suffering of both humans and wildlife that results from the destruction of the forests and watersheds.

The ecology monks are walking a fine line between their historical responsibilities as spiritual leaders and their new practice as social activists. They are consciously using the former to support and even justify the latter, to counter the criticisms aimed at their environmental efforts as inappropriate for monks. While the focus of specific activities such as tree ordinations is predominantly on local areas, the innovative use of rituals, and the implication of signs like the one nailed to the tree in Nan place the issue on a national political level. Through the use of words like *chaat*, the monks raise issues that question the responsibility of the local and national governments in deforestation and conservation.

Similarly, the practice of religion itself is being changed, even challenged, in the process. Buddhism in Thailand has become less relevant to daily life over the past century because of increasing government involvement in lay life through schools, improved health care, and development projects. The Buddhist ecology movement, following the model of the work of development monks, is not allowing the religion to become relegated to a secondary function in Thai society. It challenges the Sangha, as well as the Thai people, to reconsider its role and not to accept complacency or merely perform rituals that have no direct relevance for relieving people's suffering in daily life. It forces Buddhists to question and think about the causes of suffering, even when these causes are controversial or political. While the ultimate aim of activist monks is to relieve suffering and maintain the relevance of the religion in a changing society, this has also resulted in questioning and rethinking the function of the religion itself.

The use of Buddhist rituals (such as ordinations and the *phaa paa* ceremony), the invocation of powerful religious symbols (such as holy water and monks' robes, and the implication of words like *chaat* in the plaque on the ordained tree in Nan Province) all serve as vehicles that simultaneously preserve religious concepts and sentiments and challenge their traditional use and interpretations in Thailand. The ecology monks are responding to what they perceive as threats to or, to put it more mildly, inevitable changes in their social position. They are making conscious choices and actions, guided by long-standing religious concepts such as merit-making and kammic action, and social relations between the Sangha and the lay villagers. As a consequence, their role, the concepts and practice of the religion, and the relation between the religion (and its practitioners) and the state are all changing. The case of the tree ordination in Nan illustrates the social, political, and economic issues involved, and reveals the level at which the major changes are taking place.

This dynamic process of change is far from complete. The Buddhist ecology movement is still growing and becoming more vocal and controversial, challenging specific cases of environmental destruction caused by policies of the government or economic development plans. The responses of the government, industrialists, and general members of the Sangha, as well as the Sangha hierarchy, all need to be considered to judge the full effect of this movement on the concepts of Buddhism and ecology as they are interpreted and practiced in Thai society. It is apparent that Thai Buddhism is changing dramatically and, despite some efforts to use it as a conservative force to support the status quo and government policies, it has tremendous potential to effect social and environmental change in Thailand. The extent and success of these efforts, and the true direction of the changes involved, remain to be seen.[5]

NOTES

This chapter was originally published in *Ethnology* 37 (1, Winter 1998):1–15. It was edited for length by the author for this volume.

1. While it is difficult to determine membership in a category such as "ecology monks," as many monks are interested in environmental work but do not label themselves as such, a sense of the scope of the movement can be gained from looking at the participation in a three-day conference (held near Bangkok in July 1991) co-sponsored by 23 nongovernmental environmental and development organizations. The organizers expected around 60 monks to attend; over 200 actually registered.

2. This term is borrowed from the title of a book in honor of one of the best-known Thai monks, Buddhadasa Bhikkhu, who called for social action as an aspect of Buddhist practice (Thai Inter-Religious Commission for Development & International Network of Engaged Buddhists 1990).

3. In later projects, Phrakhru Pitak involved provincial government officials and Sangha, including the governor and military leaders.

4. I thank Dr. Thongchai Winichakul and Dr. Robert Bickner for pointing out to me the several meanings of *chaat* as used in the sentence on the plaque.

5. For more recent information on the Buddhist environmental movement, see Darlington 2003a, 2003b, 2003c, 2005, 2007, 2009, and forthcoming; Delcore 2004; and Tannenbaum 2000.

12

Javanese Women and the Veil

Nancy Smith-Hefner

When I first lived in the Javanese university town of Yogyakarta in the late 1970s and periodically walked the grounds of the prestigious Gadjah Mada University, I could not help noticing how young female university students were dressed. At that time, the coed school "uniform" consisted of Western-style knee-length skirts and short-sleeved blouses. Fewer than 3 percent of the Muslim female student population wore the veil. When I returned to Yogyakarta in the late 1990s, the transformation was dramatic. Women students had exchanged their short skirts for pants or "maxis," and the percentage of Muslim women on campus wearing the veil had risen to more than 60 percent.

The veiling style preferred by most Indonesian women today differs considerably from the loose-fitting headscarf known as the *kerudung* or *kudung*, which in previous generations was worn by pious Javanese women and is still today preferred by some older or traditionalist Muslim women. The kerudung is typically made from a soft, translucent fabric and is draped over the hair or over a close-fitting hat. Parts of a woman's neck and hair may remain visible. By contrast, the "new veil" or *jilbab*, is a large square piece of nontransparent fabric folded so as to be drawn closely around the face and pinned securely under the chin so that the hair, ears, and neck are completely covered. The fabric reaches to the shoulders, with some styles covering the chest. The jilbab is typically worn with a loose-fitting, long-sleeved blouse or tunic and a long, ankle-length skirt or loose, wide-legged pants.

There is a paradox to this far-reaching change in Muslim women's dress. Veiling has spread, not on the heels of social immobility or traditionalization, but in the wake of far-reaching changes conventionally associated in Western social theory with economic development and cultural "modernity." These developments, the impact of which first began to be felt in the late 1970s, include the expansion of mass education, the movement of women into public employment and the professions, heightened social and spatial mobility, changes in the family, and fundamental shifts in the economic and class structure of society (Blackburn 2004; Hull and Jones 1994; Robinson 2000b). As the disproportionately high incidence of veiling among female medical and technical students indicates, the practice has spread most widely among the segment of the female student body best positioned to reap the benefits of recent educational and economic changes. This makes the question of the cultural significance of veiling for Muslim women and gender roles all the more intriguing.

This chapter examines the practice and meanings of the new veiling and of Islamization for young Muslim Javanese women in the new middle class. Drawing on extensive ethnographic research in the Central Javanese city of Yogyakarta, I explore the social and religious attitudes of female students at two of the city's leading centers of higher education: Gadjah Mada University (UGM), a nondenominational state university, and the nearby National Islamic University (UIN). The ethnographic and life-historical materials discussed here underscore that the new veiling is neither a traditionalist survival nor an anti-modernist reaction, but a complex and sometimes ambiguous effort by young Muslim women to reconcile the opportunities for autonomy and choice offered by modern education with a heightened commitment to Islam.

MODELS OF GENDER AND CLASS IN JAVA

An irony of the research on women and the family in Java during the late 1970s was that few researchers, Western or Indonesian, were aware that the country was in the early phases of an Islamic resurgence. After the pioneering studies of Hildred Geertz (1961) and Robert Jay (1969), research on Javanese women and the household turned to questions of class, gender inequality, and economic development (Hart 1978; Stoler 1976; White 1976). A few years later, Valerie Hull published an important article on the changing nature of gender roles among the emerging middle class in rural Central Java (Hull 1996). Hull's work is particularly relevant here because she examined women of similar background and age as the mothers of the young Javanese women in my own study. Her work thus offers an important baseline for comparing recent changes in women's roles with those of a generation earlier.

By comparison with their counterparts in the Muslim world and the premodern West, Hull notes that Javanese women have long played a prominent role in the family and public life. For centuries, they have owned farm land, operated small businesses, and had the right to initiate divorce. When mass education first became broadly available in Indonesia in the 1950s, there were relatively few cultural impediments to women's participation in schooling. Hull recognizes that, at idealized levels of expression, Javanese do tend to see the husband as the patriarchal head of the household. However, as she also notes, in the actual conduct of everyday life, the husband–wife partnership is conceived of as complementary rather than subordinating.

Having summarized the conventional view of women's status in Java, however, Hull introduces a wrinkle into the account. This wrinkle concerns the position of women in high-status circles, especially members of the traditional aristocracy and court elite known as *priyayi*. As the ranks of the colonial bureaucracy swelled with native administrators in the late nineteenth and early twentieth centuries, the category of priyayi was extended to include not just aristocrats, but all Javanese employed in state administration. Clifford Geertz (1976) identified the priyayi as an important subcultural elite, distinguished by their concern for the Javanese arts, status-sensitive speech and etiquette, and, most important for the present discussion, their general lack of interest in Islamic piety. Although later scholars would point out that, in fact, many priyayi have been pious Muslims (Bachtiar 1973; Woodward 1989), Geertz regarded the priyayi as mystical relativists.

To this portrait, Hull added the observation that priyayi also differ from lower-status Javanese in their family and gender organization. In contrast to the traditions of their rural counterparts, the demands of family honor for priyayi women often required that women remained secluded in their homes and not be exposed to the status-demeaning bustle of the public world. Priyayi girls received only limited education and were often forced at a young age to marry a husband chosen by their parents (Coté 1995). They were not supposed to engage in demeaning physical labor, with the notable exception of that associated with the relatively prestigious, home-based industry of batik cloth painting and production (Brenner 1999; Gouda 1995).

In evaluating gender ideology and women's employment in Java during the 1970s, Hull discovered that rather than using education to propel themselves into heightened public activity, middle-class Javanese women seemed to be moving toward a neo-priyayi pattern of female domesticity and restricted public participation. Although they were gaining access to formal education and extrafamilial employment, women in the emerging middle class tended to be more, not less, focused on the household. Equally important, rather than developing greater influence or equality in the family, the authority of women in the new middle class seemed static or in decline (Hull 1996:80).

Hull discovered that middle-class women with the means to do so opted not to work outside the home, so as to devote themselves to child rearing and homemaking. In addition, these women also tended to have more children than their lower-class counterparts. In short, among educated middle-class women, Hull saw a trend toward heightened domesticity and social insularity rather than greater equality and public involvement. These developments, Hull concluded, were evidence of diminished female autonomy and social "regress" rather than "progress" (ibid., 90).

WOMEN AND CONTEMPORARY SOCIAL CHANGE

The young women who were the focus of my research in 1999 and the first years of the next century were raised in a Java significantly different from that of their mothers (the generation of women described by Hull). Among other things, these young women have benefited from the educational policies of the New Order government, which succeeded in achieving near-universal primary education and in dramatically increasing women's participation in secondary and tertiary education (Jones 1994; Oey-Gardiner 1991). These educational developments have been accompanied by a substantial movement of women into the civil service and professions.

This new generation of women are also graduates of compulsory religious courses conducted in all Indonesian schools. Since 1967, two to three hours of religious education each week has been state-mandated in Indonesian schools (from grade school through college). For Muslim students, these courses have focused on teaching basic tenets of Islamic doctrine and practice while successfully undermining those aspects of Javanist tradition regarded as polytheistic (*syrik*) and thus incompatible with Islam (Hefner 1993; Liddle 1996).

In the twenty-five years since Hull's study, the Islamic resurgence has offered young Javanese women a powerful, if complex, alternative to both the neo-priyayi and earlier modernization models of gender. The phenomenon of veiling is indicative of this change. Rather than an icon of Islamic traditionalism or anti-modernization, veiling for most middle-class Muslims is a symbol of engagement in a modern, albeit deeply Islamic, world. Although its meanings are varied and contested, veiling for most Muslim women is an instrument for heightened public participation rather than for domestic insulation. Equally significant, Muslim women themselves often contrast this pattern of Muslim mobility to what they identify as traditional priyayi values, which they describe as confining, even "feudal" (*feodal*; Dzuhayatin 2001).

THE POLITICS OF VEILING

One reason Hull and other scholars a generation ago tended to overlook the Islamic resurgence taking place across Indonesia in the 1970s is that their research focused on developments in rural as opposed to urban Java. Had Hull begun her study in the universities around Yogyakarta rather than in villages outside of town, she might have gotten a significantly different impression. At Gadjah Mada University in the late 1970s, I witnessed a new spirit of Islamic activism that, rather than just emphasizing prayer and religious study, sought to link Islam to social and political transformation. Muslim students sponsored scholarship programs for poor village youth; sent proselytization (*dakwah*) teams into neighborhoods and villages; organized cooperatives for transportation and health services; and, most generally, developed a cadre of activists dedicated to the "Islamization" of student life.

The new Islamic activism emerged in the wake of far-reaching changes in campus life. After 1978, the Suharto-led, New Order government had enacted laws aimed at "campus normalization" that effectively prohibited explicit political activity. These laws unwittingly benefited Muslim and other religious groups, since state controls weighed less heavily on religious organizations than they did on secular political bodies. Spared the full brunt of state restrictions, Muslim student organizations were well positioned to take advantage of the anti-regime mobilization that swept university campuses during the final years of Suharto's reign (Hefner 2000; Madrid 1999). Young women activists in jilbab became a familiar sight in the front lines of the demonstrations that eventually brought down the Suharto regime in May 1998. Veiling offered female activists symbolic protection from threats of violence during pro-democracy rallies. It was also intended to signal to the public that the students' cause was a moral one, not merely a matter of power politics (Madrid 1999; Rahmat and Mukhammad 2001).

Until 1991, the New Order government had prohibited veiling in government offices and in nonreligious state schools. Indonesian school children and all government employees wear standard uniforms of a designated color, style, and fabric. For women and girls, these uniforms have long consisted of a knee-length skirt and a short-sleeved blouse or jacket. Prior to 1991, there was no long-skirted, veiled option for students or government employees. Women who veiled in opposition to the state's policy faced discrimination and the derision of their fellow students, employers, and coworkers. Even more serious, they faced the possibility of expulsion from school or the loss of their job.

When the restrictions on veiling were lifted, many students reported that they came under pressure from their classmates to adopt the veil to protest against earlier government restrictions. Interviewees told me that at some high schools, virtually the entire Muslim female student body adopted the veil in a matter of days, although in the weeks that followed some women began reevaluating their decision.

Not all Javanese parents were happy with their daughters' desire to veil. They feared veiling would mark their daughters as nonconformists, hinder their chances for employment, and make it difficult to attract a marriage partner (Brenner 1996). Some of the most vigorous opposition to veiling came from families in which one or both parents were employed as civil servants. As representatives of the state, civil servants bore the brunt of policies during the early New Order; the government neither rewarded nor encouraged public piety. Many middle-aged government employees interviewed after the collapse of Suharto's New Order acknowledged their personal debt to government programs and pensions. A surprising number also admitted that they agreed with the government's earlier suspicion of "radical" or "fanatic" Islam and, as a result, were initially opposed to veiling (Alatas and Desliyanti 2002; Brenner 1996).

The early 1990s was the peak of the Islamic resurgence, and many young activists derided the Suharto government as anti-Islamic. As government policies became more Islam-friendly, however, pressures to veil as a symbol of anti-government protest diminished. In fact, as Suharto in his last years sought to wrap himself in the garb of conservative Islam, some critical women activists began to insist that veiling was only meaningful if linked to demands for democratic reform.

"BECOMING AWARE"

Although pressures to veil as a symbol of anti-government solidarity diminished with Suharto's resignation, the number of veiled women on college campuses in Yogyakarta and other university cities continued to grow. Moreover, as Javanese parents came to realize that veiling did not negatively affect their daughters' friendships, employment opportunities, or marriage prospects, many came to view veiling as a positive phenomenon, expressive of a young woman's deeper understanding of the requirements of her faith.

In interviews, the majority of young women from secular institutions (like Gadjah Mada University) who had made the *commitment* to veil told me that they did so between the ages of seventeen and nineteen, just prior to or during their first year of university classes. Almost without exception, these women describe their decision in religious and personal rather than social or political terms, as the result of a deepening religious understanding, a "becoming aware" (*menyadari*) of their religious responsibilities. Even young women who may have briefly worn a headscarf as part of a religious school uniform cited changed religious awareness as their reason for deciding to wear it constantly.

Oci, a student in her second year at UGM, described her decision to veil in just such personal and religious terms. She said that she had begun to wear the veil consistently at the beginning of her second semester of college. A few years earlier, she had attended a "modernist" Muslim (*Muhammadiyah*) high school where female students were required to wear the headscarf as part of their school uniform, but were allowed to take it off after classes— and most students did.

> I started thinking seriously about wearing the veil consistently during my first semester in college, but I was hesitant because the religious consequences are very heavy. I just couldn't decide. Finally, I did a special prayer that helps you to choose between two things, the *sholat Istikharah*. After that I decided to wear it and I've worn it ever since.

As Oci notes, the ethical standards and behavioral restrictions associated with veiling are weighty, and most Muslims regard the decision to adopt the veil as a great behavioral divide. It is widely held, for example, that veiled women should not be loud or boisterous; hold hands with a member of the opposite sex (even if he is her fiancé); go out in public after evening prayers; patronize cafés or clubs; wear makeup or fingernail polish; smoke, dance, swim, or wear tight clothing; or ride on the back of a motorcycle holding on to a male driver. If a young woman in jilbab violates any of these prescriptions, she exposes herself to public moral censure, some of it severe. She may be reprimanded by family members, friends, and co-workers, or even be challenged by total strangers on the street. Most importantly, those who decide to veil are told that after doing so they should be *konsisten dan konsekuen,* "consistent and responsible in their behavior," and must *pakai terus,* "wear it continuously"; that is, not put it on one day and take it off the next. In light of these expectations, most young women think long and hard before donning the veil. Those who do not veil describe themselves as "not yet ready" (*belum siap*) to commit to veiling's weighty ethical standards and behavioral restrictions.

Because veiling is considered a serious personal and religious commitment, women resist the suggestion that their decision to veil was influenced by social or environmental pressures, such as those made by boyfriends or family members. Although acknowledging that such pressures exist, women insist that the most important influence on their decision to veil is God's commands as expressed in the teachings of Islam. They insist, moreover, that religious responsibility must be individually embraced in order to be truly significant, and reject the notion that the obligation should ever be imposed.

VEILED INSECURITIES

Despite this widely accepted normative script of religious awareness and personal transformation, it is clear from the interviews and life histories I recorded that, in fact, social pressures and incentives do play a significant role in the decision of many young women to veil. Among the most critical influences are those related to campus life. One striking index of this fact is that at Gadjah Mada University the proportion of women veiling increases dramatically from the first year of schooling to later years. Many female students describe themselves as having been confused and insecure when they first came to university and experienced its overwhelming freedom and diversity. The sentiments expressed by one second-year student were common: "There was so much freedom (*bebas sekali*)! My parents trusted me, but I felt overwhelmed (*bingung*)." Campus religious organizations, friends and family members, religion teachers, and Islamic publications all reinforce a message of the dangers of free interactions between the sexes and press for veiling as the solution.

For many young women, college is the first sustained period away from home. Most women who live away from home move into rental rooms or boarding houses with other women students. Surprisingly, these boarding houses have few regulations concerning male guests or curfew hours. Although in the 1970s the convention was that boarding house owners would arrange for live-in housemothers for their rental properties, in the 1980s the requirement came to be widely disregarded. During those years, the combination of a booming student population and liberalizing social trends left most boarding houses with little or no adult supervision.

Even for young women who continue to live at home, taking college courses typically involves a lengthy commute alone or with a friend, on a bus or motor scooter. In the course of commuting, young women point out, they come into close proximity with many young male strangers. Some of those young men take clear pleasure in the freedoms of urban living, and feel few of the inhibitions on interaction with young women found in village or neighborhood settings. Young women complain that in these unsupervised environments they are vulnerable to unwelcome advances and even physical harassment. Veiling, as many young women insist, offers a significant symbolic defense against unwelcome male advances, while allowing young women to enjoy their freedom of movement nonetheless (see Papanek 1973).

For their own part, women widely report that veiling helps them to feel "calm" (*tenang*) and more in control of their feelings and behavior, particularly in interactions with members of the opposite sex. Others describe feeling more "self-assured" (*lebih pe-de/percaya diri*) about speaking up in class or asking questions when male students are present. Yet others describe the veil as a constant physical reminder, one that helps to keep them from overstepping the bounds of moral propriety.

These themes of heightened self-confidence and moral self-control run through all of the veiling narratives I collected from young women. While they recognize that veiling imposes certain limitations on their behavior, those who have made the commitment to veil say they have weighed their decision carefully and view the limitations as positive, not negative. While framed by women first and foremost as a personal moral commitment, the "new veiling" neutralizes at least some of the tension young women experience between urban living's freedoms and its moral threats.

CONTESTING INTERPRETATIONS

Virtually all of the young women I interviewed—veiled or not—are keenly aware of the moral ambiguities of modern urban life. Nonetheless, there is a category of Javanese women who consistently indicate that they view the act of veiling in noticeably less self-conscious terms. In particular, women in my sample from the National Islamic University, most of whom are graduates of Islamic boarding schools (*pesantren*), often have a surprisingly different attitude toward veiling than young women who come from less religious or secular backgrounds. A higher proportion of UIN students are from traditionalist Muslim families with ties to Indonesia's largest Muslim organization, the thirty-five million strong Nahdlatul Ulama (Feillard 1995). Raised in deeply pious (*santri*) Muslim families, women from these families are far more likely than their counterparts at the nondenominational Gadjah Mada University to have undergone rigorous religious socialization in their early years. Rather than being associated with a conversion-like experience in young adulthood, wearing the veil (typically the less enveloping version, the kerudung) for these women was a normalized feature of early childhood.

In contrast to their veiled counterparts from secular school backgrounds, most of these women report that they never had to make an anxiously self-aware decision to veil. Equally important, their commitment to veiling is colored by fewer political overtones than is the case for, so to speak, born-again women raised in nominally Islamic (*abangan*) families. The latter tend to see veiling as part of a religious transformation, resulting from a lengthy process of deliberation and turmoil, sometimes political, sometimes personal, and often both. In contrast, for Muslim women from traditionalist backgrounds, veiling is an important but largely taken-for-granted element of their religious upbringing and community.

A small but vocal minority among the students in this group not only question the motivations of many who have recently chosen to veil, but have also begun to question the meaning and necessity of veiling itself. In public meetings and student publications, these neo-traditionalist activists have begun asking whether the stricter forms of veiling promoted by militant student groups represent an effort to impose "Arab culture" on Indonesian women who already have their own more authentic tradition of veiling and modesty. A few even question whether it is necessary for Muslim women to veil at all. In this regard, it is interesting that the most assertively feminist of young Muslim women in Yogyakarta consistently come not from the campus of the secular Gadjah Mada University, but from the National Islamic University, where the great majority of students are from staunchly Muslim backgrounds.

BEYOND THE VEIL

Though their effect may be less immediately apparent, contemporary social developments other than veiling have had an equally dramatic impact on young Muslim women's lives. Many of these developments have to do with the increased educational and employment opportunities that were unavailable to women a generation ago (cf. Smith-Hefner 2005). Most of the young women I interviewed are the first generation of women in their families to receive a college degree. Ina, for example, is a fourth-year student at UGM. Her mother never completed high school because her parents forced her into an arranged marriage at age seventeen. Despite her limited schooling, Ina's mother encouraged all her daughters to put off marriage and continue their education; her two oldest have graduated and now work in Jakarta. Ina, like the majority of young, middle-class women today, also intends to finish her university studies before marrying. Moreover, when she and her friends do marry, they fully expect it will be to a man of their own choosing.

Recognizing their lessening control over the choice of a marital partner for their offspring, middle-class Javanese parents have begun to emphasize the importance of their daughters being able to work so they can take care of themselves and their children should things go wrong. Parents underscore the sacrifices they have made to educate their children; the great majority also affirm that for a young woman to get a college degree and then not work would be an enormous waste of time and money. Equally surprising, many parents state that they want their daughters to educate themselves and work "so that they will not be too dependent upon their husbands." This practical counsel, with its cool-headed assessment of women's vulnerabilities relative to unreliable husbands, stands in striking contrast to the pattern reported for Javanese by Hull a generation earlier (Hull 1996).

Veiled or not, a full 95 percent of the university women I interviewed reported that they expect to work both before and after marrying. Women echo the concerns of their parents. They want to work so that so that they will avoid being completely dependent on their husbands and so that their relationship will be "more equal." They are also aware of the sacrifices their parents make in order to finance their educations; by working, they hope to repay some of that debt. Others plan to help in the educational support of a younger sibling or other relative. On a less idealized level, most young women also observe that in a modern economy, a woman's income is required to maintain a family according to a reasonably middle-class standard.

All this is to say that women who, as Hull reported a generation ago, prefer not to work and plan to stay at home to care for children, are today a fast-dwindling minority. Phrased in cultural terms, many middle-class women have clearly caught wind of a new narrative of self and personal development. They cite the solitude and boredom of staying at home all day (like their mothers) and talk about their desires for "self actualization" and "realizing their potential." This complex mix of motives—monetary, religious, individualistic, and self-actualizing—reminds us again that, like the Islamic resurgence as a whole, veiling has heterogeneous influences, responsive both to the desire for greater religious piety and for the mobility and prosperity of the new middle class.

NOTE

The materials presented here are part of a larger project on Muslim Javanese youth and contemporary social change in Yogyakarta. Research was funded by a Fulbright-Hays Faculty Research Grant and a Spencer Foundation Small Grant; write-up was supported by the National Endowment for the Humanities.

This chapter was originally published in the *Journal of Asian Studies* 2007 66(02): 389–420. It was edited for length by the author for this volume.

13

Everyday Catholicism: Expanding the Sacred Sphere in the Philippines

Katharine L. Wiegele

For nearly fifteen minutes we pass face after face, in every direction. We walk silently, at a steady pace. Were it not for the landmarks in the distance—the city's skyline on one side, the orange sunset dusting Manila bay on the other—we might be disoriented on our journey toward the rally stage. The crowd of half a million is calm but expectant as they go about settling in on the vast rally grounds. Some listen to the radio broadcast from the grandstand or browse the vending stalls. Others carefully write down their needs, worries, and dreams on prayer-request papers that will be prayed over, when the sky grows dark, by the charismatic Brother Mike from his glowing electric stage in the distance. And somewhere behind the stage curtains, his features artfully outlined with makeup, Brother Mike is stiff with performance jitters that only his wife and his closest aids witness. Up close, with his neon plaid suit and his stage face, he looks fantastically larger than life.

Father Bert, a Filipino Catholic priest, has come with me to this national El Shaddai rally to watch "Brother Mike," who preaches and heals the faithful here, every Saturday night. Father Bert is not a member of El Shaddai. In fact, he explains, he is against what El Shaddai stands for because he feels it runs counter to liberation theology.[1] Nonetheless, he wants to attend just once to "see how it is done." How does Brother Mike create moods of elation, moods in which one can feel the Holy Spirit moving, moods so powerful that people, men and women alike, come from all over the nation to experience a "prayer and healing rally" lasting five or six hours, sometimes ten, until dawn, and even in the rain? How does he motivate millions of impoverished Filipinos to tithe 10 percent or more of their incomes to an organization that has not even so much as a church building? How does he inspire millions to testify, often publicly, that they have been radically transformed, and that miracles have graced their lives?

Father Bert has listened to tapes of American evangelists like Jimmy Swaggart in an attempt to spice up his oration style, but he still has not managed to fill his church and its coffers to overflowing, nor has he heard any testimonies of miracles, nor of lives dramatically transformed. How do Brother Mike and his preachers do it? After the rally, as we weave through the crowds and traffic on the way home, Father Bert tells me vaguely that experiencing the rally will be helpful in his community organizing, but exactly how, he cannot say.

At the same time, I realize I have just witnessed one of the many faces of Roman Catholicism in the Philippines. Not just Father Bert, but Brother Mike, too. Who is he? Flashy televangelist? Yes. Charismatic leader of a religious movement? Yes. Wealthy businessman turned preacher of prosperity? Yes. *Redefining Catholicism for millions of ordinary Filipinos?* Yes again.

Of course, it is true that a practicing Catholic from anywhere in the world would likely feel right at home walking into a mainstream Catholic mass or baptism at any church or cathedral in the Philippines. They would likely feel they share many of the same formal prayers and rituals, and perhaps similar moral values. But if they stayed long enough, they would realize that being Catholic is not really the same in every place. Local traditions and ideas contribute to the making and doing of religion everywhere. All religion to some extent springs forth from the cultural context in which it is practiced. In the Philippines, this means that Filipinos have always made Catholicism "their own."

In this chapter, I explore the appeal of El Shaddai for millions of Filipinos who, by enthusiastically following Brother Mike, have created a veritable religious movement. What is El Shaddai? Why has it recently taken off like a rocket in the Philippines? But first, let us explore how El Shaddai is but one example in a history of Filipino adaptation of Roman Catholicism to local culture and to the current concerns of its people.

A BRIEF HISTORY OF RELIGION IN THE PHILIPPINES

The Philippines and East Timor are the only predominantly Christian countries in Asia. According to the 2000 Census, the Filipino population of 81 million at the time was 80.9 percent Roman Catholic, 11.6 percent other Christian, 5 percent Muslim, and 2.5 percent other affiliation. In all, 92.5 percent of Filipinos are Christian. Filipinos were mostly animistic prior to the arrival of Christianity in the sixteenth century. Local religious practices, which varied from place to place, typically involved a variety of malevolent and benevolent environmental spirits, the veneration of spirits of departed ancestors, and worship of other gods and goddesses. Rites and offerings ensured good health, harvests, luck, and cosmological balance. Individuals with healing abilities, great warriors, and *datu* (village headmen) earned respect and wielded some authority.

Christianity first arrived via Ferdinand Magellan, a Portuguese explorer sailing for Spain. He reached the island of Cebu in the central Philippines in 1521, laying the foundation for more than three and a half centuries of Spanish colonization. With the exception of certain mountainous areas, such as the Luzon highlands, and Muslim areas in the southern Philippines, the Spanish established political dominance throughout the archipelago and converted the majority of its people to Roman Catholicism.

But Filipinos have never been simply empty vessels for imported ideologies, religious or otherwise. Vicente Rafael (1998) describes the process of Tagalog[2] conversion to Roman Catholicism under early Spanish rule as one of *translation*. That is, in the conversion process, Filipinos interpreted events and symbols through their own local categories, sometimes producing entirely unexpected and new meanings of Catholic rituals and colonial power relations. Pre-colonial native notions of reciprocity and debt, for example, combined with Roman Catholicism to form uniquely Filipino concepts and practices within, and sometimes in opposition to, Catholicism and Spanish rule. Concepts such as *utang na loob* (debt of gratitude) and *hiya* (shame)—central to reciprocity and the formation of social relationships—colored Tagalogs' relationships with the Christian God and Catholic religious authorities. According to Rafael, Tagalogs conceived of God as a benefactor to whom they were constantly in debt, a debt that could be repaid only at death. This perspective bound the Filipino in an obligatory relationship with God and the church.

Religion in the Philippines has always been part of the language through which power relationships and political and economic change have been understood, manipulated, and resisted. For example, Spanish colonialism and the penetration of foreign merchant capitalism in Negros, a Visayan island, was understood by Filipinos as a "clash of spirits" between competing cosmic forces—the foreign merchant capitalists on one side and the Spanish friars on the other (Aguilar 1998:26). Tagalog grassroots resistance movements utilized local interpretations of the passion story of Christ (*pasyon*) in their struggle against colonialism from 1840 to 1910. While Spanish clerics intended the pasyon to encourage acceptance of suffering and submission to Catholic doctrine and colonial power, Filipinos mobilized the story dramatically for revolution and confrontation (Ileto 1979).

In 1898, after Filipinos had waged a long fight for independence from Spanish rule, the United States intervened in the islands. Following the Spanish-American War, Spain ceded the Philippines to the United States. Filipino resistance continued during the American colonial period, which finally ended with Philippine independence in 1946. Under American rule, Protestant missionaries and teachers arrived and had relatively modest success in conversion compared to their Catholic predecessors. Their most significant impact was in the transmission of American values and institutions in Philippine society.

During the late 1970s and early 1980s, the Philippine Catholic Church became increasingly involved in political activities in response to widespread abuses of power by the regime of Ferdinand Marcos, eventually expressing open opposition to the dictatorship. As an independent institution, the Church was one among many oppositional forces that led to the 1986 People Power Revolution, which ousted Marcos and restored a democratic form of government. In recent decades the Church has continued to be a moral and ethical voice in politics.

Today, the country remains overwhelmingly Catholic. However, since the 1970s, and especially since the 1980s, the growing popularity of Pentecostalism, Evangelicalism, and charismatic Christianity (a Catholic version of Pentecostalism) has become a major current in the Philippine religious scene, reflecting worldwide trends, especially in the southern hemisphere. As Kessler and Ruland have noted, "While elsewhere in the world Protestant Pentecostals and Evangelicals are the main actors in religious revivals and Christian growth, in the Philippines, this phenomenon is dominated by Catholic Charismatic Renewal" (Kessler and Ruland 2008:2). The El Shaddai group is the largest of the Catholic charismatic groups in the Philippines today.

AN INTRODUCTION TO EL SHADDAI

El Shaddai, founded in and based in Manila, began in 1984 as a nondenominational Christian radio program. Within fifteen years, the group had blossomed into a substantial movement with millions of followers (estimates range between 5 and 10 million).[3] It has chapters in nearly every province in the Philippines and in more than thirty-five countries. Approximately 80 percent of El Shaddai's members subsist below the national poverty line, paralleling overall poverty rates in the country. The group is most known for its massive outdoor Saturday night rallies in Manila that attract a half million to one million followers each week. These "prayer and healing rallies," featuring emotional preaching by "Brother Mike" Velarde, the group's founder and "Servant-Leader," are broadcast on television and radio throughout the country. Local Shaddai chapters also hold smaller weekly prayer meetings.

Brother Mike is a businessman turned preacher, without formal religious training. His evocative and entertaining preaching style, his populist persona and message, and the belief that he can channel miracles to the faithful, allow him to attract crowds and monetary collections that are the envy of clergymen. He and his congregation have been influential in national politics over the past twenty years. Brother Mike even seriously explored running for president of the country in 2010, but decided against it.

El Shaddai is recognized by the Philippine Roman Catholic Church as a Catholic lay movement. Like other charismatic and Pentecostal groups, El Shaddai emphasizes the workings of the Holy Spirit (i.e., faith healing, miracles, and emotional worship experiences) over doctrine (Poewe 1994:2). El Shaddai is a "prosperity" charismatic group (also called "neo-Pentecostal"), due to its acceptance of material prosperity and its appeal across social classes and religious denominations (Coleman 2000). Like other prosperity groups, members practice *seed-faith* (the idea that giving tithes with faith will result in miracles) and *positive confession*, done in part through written "prayer requests" for miracles. As a result, El Shaddai members often interpret everyday life events as miracles, and may publically testify to their miracle stories at rallies and prayer meetings.

In a mainstream Catholic church in the Philippines, one might hear a sermon about "taking up the cross"—the idea that there is spiritual value in suffering and hardship. In contrast, Brother Mike teaches that suffering and poverty can be alleviated by faithfully following God's principles, such as tithing. As such, the "prosperity gospel" affirms the desire for upward mobility. It teaches that paradise can and should to be achieved now, not postponed until after death.[4] During the decade or so immediately following the People Power Revolution of 1986, the aspirations expressed in this prosperity theology seemed to fit with attempts in national government to focus energies on development and material well-being ("The Prophet of Profit: El Shaddai's Mike Velarde Brings Religion down to Earth," 1996). In addition, the vacuum of power created by the end of the Marcos dictatorship, the ultimate disappointment with the subsequent leadership's ineffectiveness in dealing with poverty, corruption, land reform, and human rights abuses, and the weakening of the communist insurgency in the 1990s and early twenty-first century provided the sociopolitical context for the emergence of Brother Mike, whose populist message emphasized not only prosperity, but also self-reliance and hope.

El Shaddai's Catholic affiliation confers some legitimacy within this predominantly Catholic country. Although El Shaddai operates as if it were an independent church, local chapters are linked with local Catholic parishes, and the movement has a Catholic priest as a "spiritual advisor." A portion of its collections go to the church, and mass is said at El Shaddai rallies. However resident El Shaddai healers in Manila neighborhoods conduct healing rituals that merge local shamanic or folk traditions with ritual elements of Catholicism and charismatic Christianity, producing what some residents see as "authentic healing power."

BECOMING "LIVE"

Early on, El Shaddai's initial radio listening audience evolved into a rally audience as people gathered outside the radio station in thanksgiving for miracles. This gathering became a weekly occurrence, and eventually developed into mass rallies. The radio (and later television) programming expanded greatly to become hallmarks of the movement.

DWXI, El Shaddai's radio station, is one of the more popular AM band radio station in Metro Manila. The group also buys television and radio airtime on stations throughout the Philippines. The predominance of radio and television in El Shaddai religiosity differentiates it from the mainstream Catholic experience. The El Shaddai community is, to a large extent, a mass-mediated community. Despite the fact that El Shaddai outdoor rallies and other events are now also experienced "live," mass media actually produce this "live-ness." As we will show, the boundaries between these two "communities" (radio and live rally) are blurred both conceptually and spatially.

Going to an El Shaddai mass rally on a Saturday in Manila involves merging the world of the mass media community with the anonymous but physically manifest congregation of El Shaddai devotees in the huge open field that El Shaddai ministries rents for its rallies. The description below, adapted from my field notes, provides an experiential account of this process.

I am the last person to arrive at Eddie's dwelling—a two-room section of a house in a cramped semi-squatter area in the heart of Manila. Eddie's wife, Celia, and their two children, are still preparing for the El Shaddai rally, as their neighbor Josie and two other young women wait on the couch. The TV in front of them is on, competing for attention amidst the bustle of the rally preparations.

The TV is tuned to the live broadcast coming from the stage at the rally site. The rally has not actually begun yet, but on TV we can see the activity on the stage. A series of individuals give short, impassioned testimonies of miracles they have received, a choir from a provincial chapter sings religious songs, and an emcee mediates each transition with introductions, announcements, short prayers, and pep talks about the exciting rally, or "Family Appointment with Yahweh El Shaddai," that will begin in several hours. As the cameras pan the crowds, we see the commotion of hundreds of thousands of followers getting settled in the open-air field for the evening. Peddlers sell plastic mats, food, and other necessary supplies. Ushers keep people from sitting in the roped-off aisles, and hand out envelopes for "prayer requests" and tithes. On the fringes, people wait in line to use portable toilets. As the emcee on stage pauses to lead a short prayer, Josie and the others present in the living room fall silent and listen, concluding the prayer with an "amen" spoken out loud, in unison with the emcee. Josie joins in, momentarily, as the choir sings the popular song, "We will serve the Lord." Josie's friend, Nhelin, sits beside her on the couch and writes her "prayer request."

When Eddie's family is ready to go, he lowers the volume of the TV, and we join hands in a circle for a "binding" prayer with each other. Then Eddie turns off the TV. Although the house is less than two kilometers away from the large open field along the coast where the rallies are held, it will take us over an hour to navigate our way via public transportation to our final destination: a spot on the rocky lawn, close enough to see the stage area, but far away enough to be able to sit comfortably, with enough fresh air.

Celia flips on the radio as we begin the journey, tuned to DWXI, where the rally is being broadcast live. We leave the house, and then the "interior" of Sinag by walking through the many *iskinita*, or narrow corridors between houses and buildings—the dark urban footpaths that wind around and between the two- and three-story buildings. Neighbors greet us as we pass through the densely populated neighborhood where according to the local priest, at least 85 percent of the residents live below the national poverty level. One neighbor greets us with "See you there, sister!" even though she knows she'll never find us in the crowds at the rally. A young man, half-mockingly, hums the first line of the El Shaddai theme song.

After fifteen minutes waiting by a major thoroughfare, a jeepney (public jeep) finally stops for us, and the eight of us get on. As we sit in the cramped jeepney, we listen to a woman's humorous testimony coming from the radio. She is talking about her husband, exaggerating his former bad qualities, and then testifying to his transformation. My companions laugh and say, "Amen! Praise God!" as we imagine those in the crowd at the rally are doing the same.

Forty-five minutes and two jeepney transfers later, we arrive outside the Harrison Plaza shopping mall. By now, all of the passengers are hot, grimy, and a little light-headed from the humidity, heat, and air pollution. Here we pile out and walk three blocks on the side of the street to a designated spot outside Rizal Baseball Stadium, where enterprising jeepney drivers have formed a new jeepney route. These jeeps go from here, to the rally grounds, and back to Harrison Plaza, all day long, every Saturday. This particular route has expanded in recent years to accommodate the hundreds of thousands of travelers going to the El Shaddai rally.

As we wait in line, along with at least a hundred other people, for space on the next public jeep, radios of various volumes can be heard throughout the crowd, all tuned to the live broadcast from the rally stage. There is a feeling of camaraderie amongst the people waiting in line. People greet each other as El Shaddai followers—with the titles "Brother" and "Sister."

Everyone inside the jeepney is going to the rally and a more powerful "boom box" blasts the live transmission. Within ten minutes we are inside the grounds, slowing to avoid hordes of pedestrians. We are dropped off near one of the parking areas and walk the rest of the way.

Outside the rally grounds, El Shaddai activity extends as far as the highway—a good twenty-minute walk from the stage. On Saturdays the area of the city surrounding the field becomes, in effect, El Shaddai space. Not only are decorated and bannered jeeps, taxis, cars, tricycles, bicycles, buses, and mobile vending stalls blocking movement and traffic, but pedestrians and vendors adorned with markers of El Shaddai membership—El Shaddai handkerchiefs, portable chairs, tee-shirts, candles, hats, and blasting radios—seem to flow from every corner en masse toward the grounds. Those passersby stalled in traffic on the highway can sometimes gaze at vending stalls with El Shaddai religious items, which include wall calendars, banners, El Shaddai cassette tapes, and ritual items for the day's rally, such as eggs or flowers. El Shaddai participants get a small kick out of inconveniencing the unconverted through these huge weekend traffic jams. To them, it is a form of evangelism.

As the crowds get thicker and the back of the grandstand area is in sight, we no longer need our radio—we can hear the live transmissions from countless radios around us, of people who have decided to sit down here on the fringes. Some people can't even see the grandstand at all because their view is blocked by another building in the rally compound. Nonetheless, when Brother Mike begins speaking in several hours, these people will listen to the live radio and face the grandstand while going through all the same motions as everyone else, actively participating in the rally.

As we head toward the grandstand, the sounds of portable radios are gradually replaced by the sounds coming from the loudspeakers near the stage. Soon we can actually see the emcee on the stage as we squint in the brightly lit area. We are now part of the "live" rally. Huge stands with camera and audio equipment block the view of the stage as we get closer. The area directly in front of the stage is blocked off and reserved for the "very sick"—those with terminal illnesses or deformities—so that they can receive the strongest healing power coming from Brother Mike on stage. There is a feeling of excitement, of being part of history, as a video camera's gaze passes over us and simultaneously transmits our image to people across the country. Josie told me once that she loves going to the rally here, as opposed to the smaller rally in her local chapter, "because it's live!" Were it not for the cameras, the simultaneous broadcast, and the instant playback (after the event is over), this "live" feeling would not exist. In the floodlights and in the camera's gaze, we have come out of the "interior" into the spotlight. For a few hours this evening we are, it seems, significant, and in a sense demarginalized.

As the crowds of people leave the area and journey home after the rally around midnight, many radios will be tuned to the playback, a repeat broadcast of the event that just occurred.

DWXI announces the upcoming rally all week. Followers journey to the rally from sections of Manila and from far-flung provinces. Yet the ritual sphere of the rally extends beyond its immediate locale because radio and television are played constantly, before and after the event. Since the broadcast is live, one begins experiencing the event even while still at home. Listeners can "tune in" by listening to radios or watching oversized film screens on the perimeters of the massive rally lawn. Many watch or listen to rallies without even attending them, but go through the motions, the songs, and the prayers as if experiencing them "live." Within the rally grounds, radios serve as links to Brother Mike at the center. During the journey, the mass mediated community is gradually transformed into the more immediate, physical community of the rally. As the crowd leaves the rally, the opposite occurs. The rally community is transformed once again into the media audience.

Mass media help to create a "live" feeling at the rally, which becomes "live" when participants enter a zone they understand to be mediated to oth-

Figure 13.1: Singing and praying at an El Shaddai rally, 1996.

ers watching or listening "out there." This brightly lit, colorful sphere presents a larger-than-life, amplified reality that doesn't stop with the self, but flows outward. This feeling is enhanced by Brother Mike on stage, who is aware of this outward flow as he directly addresses people at home. "There is a woman in Naga City listening right now who is in need of a miracle. She has been suffering from cataracts for several years. Woman, you will be healed, and you will see your son graduating from high school next year!" (Inevitably a person fitting this description will surface later to publicly tell a miraculous story of healing.) Many followers I interviewed testified to having been healed through radio or television, from blessings Brother Mike gave either during a live rally broadcast, or during a radio program. Some hold up objects to the radio or television to be blessed—similar to what is done at rallies—or use the radio or the television to keep evil spirits away from the house, for example spirits that are said to bring drugs into the neighborhood or cause discord within families.

RITUAL SPACE, COMMUNITY, AND THE HOLY SPIRIT

By expanding the boundaries of ritual space through the airwaves, El Shaddai creates a direct experience of sacredness, ritual, and the Holy Spirit in the home, within a very personal sphere. Blessings can travel through the airwaves, unmediated by traditional Catholic channels such as priests, saints, the Virgin Mary, the Eucharist, statues, or rosaries. Brother Mike told me that his ministry's calling was to "free people from the bondage of religion." He values traditions such as the sacraments and mass attendance, but says the Church and its clergy are bogged down with intellectualism and ritual. Furthermore, while Catholic priests' connections with God are "man-made" (the result of studying), Brother Mike see his as unstudied and "spiritual."

"This is no longer the work of man," Brother Mike told me personally. "We are just willing vessels. Like me—I have a covenant with God that no man can ever understand."

Furthermore, followers see the media airwaves and the open air of the rally as conducive to the free movement of the Holy Spirit. As one El Shaddai member said, "At church, God is near. At the rally, he is actually there." They say they can "feel" God at the rally, in the open space—as energy, as heat running through their veins, as rain water on their skin (when it's not raining), or as wind (when there's no wind blowing). Moreover, they say that the feeling of God's presence follows them into their everyday lives, whereas going to a church (i.e., in a Catholic church) is seen as limited in space and time: "you go in, you go out," or "after one hour, it's over."

It is understandable that followers enjoy the rallies in this open space on the coast, and that they "feel God" there. One emerges from Manila's cramped, tunnel-like streets and neighborhoods[5] to a rare, wide open space with a view of the sunset, and on the horizon, one sees a partial view of the city's skyline in the distance. The fresh air, sea breeze, open space, and stars signify a different, liberating sort of existential state to many of those who come to spread blankets on the ground.

In this space, El Shaddai members get a perspective not only of the city, but also of themselves and their own critical mass. They are able to express the force of this mass to outsiders by disrupting the city and its imposed "order" and by occupying, even reclaiming, public spaces. They create massive traffic jams at unusual times and take over the clean, posh segments of the city. In the interior *barrios*, El Shaddai's mass is dispersed and unseen, but a rally crowd is a totality that can be seen and felt. As part of this collectivity that is simultaneously broadcast on national television, El Shaddai members are in a sense de-marginalized. Seeing El Shaddai's impressive assembly, especially from atop the steps of the Film Center building (within the rally grounds) or through the TV cameras above the stage, gives participants a sense of significance, even empowerment. This view of "the numbers" is, in part, what makes El Shaddai seem awesome to outsiders as well.

In coming out from the barrios, El Shaddai members also enter a space where mediation with the elites and the power brokers of Philippine society seems possible. People in the rally audience are courted by politicians and candidates who "perform" for them on stage, address them directly, and banter with Brother Mike. In El Shaddai/rally space, formerly invisible people now exist, at least on some limited level, for the nation—they are on the national political map and in the national consciousness. Not only do politicians, candidates for political office, high officials of the church, prominent businessmen, and other prominent people regularly visit them, giving them a sense of importance, but these visits reach a national audience through mass media.

CONCLUSION

Congregation, sacredness, and community have been transformed and expanded in El Shaddai contexts to create forms of religious experience that are very different from those of the mainstream Church. Most notable are the ways El Shaddai' followers see their relationships with God and with others in the religious community, their experience of ritual, their emphasis on the spiritual manifestations of God, and their orientation toward Brother Mike as a conduit to God. By using mass media and open air rallies, Brother Mike also puts El Shaddai ministries in a strategically favorable position with the Church institution, allowing El Shaddai to remain both independent and under the wing of the Church at the same time. This gives El Shaddai a perceived distance from Catholic orthodoxy, while allowing it to capitalize on the sense of legitimacy derived from its Catholic identity. El Shaddai members' use of religious programming, combined with their participation in mass rallies, extend the sacred and ritual sphere beyond the immediate locale into the home and the body, blurring the boundaries between mass mediated religious experience and more temporal forms of religious practice.

Interestingly, on August 20, 2009, Brother Mike opened the El Shadddai International House of Prayer, a $20 billion worship structure with a floor area of one hectare (more than two acres) in the Brother Mike-owned Amvel City San Dionisio, Paranaque City (within metropolitan Manila). The structure reportedly has a seating capacity of 15,000, with a standing-room capacity of 25,000, and an overflow capacity of 200,000. It claims to be the biggest place of worship in Asia. Will this alter the essential nature of the El Shaddai religious experience? Will El Shaddai continue to be as distinctive and relevant? What is the future of the open-air, boundless El Shaddai with a church?

NOTES

Parts of this chapter previously appeared in Wiegele (2005) and Wiegele (forthcoming).

1. Liberation theology is a theological movement that emphasizes the church's role in changing oppressive social, economic, and political structures.

2. Tagalogs are one of the major ethnolinguistic groups in the Philippines.

3. The group does not stress official registration of members, so many participants are not "official" members. Therefore, official membership numbers are much smaller: 252,463 as of September 19, 2005 (Personal interview, El Shaddai headquarters, Makati City, September 2005).

4. The prosperity gospel's emphasis on worldly over eternal concerns has been a major point of contention with mainstream Filipino Roman Catholics and clergy.

5. At the time of this research, the population of Metropolitan Manila was approximately 9.5 million. If one includes the surrounding suburbs, that figure nearly doubles.

PART FIVE

Communicating Ideas: Popular Culture, Arts, and Entertainment

Southeast Asia is rightly celebrated for the rich diversity of its artistic, expressive, culinary, and entertainment traditions. Many American and European scholars were initially drawn to Southeast Asia via chance encounters with the region's music, dance, material culture, or martial arts. One of this volume's editors (Adams) still vividly recalls a European train ride she took as an undergraduate on which an Indonesian family introduced her to their homeland by pulling out from their suitcases an array of brightly colored batik textiles and postcards of their elaborately carved ancestral houses. When they learned that Adams was an anthropology major, the family declared Indonesia to be a dream nation for anthropologists interested in the arts, as the country is home to a multitude of cultural groups, each with its unique genre of textiles, music, and carvings, not to mention foods and leisure activities. This family's assessment of the richness of Indonesian expressive forms is equally applicable to other regions of Southeast Asia.

In Southeast Asia, as in other parts of the world, popular culture, the arts, sports, and even food preferences express a myriad of personal, communal, spiritual, and political concerns. Some performative and artistic traditions may have their roots outside the region, as is the case with the famed puppetry and dance performances based on the Indian epics of the *Ramayana* and the *Mahabharata* or stories recounting episodes of Buddha's life. However, as with all cultural borrowings, these imported epic narratives rapidly became infused with local cultural themes. Today these imported traditions are part of the expressive landscapes of Java, Bali, Thailand, and other regions of mainland Southeast Asia. The Indian tales of the *Mahab-*

harata or the *Ramayana* may be performed accompanied by *gamelan* percussion orchestras as shadow puppetry epics (*wayang*) at all-night village-based celebrations (such as weddings or purification ceremonies), as they were in the past on Java and Bali. Or the epics might be condensed, updated, and staged at prestigious performing arts venues in national capitals, adapted to make trenchant commentary on social issues, as the Indonesian artist Kumoratih Kushardjanto recently did in his adaptation of the *Mahabharata* ("Boma"), which spotlighted the profusion of homeless children on the streets of Jakarta.

In her contribution to this section, Sandra Cate (chapter 16) examines the ways in which several contemporary Thai artists in Bangkok and Chaing Mai craft interactive art forms drawing on ancient Theravada Buddhist forms or other "traditional" Thai icons (including the elephant or the symbolic color of yellow, associated with a revered king of Thailand) to problematize official national narratives of Thai history. These official national narratives suppress evidence of state-sponsored violence against Thai citizens and celebrate mythologies of benevolent rulership. Participatory art in Southeast Asia may also offer less disturbing, more easily digestible lessons. Cate's chapter also addresses the ways in which contemporary Thai artists such as Rirkrit Tiravanija and Pinardee Sanpitak draw on performance and participatory art to celebrate how the preparation of foods such as *pad thai* (the epicurean embodiment of Thai identity for many American frequenters of Thai restaurants) can be reconceptualized as part of the social, interactive "art of living." A bottom-line point embodied in these performative pieces is that we need not limit our conception of "art" to objects and paintings. In a related vein, Nir Avieli (in chapter 17) spotlights food, approaching the Hoinese everyday meal as a kind of cultural artifact that conveys much about Vietnamese conceptions of the cosmos. That is, when viewed as a communicative cultural form, a simple meal of rice, fish, fish sauce, and other leafy or aromatic greens is far more than mere caloric nourishment. Rather, underlying such a meal are important ideas about cosmic principles (*yin* and *yang*, *am* and *duong*) and the ways in which diet can forge balance between these principles. In essence, as Avieli's anthropological analysis suggests, Vietnamese food is interwoven with cultural and metaphysical ideas, even when not consciously articulated by those consuming it.

Thus far we have spotlighted performative, immaterial expressive forms and how these expressive forms may "speak" to various spiritual, political, or historical themes. What of more concrete types of material culture? Various writers have addressed the ways in which ancient monumental architectural displays in Southeast Asia embody visions of the cosmos. For instance, the Hindu-Buddhist temple of Borobudur in central Java (Indonesia), whose construction began in approximately 760 CE, is a three-dimensional representation of Buddhist worldview: seen from the air, its overall form is that of a mandala. As pilgrims progress through the levels of the temple, approaching an enormous stuppa at its summit, they trace a path toward spiritual enlightenment. Borobudur's overall form, the chiseled stone depictions of the life of Buddha on its walls, its division into three spheres (from the sphere of desire at its base to the sphere of formlessness at its summit), and its sculptural representations all communicated themes in Buddhist doctrines to the early Javanese pilgrims who made it their destination. Likewise, as has been noted, the expansive Khmer site of Angkor, whose major temples were constructed between the ninth and fourteenth centuries, also replicates Hindu conceptions of the cosmos, with its enormous "moat" surrounding the central point of Mount Meru (see Part 4).

Architectural representations of Southeast Asians' varied worldviews are not limited to regions where imported world religions dominate. A consistent theme explored by anthropologists is how indigenous architectural forms may embody the worldviews, social organizational principles, or religious perceptions of their builders. In the 1960s, Clark E. Cunningham (1964) wrote a classic article examining the ways in which the traditional house architecture of the Atoni of Timor is tied in to broader symbolic systems relevant to Atoni society. More recently, Roxana Waterson (1990) has written a wide-ranging anthology of the ways in which various indigenous Southeast Asian architectural forms embody visions of social and symbolic worlds. Such visions are not limited to the traditional architecture of rural societies in Southeast Asia. Consider, for example, the use of feng shui in constructing new skyscrapers in Singapore.

In her contribution to this section (chapter 14), Kathleen M. Adams examines the ways in which Toraja carvers (on the island of Sulawesi, Indonesia) artistically articulated their concerns about Indonesia's fall into interreligious strife at the end of Suharto's New Order regime. The carvers drew on a repertoire of symbols derived from the carved façades of their ancestral houses in order to sculpt a new genre of "carved paintings that speak." The encoded messages of their artistic productions are not only about crafting harmony among individuals, groups, and religions, but also project to the world these Toraja artists' pride in the wisdom of their ancestors.

An introduction to our section on arts, popular culture, and entertainment in Southeast Asia would not be complete without mentioning Bali and the role it has played in anthropological examinations of the arts. Within Indonesia, Bali has long danced in the imaginations of tourists and scholars alike as a mesmerizing center of artistic creativity. Thanks to the legacy of early anthropologists such as Margaret Mead and Gregory Bateson, and artist-ethnologist Miguel Covarrubias, many Americans of a certain generation shared an idyllic image of Bali as a tropical paradise in which there was no word for "art" yet nearly all parents reared their children to engage in artistic endeavors on an almost daily basis. While the tumultuous Indonesian events of the late 1990s and the much-publicized 2002 Bali nightclub bombings have somewhat attenuated these romanticized Western images (and have also thrust Bali scholarship in new directions), for many foreigners Bali remains the quintessential artistic Mecca and perhaps the island whose arts have been most intensively researched.

Mead and Bateson were among the first generation of anthropologists drawn to Bali to study artists at work, ritual performances, and even dance (in 1952, they produced the classic film *Trance and Dance in Bali*). While Mead and Bateson drew on their studies of Balinese arts to explore the linkages between culture and personality, a popular anthropological topic at the time, subsequent scholars such as Hildred Geertz (1994, 2005) have offered fine-grained analyses of the life history and productions of particular artists in order to foster our appreciation of the ways in which Balinese religious, artistic, and expressive practices are entwined with the "pragmatic goals" of amassing spiritual strength and gaining protection from the unseen world of nonhuman spirits. Other scholars, such as J. Stephen Lansing, have examined how Balinese ritual traditions, such as the crafting of exquisitely beautiful food offerings for various deities tied to water temples, are related to an elaborate and ingenious system of water management on the island. In this system, water temple rituals—the dances, musical performances, carefully crafted offerings, and priest incantations—are tied to regulating water flow to fields and temples farther down the mountainside, thereby ensuring optimal water sharing and rice-paddy irrigation (for a fuller account, see Lansing 1983, or the film *The Three Worlds of Bali*). Still other scholars have examined how the island's intensive history of tourism has contributed to the shaping of Balinese culture, leading to an efflorescence of the arts—a kind of cultural self-consciousness that Michel Picard has dubbed "touristic culture" (Picard 1996; for a related observation, also see McKean 1976).

As with more formal arts, many dimensions of everyday life and leisure entail reproducing and recreating systems of belief and social relationships. Nir Avieli notes how the very act of eating a meal together reproduces Confucian social relationships, with seniors eating from the bowls of food first (chapter 17). Pattana Kittiarsa (chapter 15) introduces us to *muay thai*, now a famous international sport. As he notes, muay thai works to reproduce Thai conceptions of masculinity. The Thai boxer is an exemplar of maleness, male power, skill, toughness, and determination, especially of male dignity. As Kittiarsa points out, these standards of maleness are tragically ephemeral, based as they are on levels of strength and coordination that cannot be maintained throughout life. Muay thai is also a national emblem of Thai toughness in the face of more powerful neighbors trying to overcome the nation. The *Ong Bak* series of popular movies, in which a poor rural Thai boy conquers thieves and murderers from Burma, Thailand, Australia, and the United States, have become an international phenomenon and thus a further point of national pride. The boy triumphs because he is pure of heart, a Buddhist, and incredibly skilled. As might be imagined, Burmese contest Thai national claims to this art of boxing.

A wide range of other art forms in Southeast Asia could also be addressed here, had we the space. We have not examined the rich musical traditions of Southeast Asia, nor have we addressed the ways in which contemporary music and film from other nations are absorbed and retooled for and by Southeast Asian consumers (for a lively exploration of music in Southeast Asia, we recommend Craig Lockhard's *Dance of Life: Popular Music and Politics in Modern Southeast Asia* [1998]). In our current globalized era, art is a key avenue for intercultural interactions: tourists from around the world travel to Southeast Asia to study Balinese dance, to practice muai thai, and to "jam" with Southeast Asian musicians. Likewise, Western and Middle Eastern forms of music travel to Southeast Asia, where they are enthusiastically embraced and also transformed, as they become imbued with locally relevant meanings. We have only touched the surface of these varied and complex art forms.

14

Cultivating "Community" in an Indonesian Era of Conflict: Toraja Artistic Strategies for Promoting Peace

Kathleen M. Adams

A TALE OF VIOLENCE AVERTED

On a brisk morning in 1997, a convoy of trucks rumbled into the rural pre-dominantly Christian Toraja town of Rantepao, in upland Sulawesi, Indo-nesia. The trucks screeched to a halt at the town's dusty main intersec-tion, where sarong-clad villagers awaited public transport to the market and unemployed Toraja tourist guides lingered alongside snoozing immigrant *becak* drivers. The ordinariness of the morning was abruptly shattered, as fierce-looking young men poured out of the trucks in front of the Chinese-owned businesses lining the main street. The Toraja souvenir vendors in ad-jacent shops, bank tellers at the imposing People's Bank of Indonesia, and the cluster of people catching up with friends in front of the post office all snapped to attention. All had seen televised images of violent anti-Chinese outbursts on Java and in their provincial capital of Makassar, and all had a framework for imagining what appeared to be on the verge of happening in their own homeland. Hurling anti-Chinese curses, these strangers began to move menacingly toward the largest Chinese-owned business, as fright-ened Chinese shop-owners snatched up their outdoor displays and franti-cally yanked down heavy metal security doors. However, the sequence of events that unfolded next did not follow the same path of violence and de-struction that had seemed so inevitable and uncontrollable elsewhere in In-donesia. Dozens of Torajas quickly locked arms, forming a human barricade between the muscular invaders and the Chinese businesses. As I was later told by Toraja friends, these Toraja were unfazed by the rocks and sticks the men brandished. Instead, they resolutely declared, "You cannot harm the Chinese in Tana Toraja, for these are our brothers (*saudara*). You have to go through us to get to them. Go home, and leave our brothers alone." After a tense standoff, the men grudgingly returned to their trucks and drove away.

When I returned to Tana Toraja in May 1998, during a period of violent clashes throughout Indonesia, many people in the community recounted this story to me. Two of my closest Toraja friends enthusiastically shared detailed, riveting accounts of this narrowly averted conflict, knowing it would pique my interest. Although the tales of the incident varied in detail, all celebrated the theme of Toraja–Chinese Christian brotherhood (*persaudaraan*) and many suggested the muscular men were outside agitators, either military, Muslim Javanese, Makassarese, or Bugis (neighboring ethnic groups in South Sulawesi).

Chinese merchants in Rantepao told the tale more soberly, some trembling as they spoke. Many conveyed their fears for the future, and some were considering abandoning their lifelong homes in Indonesia. As one merchant, Pak Budi, told me, "This time around, we were protected. . . . But will our Toraja neighbors be able to protect us when these outside agitators return with knives or guns?" As he spoke, it seemed telling that, unlike my Toraja friends, Pak Budi opted to use the term "neighbors" (*tetangga*) rather than "brothers" (*saudara*). His sense of vulnerability became still more palpable when he recounted that his children were unable to sleep soundly since the incident. Their nightmares triggered his own fears, and his evenings were spent making costly long-distance calls to lay plans for an emergency escape, should one be needed. In the meantime, Pak Budi was trying to smile charitably when testy customers growled at him because of the spiraling prices of his merchandise, prices driven up by the seemingly out-of-control inflation that was sweeping Indonesia at the time. For Pak Budi, Torajas' 1997 defense of their Chinese "brothers" generated relief and gratitude, but he did not feel that he could expect their help in the future.

One Muslim family, who had migrated two decades earlier from the impoverished adjacent region of Duri, also recounted the story of the averted clash to me, conveying their own distinct fears. On my first visit to their home after a two-year absence, Bu Hasan, her teenaged daughter, and I sat on a woven mat on the dirt floor of their modest plywood home, catching up over sweet tea and fried bananas as the television hummed in the background. Bu Hasan, a plump widow in her fifties, reported that since the incident business had evaporated at the small noodle soup kiosk she ran out of her home's crammed front room. Previously, Bu Hasan had spent her afternoons scurrying between the caldron of aromatic soup simmering outside her back door and the front-room noodle shop, where benches were filled with animated Toraja high school students and neighbors taking breaks from chores. On my earlier visits, Bu Hasan was always dashing about, juggling heaping trays of *lemper* (rice packets wrapped with banana leaf) and steaming bowls of the soup for which she was locally famous. On this day, however, she was idle, the wobbly wooden benches were empty, and the front room was disturbingly silent.

Bu Hasan distractedly smoothed a wrinkle in her batik housedress, as she described her recent economic and personal hardships. Remorsefully, she confided that she was ready to abandon the soup kiosk and turn her efforts to selling used charity clothing supplied by her coastal Muslim relatives. I stole a second, closer glance at her front room and now noticed that the two long tabletops, where Christians and Muslims once sat slurping noodles elbow-to-elbow, were spotlessly scrubbed, without the usual soup splashes and abandoned banana-leaf wrappers. The glass snack jars and containers of hand-folded, kite-shaped napkins were filled to their brims. I imagined Bu Hasan and her daughter folding countless paper napkins and baking heaping mounds of sweets in hopes of luring back their customers. Their efforts, however, were in vain: a faded portrait of President Suharto and the tattered posters of Indonesian pop stars presided over a silent, empty room. In a soft voice, Bu Hasan shared her fears that, as Muslim outsiders, her family was now being lumped with the anti-Chinese agitators. The televised images of looted, torched Chinese stores elsewhere in Indonesia both sparked her pity for these fellow "outsiders" and prompted fears about what might befall her own family. My feeble attempts at reassurances were met with a reminder that, as Muslims, her family did not share the same kind of "brotherhood" with the predominantly Christian Torajas. A few weeks later when I revisited Bu Hasan, she confided that her family was contemplating returning to their impoverished Duri homeland.

On that 1998 visit, I was alternately moved, alarmed, and intrigued by the discussions prompted by this episode of narrowly averted interethnic violence. I open with this incident because it embodies several themes concerning ethnic–religious clashes and accommodations framing this chapter.

The first theme is that of the complexity of discussing religious identities in Indonesia and elsewhere in contemporary Southeast Asia. As suggested in this Toraja story of violence averted, a variety of conflicting and entwining identities were at play: ethnic, religious, political, and regional residential. Although Christianity and Islam have become increasingly important dimensions of identity in Indonesia in recent years, and are often reported to be prime motivators in current situations of conflict, one must keep in mind the constructed and myriad nature of identity. Not only does each Indonesian have a variety of entwining, sometimes competing religious, ethnic, and regional identities that must be considered in analyzing ethnoreligious strife, but these identities are also not inert and primordial. Rather, identities are dynamic: they are shaped in particular historical and political circumstances (cf. Keesing 1989). Identity is always in the process of being formulated, challenged, or reaffirmed.

While popular media commentators often paint Indonesia as an explosive volcanic hotbed of ethnic and religious resentments, as a nation comprised of cultures programmed to run amok, or as a land of devout Muslims revolting against the forces of globalization and Westernization, scholars such as Sidel (2001) and Bubandt (2001) suggest that such explanations are erroneous. Rather, we need to understand how historical processes of capitalist development, class relations, and religious policies in Indonesia underlie the recent eruptions of violence. One broader theme in this chapter is on spotlighting these sorts of local histories to better illuminate dynamics in current ethnoreligious conflicts.

Another theme in this chapter concerns the production of peace and pan-identities. The Rantepao event is an instance in which violence was averted, where ethnic divisions between Chinese and Torajas were momentarily erased, presumably due to shared Christian identities and common residential or regional identities. Although many commentators have concentrated on documenting and analyzing violence in Southeast Asia, I wish to focus on the ways in which peace is produced, however tenuously. Just as it is important to ask why some places have been torn by religious, ethnic, and class violence, it is equally important to ask why many places in the same nation seem to remain comparatively peaceful, despite economic and employment woes.

The third theme of this chapter centers on how stories and material objects can become resources for ethical responses to conflict and the threat of violence. On the many occasions during which I heard the story of Toraja resistance to outside provocateurs, it was clear that this tale had become imbued with meaning as a model for Toraja conceptions of identity and ethical behavior. The emphasis on the Chinese as *"saudara,"* a term laden with Christian connotations, also hints at the role of language in producing and underscoring emergent kinds of "we" identities, uniting ethnic communities under a religious umbrella. In Indonesia, how do some expressive and artistic practices foster reflections on ethical behavior in contemporary times? Specifically, this chapter explores how material creations become vehicles for imagining ways to engage harmoniously (and sometimes not so harmoniously) with other groups.

CARVING NEW RELIGIOUS DIALOGUES IN TANA TORAJA

The Sa'dan Toraja are a minority group of approximately 350,000 living principally in the South Sulawesi highlands (Indonesia). They make their living through wet-rice agriculture, coffee planting, gardening, civil service work, and employment in the tourist trade. In contrast to the Islamicized lowland Sulawesi kingdoms of the Buginese and Makassarese, Toraja lived in small mountaintop kin-based settlements and did not envision themselves as a single ethnic group until Dutch colonialization and missionary activities in the early 1900s fostered these sensibilities (Bigalke 1981). Today, Christianity has become a key dimension of Toraja identity (more than 80 percent are Christian), and also serves as a source of feelings of vulnerability in predominantly Muslim Indonesia. Although small communities of Muslim immigrants reside in the Toraja homeland, most residents are Christian, including most Chinese merchants in the regency.

By the 1980s, the Toraja highlanders were "discovered" by domestic and foreign tourists. This flow of outsiders into the Toraja homeland offered new economic possibilities (as well as competitions with neighboring Muslim groups) and enhanced many Torajas' sense of ethnic pride (Adams 1998; 2006). In the mid-1990s, over 140,000 tourists were visiting the Toraja homeland annually. But in recent years, the tourist flow has been hindered by incidents of terrorist bombs targeting hotels and discos elsewhere in Indonesia, as well as by fears of Avian virus outbreaks.

When I began research in Tana Toraja in 1984, I was intrigued by the relationship between Toraja traditional carvings and ideas about identity and social order. Toraja elders were fond of telling me that all of Toraja philosophy, values, and worldview could be "read" in the carved motifs of traditional Toraja houses, or *tongkonan*. At that time, most carvings produced for locals and tourists depicted traditional houses, funeral scenes, parading domesticated animals, or geometric Toraja motifs (each with its own name and meaning). When I returned to Tana Toraja in the mid-1990s, however, I found that a new genre of Christianized Toraja carvings had blossomed.

In the mid-1980s, I knew only one tourist carver, a pastor's son, who routinely infused his works with Christian imagery. He was especially gifted at crafting trays depicting tongkonans that had been reconfigured to showcase dimensions of Christian spirituality. These trays highlighted the tongkonan's cross-shaped front support beams and many included halo-like sunburst motifs (a Christianization of a motif called *pa' barre allo*) above these traditional houses. His trays had a spiritual feel and were regularly found on the shelves of local souvenir stands, as they sold well to urban Toraja tourists. Aside from the creations of this carver, however, Christianity was a relatively rare theme in the Toraja handicrafts of the 1980s.

In the mid-1990s, as Indonesia's public terrain grew more Islamicized, a novel genre of Christianized Toraja carvings began to blossom. Many of these new creations took the form of carved pictorial works. In some, the Christian elements, such as crucifixes or Christ's head, are cleverly worked into larger traditional landscapes: for instance, a carved pastoral scene depicting tongkonans, rice barns, and traditionally clad villagers might feature highlighted pathways forming Christian cross shapes. During the same decade, the living rooms of several of my more devout Toraja acquaintances displayed traditionally embellished carved wall plaques depicting Christ figures and crosses.

For instance, one particularly eye-catching image (Figure 14.1) displayed by a Rantepao friend showed a benevolent-faced Jesus cloaked in a flowing brown robe. His arms were extended, as if preparing to embrace the viewer. An open Bible lay at his feet, alongside a wooden pedestal bowl (*dulang*),

Figure 14.1. Christianized Toraja carving depicting Jesus.

the sort traditionally used for ritual offerings to the gods. Three gleaming white candles glowed in the bowl. Off in the background, the carver had depicted a tidy modern church. Most striking, however, was the carver's framing of Jesus' head with a whitened tongkonan façade, evoking a halo effect. Behind this, the carver had depicted the profile of yet another large tongkonan rooftop, further enhancing the halo imagery and presumably alluding to the Toraja description of the church as the "big tongkonan." In this instance, we see an array of traditional motifs conscripted to project Christianized messages about community and spirituality.

In tandem with the increased Islamicization of Indonesia's urban landscape in the 1990s, these carvings and other Torajanized church embellishments seem to be further Christianizing Tana Toraja's landscape. Muslim Torajas, who constitute roughly 10 percent of the population, noted this Christianization of Toraja motifs. When I returned in 1998, some Muslim Toraja in Rantepao were drawing on Toraja carving motifs to display their own religious identities. For instance, the exterior rafters of Rantepao's Islamic school had been Torajanized, incorporating carvings of the Islamic star and crescent, bordered with a fringe of geometric motifs drawn from tongkonans. Rather than adhere to the classic Toraja carving colors of red, yellow, white, and black, however, the white crescent and yellow stars floated on a background of vibrant green, the emblematic color of the Muslim faith. In a sense, a symbolic interfaith dialogue about the nature of Toraja identity was transpiring in these public outcroppings of religiously infused Toraja carvings.

ETHICAL CARVINGS: REFRAMING LOCAL, INTERETHNIC, AND INTERRELIGIOUS RELATIONS

It was in this context of increasing religious self-consciousness and burgeoning religious, economic, and political tensions in Indonesia that I became aware of how some Toraja were promoting ethical responses to conflict and turmoil, both locally and nationally, through their carvings. Upon arrival on a research visit in 1998, I stopped by the rural home and workshop of one of my Toraja "siblings" to catch up on family news. This brother, Ambena Landang,[1] was now in his fifties and with each passing decade he seemed to become increasingly reflective and political, pouring his energies into sculpting a better world. Always a charismatic man with a deep concern for ethnic equality, as well as for ethical behavior, by 1998 Ambena Landang was finally becoming recognized as an intelligent local leader.

The pounding of distant carvers' mallets echoed in the bamboo glen as I came down the narrow path leading to Ambena Landang's home and studio on a damp June morning in 1998. I found him seated at a sturdy old wooden table in the center of his breezy workshop, his head bent over papers. From the entryway, I surveyed his studio, which was greatly changed since my last visit. Scattered around the workshop were dozens of figural sculptures: hunchbacked elders with enormous canes, elegant traditionally clad women in funeral finery, and even miniatures of squatting gray-haired grannies clutching betel nut bags crowded the benches and corners of the space. The walls were covered with striking three-dimensional carved paintings, many unlike any I had ever seen before: some shimmered with new colors atypical of the Toraja palette; innovative metallic gold- and silver-saturated scenes magnetically drew my eyes. Still others glistened with a layer of shellac, and many were framed. Astonished by this outpouring of creative productivity, I paused to absorb it before calling out the Toraja greeting, "*Manasumorekka?* [Have you cooked rice yet?]"

Ambena Landang's bespectacled head bobbed up. He flashed a grin along with the standard reply, "*Manasumo!* [The rice is cooked already!]," and gestured for me to come in and chat. We plunged into the important family news—updates on deaths and funerals in the community during my absence. Finally, Ambena Landang turned to discuss his new carvings.

Several years earlier, Ambena Landang had observed trouble brewing among the youth in his rural district. Many had graduated from high school or college, but had returned home to face unemployment. They were alternately depressed, dejected, and resentful that their years of schooling had not brought them jobs. As Ambena Landang observed, with empty pockets and time on their hands, these youths were veering toward gambling and petty crime. Recognizing their need for income and productive activity, Ambena Landang established a carving workshop for these unemployed youths. Gathering a few idle teens from his hamlet, he mentored them on carving, reasoning that if they were kept busy carving, they would soon forget about gambling. With a furtive smile in the direction of his wife, he reminded me, "I used to gamble, to the point where gambling became my profession. Hopefully, this workshop will give them . . . a profession that will not torment the spirits of their wives and children."

Initially, working under Ambena Landang's tutelage, the teens at the workshop produced the standard touristic wall plaques and trays. Several of the young carvers routinely chipped away at their creations while perched on the studio's airy front porch. The workshop's location alongside a trail to a much-visited gravesite meant that tourists often paused for snapshots of these photogenic young carvers. Ultimately, the visitors would be drawn into the workshop and purchases would soon follow. Between Ambena Landang's careful quality control and the studio's ideal location, the workshop was soon financially viable. Gradually, Ambena Landang began experimenting with new carving styles and genres, infusing seemingly innocent landscapes with embedded political and ethical messages. Drawing on the traditional vocabulary of Toraja symbols, he sketched models for his new visions, then relinquished them to the workshop carvers who made these visions come to life in multidimensional carved "paintings."

As Ambena Landang declared,

> [Through our carvings] we want to communicate to our fellow citizens and to all the peoples of the world that there *is* a Toraja philosophy of life that was recorded in carvings in the eras before writing existed, and that this Toraja life philosophy still has relevance for us all. All that you see here, it's all our philosophy.

Ambena Landang pulled a large, meticulously executed piece off the wall (Figure 14.2). Whisking off the dust with his palm, he placed it in front of me for closer inspection. "Take a look at this one, Katlin," he instructed. Carefully, I studied the images on the painting. Dominating the center was the façade of a traditional ancestral home, a tongkonan, overlain with a sculpted image of a *bate manurun* structure. Bate manurun are sacred, ladder-like objects constructed of bamboo and cloth banners. They are erected during great *maro* rituals, rituals that were traditionally held to restore order following a disturbance (Nooy-Palm 1979:221). Bate manurun translates as "the flag that descended from heaven." For adherents to ancestral religion, this massive structure was lowered by the gods from the heavens to protect humans from various dangers. Some interpret this ritual architectural structure as a "helping hand extended by heaven to mankind on earth" (ibid., 222). Above the bate manurun, at the apex of the house, a large cockerel (*pa' manuk londong*) stood poised atop a sunburst motif (*pa' barre allo*). Menacing the cock was a fork-tongued serpent (on the painting's upper-left side). To the cock's right, behind its tail feathers, Ambena Landang had sculpted a pair of animals—the *kabonga* (water buffalo head) and the *katik* (a mythical long-necked crested bird).[2] The background of this upper portion of the painting was filled in with the betel nut leaf motif (*pa' daun bolu*), a motif Kesu' area carvers I interviewed said was associated with offerings to the gods and spirituality. At the painting's base, under the bate manurun structure, a roughly hewn nude man stood with arms extended, grasping two sinuous serpents. Each enormous serpent appeared poised to swallow a small frog. Although unpainted, the entire carved scene was enthroned on a colorful frame embellished with traditional Toraja iconography.

After I had surveyed the painting for a moment, Ambena Landang began his explanation. Tapping his finger on an area around the apex of the bate manurun structure and the tongkonan (which elites in this hamlet associated with the power of the gods and ancestors), he explained, "See *here*? Power resides *here* at the top. But next to it, there is *Setan* (Satan)—the powers of *Setan*." He gently tapped the forked-tongued serpent to underscore his point. Turning to the painting's upper center and indicating the rooster, he

Figure 14.2. Ambe Landang's new genre carving.

continued, "The rooster is our symbol of law and justice. See here, next to it, Setan [in serpent form] is trying to lure it into temptation. But the rooster is saying 'there is power behind me.'"

Ambena Landang paused to point to the mythical katik bird, the buffalo head, and the betel nut leaf motif, reminding me of their associations with the power of the gods and ancestors. As I reflected on the various sorts of powers to which these motifs alluded, Ambena Landang continued unpacking the carved painting's meaning.

"Here, in the bottom part, humankind is always in motion . . . and temptation is always hovering, trying to goad humans' desires." I squinted at the painting, initially perplexed, until I realized that the tongkonan dominating the painting's center, as well as the bare man clutching the serpents, alluded to human activities and temptations. Pointing to the small frogs near the serpents' mouths, Bapakna' Landang moved on,

> See the frogs? Man is giving the frogs to the snakes. He is telling the snakes, "Just eat these frogs—don't make me your target." Nah, beginning at that moment, Toraja people started wanting to be as good as they possibly could.

Gesturing to a pair of roosters near the center of the painting that I had previously overlooked, Ambena Landang elaborated:

> You remember, Katlin, how usually a pair of roosters is carved at the top of tongkonan? Those roosters are continually crowing to each other, delivering messages for us all to remember. These roosters here are crowing reminders of this story, crowing to everyone that we are *one* community and that we must treasure each other, and celebrate our community. So the picture is giving us a lesson about how to live.

He paused for a moment, puffing on his cigarette while I reflected on the carved painting's overall message. Although he hadn't directly addressed the bate manurun dominating the center of the painting, I now understood the reason for its presence. Indonesia had fallen into a period of violence and disruption, and the bate manurun was a structure erected as part of traditional rituals designed to restore order to the community. In essence, Ambena Landang was invoking this traditional "helping hand" from the heavens to restore order to the broader community. He was adeptly invoking a pantheon of traditional images to sculpt a message about living harmoniously in today's complicated world.

Turning more directly to the context of South Sulawesi, Ambena Landang resumed:

> I started this sort of carving to help poor people here make a living. But now I'm seeing that we need to do this to support ourselves in other ways. If our carvings are liked by others, people [from other groups] will automatically

respect us. We don't want what happened back in the 1950s to repeat itself—when Torajas made shoes for people in Makassar and those people [Muslim Bugis and Makassarese] used those shoes to stomp on us. Right?

Ambena Landang's eyes sparkled as he proceeded to tell me about the next part of his vision, which he hoped would carve a new path for Toraja relations with their lowland rivals:

My plans are to start carving tables to give to people in Makassar. Soon, they'll be sitting before *our* tables. If they enjoy eating and drinking from our carved tables, when we Toraja appear, they'll be saying *"silahkan . . ."* [please come sit and join us]. Nah, that's what I'm doing next!

As I listened, I realized that for Ambena Landang, these furniture-carving plans embodied an attempt to manufacture more harmonious relations between Muslim Makassarese and Christian Toraja, relations that would bring them together over shared food and drink.

FINAL REFLECTIONS

Ambena Landang group's new genre carvings were not simply decorations, but also articulated messages about ethical behavior in challenging times. Just as the tale of Toraja defense of their Chinese "siblings" recounted at the beginning of this chapter celebrated an instance where local-level cultural differences were bridged and violence averted, so did these new carvings offer embedded lessons about how to live with dignity in an increasingly conflict-laden world. Of course, there is another dimension to Ambena Landang's endeavors. As some observers might suggest, questions arise as to whether these Toraja carvers are simply trying to create interethnic bridges via their carvings or whether they are trying to "turn the tables" on their lowland rivals. That is, in furnishing lowland Muslims' homes, Torajas would be making themselves ever-present in their rivals' daily lives. Whichever perspective one embraces, Ambena Landang's new genre carvings constituted an avenue for reimagining and reframing histories of past ethnic and religious tensions.

In this chapter, I have tried to chronicle how Toraja people have drawn upon stories and carvings to envision and propel ethical approaches to coexistence, bridge-building, and in some cases "brotherhood" with other groups. It would be an exaggeration to suggest that these bond-forging moves have been entirely successful: in the years since 1998, some fights have broken out in the Toraja highlands, though at present these small-scale clashes have not erupted into riots. People in Tana Toraja remain anxious and fearful as they watch religious and ethnic conflict explode in nearby cities and regions.

However, in the artistic strategies chronicled here, we can see some local people's attempts to develop ways of speaking to, connecting with, and redefining potential enemies. In these modest efforts may lie lessons for us all.

NOTES

1. A pseudonym.

2. This pair of animals could traditionally adorn only those tongkonan that had held the highest-level rituals. Today, however, these symbols are increasingly found on tongkonan that have never hosted these rituals. For instance, a little over a decade ago, the Toraja Church erected a tongkonan on their Rantepao grounds—this tongkonan prominently displays these symbols, even though their original association is with *aluk to dolo* (Toraja ancestral religion) rituals that never have been and never will be celebrated in this Protestant building.

15

The Fall of Thai Rocky

Pattana Kitiarsa

Thai-style boxing (*muai Thai*) is perhaps Thailand's most popular national pastime and its best-known international sport. Thais are immensely proud of their boxing tradition. In the past, boxing skills formed a core part of military training known as the art of bare-hand weaponry (*phahuyuth*; see Bua 1989 and Khet 2007). Many legendary Thai boxing warriors employed these arts of fighting and physical prowess to defeat their foreign opponents and were accorded national hero status (Vail 1998). In modern times, boxing has become a professional spectacle sport, an internationally renowned martial art form, and a prizefighting competition for the gambling and tourist industries.

I use the term "Thai-style boxing" (*muai Thai*) to distinguish it from the international style of boxing (*muai sakon*). Muai Thai is sometimes known in the martial arts community as "kick-boxing," but many practitioners and specialists do not agree with this Western generic branding, arguing instead that muai Thai is perhaps the only true full-contact form of boxing. In muai Thai, most parts of the body can be used as sophisticated weapons with devastating impact; its methods include kicking, kneeing, punching, and elbowing. Although the world has recognized the bloodiness and distinctiveness of Thai boxing (Panya and Pitisuk 1988; Rebac 1989), few are informed about the complexities of the tough life of young men who practice this full-contact sport. Nor are many fully aware of the everyday masculine cultural forces and social institutions that have reinvented it, sustained it, and elevated it from a Southeast Asian local setting to the global market of popular culture.

I offer Thai boxing culture as an example of how masculine aspects of everyday life are practiced through a cultural model that regards human prizefighters as "hunting dogs" (*maa lai neua;* Pattana 2003; 2005). Thai boxing culture is highly gendered and embedded in the masculine domain of power relations. Robert Connell reminds us that "masculinity is not just an idea in the head, or a personal identity. It is also extended in the world, merged in organized social relations" (1995:29). Everyday life is far from being a cultural space of smooth and homogeneous meanings; it is important to complicate the domain of everyday life as a gendered and problematic lived experience. Boxing culture in Thailand is a site for contesting masculinity. It has inspired generations of poor, young boys to become breadwinners for themselves and their families, as well as to compete fiercely, in their short-lived careers, to attain male honors available only to "a few good men." I cite a real-life tale of a muai Thai champion, who was once affectionately known to the media and fans as Mahahin (the Invulnerable Rocky), to illustrate how this form of everyday life serves as a space of masculine ideological practices in contemporary Southeast Asia. In his prime, Mahahin won championships in four different weight categories at Lumphini Stadium. He was twice bestowed the Boxer of the Year Award by the Sports Authority of Thailand (SAT), in 1999 and 2001, and was also the title holder of the 115-pound Junior Bantamweight organized by the World Muai Thai Council. These feats were accomplished by a native of a poor upcountry village from Nakhon Ratchasima, some 275 kilometers northeast of Bangkok.[1]

INTRODUCING THE THAI ROCKY

In mid-2008, the Thai Rocky was an aging former boxing champion. However, he is the Thai version of Rocky Balboa, the Hollywood-enshrined American hyper-masculine fictional boxing hero portrayed by Sylvester Stallone. Like his American counterpart, the Thai Rocky's heart is said to be made of rock and steel. He withstands all pain when he fights his opponents in the ring; he is a proud, enduring fighter. If we apply the Thai cultural metaphor that compares prizefighters to hunting dogs, he started as a novice hunter who eagerly climbed up the professional ladder while tirelessly sharpening his match-fighting skills. His active career spanned over two decades, an unusually long time for most boxers in Thailand. But at thirty-six, he is a spent body beyond his prime, at the dead end of his career. He is now a toothless and useless hunting dog.

Thai Rocky's lucky boxing name (*chue chok muai*) is Thongchai To Silachai. The name Silachai is adopted from the name of his boxing gymnasium or camp. It is an old tradition in Thai popular performing arts, such as boxing, folk opera, music, and films, that performers training and working under the same master share a stage surname, giving them common identities, a kin-like sense of bonding and belonging. The boxer chooses his first name, in many cases a fictionalized one. Most Thai boxers choose auspicious, ferocious, or motivating stage names of heroic fighters such as *Insidam* (Black Eagle), *Nakrop* (Warrior), *Falan* (Shaking the Sky), or *Phadetsuk* (Winning the Battle). Many pick the name of their birthplace or hometown as a boxing name. Others simply use their personal given names, such as Thongchai, which means "the banner of victory."

My colleagues and I first met Rocky in late March 2001 while doing ethnographic fieldwork on Thai boxing in Nakhon Ratchasima. It was a typical training day at the To Silachai training ground, located inside the residential compound of the First Air Force Unit. The owner of this boxing gym is a former muai Thai fighter currently serving in the Royal Thai Air Force. Rocky, who was in a relaxed mood, had just completed a month-long intensive training session to regain his freshness and strength prior to a match. After helping his trainer supervise younger colleagues, he gave us a short interview in which he offered an account of his life.

> I was born in 1972. I came from a very poor family. No children in my family went to school beyond the compulsory Primary 6. My father was my first trainer. He is a self-taught boxing trainer. He never fought in the ring when he was young, but boxing was always in his blood. He trained me to fight in the local temple fairs when I was eleven. I was still a primary school pupil when I fought in the ring for the first time. I was defeated in my first boxing match, but I received 40 baht [USD 1.1] for my three-round fight. I was so proud of myself that I could earn some money from my boxing skills. In 1984, my father brought me to the To Silachai boxing camp in Nakhon Ratchasima, where my older brother had trained as a live-in boxing understudy. My father was close to the owner of the camp. I trained hard day in and day out and my career began from there. Like most of the young fighters from the countryside, I had to accumulate experience by fighting in countless temple fair boxing competitions. Every boy always keeps in mind that only talented fighters will earn a chance to fight in Bangkok's Lumphini or Ratcha Damnoen Stadiums.

The Thai Rocky's early biography tells us two things about boxing culture in Thailand. First, poverty produces muai Thai fighters. Boxing is a tough career sought almost exclusively by poor young boys from working-class backgrounds; boxing serves as an escape from poverty and a venue for geographical and socioeconomic mobility. Boys from higher socioeconomic classes would not dare to enter this bloody and bone-breaking trade. Second, most young boys have their first encounter with boxing in rural villages and at small town temple fairs, initially as fans and then as amateur fighters. In the past, sons of farmers or wage laborers often learned to box from their peers or elder "brothers" in the empty space of a rice field or vacant ground in their villages. The rural periphery is where a mass of raw talent is nurtured, through boys' alluring dream of success through boxing.

As in most professional male sports in Thailand, young boxers-to-be are identified and recruited at a very young age. Rocky first learned to box when he was ten or eleven. The pre-teen or just-pubescent boy is considered to be at a perfect age to start muai Thai lessons. Choi, a veteran boxing trainer in Nakhon Ratchasima, suggested that a twelve-year-old boy is at the ideal age to become a muai Thai trainee:

At this age, the boy is still obedient. He listens to and remembers by heart whatever we teach him. I never want to train kids from well-to-do family backgrounds; I want boys from very poor families as my boxing trainees. I believe poor boys take boxing more seriously. They are more persevering and able to endure hardship and pain. They have witnessed their parents' real-life difficulties. That's the best motivation for them to be their family saviors. It inspires them to train hard and take every fight as the fight of their life.

Rocky's boxing background illustrates some major classifications of muai Thai. Muai Thai broadly combines amateur and professional training and fighting styles. Many boys even acquire their fighting skills at the local Buddhist temple grounds, where young Buddhist monks and abbots teach young disciples to fight as muai Thai boxers; furthermore, the temple ground is always open to the public for outdoor training space. Two important Thai colloquial classifications of boxing styles are *muai wat* (temple-trained boxing) and *muai ban* (village-trained boxing), respectively. These terms imply a casual and unsophisticated fighting style in comparison to *muai khai* (professional camp-trained boxing). The latter suggests a serious professional boxing style under the supervision of experienced masters or trainers with unique fighting traditions and identities. Some well-known traditional muai Thai traditions are associated with outer cities such as Chaiya, Lopburi, and Khorat.

Phong, Rocky's trainer, pointed out that experience is one of the most important factors for a successful boxer:

You must begin your muai Thai lessons at an early age. I mean the lessons in the ring. You must fight in the village or temple fair boxing competitions at least ten bouts before you can move on from muai wat/maui ban to muai khai. You train hard and you must pass the fighting test at the local fights in order to move on to another professional level. The road for all boxers always leads from the countryside (*phuthon*) to Bangkok. It is now national legislation [since 1999] that your body weight must be at least one hundred pounds in order to fight legally in major stadiums in Bangkok.

Rocky had no formal education after he completed primary school at age twelve. From that point on, he devoted himself to fitness and improving his fighting skills. Thai boxing culture holds that a great champion must possess three great properties: (1) the right attitude and self-discipline for intense training; (2) fighting intelligence; and (3) a never-say-die spirit. Rocky was the rare boxer with all three of these fundamental ingredients. As an intelligent and gifted boxer, he was known in Thai as *phonsawan* (talented, implying a heavenly blessing), a talent that distinguished a great champion from ordinary boxers. This divine "gift" goes hand in hand with intelligence. A gifted boxer elevates his trade into a gracious and artful fighting style that goes beyond performing a simple physical or violent game. Phong holds Rocky up as a boxer with rare natural talent or "gift," who knows how to outwit and outmaneuver his opponent in critical moments. "If you are gifted, it is not difficult to be coached. Gifted boxers are usually intelligent. A good brain and sharp memory are vital in both training and on the ring. Gifted boxers, like Rocky, pick up lessons quickly and are able to steadily improve themselves, just as clever kids do in school."

Rocky strongly believes in a rigorous training regime in order to achieve his best physical and mental condition. At the To Silachai camp, he trains twice a day in morning and afternoon sessions. Each session lasts two or three hours. The training routine begins with a ten-kilometer jog as a warm-up prior to tactical drills in the gym. After jogging, Rocky and his fellow boxers do a ten-minute air-punching exercise, followed by five rounds of full-contact kneeing drill with a partner for a total of forty minutes. After a short break, boxers practice their kicking drills by spending twenty minutes on the heavy punching bag and another thirty on kicking-pad drills. They finish their training routine with a combination of workout exercises such as push-ups, pull-ups, and weight-lifting. This boxing camp requires that a boxer go through a heavy and continuous training regimen for at least twenty days before each scheduled match. Each boxer is given a total of three days before and after the bout to prepare or restore his physical and mental fitness. If a boxer is defeated by a technical knockout or sustained injuries, the rest time might be extended.

A painstaking regimen of hard training "turns the body into the weapon and target of deliberate assault" (Wacquant 1995:136). Food and diet are carefully regulated in order to control body weight. Rocky once told me that the most excruciating part of training did not come from an opponent's weapons on the ring, but through the pitiless efforts to reduce his body weight (*rid namnak*) for the pre-fight weigh-in. Body-weight treatment techniques include jogging, rope-jumping, sitting in a sauna, fasting, and the use of diuretics. It is commonly thought in Thai boxing that the more body weight a boxer sheds from his regular body mass before weigh-in, the greater the advantage he will enjoy during the actual encounter. After the weigh-in, the boxer regains his body weight and strength by eating heavy meals, with foods believed to be nutritionally rich, and full rest so that he is fresh and ready for the fight.

Thai boxers start to learn their trade at a tender age in order to accumulate and strengthen their *kraduk* (literally, bone), the core of experience. This also gives a young fighter time to earn his reputation and the right to fight as a professional boxer in the provincial, regional, and finally national capital rings in Bangkok. In this movement through the rigid channel of social mobility, the young boxer also earns increasingly higher wages. In 1988, the young Rocky had his first bout at Lumphini, Bangkok's most prestigious boxing stadium. His body weight then was 43 kilograms (94.6 lbs.). As a top junior boxer in his hometown, he was a sixteen-year-old rising star. He outpointed his opponent in the first match and pocketed 1,500 baht (USD 43) as his wage (*kha tua*, the performance fee, but literally, the "body price"). Between 1988 and 2001, he became a star boxer. Within the first ten years of his career, his wage rose to 10,000 baht (USD 293) and then 100,000 baht (USD 2,928) per bout. When my colleagues and I met him in 2001, he was earning 160,000 baht (USD 4,685) per bout, the highest wage a boxer could enjoy. He usually fought once or twice a month and his earnings were split equally between his trainer and himself. The trainer needed money for his own profit as well to pay the daily expenses for all the boxing trainees living in his camp. Rocky told us that he was extremely happy with his earnings and overall career:

> I have a good and stable income for my family because of muai Thai. Boxing may take a toll on your body and you have to sweat blood and suffer pain from the fight, but I am proud of myself. I can earn a living and achieve something by winning several major championships and awards. A poor boy from a humble background with low education like me could not have asked more from life.

Rocky is a fighter with a "diamond heart" (*chai phet*). Phong points out that his fighting spirit (*chai su*) is perhaps Rocky's most outstanding quality:

> Rocky simply refuses to lose. He has a very big heart and gut. He can always endure a painful or bloody fight. He shows no pain when he is on the receiving end during the fight. His heart knows no pain and the word "giving up" (*yom phae*) has no place in his boxing dictionary.

A boxing fan and admirer of Rocky observed that "Rocky's heart is as strong and tough as a rocky mountain. He can always stage a comeback to beat his opponent toward the end of the final round despite being far overwhelmed as an underdog." The boxer performs the poetics of boxerhood by fully demonstrating his powerful will to finish off his opponent. He displays his great spirit in overcoming his own physical limitation and gamely dealing with his adversaries. Rocky's example reminds us that in boxing, a model boxer is admired not because he is a gentleman, but because he is a killer or a punisher. It is this extraordinary quality of fighting spirit that guided Rocky's career. He rarely suffered a knockout blow and never knelt down before any opponent. Boxing promoters, media, and fans in Bangkok admired him for his distinctive fighting spirit. In the Thai boxing fraternity, Rocky's popularity and reputation spread on and off the ring.

ROCKY AND "*SAKSI LUK PHUCHAI*"

Boxing as a type of fighting skill and a social ideology constitutes a key part of the Thai concept of masculinity (*khwam pen chai chatri*). According to

Khet Sriyaphai, a prominent muai Thai master, a masculine man (*chai cha-tri*) in the pre-modern Thai tradition should possess at least five properties: (1) learned secular knowledge and right livelihood; (2) politeness and being respectful; (3) good morale and perseverance; (4) religious and supernatural knowledge; and (5) physical prowess and skill in the arts of self-defense, including boxing (Khet 2007). After years of training and fighting, Rocky is a boxer to the core of his being; he has the speech, looks, thoughts, and manner of a boxer and is the consummate muai Thai boxer. In his prime, Rocky had a reputation as a principled young man. "Rocky, what do you think is the most important principle for a successful boxer?" I asked him in late March 2001. He replied, "discipline, passion, honesty, perseverance, and gratitude to people around you, that is, parents, teachers, and trainers. They all are important to every boxer. You cannot survive in the tough boxing world all by yourself. You also need to stay healthy and injury-free." I felt, however, that Rocky had given me a textbook answer rather than his genuine, reflective opinion. Some might wonder, "Why would he comment differently? Isn't he a model boxer after all?" Nonetheless, I was curious about any opposing thoughts he had: "What don't you like about muai Thai as a boxer and as a person?" He said, "I hate match-fixing. The boxer who fixes his fight is a traitor to his career. He is selfish, money-oriented, and short-sighted. He has no future. He has no dignity as a boxer (*mai mi saksi nak muai*). He loses his head, heart, and fighting spirit when he is judged a boxer fighting below his full capability and with no respect to the dignity of the sport (*chok mai som saksi*)."

Boxing is a laudable sport for men, symbolically connoted by the concept and practice of *saksi* (dignity, honor, or pride). Saksi is a gendered cultural concept. In the past, Buddhist monkhood provided a religious path to honor for men, while women took common venues of motherhood and nurturing crafts to negotiate their culturally defined selfhood and their gender roles. Saksi is a key cultural paradigm that moves Thai boxing from raw aggression to the "art of boxing." Saksi serves as a spiritual mode of professionalism and a means of training for every muai Thai fighter from day one. It motivates two opponents to fight in the ring to their full capability. Most importantly, it is what distinguishes the art of fighting from raw aggression. Thai men are considered symbolically disgraced when they have committed a social act that deprives them of saksi. When Rocky alludes to the term, he raises an important matter related to boxing and masculine culture in Thailand. Saksi in general and *saksi luk phuchai* (men's honor, prestige, status) in particular form the heart and soul of Thai masculine ideology, the standard of pride, honor, and dignity.

A boxer's disgraceful acts on and off the ring, such as match-fixing, underperforming, and misbehaving, are described as "dishonor," "shame," or a serious offense to the saksi. In muai Thai, if one boxer is judged to have committed a dishonorable offense, he might have to face accusations of disrespecting and violating (1) the boxer himself (*saksi nak muai*); (2) Thai boxing as a collective sport entity (*saksi muai Thai*); and (3) the Thai nation that claims the ownership of national sport (*saksi chat Thai*). According to the 1999 Muai Thai Act, participants involved in match-fixing or influencing the fight are subject to legal sanctions established by the 1999 Boxing Act of Thailand. In other words, acts defined as disgracing and disrespecting the saksi of muai Thai are punishable by law and can lead to sanctions by the professional boxing community.

Muai Thai as a representation of masculinity is highly situated in the country's discourses of race and nationalism. The multiple practices of saksi function to legitimate the assurance of national masculine superiority. Champions have traditionally been glorified as symbols of national and racial superiority. Everywhere, from rural village temple fair fights to premier boxing competitions in Bangkok broadcast live on national televisions, the ring announcers tirelessly repeat to their audiences the nationalistic myths of how forefathers of the sport used the art of muai Thai to defend the homeland of the Thais against foreign intruders, especially the Burmese; how with their superior boxing skills, Thai men defeated larger opponents in the ring despite their physical disadvantage. The Thais are "small but terrible" or "small but very spicy like chili" (*lek prik khinu*). Since the early 1980s, Songchai Rattanasuban, the country's top boxing promoter, has heavily marketed muai Thai to both domestic and international audiences as "the Thai Treasure, the World Heritage" (*muai Thai, moradok Thai, moradok lok*). Rocky was one of Songchai's top model fighters for more than fifteen years.

Saksi is thus a product of embodiment, molded into the body of young boxers. A boxer's saksi represents a form of working-class discipline, encouraging young boxers to dream of a better tomorrow through the rigors of the manly body, or as Loic Wacquant puts it in describing African American boxers, they are "small entrepreneurs in risky bodily performance" (1995:11). At the same time, the loss of saksi publicly condemns any boxer or man who has been judged as dishonored, a traitor, or a loser. A saksi-less boxer is a person who fast falls out of hegemonic rules of manhood.

ROCKY'S FALL AND THE QUESTIONS OF EVERYDAY MANHOOD

On July 3, 2008, Rocky was arrested and charged for petty drug smuggling. The police reported that he had used and traded amphetamine (*ya ba*). While he admitted to using the drug in small amounts in the past two years, he insisted that "I am not a drug addict" (reported in *Muai Siam* 2008). Rocky was bailed out by his trainer and parents. The news of this fallen boxing hero hit the boxing world and the public like an avalanche. Since the late 1990s, almost every boxing program (many of which featured Rocky) had been organized as a part of a nationwide antidrug campaign. How could the life of a famous ex-boxing champion go so terribly wrong? Overnight, Rocky was transformed into a villain. His boxing fame, which he had amassed for years, quickly evaporated as the news of his arrest made national headlines (*Thairath Online* 2008). How could a great boxing champion become a drug dealer and finish his illustrious career behind bars? The rise and fall in the boxing career of Rocky was nothing short of a real-life drama: a young boy from a poor family background fighting through blood, sweat, and tears to earn money to support his poverty-stricken family and to achieve the highest honors available in Thailand's boxing world turns to drugs, and before long falls prey to this evil.

Rocky was deeply apologetic when he talked to a boxing reporter:

> My sincere apology goes to all my supporters and fans. I broke into tears when I first met my trainer [Metprik To Silachai], who had taken care of me for years. I said sorry to him. It is purely my own fault. It is my bad decision in life. I have to retire from boxing immediately because I can't stand going back to see my boxing fans face-to-face. They have supported me for years and deserve much better from me. I can never win their faith and love again. It is sad that I have to end my boxing career this way. (*Muai Siam* 2008, July 9–15:6–7)

In another interview account of his tragic event, he told the reporter:

> I have never betrayed my supporters and fans. I always fought to my best capability in the ring. I never fixed any of my fighting bouts, even though I was offered a very large sum of money. Money can't buy saksi. My involvement with drugs happened quite recently in the last two years. (*Muai Siam* 2008, July 9–15:8)

By ruling himself out of match-fixing, Rocky insists that he has upheld professional dignity throughout his career. In his plea to the public, he desperately wishes to ensure that his saksi and reputation are still intact, and he relegates his drug scandal to a minor and unfortunate incident, a nonboxing matter that occurred outside the ring, the site of his construction of his saksi. It is a twisted paradox. Indeed, there are many ironic layers in Rocky's fall: a proud breadwinner and hero ending up in jail, and a model boxer in the national antidrug campaign turning to drugs himself when his body cannot keep pace with the physical demands of the ring. Saksi is a fundamental notion in the boxing profession and the life of a young boxer, but it can be upheld only through performance in the ring. Who defeats the mighty Rocky? Who exploits the hunting dog?

While the media and the public blame Rocky for his shortsighted greed and lack of morality, analytically we must recognize that what causes the fall of Rocky and other hundreds of muai Thai boxers is not that simple to define. It is an inescapable truth that the boxer's body betrays his desire to stay an eternal winner. He cannot stop his body's deterioration, nor freeze it at the peak of his physical strength. Professional muai Thai boxing is one of the most physically demanding sports in the world. The looming anxiety and fear for an aging boxer is that he has to work with a deteriorating tool, his body. Saksi raised Rocky and brought him down; it had a dual function in encouraging Rocky to fight and to maintain his boxing standards as proof of possession of saksi. Simultaneously, a demonstration of the consequences of lack of saksi are evident in his loss of power and skill. Members of the boxing community, from trainers, fellow boxers, promoters, fans, and media, down to audiences at large, play their parts in supervising and monitoring behaviors of upholding or withdrawing saksi. They judge. They quickly side with the winner and cut the loser's throat with their words, knifelike glances, cold social distance, and silence. Their success depends on the boxer's blood and sacrifice, the proof of his saksi. Third, the boxing culture defeats Rocky. Like other sports, boxing as a form of cultural practice continuously breeds new successors to feed hard-to-please fans and industry. It blindly glorifies the winner. Finally, drugs and boxing have coexisted for years; using drugs and stimulants is endemic, as in many modern professional sports. Rocky's arrest exposed this blemish in the Thai boxing community. The fact that Rocky's crime took place outside the boxing ring serves to encourage this culture of silence and secrecy, leading to blaming one person's moral failings rather than the system itself.

Everyday life is a cultural space full of real-life events and characters, with ordinary voices to be heard and stories to be told. Rocky's life is a dramatic display of the twists and turns in the boxing career and life of poor underclass men in Thai society. The hegemonic form of masculinity occupies a paramount position in the Thai boxing culture much as in other social fields across the Thai hierarchical social spectrum. Rocky is almost voiceless within these power relations; he conforms and speaks the language of hegemonic masculine power. He is only a small individual who, at one moment, emerged as a winner in the theater of Thai masculine honor and pride, but, at another moment, had to come to terms with life out of the ring and beyond as a retired "hunting dog."

NOTE

1. This ethnographic fieldwork on Thai boxing was carried out in Nakhon Ratchasima, Thailand in 2000 and 2001 with a research grant from Research and Development Institute and Institute of Social Technology, Suranaree University of Technology. Quotations from the boxers in the text come from the team's research, unless otherwise noted. Additional data, such as dates of victories, come from *Muai Siam* [Siam Boxing Magazine]. In addition, I have drawn on Thai literature on boxing,

such as Bua 1989 and Khet 2007, for further information on the history and culture of muai Thai.

The author is grateful to Suriya Smutkupt, Preecha Srichai, Natthawut Singkun, Siriphon Chailert, and Chantana Klaewkla for their assistance to the project. The romanized spellings of Thai terms and names in this chapter follow the general guidelines for transcription issued by the Royal Institute of Thailand (Ratcha Banditthayasathan). Interview transcription and translation from Thai-language sources are my own unless otherwise indicated. Statements from the boxers in the text come from the team's research, unless otherwise noted.

16

Everyday Life as Art: Thai Artists and the Aesthetics of Shopping, Eating, Protesting, and Having Fun

Sandra Cate

BLOWING UP NATIONAL NARRATIVES

The collective shock of the 1997 economic crisis in Thailand stimulated a number of young artists to confront Thai social realities through installations and the "new media" of film and video, performances, and interactivity. With the collapse of the Thai baht currency, the promises of globalization had faltered and stereotypes of Asian economic prowess collapsed—a theme that artist Sutee Kunavichayanont explored literally in his interactive series *Breath Donation* (1997–2000) with inflatable silicone forms. Each form symbolized Thai national identity: a deflated "Asian tiger" referred to the name given the Asian economies that had boomed so wildly during the 1980s and 1990s, the water buffalo an icon of rice-growing Thailand, and the sagging elephant representing the nation itself and one of the most common motifs in Thai art and craft. Viewers blew through tubes to inflate the forms, giving them "life." The flaccid elephant had to receive continuous "breath donations" to remain inflated, suggesting Thailand's dependence on outside investments for its stability.

Sutee's inflatable Siamese twins making the *wai*, the Thai sign of respect, appeared in front of the Hard Rock Café in Bangkok's Siam Square and also at Wat Pho, a popular tourist attraction. One twin was white and the other yellow, a racializing gesture that implicated both Asians *and* Westerns in the economic crisis, showing them conjoined in global economic processes. In these spaces, as far as passers-by were concerned, his inflatables lacked a frame declaiming them as "art." Many were eager to participate, to "play" with the figures, erasing any distance between the viewer and the art object. In contrast, Sutee told me, if these inflatables had been on display in a gallery or museum, many Thai people would have been "afraid to touch them." Sutee's inflatable figures and subsequent installations have a dual purpose:

not only to critique aspects of contemporary Thai society and politics, but also to overcome a Thai reluctance to go into the "white cube," a popular Anglo Thai reference to museums and galleries (Sutee 2008a). Sutee and other Thai artists have instead turned to works based on everyday activities and installation/collaborations in accessible public spaces as both artistic inspiration and as a strategy for bringing their art to a wider Thai public.

THAI ART/THAI EVERYDAY LIFE

In 2007, when I began to question Thai artists in Bangkok and Chiang Mai about participatory art and to attend these events, one of my first conversations detoured to the subject of comparative linguistic features of Thai and English. The conjugations of English verbs, the artist observed, always place a person and event in time. Thai verbs are tenseless; to indicate time one adds a qualifying phrase. But English allows really only one form of a personal pronoun as subject: "I." Thai has several words for "I"—*phom, chan, ku*—each context dependent. The choice of the "I" always places the self in relation to the other—by gender, age, social status, or distance—whereas English always places the self in relation to time. That, he observed, makes Thai people "different" in that "we know how to manage and locate in the present time very well" (Wit 2008). And, one might add, Thai linguistic features emphasize social relationships as *the* prominent feature of Thai everyday life, whether expressed in a finely graded social hierarchy of superior–inferior kin-like relationships (cf. Keyes 1987) or in a notable propensity for hanging out, eating, shopping, protesting, traveling together (*pai thiaw*), and generally having fun (*tham hai sanuk*) with ones' friends and colleagues (Phillips 1966: 56–60, 1987:34; Mills 1999). That contemporary genres of participation art—also called relational or interactional art (see essays in Bishop 2006)—emphasizing social relationships and tactile involvement with objects rather than the passive spectatorship of an art work—would become a popular form in Thailand is thus no surprise. Wit Pimkanchanapong, member of the Thai/Japanese SOI collective, told me,

> People here [in Thailand] have the idea of art, but it must be within the frame of art. I want to have a conversation with the people. I want to show what I have done to people on the street. These are the people I live with, who have no background with art, but love to see something strange and wonderful, but not too complicated. (Wit 2008)

As an example of his concept—although still set within the "white cube"—in a 2006 exhibition at Bangkok's Queen Sirikit Gallery, Wit provided visitors with stacks of paper model patterns, glue, and a place to assemble the patterns into Rocket Cabs (Fig.1). The hundreds of paper rockets were then strung together and hung to fill the five-floor central atrium of the building, to complete this playful, collaborative work of art.[1]

HISTORY CLASS

Official denials or distortions of contemporary Thai political history have propelled Sutee to question, with increasingly complex, interactive installations in public spaces, the received wisdom and hegemonic national narratives that Thai schoolchildren learn as "Thai culture" and "Thai history" from standardized textbooks. Despite a decade of educational reform stressing international education and the creation of a "learning society," the "master narrative" of Thai history has created a public mythology of benevolent rulership, but in fact ignores or suppresses the historical evidence of state-sponsored violence against Thai citizens (Thongchai 2002:263), specifically during protests against military dictatorships in 1973, 1976, and 1992. These events are simply not taught to schoolchildren.[2]

Sutee installed his *History Class* on the sidewalks of Ratchadamnoern Avenue, across from the Democracy Monument where protests, violence, and killings had taken place in both 1973 and 1992. The work comprised fourteen wooden school desks the artist had found in an antique shop, exactly like those he had used as a child in primary school. Focusing on forgotten or suppressed episodes from Thai history, he inscribed each desk with symbols, scenes, or quotations from prominent kings and other historical figures, much as children inscribe their own names to "mark" their history at the desk. For example, one carving was an excerpt from an infamous 1976 interview with Phra Kittivuttho, a right-wing Buddhist monk. The reporter had asked,

> "Is it wrong to kill the leftists or communists?" Of which the monk said, "I believe it is the right thing to do. Even though Thais are Buddhists, we do not consider this action as murder. Anyone who is trying to destroy our nation, our religion, and our monarchy is not a whole human. We must focus on the fact that we are killing demons. This is every Thai's duty." (cited in Cheng Zu 2001)

Sutee provided paper and charcoal for visitors to make rubbings of the desk surfaces that made visible, literally, the opaque and little known history of the nation. Casual passers-by expressed their nostalgia and delight in seeing the old-time school desks. Many indicated that they were "too young" to know about the events referred to in the carvings or that they knew the history, but had received the "wrong version." But their creative responses to the installation surprised Sutee. "What people did, they combine images

Figure 16.1. Students assembling rocket cabs. Photo courtesy Wit Pimkanchanapong.

Figure 16.2. Making rubbings in Sutee's *History Class*. Photo courtesy of the artist, Sutee Kunavichayanont.

from different tables on their respective prints. They swap and they make new sentences," he told me, suggesting an act "much more creative" than "making a copy of what I gave them" (Sutee 2008a). Their creativity contrasts directly with the classroom experience, about which one Grade 10 student observed (in a public conference on educational reform), "I sometimes think school is teaching me to be a tape recorder" (cited in Fry 2002:24).

In a 2008 installation in the courtyard of the Pridi Banomyong Institute, Sutee provided visitors with school blackboards and moveable magnetized phrases such as "On the morning 6th October, 1976 at Thammasat University," "the students," "murdered," and "right-wing 'patriotic' groups." With these phrases, viewers could construct their own versions of the events of Hok Tula (6th October)—the student protest at Thammasat University in 1976 where students had been brutally tortured and murdered by police and paramilitary agents. This art installation, part of *Flashback '76: History and Memory of October 6 Massacre*, mimicked the rewriting of history that had galvanized four artists to make the exhibit. Prime Minister Samak Sundaravej, Deputy Interior Minister in 1976 and Prime Minister in 2008, had actively urged police to crack down on student demonstrators. In a 2008 CNN interview, Samak had proclaimed that only "one unlucky guy" was beaten and burned at the Hok Tula protests—revising the history in which he had had an active role (TalkAsia 2008). Yet in 1977, just after the event, Samak had admitted to Thai students in France that *forty-eight* people had died that day at Thammasat (Manit 2008). Sutee's act of deconstruction—of breaking into small pieces one key official's revised narrative about 1976—became participants' *reconstruction* of that event as they made their own sentences, demonstrating that history requires one to be an actor oneself, implicating them directly in the social processes that remember or forget the traumatic events of the past.

Sutee and fellow artists Manit Sriwanichpoom, Ing K., and Vasan Sittikhet have put these events and the issue of memory at the center of their recent visual work. Their "trauma art" represents a shift from outrage and calls for vengeance, prominent in earlier political art, to challenging the publicly manipulated processes of remembering and forgetting (Sudarat 2010). In Sutee's words, their artwork is necessary, for "learning [that] to deal with cruel and repulsive aspects of one's historical memory is part of learning about oneself" (Sutee 2008b:8). Further, as Sutee claims, the desktop rubbings "connect the obscure days of the past to manufacture a present" (Cheng Zu 2001).

THAI PARTICIPATION

Everyday gatherings in Thailand besides in school classrooms might be seen as cultural analogues of participatory art events. The public spaces of Buddhist temples or *wat* contain multisensorial religious installations created or donated by the devout: murals, lacquered cabinets, hanging banners (*tung*), statues of the Buddha, flowers, and peacock feathers. Often monks' chanting or gongs and bells ringing fill the aural space. To make merit, worshipers perform in these spaces and with these objects, offering food, flowers, incense, candles, and money, and applying tiny squares of gold to sacred images. Preparing for temple ceremonies, friends and neighbors spend hours cooking food for monks and constructing elaborate, decorative *bai sii* of folded banana leaves and flowers to offer to the Buddha during the ritual.

Street politics in Thailand have also become routine, everyday performances utilizing skits, color, and altar-like installations. For decades, protesters with a wide array of social grievances have gathered regularly before the national Government House in Bangkok. Their encampments become daily life—they are found sleeping, eating, and even bathing. Their actions—including two men pouring buckets of pig feces over themselves to protest the loss of their savings in the 1997 crisis—become street theater, as documented by the photographer Manit Sriwanichpoom (2003). In the days following the 1992 massacre of pro-democracy protestors, Ratchadamnoern Avenue became a "charnel ground" and another collective installation, with improvised memorial altars, billboards pinned with images of the carnage, banners, tiny black stickers proclaiming "5,000 Dead" and "Liar-Free Zone," bits of bloodied clothes, abandoned shoes, and even bodies, tape recordings of chanting monks, as well as sidewalk hawkers selling photographs and videos of the police actions (Klima 2002:134–40).[3] These material representations of the violence, produced by ordinary people horrified and enraged by police actions, countered the official media censorship of television and radio coverage. As Klima has noted, "Now was the time when establishing what had happened would have its greatest impact, when there was the most interest in knowing the truth, and the most consciousness of the fact that it was an event worth remembering" (ibid., 134).

While framed by "religion" or "political protest" and not "art," these activities suggest that the boundaries by which we define these activities are arbitrary and often blurred. They also provide indigenous Thai models of active sensory engagement between people and objects in public spaces that resonate with the forms and goals of Thai artists in presenting relational or participatory art. Thus, in analyzing these spatial transformations, one might glance away from the objects per se to focus instead on congruent processes in art and everyday life that materialize social values and relations as objects and performances with objects. They show "how the things that people make, make people" (Miller 2005:38) in their expressive lives.

The memorial to the October 1973 massacre at the Democracy Monument dedicated and extended the notion of participation into its very construction. According to one of the artists responsible for its design, Chatchai Puipia,

> I helped shape the idea of walling the base of the monument with small terra cotta panels each bearing the heroes' names, and with other impressions of the event by artists and ordinary people.

I don't think a monument for such a dynamic event should be an architecture that is complete in itself. I would like to involve people, to encourage participation. The terra cotta tiles, therefore, came into the picture.

Terra cotta has the right feeling. We can write names, make traces or record anything on it. The panels will incorporate elements from a wide base of people. It will become a live sculpture, something like conceptual art. We won't be able to predict what the outcome will be.

I do believe the beauty of the monument lies not in its form or fixed design, but in the participation and cooperation that goes on behind its construction. . . . It is the truth and feelings expressed by real people that matter, not any theory about art and aesthetics. (*Bangkok Post* 1998)

Artists' public works of participatory history-making and social memory continue the "civil society activism"[4] prominent in the 1990s in Thailand, and have been magnified mightily in the street politics of the present: the 2006 military coup that threw out Thaksin Shinawatra, an elite-dominated opposition (the People's Alliance for Democracy or PAD), all culminating in the 2008 takeover of the Government House and Bangkok's two airports and the downfall of two elected governments, and counter-demonstrations in 2009–10. These protests, thick with posters, cartoons, cutouts, and shrines (many captioned in English, to make their messages accessible to an international audience), were visually dominated by color. The PAD demonstrators wore and displayed yellow, the color most associated with Thailand's revered King Bhumiphol and deployed in these protests to assert national and royalist loyalties (see White 2009). The color red dominated clothing and banners in the subsequent counter-protests in 2009-10 by the amalgamated Red Shirt forces made up of Thaksin loyalists and activists seeking the restoration of democracy. These recent, highly visual demonstrations suggest that direct action, rather than the unsatisfactory workings of electoral politics and a state-controlled media, may be writing the new history of Thai politics.[5]

ART, MOVING OUT OF THE WHITE CUBE

In the 1990s, the ways in which their art expressed cultural and national identity had become the central issue for contemporary Southeast Asian artists seeking international success (Apinan 1993; 1996, Turner 1993, Clark 1998). The Thai artist Rirkrit Tiravanija had already cooked *pad thai*, the quintessential Bangkok street stall noodle dish, and served it to visitors in New York's Gallery 303 as *Untitled 1990 (Pad Thai).*[6] Positioning this event as "somewhere between performance art and gastronomy," one art writer said, "Tiravanija's art has to do mainly with social experiences and interactions, not painting or sculpture" (cited in Tomkins 2005:82). Another critic called Rirkrit's work ". . . the art of living, although I'm not sure I could explain the difference between that phrase and 'life'" (Hainley 1996:56). The take-away lessons from Rirkrit's act—that art need not be about an "object" and that galleries can generate social relations beyond sales[7]—have now taken root throughout the international art world.

Rirkrit's impact on the Thai scene was less immediate. His challenge to the culturally constructed boundaries between "art" and "life" made sense in New York, but Thais could not really see that boundary. One Thai intellectual questioned the authenticity of his ingredients and thus the cultural ground of his act (Pandit 2006:100). Another curator asked, "What difference did it make between his 'Pad Thai' and the one cooked by the vendors on the street in Bangkok?" (Gridthiya 2001).

The conceptual basis of Rirkrit's cooking—establishing a social relationship between artist and "viewer" rather than between viewer and objects on display—did make sense to artists in Thailand, who were long frustrated with the weak infrastructure of the Thai art world. Curators of Bangkok's three most innovative alternative art spaces of the 1990s (Project 304, About Studio/About Café, and Tadu Contemporary Art) had moved on to other projects. Most Thai art collectors, sensitive to paintings' investment or status value, favor the Buddhist-inflected neo-traditional paintings of a Chalermchai Kositpipat or Thawan Duchanee (Gridthiya 2001, Cate 2003) over works showing international influences. The more cutting-edge art galleries promote their stable of artists and their works to foreign collectors. International curator Apinan Poshyananda, as director of Office of Contemporary Art and Culture, has produced exhibits such as *The Art of Corruption* (2008) that make strong social critiques. But at other major art venues such as the Queen Sirikit Gallery or the newly opened Bangkok Center for Contemporary Art, exhibits remain safely oriented to "the center," with works tied to anniversaries or activities of the royal family or promoting Buddhist doctrine (Thanom 2007). An anemic arts infrastructure with minimal government support, limited sources of funding, no arts-related tax deductions, little public art education, few Thai-language art critics, and a dearth of professionally managed public arts institutions has thus required artists to seek new venues (Pettifor 2007, Teh 2006). As everyday activity, "art" and gallery/museum going has largely failed in Thailand. So artists now seek to reverse the equation, to present everyday life as art, by addressing ordinary people who might unexpectedly encounter their works in Bangkok's 24/7 bustle of working, banking, schooling, protesting, shopping, and eating. Their projects involve viewers in creating the work and also draw on familiar social forms to bring "art closer to everyday life" (Bishop 2006:10).

Most of the artists and historians I interviewed trace the genealogy of Thai participatory art to artists' exchanges and exhibition trips abroad, to art books circulating in Thailand, and more recently to the international successes artists including Rirkrit and Surasi Kusolwong. Artist Wit Pimkanchanapong calls Rirkrit and Surasi the "superstars" of Thai relational art and compares them to Pélé. But, he added, "Everyone in Brazil is good at football"; and noted that participatory art is "coming out of the Thai way of life" (Wit 2008). When young Thai artists saw interactive art forms on their travels abroad, their exposure encouraged them to look "at something we already have" in Thai social relations and cultural forms, says Sutee (2008a). They credit Montien Boonma with having a seminal influence on audience engagement; in the mid-1990s, he built "environments," often outdoors, that evoked Buddhist forms and practices in the ways that viewers entered and experienced them. As he came to terms with his wife's and then his own terminal diseases, his built spaces (see his *Nature's Breath: Arokhayasala* in Apinan 1996) became more meditative and healing, infused with the aroma of medicinal herbs. His installation *Melting Void: Molds for the Mind* (1999) replicated the mold for casting a large head of the Buddha in which people could stand, but reversed to create a void within, ". . . a place of refuge for mindfulness of viewers who wish to be in [a] condition of calmness and contentment." (Apinan 2003:35). From my observations, viewers' experiences of Montien's work at various Bangkok venues attained those precise conditions.

Building on his move toward active audience engagement and nontraditional settings, Montien and his students and colleagues initiated the *Chiang Mai Social Installation* (CMSI). Produced three times from 1992 to 1994, CMSI included site-specific installations, performances, and lectures on social issues involving the public in familiar, noncommercial spaces: temples, cemeteries, private residences, public buildings, streets, rivers, canals, and open spaces. This turn (and others) toward localism emphasized the potential of everyone to be a cultural producer; it provided a contrast to the production of art commodities for the market (Apinan 1996:108; Pandit 2006:100) and enabled the development of a new definition of contemporary art that "fits to Thai society" (Sutee 2008a). While remaining largely oriented to an urban elite, CMSI events did disrupt the flow of daily life in Chiang Mai, by startling people going about their business with unexpected installations and performances (Pandit 2006:101). The Indo Thai artist Navin Rawanchaikul installed a boat in front of the Ched Yot temple. A familiar Buddhist motif, boats carry believers in the Dhamma toward Nirvana or Enlightenment. Navin's boat was loaded with the detritus of the secular world: clothes, photographs, pens, and "consumed" objects such as socks, pills, and hair clippings. Probably seen as disrespectful of Buddhist teachings, it was demolished anonymously within a week (Pandit 2006:103). Navin's subsequent work, the *Navin Gallery Bangkok* (1995–1998), engaged the public in a less culturally threatening way: he outfitted a taxicab with paintings, art objects, and video monitors as a mobile art gallery, plying the streets of Bangkok. Unsuspecting riders hopped in to receive a quick dose of "art" while stuck in Bangkok's infamous traffic. The unpredictability of the encounter not only subverted the intentionality of a gallery-going experience, but it also pierced the domain of "work" and replicated the realities of everyday life in Bangkok in the mid-1990s before the mass-transit Skytrain overhead railway was completed (Worathep 2008; Cate 1999).

PINAREE SANPITAK, *BREAST STUPA COOKERY PROJECT*

Pinaree Sanpitak, a renowned artist working with interactive art, silk, and food, articulates the multilayered experiences of being a woman while challenging conventional attitudes toward the female body. Through one shape referencing both the female body and an icon of Theravada Buddhism, the breast stupa, she explores boundaries and relationships between the sacred and the profane, art and craft, self and other, artist and audience.[8]

As stuffed silk or organza cushions, Pinaree's breast stupas invite viewers to play. To promote breastfeeding, *noon-nom* (2001–2002) was installed in Bangkok's Discovery Centre, a popular shopping mall—one of the new social spaces of Bangkok (Wilson 2004:110) and a popular youth destination. The installation—an enclosure filled with breast-shaped cushions—asks the viewer to "just take off your shoes and go into the piece and do whatever you want. You become part of the artwork" (Pinaree 2008). At *Temporary Insanity* (2004), installed at the Jim Thompson Art Centre, breast cushions contained sensors that set them quivering and vibrating in response to viewers' voices and movements.

In her ongoing *Breast Stupa Cookery Project* (2005–present), Pinaree cedes artistic control and reimagines the nature of the "art object" as ephemeral rather than enduring and monumental (qualities inherent in the stupa form). Nourishing collaboration, creativity, and fun, she invites chefs to produce meals using cast aluminum and glazed stoneware breast molds, each a different shape and size; each meal is videotaped. At these events, the locus of value and meaning shifts from the artist's intention or art writer's critical assessment to the moment and its myriad potential for those involved. Pinaree also elicits direct reactions to her ideas, saying, "It's my way of asking back, 'What do you think of this form?'" (Pinaree 2007). Thai chef Benya Nandakwang was eager to participate, saying "I thought it would be fun and wanted to unmold something that was textured with beautiful colors" (Fig. 3). Responding to the breast stupa as container, Chef Benya invented a breast-molded aspic using quail eggs and Chinese herbal soup. But upon reflection, she realized that eggs in aspic "is something about giving birth to life" (Bunnag 2005). When the dish was unmolded, the viewers responded with "*suay*" (beautiful) and "*sanuk*" (fun). The *Breast Stupa Cookery Project* has taken place in diverse public and private contexts around the world—in Paris, Singapore, Tokyo, San Francisco, Bangkok, and Beijing, continually expanding Pinaree's art public through everyday acts, allowing her to "cross boundaries" instead of only mingling with curators and other artists (Bunnag 2005).

Figure 16.3. Breast Stupa Cookery Project guest chef, Benja Nandakwong. Photo courtesy Pinaree Sanpitak.

CONCLUSION

Nicolas Bourriaud, the French theorist of relational art, has said, "For art does not transcend our day to day preoccupations; it brings use face to face with reality through the singularity of a relationship with the world, through a fiction" (2006:168). Thai artists have accomplished this "fiction" through utilizing their own realities. In Bangkok, Sakharin Krue-On's *Temple* (2000) invited viewers to stencil their own versions of religious motifs on the temple-red walls of the About Studio/About Café, transforming the ordinary into a version of the sacred by echoing age-old stenciling techniques used by Thai temple muralists. Sutee's *History Class* and his inflatables reference the visual culture embedded in the Thai everyday, but pointedly question and challenge the public education that generates distorted versions of Thai history and culture. Pinaree's *Breast Stupa Cookery Project* reflects upon and re-enacts in diverse settings, the sociality and collaboration that Thais value. Because these projects are so grounded in mundane experiences—going to the temple, sitting in a classroom, cooking/sharing food—their concepts also travel easily across cultural borders, even though the specific motifs stenciled on temple walls, carved on the school desks, or forming the stupa/chedi shape may lack referential power in translation.

The Thai artists discussed here produce their projects in Thailand, Europe, Australia, Japan, the United States—globally. Rather than constituting extraordinary exceptions, artists' participation in this expanded art world has become part of *their* everyday modes of travel and work. So both at home and abroad, interactive, participatory art events derived from the practices of everyday life allow Thai artists to foreground aspects of "being Thai" (the historical narratives, the breast stupa forms, or the temple practices), without necessarily reproducing exotic cultural stereotypes or predictable artistic forms and motifs. Pushing at the boundaries of their own art worlds, both local and foreign, Thai artists seek to shrink the distance between artist and audience, and to expand their public by leaving "the white cube," invading the spaces of the everyday (Warner 2002).

NOTES

1. For photographs of the assembly process and final installation of Wit's Rocket Cabs, see http://bangkokok.typepad.com/platform/2006/11/installing_abou.html.

2. In 2001, Thailand's Ministry of Education commissioned a leading Thai poet to write a supplementary textbook account for students of the 1973 events, but, due to politics (one editor was the son-in-law of a member of the 1973 military dictatorship), it has not been published (Fry 2002, Singh and Gearing 2000).

3. These Thai versions might be compared to the Western shrines and memorials that sprout up spontaneously at sites of gang shootings, fatal bicycle or car accidents, or to honor deceased celebrities such as Princess Diana or Michael Jackson.

4. Chang Noi (2009).

5. For a succinct account of the Thai political situation, see Chang Noi (2009) and Montesano (2009).

6. Rirkrit, born in Argentina of a diplomatic family, was educated in Canada, and has lived in Ethiopia and the United States, as well as Thailand.

7. Anthropologists have long studied art objects as mediators, creators, or outcomes of social relationships. For an influential formulation of this proposition, see Gell (1998). Also see Adams (1998).

8. The stupa, a sign of Buddhist doctrine and a form prevalent throughout Theravada Buddhist culture, encloses relics or the ashes of holy or important figures, including the Buddha (Woodward 1993).

17

Eating Lunch and Recreating the Universe: Food and Cosmology in Hoi An, Vietnam

Nir Avieli

It was 11:30 AM and Quynh said that lunch was ready. We all took our seats on the wooden stools by the round wooden table: Quynh and her husband Anh, his mother and sister, Irit (my spouse) and I. The food was already set on the table: a small plate with three or four small fish in a watery red sauce, seasoned with some fresh coriander leaves, a bowl of morning-glory soup (*canh rau muong*) boiled with a few dried shrimps, and a plate of fresh lettuce mixed with different kinds of green aromatics. There was also a bowl of *nuoc mam cham* (fish sauce diluted with water and lime juice, seasoned with sugar, ginger, and chili). An electric rice cooker was standing on one of the stools by the table. There were also six ceramic bowls and six pairs of ivory-colored plastic chopsticks.

We took our seats, with Anh's mother seated by the rice cooker, and handed her our rice bowls. She filled them to the rim with steaming rice, using a flat plastic serving spoon. Quynh pointed at the different dishes and said: "*com* [steamed rice], *rau* [(fresh) greens], *canh* [soup], *kho* ['dry'—pointing to the fish]." Then she pointed to the fish sauce and added "and *nuoc mam*."

In this chapter, I discuss the Hoianese[1] daily, home-eaten meal as a cultural artifact, as a model of the universe (Geertz 1973): a miniature representation of the way in which the Vietnamese conceive of the cosmos and the ways in which it operates. This is based on anthropological fieldwork conducted in the central Vietnamese town of Hoi An since 1998.

THE BASIC STRUCTURE OF THE HOIANESE MEAL

The Hoianese, home-eaten meal is basically composed of two elements: steamed rice (*com*), served with an array of side dishes (*mon an* or "things [to] eat"). It could be argued that this meal is structured along the lines of a Levi-Straussian binary opposition: an amalgam of colorful, savory toppings

Chart 1. The "twofold-turn-fivefold" structure of the Hoianese daily meal

Rice			"Things to Eat"		
Rice	Greens	Soup	"Dry" dish	Fish sauce

juxtaposed over a pale, bland, staple grain. Moreover, the relations between the rice and mon an could be analyzed within the nature–culture dichotomy that underlies Levi-Strauss's work, with the hardly transformed rice standing for "nature" and opposed to the deeply manipulated dishes that stand for "culture." However, the Hoianese meal is better understood within the context of Vietnamese culture.

The mon an ('things to eat') are of a more varied and dynamic nature than the rice. The Hoianese mon an are made of raw and cooked vegetables and leafy greens and a small amount of animal protein, usually that of fish. The mon an adhere to the four categories mentioned by Quynh: *rau*—raw greens, *canh*—boiled soup, and *kho*—a "dry" dish (fried, stir-fried, or cooked in sauce), which are always accompanied by nuoc mam (fermented fish sauce).

The basic structure of the Hoianese home-eaten meal is therefore that of a dyad of rice and "things to eat," which further develops into a five-fold structure encompassing five levels of transformation of edible ingredients into food: raw, steamed, boiled, fried/cooked, and fermented.

This "twofold-turn-fivefold" structure is a Weberian "ideal-type." Ashkenazi and Jacob suggest that such basic meal structures should be viewed as "schemes" for a meal "which individuals may or may not follow, but which most will recognize and acknowledge as a representation of the ways things should be" (2000:67). Thus, though Hoianese meals routinely adhere to the "twofold-turn-fivefold" scheme, there are innumerable possibilities and combinations applied when cooking a meal.

Let us now turn to the ingredients and dishes that constitute the meal: rice, fish, and greens, and show how they conjure into a solid nutritional logic, firmly embedded in an ecological context.

Com (rice)

"Would you like to come and eat lunch in my house?" asked Huong, a sales-girl in one of the clothes shops with whom we were chatting for a while. I looked at Irit and following our working rule of "accepting any invitation" said "sure, why not!"

We followed Huong toward the little market near the Cao Dai temple and turned into a paved alley that soon became a sandy path and ended abruptly in front of a gate. "This is my house!" Huong exclaimed proudly, pushing her bike through the gate and into the yard.

The small house was whitewashed in pale blue and looked surprisingly new. Huong invited us into the front room and offered us green tea. She told us that her parents had left the country several years previously and had settled in the United States. Huong was waiting for her parents to arrange her immigration papers, while her younger brother was about to marry his Hoianese girlfriend and was planning to stay in town. The newly built house—with its ceramic-tiled floor, new wooden furniture, and double-flamed gas stove—was purchased with money sent by the parents in America. We browsed through some photo albums, sipped tea, and chatted.

Shortly before 11:30, Huong said that it was time for lunch and went to the kitchen. In the small kitchen, the brother's fiancée was sorting fresh greens. Rice was ready, steaming in an electric rice cooker. On the gas stove there were two tiny pots, one with a couple of finger-sized fish simmering in a yellow, fragrant sauce, and the other with a single chicken drumstick cooking in a brown sauce, chopped into three or four morsels. There was nothing else. "Is this all the food for lunch for the three of you?" I asked Huong, feeling surprised and embarrassed. "Yes," she replied.

I returned to the main room and told Irit in Hebrew that there was very little food in the house, certainly not enough for guests, and that we shouldn't stay and eat the little they had. We apologized and said that we hadn't noticed how late it was and that we had to leave right away. Huong seemed somewhat surprised for a moment, but then walked us to the gate and said goodbye. She didn't look angry or offended, so I thought that she was relieved when we left, as she avoided the humiliation of offering us the meager meal.

That afternoon, we recounted this incident in our daily Vietnamese language class. I remarked that the house didn't look poor at all, so I couldn't understand why this family was living in such deprivation, with three working adults having to share two sardines and one drumstick for lunch. Our teacher, *Co* (Miss/teacher) Nguyet, looked puzzled for a while and finally asked: "Why do you think that this was a small lunch—didn't they have a whole pot of rice?"

Rice is the single most important food item in the Hoianese diet. The most meager diet that "can keep a person alive" is boiled rice with some salt. Rice is the main source of calories and nutrients, and constitutes most of a meal's volume. In a survey of the eating patterns I conducted in 2000, the ten families who reported daily for six months on their eating practices had steamed rice (*com*) or rice noodles (*bun*) twice daily (for lunch and dinner), six to seven days a week. In addition, most of their breakfast items (noodles, porridge, pancakes), as well as other dishes and snacks they consumed in the course of the day (sweetmeats, crackers, etc.), were made of rice or rice flour.

Rice has been cultivated in Vietnam for thousands of years. Grains of *Oryza fatua*, the earliest brand of Asian rice, were cultivated by the proto-Vietnamese Lac[2] long before the arrival of the Chinese (Taylor 1983:9–10).

Cultivating rice is the single most common activity in Vietnam (Nguyen 1995:218). A total of 80 percent of the population live in the countryside and roughly 80–90 percent farm rice. The rural landscape is of endless green expanses of rice terraces. Roughly 125 days per annum are spent directly in rice production, and most other rural activities revolve around the exploitation of rice residues (Jamieson 1995:34) or in supplementing its nutritional deficiencies. Peanuts, beans, and coconuts supply proteins and fats; leafy greens and aromatic herbs provide the vitamins, minerals, and fiber lost in the process of polishing; pigs are fed with rice bran and meals' leftovers, mostly rice; ducks are herded over the newly harvested rice fields. Every grain ends up in the human food chain. Even the dogs are fed rice. Traditionally, when a farmer died, he was buried in his own rice field, returning symbolically and physically into the "rice-chain" that is the source of human life.[3]

In Vietnam, there are two kinds of rices: *gao te:* ordinary or "plain" rice, and *gao nep:* "sticky" glutinous rice. Sticky rice, the staple of many of the ethnic minorities in Vietnam, was domesticated thousands of years before the development of the hard-grained "plain" rice. Plain rice is cultivated nowadays on a much larger scale, as it yields significantly bigger crops, yet sticky rice is considered the "real" rice, hence its prominence in religious and social events. The distinction between plain and sticky rice in Vietnam is so important that the term *nep-te* ("sticky rice–plain rice") is used to express oppositions such as "good–bad," "right–wrong," and even "boy–girl."

The centrality of rice is evident in the language. Vietnamese features a wide variety of terms for rice in various states of cultivation, process, and cooking: rice seedlings are called *lua*, paddy is *thoc*, husked rice is *gao*, sticky rice is *nep* (and when boiled, *com nep*), steamed sticky rice is *xoi*, rice porridge is *chao*, and steamed (polished) rice is *com*. *Com* means both "cooked rice" and "a meal." *An com*, "[to] eat rice," also means "to have a meal," and this term is used even in cases when rice is not served. *Com bua*, literally "rice meal," means "daily meal."

The most prominent aspect of Vietnamese rice culture is the great quantity of grain consumed daily. Though the total amount of food eaten in a meal is far smaller than that consumed in a parallel Western meal, the amount of rice is very large: 2–3 bowls of cooked rice per adult per meal, approximately 700 grams of dry grain daily, or roughly 1.5 kg of cooked rice, exceeding 2,000 calories.

Cooking rice is a serious and calculated process. The rice is first rinsed thoroughly so as to wash the dusty polishing residues. If left to cook, this dust would make for a sticky cement-like texture that would disturb the balance between the distinct separation of each grain and the complete wholeness of the mouthful of rice. Water is added in a 1:2 ratio and the pot is placed over the hearth. When the water boils, the pot is covered and the rice is left to cook for about twenty minutes. The rice is then "broken" or stirred with large cooking chopsticks and is left in its own heat for a few more minutes before serving.

Since the 1990s, when electricity became a regular feature in Hoi An, most Hoianese, urban and rural, have used electric rice cookers. These appliances regulate the proper temperature, humidity, and duration of cooking. In the suburbs of Hoi An, where the dwellers were mostly farmers shifting into blue-collar and lower-middle-class urban jobs, traditional wood-fed hearths were gradually replaced by gas stoves and electric rice cookers, and rice is no longer served from large, smoke-blackened pots but from smaller, lighter, bright tin ones. Still, people rely on their own expertise and experience even when using rice cookers.

Although rice makes the event of eating "a meal," rice does not call attention to itself (Ashkenazi and Jacob 2000:78) with its white blandness, mushy consistency, moderate temperature on being served, and subtle fragrance. Yet, for the Hoianese rice undoubtedly constitutes the essence of a meal. The very act of eating a meal shows respect toward rice and reproduces Confucian patterns of seniority and status in the order with which people take the first bite of rice.

Rice must be supplemented with other nutrients, notably protein, fat, vitamins, and fiber. The Vietnamese overcome the nutritional deficiencies of rice with ingredients abundant in their ecosystem: fish and seafood, coconuts and ground nuts, and a variety of leafy and aromatic greens.

Ca (fish)

Khong co gi bang com voi ca	Nothing is [better than] rice with fish
Khong co gi bang me voi con	Nothing is [better than] a mother with a child

Vietnam has more than 3,000 km of coastline, several large rivers, and an endless system of irrigation canals and water reservoirs. These provide a fertile habitat for a rich and diverse variety of fish, seafood, and aquatic animals such as frogs, eels, and snails.

The intimate relations of the Vietnamese with water and waterways can be discerned from the very early stages of their history. The Vietnamese terms for a "country" are *dat nuoc* (land [and] water), *nong nuoc* (mountains [and] water), or simply *nuoc* (water), while government is *nha nuoc* (house [and] water). It is easy to understand why under such socioecological conditions aquatic animals are essential components of the diet.

Coastal and freshwater fishing are extremely important; many farmers are part-time fishermen and some have recently turned their rice fields into shrimp ponds. Almost all farmers exploit aquatic resources within the rice system, regularly trapping frogs, snails, eels, fish, and crabs that inhabit the rice terraces and often compete with the farmer over rice seedlings and paddies. Many practice "electric fishing," using electrodes powered by car batteries so as to shock and collect fish and amphibians at night (at great personal danger, they say, as they risk the bites of poisonous snakes as well as encountering hungry ghosts that roam the swamps at night).

Often, much time and effort were invested in fishing a few, miniscule fish. Whenever I was in town during the Hoianese flood season (November and December), I would see many of my neighbors pole fishing in the raging drainage canals for a few hours each afternoon. They never caught more than a handful of small fish, yet were obviously content with their catch, which was promptly cooked for dinner. This led me to pay more attention to the quantitative relations between the fish and the rice eaten at every meal. For Israeli or Western diners, serving such a small amount of fish would probably seem insulting. For Hoianese, however, half a dozen finger-size fish, approximately equivalent to a single sardine can, were clearly perceived as sufficient for a family meal.

Fish are commonly cooked into a "dry" dish or soup. As a "dry" dish, fish and other kinds of seafood can be fried and then boiled in tomato sauce, lemongrass, or garlic, or may be steamed or grilled (another local specialty is grilled fish in banana leaves, but this is a restaurant meal). Small fish and shrimp are often cooked with leafy greens into canh (soup). However, the most popular method of fish consumption is in the form of nuoc mam, the Vietnamese fish sauce.

Nuoc mam (fish sauce)

> Lanh lives with her husband and daughters in her in-laws' shop-house opposite the pier, just by the municipal market.
>
> Lanh quickly realized where my interests lay and often invited me to come for a meal. We often went to the market and shopped together. Her home was at the top of a flight of stairs; I learned to take a deep breath and hold it as long as possible as we climbed up. When I couldn't hold my breath any longer, I would silently empty my lungs and then, slowly and cautiously, breath through my mouth. However, this did not help. The thick, salty stench of fermenting fish would hit me. On my first visit, still unprepared, the stench was so heavy that I almost fainted.
>
> At the corner of the room stood a large cement vat. Drops of amber liquid slowly dripped from its tap into a large ladle. "This is my mother's nuoc mam," said Lanh proudly, "the best in Hoi An!"
>
> Lanh's mother-in-law bought a few kilograms of *ca com* (rice fish or long-jawed anchovy) every spring and mixed them with salt. The salt extracted the liquids out of the fish, while the tropical heat and humidity facilitated fermentation of the brine. After three or four weeks, the brine mellowed and cleared. Normally, this was the end of the process and the liquid was bottled and consumed. In order to further improve its quality, Lanh's mother-in-law kept the liquid "alive" by pouring it over and over again into the vat, allowing for a continuous process of fermentation that enhanced its flavor (and smell!). The result is an especially potent nuoc mam *nhi* (virgin fish sauce). Lanh told me that "only Vietnamese people can make nuoc mam because only they can understand! . . . Now you know why my dishes are so tasty,"

she added. "The secret is in the nuoc mam. Don't worry, when you go back to your country, I'll give you a small bottle. My mother always gives some to our relatives and close friends for *Tet* [the New Year festival]."

The tropical weather means that fresh fish and seafood spoil very quickly. Hence, rational practicality partly underlies this culinary icon, which is essentially a technique of preservation. However, nuoc mam embodies much more than nutritional and practical advantages, as it is the most prominent taste and cultural marker of Vietnamese cuisine.

Nuoc mam is used in different stages of cooking and eating: as a marinade before cooking, as a condiment while cooking, and as a dip when eating. In each stage, fish sauce influences the taste in a different way: in a marinade it softens the ingredients and starts the process of transformation from "raw" into "cooked"; nuoc mam is added to most dishes while cooking in order to enhance their flavor, to make the dish salty and, most importantly, to give the dishes their crucial "fishy" quality; at meals, nuoc mam is always present on the table, mixed with lime juice, sugar, crushed garlic, black pepper, and red chili into a complex dip.

The diners dip morsels of the "side dishes" in the sauce before placing them on the rice and sweeping a "bite" into their mouths. Since it is impolite for diners to adjust the taste of a dish with condiments, as it implies that the dish is not perfectly cooked, providing a complex dip allows for a polite and acceptable personal adjustment of the taste of a dish.

Finally, the nuoc mam bowl is the agent of commensality in the family meal: rice is dished into individual bowls and the side dishes are picked out of the shared vessels, but everybody dips their morsels of food into the common fish-sauce saucer just before putting them into their mouths.

Leafy Greens and Aromatics

No Vietnamese dish and certainly no Hoianese meal is served without fresh and/or cooked leafy greens: a dish of stir-fried or boiled *rau mung* (water morning glory), a tray of lettuce and aromatic leaves (*rau song*), or just a dash of chopped coriander over a bowl of noodles would do. Polished rice and fermented fish lack fiber and vitamins, specifically B1 (thiamin) and C (Anderson 1988:115). Lack of fiber causes constipation in the short term and might contribute to serious digestive maladies, including stomach cancer (Guggenheim 1985:278–82). Lack of vitamin C can cause, among other maladies, scurvy (ibid., 176); and lack of thiamin might result in beriberi (ibid., 201). For the rice-eating Vietnamese, the consumption of greens, and especially of raw greens, is therefore essential for balanced nutrition.

A variety of fresh, mostly aromatic, greens are served as a side dish called *rau song* (raw/live vegetables). There are regional variations in the composition of the greens. In the north, the purple, prickly *la tia to* (*perilla*) and (French-introduced) dill are often served. In the center and south, lettuce leaves (*xa lach;* note the French influence) are mixed with bean sprouts (sometimes lightly pickled), coriander, and several kinds of mints and basils. In the south, raw cucumber is sometimes added. In Hoi An, *ngo om* (a rice-paddy herb) and *dip ca* ('fish leaves," dark green heart-shaped leaves that, according to the locals, taste like fish) are often included in the platter. In the countryside, farmers tend small plots of greens right next to the house, creating convenient kitchen gardens. Urban dwellers buy the greens in the market just before mealtime.

Ba (Grandma) Tho, lips red from her constant chewing of *trau cau* (betel quid), handed me a bag of *rau song* just bought in the market and told me to wash them. The greens are harvested young and tender: a lettuce head is no bigger than a fist and the other greens are not higher than 10 cm and have only a few leaves. When lettuce is cheap, there is plenty of it in the mix, but when the price goes up, cheaper greens make up the volume.

I squatted on the cement floor near the tap, filled a plastic basin with water, and soaked the greens. The old woman placed a strainer near me and instructed me to carefully clean the leaves and throw away anything that was black, torn, old-looking, or seemed to have been picked at.[4] If the leaves were too big for a bite, I was to break them into smaller bits. Only the good parts were to be put in the strainer for a second wash.

The bag contained no more than a kilo but it took me a while to go over it thoroughly. The mound of rejected leaves was constantly larger than the pile of perfect, crunchy greens in the strainer.

Grandma Tho, obviously unsatisfied, asked me why I was taking so long and why I was throwing away so many good greens. She picked up the pile of rejected leaves and went to the back of the kitchen where, at the narrow space between the toilet wall and the fence, stood her beloved chicken coop. She threw the leaves in and contentedly watched the chicks fight over them.

Greens are served fresh and crunchy, fragrant, cool, and bright, and their contribution to the taste, texture, and color of the meal is substantial. They are picked up with chopsticks, dipped in nuoc mam, sometimes mixed with rice or other side dishes, and then eaten.

As they are so fragrant and aromatic, it seems obvious that the greens are there for their taste and smell. However, a specific taste is not the main objective. The prominence of the bland nonfragrant lettuce and bean sprouts further hints at other aspects of the greens. Here I recall my own eating experience: the cool crunchy greens adjust and balance the texture of the meal. The moist rice and the slippery, almost slimy, fish are counterbalanced, "charged with life," so to speak, by the fresh crispness of the greens. The aromatic greens cool down the dishes, not only by reducing the temperature, but also by adding a soothing quality that smoothes away some of the sharp edges of the other tastes. The random mixing of aromas and tastes adds a new dimension to every bite: a piece of *ca tu* (mackerel) cooked in turmeric and eaten with a crunchy lettuce leaf is a totally different from the same bite of fish eaten with some coriander. Here again we see how the structured rules of etiquette, which prevent personal seasoning and stress common taste, are subtly balanced by a setting that allows for personal modification and constant, endless variation and change.

MEAL STRUCTURES AND COSMOLOGY

Chi, a local chef and one of my most valuable informants and friends, suggested on several occasions that the basic dyad of "rice" and "things to eat" "is *am* and *duong*" (yin and yang). A similar point was made by Canh, another prominent Hoianese restaurateur, when we discussed the medicinal and therapeutic qualities of his cooking, while Tran, a Hoainese scholar, also suggested that *am* and *duong* shape the ways in which dishes and meals are prepared.

Yin and yang is an all-encompassing Chinese Taoist principle that champions a dynamic balance between the obscure, dark, wet, cold, feminine energy of yin and the hot, powerful, shining, violent, male energy of yang (Schipper 1993:35). This cosmic law maintains that harmony is the outcome of the tension between these opposites, which are the two sides of the same coin and existentially dependent upon each other, as there would be no "white" without "black," no "cold" without "hot," and no "men" without "women." Jamieson, in his insightful *Understanding Vietnam* (1995), claims that the principle of yin and yang is the key to understanding the Vietnamese society, its culture and history. He particularly points out that "Diet could . . . disrupt or restore harmony between yin and yang" (1995: 11), stressing the essential relationship between this cosmological principle and the culinary realm.

As pointed out earlier, am and duong were mentioned by my informants on several occasions when discussing food and, specifically, when I asked them about the structures of meals and dishes. They suggested that the bland, pale, shapeless rice was compatible with the notion of am (with rice related to femininity, as the senior female is the one who serves rice to the others), while the colorful, savory, varied mon an adhere to the definition of duong as flamboyant, savory entities to which men have privileged access. Moreover, the meal is wholesome only when both rice and mon an are presented on the table or tray, making for a material representation of am and duong, with a bowl of rice and mon an resembling the famous graphic symbol of yin and yang.

Am and duong, however, were actually mentioned by my informants quite rarely, and only by highly skilled cooks or educated professionals. The popular and common discourse was mainly concerned with the therapeutic qualities of food, within the medical cold–hot paradigm, according to which all dishes, ingredients, seasoning, and cooking techniques are either "heating" or "cooling." According to this theory, a dish should be balanced, combining hot and cold elements (as in the case of sweet-and-sour dishes) so as to maintain the diners' physical and emotional harmony.

In some cases, heating or cooling are desired, usually due to some health problems, as in the case of colds and flues, when ginger is used so as to "heat" up the dish and, as a consequence, the eater, so as to help him or her overcome a cold condition. In other cases excess is sought, as in instances when enhanced masculine sexual potency is desired. In such circumstances, aphrodisiacs such as snake, he-goat meat, or duck embryos, which are extremely "heating," would be consumed so as to enhance the level of duong.[5]

While the hot–cold paradigm for food was mentioned often, very few were aware that it is an implementation or implication of the am and duong theory. It seems, then, that in between abstract cosmological notions and lived experience there exists a third, mediating level, concerned directly with practical knowledge of the body and its well-being. While only a few people talk confidently about am and duong, the "hot-and-cold" paradigm is often evoked in discussions about food and cooking. The important point is that although the Hoianese only rarely linked the meal structure directly to the cosmological theory of am and duong, they did refer often to its practical implications of "hot and cold."

If the twofold structure of the Hoianese meal is a manifestation of the cosmic principle of am and duong, it would be reasonable to argue that the fivefold structure into which it evolves also stands for a cosmological principle. Here, I suggest that this fivefold structure is a representation of the cosmological theory of *ngu hanh* or "the five elements."

The five elements (or phases): water, fire, wood, metal, and earth, are finer subdivisions of the am and duong and "represent a spatio-temporal continuation of the Tao" (Schipper 1993:35), standing for the cardinal directions, the seasons, the planets, the viscera, and for everything else that exists. Hence, "like the yin and yang, the five phases are found in everything and their alternation is the second physical law [after yin and yang]" (ibid.). The five elements are interrelated in cycles of production and destruction (e.g., water produces wood and extinguishes fire); their relations and transformations generate the movement that is life.

Though my Hoianese friends never said that the five components of the Hoianese meal are representations of the five elements, when I suggested that this was the case, several of the more knowledgeable ones (e.g., Chi, the chef, and Co Dung, my Vietnamese language teacher) thought that I had a point. They were not able, however, to help with a formulation of the elements into a culinary matrix. The only clear reference was to rice, which is the centerpiece of the meal and corresponds to the "center" and, as such, to the "earth" element. I assumed that the soup corresponds to "water" and the

Chart 2. The "twofold-turn-fivefold" structure of the Hoianese meal as an expression of the cosmological principles of *am* and *duong* and *ngu hanh*

Am			Duong	
Rice Bland Pale/Colorless Mother			'Things to Eat' Savory Colorful Father	
Earth	Water	Wood	Metal	Fire
Rice Steamed	Soup Boiled	Greens Raw	"Dry" dish Fried/Grilled	Fish sauce Fermented

greens to "wood," but was not sure which of the other two, the fish sauce and the "dry" dish, corresponded to fire and which to metal. However, since the fish sauce is a fermented substance used in different stages to transform other ingredients, I would attribute it to "fire," while the "dry" dish corresponds to "metal." The fivefold structure also encompasses the five possible states of transformation of edible matter into food: raw, steamed, boiled, fried/grilled, and fermented.

The "twofold-turn-fivefold" structure of the Hoianese daily home-eaten meal presented in Chart 2 is both an outcome and a representation of the two most important Vietnamese cosmic laws. The Hoianese meal can be seen as a model of the universe: an abstract, condensed version of the ways in which the universe looks and operates. In similar lines to Eliade's (1959:5) claim that "all the Indian royal cities are built after the mythical model of the celestial city, where . . . the Universal sovereign dwelt," and to Cohen's (1987) suggestion that the cross pattern employed by the Hmong in their textile design, as well as specific pattern of face piercing applied by devotees during the vegetarian festival in Phuket (Cohen 2001), are cosmological schemes, I argue that the Hoianese meal is also a model of the universe and of the ways in which it operates.

Thus, whenever the Hoianese cook and eat their humble daily meal, they make a statement about the ways in which they perceive the universe and, when physically incorporating it, reaffirm the principles that shape their cosmos, endorsing them and ensuring their continuity. As with Indian Royal cities, Hmong embroidery patterns, or Thai piercing, most Hoianese are unaware of the cosmic meaning of the food they prepare. However, cooking and eating, just like piercing or following specific architectural designs, is a practice that encompasses "embodied Knowledge" (Choo 2004:207), knowledge that exists but not always intellectually and reflexively.

NOTES

1. Though my analysis could be applied, at least to a certain extent, to the daily meals of most Vietnamese and possibly to other Southeast Asian meals, this chapter is concerned only with the Hoianese meal. When discussing broad issues such as nutritional requirements or cosmological theories, I talk about "the Vietnamese" or about "rice-eating cultures," but I repeatedly point to minute details (e.g., specific kinds of fish and herbs or local weather cycles) as the elements that distinguish the Hoianese meal as a unique artifact embedded in specific space and time.

2. *Lac* probably derives from the Vietnamese word *lach*, which stands for ditch, canal, or waterway (Taylor 1983:10). Thus, the early Vietnamese named themselves after the rice-irrigation system they have developed, stressing the utmost importance of rice farming in their culture.

3. Nowadays the law requires that the all the dead must be buried in cemeteries, which are still often located among the rice fields.

4. While leaves that were damaged by birds and bugs were considered of low quality and discarded up until recently, in 2006 I was told by some friends that they only buy greens where they see some damage from bite marks: "nowadays farmers use extremely poisonous pesticides, which make for perfect leaves but poison the eaters. So we prefer bitten leaves, as bug-bites suggest that these chemicals were not used. . . ." Paradoxically, then, defective produce is regarded as of higher quality under free-market conditions.

5. Such aphrodisiacs do not function immediately as, for example, Viagra does. A Singaporean Chinese colleague pointed out when discussing diet as medicine that "the physical and curative effects of a given diet are accumulative. . . ."

PART SIX

War and Recovery

For young tourists and travelers today, Southeast Asia is a place of beauty, pleasure, and peace. It has not always been so; as with other regions, the area has experienced wars. The warfare of early states in Southeast Asia tended to focus on limited goals. For instance, the aims of mainland warfare were not so much to capture territory, but to capture populations. As the saying went, "Gather vegetables into baskets, gather people into the *mueang* [domain]." Given low population densities, the precious resource was labor, not land. There was little, if anything, to be gained by wholesale slaughtering of populations.

As we have seen, colonialism not only transformed political structures, but also transformed the ways in which violent conflict was carried out and resolved. One of us (Gillogly) read many British colonial reports on Burma and southwestern China as part of her research, and was amazed at the colonial phenomenon of the punitive expedition, a military expedition meant to punish a group of people (a village, a town, a state) for failure to adhere to rules established by the colonial power. As colonial powers extended their control across the landscape of Southeast Asia, people were increasingly drawn into regimes of governance that they experienced as heavy-handed and authoritarian. The effect of colonial taxation on the village "moral economy" is documented by James Scott in *The Moral Economy of the Peasant: Rebellion and Subsistence in Southeast Asia* (1979). He discusses the pre-colonial peasant village norms of reciprocity and the moral ethic of the right to subsistence. Colonialism, state taxation, and capitalism brought about a reorientation toward cash and commodities that undercut the "traditional" safety mechanisms preventing any given household from suffering devastating poverty and famine. These conditions worsened in the global economic depression of the 1930s. At the same time, many Southeast Asian urban elites, increasingly educated in the standards and worldview of colonial masters, began to rebel against colonial control. Colonial governments sent particularly promising students from the colonies to Europe and the United States to continue their education, with the expectation that these students would then return to serve as colonial managers and bureaucrats. In the Philippines, for instance, the students funded to pursue higher education in the United States during the first three decades of the twentieth century were known as *pensionados*. One unanticipated outcome of such studies abroad in the colonists' homelands was that Southeast Asian students became schooled in the idea of nationalism. When studying at European universities, they met other students from other colonies and came to recognize their shared status. The language of national identity served as a vehicle for calls for independence from Britain, France, Portugal, and the Netherlands.

World War II was a watershed for Southeast Asians in the trajectory toward independence. In some Southeast Asian nations, when the colonial powers fell before the onslaught of the Japanese empire, the colonialists' claim to rule was perceived as empty. Many Southeast Asians fought with the Allies against the Japanese, some landed in POW camps, and others perished. When the war ended, they believed they had won the right to determine their own future courses. As colonial powers attempted to hold on to their overseas territories, Southeast Asia became a game board on which world powers competed for political power, resources, and diplomatic alliances.

The Vietnam War (known in Vietnam as the American War) looms large in the American political imagination. The modern history of this war is complicated. The fight for independence in French colonial Indochina led to a particularly long and brutal war. One critical point occurred in 1954, when the French lost the battle of Dien Bien Phu to Viet Minh forces, the national independence movement founded in the early 1940s (a continuation of a nationalist independence movement of the 1930s). At the Geneva Conference that same year, the French Indochina war ended. The Geneva Accords recognized the territorial integrity and sovereignty of the countries of Indochina—Vietnam, Laos, and Cambodia. A ceasefire was established, and a provisional military demarcation line was established between the north, where the Viet Minh had established control, and the south of Vietnam; the ultimate goal was unification upon free democratic elections. The Viet Minh were identified as communist, and the United States chose to support the alternative government in the south as part of its Cold War strategy based on the domino theory, which surmised that if one country fell to communism, then all of the surrounding countries would follow. Hundreds of thousands of Catholic Vietnamese from the north fled as refugees to the south (some contend that they were instigated by the U.S. Central Intelligence Agency).

As the French withdrew, the United States took their place in supporting the government of the south. The south refused to participate in national unification elections and became the State of Vietnam, while the north became the Democratic Republic of Vietnam. Insurgent South Vietnamese who opposed the U.S.-supported government of the south formed the Viet Cong. They were supported by the Vietnam People's Army of the north. The state of war continued to escalate throughout the late 1950s and into the 1960s. In August 1965, the United States claimed that its navy had been attacked by the north, and this served as the rationale for a dramatic escalation of U.S. involvement in the war. The Tet Offensive of 1968 was a turning point. The northern forces showed themselves to be militarily successful, and the high death rates helped to turn the American public against that war. Antiwar demonstrations against U.S. involvement in Vietnam probably dominate most readers' knowledge of the era—that, and the pro-war discourse implicit in items such as the *Rambo* series of movies. Approximately 8 million Americans fought in the war in Vietnam and 58,159 U.S. soldiers died (the original number listed on the Vietnam Wall; names have been added since its memorial dedication in 1982) until the U.S. withdrawal in 1975 and the fall of the south to the north, bringing about unification.

While the gaze of Americans has been on their own troops and the effects on their country's policy of military intervention, the war was even more horrific for the people of Vietnam. Under programs to remove rural peoples from the influence of the Viet Cong, villagers were at times expelled from their residences and placed in compounds far from their fields, domestic animals, and means of earning their livelihood. Neighbor turned against neighbor; military forces could not tell who was on which side; innocent civilians in both the north and south were killed and maimed; atrocities such as My Lai were committed, as discussed by Shaun Malarney (chapter 18); Le Ly Hayslip's autobiographical *When Heaven and Earth Changed Places* (1989) documents the chaos experienced by the people of the south; Bao Ninh's novel *The Sorrow of War* (1993) tells the story of loss from the northern perspective. The people of Hanoi were subjected to unprecedented levels of bombing; the peoples of Laos and Cambodia suffered the same fate, as the U.S. military attempted to stop the flow of supplies to the Viet Cong and North Vietnamese forces in the south along the "Ho Chi Minh trail" (actually, many trails) through Cambodia and Laos. When Gillogly first flew into Hanoi in 1989, she was astounded by the neat squares of rice fields interspersed with hundreds of little round pits. She first took these to be fish ponds—until she realized that these were bomb craters, the scarred landscape of an air war. Similarly, in southern Laos, her research team was explicitly warned by Lao villagers of the risks of stepping off the trails because of the danger of unexploded ordinance. Approximately 7 million tons of bombs were dropped on Vietnam, Laos, and Cambodia during this war; in comparison, about 2 million tons of bombs were dropped in World War II. To this day, Laos is believed to be the most heavily bombed country in history. And those bombs still go off. Cluster bomblets often failed to detonate—leaving them to explode long after the war ended, creating a legacy of death and crippling injury well into the end of the twentieth century. Despite the American concern with their own war dead and missing, then, imagine how much higher the death and casualty tolls must have been for the people of Vietnam, Laos, and Cambodia. An Agence France Presse (1995) news release on the occasion of the twentieth anniversary of the end of the war estimated that nearly 5 million Vietnamese, from both the north and south, died in the war. As Malarney points out, "War dead are a ubiquitous and readily visible part of contemporary Vietnamese society. . . ."

A discussion of war dead in Vietnam is not complete without an appreciation of cultural ideas surrounding death and ancestors. Ancestors are important in patrilineal societies, and certainly so in Vietnam (as well as in Chinese Singaporean society and in overseas Chinese communities elsewhere in Southeast Asia). People use patrilineal connections to build networks, for investment, and for other utilitarian strategizing; patrilineal kin in other towns and villages have an obligation to help members of their patrilineage. In fact, a sense of trust is inherent in the patrilineal relationship that does not exist as easily with non-kin. It is also a formal legal identification in the Vietnamese state. Each patrilineage has its ancestor hall. In rural villages, each household of the local patrilineage contributed funds toward the upkeep of the ancestor hall and its grounds; people paid respect to ancestors at their shrine twice in the lunar month. Lineages held at least one main feast to commemorate their founding ancestor, usually at Tet, the Vietnamese New Year, at the village of the senior male of the lineage. There were also feasts on the death anniversaries of respected ancestors. Lineages undertook joint activities such as maintenance of lineage cemeteries, upkeep of the lineage hall, and collection of funds for funerals and weddings (Hoa et al. 1993). In northern Vietnam, countless young men left their homes never to be heard from again—as many as 300,000. The location of the war dead is a great obsession for many Vietnamese and much effort can be put into finding the remains of ancestors—a difficult if not hopeless task, given how quickly organic material breaks down in the tropical forests of the south. In the face of these challenges, Vietnamese families in the twenty-first century sometimes draw on supernatural means to attempt to find their war dead.

In Cambodia, as bad as the secret bombings of eastern Cambodia had been, worse followed after the American withdrawal. Little had prepared the ruling elite of Cambodia for the massive social dislocation and influx of refugees fleeing the American bombings of April 1970—if any society could ever have been prepared for such chaos. The French colonial government had not developed the kind of bureaucratic infrastructure it had established in other colonial territories; hence, locals initially did not experience the same level of disruption to their "traditional" ways of life under colonialism. As Penny Edwards points out, "Cambodge" became an oasis of tradition and beauty and remoteness (2007), the exotic other to the French; colonials' energies were focused on maintaining what they saw as reviving and purifying Khmer traditions. In Cambodia, the nationalist movement of the 1920s and 1930s was also associated with communism, but this morphed into a form of romanticized communalism under the guise of calls for a return to the "original Khmer" ways. The Khmer Rouge (Red Khmer) was founded in 1960 and came to control large swathes of territory in rural Cambodia (see the essay by Eve Monique Zucker, chapter 20). After the American bombings, King Norodom Sihanouk was deposed by a military coup and joined forces with the Khmer Rouge. When Phnom Penh fell in 1975, the Khmer Rouge took over the capital and the country and removed all inhabitants from the cities; in Phnom Penh alone, nearly 2 million people were removed within days. This was followed by many years of forced labor, mass murder, and atrocities in what came to be known as the Killing Fields. Children were taken from their parents to be raised in separate forced labor camps; factories, schools, and hospitals were shut down; educated and professional people—and anyone else perceived as being opposed to the Khmer Rouge—were killed along with their extended families. Approximately 1.7 to 2 million Cambodians (Kiernan 2003; Genocide Program 2010) were killed or starved to death under Khmer Rouge rule until 1979. The horror of this time is vividly depicted in *The Killing Fields*, a film based on Dith Pran's account of his survival of the Khmer Rouge atrocities. In the Tuol Sleng Prison, the Khmer Rouge systematically photographed, tortured, interrogated, and killed as many as 30,000 prisoners—the site is now a genocide museum.

Island Southeast Asia's newest nation, East Timor (Timor Leste), experienced a different, though equally traumatic, path to independence. In her contribution to this section, Elizabeth G. Traube (chapter 19) examines that path through the lens of local people's eyes, spotlighting how one ethnic group on East Timor, the Mambai, draw on ancestral origin narratives not only to explain the origins of colonial rule on their island, but also to formulate and express their expectations for the future. When Traube began her research in the 1970s, Portugal was readying Portuguese Timor for decolonization, following several centuries of colonial rule. However, within weeks of gaining independence from Portugal, East Timor had become a colony once again. The Republic of Indonesia invaded East Timor in 1975, and twenty-four years of brutal occupation and guerrilla warfare (waged by the FALINTIL) ensued. It was not until 1998, following the collapse of Suharto's New Order regime in Indonesia, that East Timorese were promised an independence referendum. Despite the Indonesian military's campaign of terror to discourage pro-independence voters, East Timorese overwhelmingly voted for independence in 1999. Traube's chapter examines the cultural dynamics of national identity formation before, during, and after the Indonesian occupation. She movingly spotlights how Mambai invoke traditional origin myths (which represent elders as suffering lifegivers entitled to receive compensation) as metaphors for their current situation. Traube's contribution shows us yet again how new identities and visions for the future are forged out of old cloth.

18

Living with the War Dead in Contemporary Vietnam

Shaun Kingsley Malarney

Two of the most common sites visible across Vietnam are cemeteries for soldiers and monuments that instruct the living to remember their debts to dead soldiers. These symbolic reminders of the presence of war dead can be found in virtually every Vietnamese community, yet other reminders are visible as well in the names of schools, streets, and national holidays. They are also present in photographs on family ancestral altars and in government-issued certificates acknowledging the death of a soldier in battle that are hung on the walls of homes. Stated simply, war dead are a regular and visible part of everyday life in Vietnam. Their ubiquity creates an initial impression that Vietnamese people think about, categorize, and engage them in similar ways. However, as this chapter will demonstrate, war dead mobilize many significant cultural ideas, unique sources of anguish, and political complexities. Moreover, their presence both reveals and conceals significant consequences of the decades of warfare that Vietnam experienced in the mid- to late twentieth century.

THE BACKGROUND TO WAR DEAD IN VIETNAM

Over the course of its history, Vietnam has been involved in numerous wars, most notably with its northern neighbor China. The Chinese successfully conquered the northern parts of Vietnam and turned it into their southernmost province from 111 BC to 938 AD. They then reinvaded several times in subsequent centuries. In the period from 1946 to 1989, Vietnam experienced a series of wars that took the lives of millions of its citizens: first in the eight-year war against the French (1946–1954); second in the prolonged war of reunification that pitted the northern Democratic Republic of Vietnam against the southern Republic of Vietnam and its allies, notably the United States (1959–1975); next in the brief border war against the Chinese (1979–1980); and finally in the war in Cambodia after the Vietnamese overthrow of the

Khmer Rouge (1979–1989). These latter wars involved the deaths of hundreds of thousands of Vietnamese soldiers, but they also involved the deaths of over at least one million civilian noncombatants.

The frequency of Vietnam's wars, combined with the fact that the majority of their wars have been fought on their own soil, has led to the cultural celebration of heroes (anh hùng) who have resisted foreign aggression. Over the centuries, a wide variety of individuals have gained fame for fighting foreign invaders, such the Trưng Sisters, who lost their lives after they successfully overthrew Chinese rule in 40 to 43 AD; Triệu Thị Trinh, who also lost her life after leading another revolt against the Chinese in 248 AD; and Trần Hưng Đạo, the general who devised the strategy that halted the Mongol invasion of Vietnam in 1285. These and other heroes are widely celebrated in popular culture for their "meritorious works" (công) in trying to protect Vietnam from aggression and occupation.

Although fighting to defend Vietnam is accorded tremendous prestige, the greatest prestige is given to those who give their lives in doing so. Such individuals are regarded as having "sacrificed" (hi sinh) their lives, an act that gives them great distinction in the community of the dead. The process of being socially recognized as having sacrificed one's life for Vietnam, however, begins to illustrate the complexities associated with Vietnamese war dead. The most prominent and prestigious members of this community in contemporary Vietnam are those referred to as "revolutionary martyrs" (liệt sĩ). The term liệt sĩ has a long history in the Vietnamese language, but in the mid-1920s the Vietnamese communists redefined it as an individual who had "sacrificed" his or her life in support of the revolutionary cause. Benoit de Treglodé, based upon an official document from 1957, gives a compelling description of the revolutionary martyr as "a person who died gloriously on the field of honor in the struggle against imperialism and feudalism since 1925." He further noted that the revolutionary martyr was someone who had "courageously fallen at the front in the defense of the work of the national revolution" (Tréglodé 2001:267). It is important to note, however, that it was initially the Communist Party and later the government of North Vietnam that decided which individuals were classified as revolutionary martyrs. There were no restrictions based upon age, gender, or even Communist Party membership, but the designation could only be earned through official scrutiny and confirmation.

The Vietnamese communists began creating their list of revolutionary martyrs in 1925. After the outbreak of hostilities against the French in 1946, their numbers began to grow and later did so at a tremendous rate during the period of the American War. From the Vietnamese communist's perspective, soldiers dying in battle presented a number of dangers, particularly one that the living would perceive their deaths as meaningless, which in turn could erode support for the war effort and ultimately the government. In order to counter these dangers, a variety of measures were introduced over the following decades to reinforce the idea that these soldiers' deaths were meaningful. At the simplest level, revolutionary martyrs were integrated into the larger community of heroes who fought against foreign aggression. General Võ Nguyên Giáp, the famous commander of Vietnamese forces in their historic victory over the French at Điện Biên Phủ in 1954, noted that "The contemporary ideas of our party, military, and people for the offensive struggle cannot be separated from the traditional military ideas of our people. During our history, all victorious wars of resistance or liberation, whether led by the Trưng Sisters, Lý Bôn, Triệu Quang Phục, Lê Lợi, or Nguyễn Trãi, have all shared the common characteristic of a continuous offensive aimed at casting off the yoke of feudal domination by foreigners" (Vietnam Institute of Philosophy 1973:269). Those fighting and dying in the struggle against foreign aggression were thus part of a longer, noble line of patriotic combatants. Martyrs' deaths were also described as "honorable" (*vinh dự*). Finally, the state publicly glorified the personal courage and sacrifices that revolutionary martyrs made. Communist Party General Secretary Le Duẩn stated in 1968, "Without the virtuous willingness for sacrifice, one is not an authentic revolutionary. If you want to realize the revolutionary ideal, but will not dare to sacrifice yourself, then you are only speaking empty words" (ibid., 275). Such statements publicly reinforced the martyrs' virtues and helped give them tremendous prestige in social life.

Issues of language aside, war dead in Vietnam have become so prominent because the socialist government developed other policies to insert them into public life. One of the earliest manifestations of this agenda was the designation in 1947 of July 27th as War Invalids and Martyrs Day (Ngày Thương Binh Liệt Sĩ). On this day, government officials, ranging from local communal administrations to the national government, organize and sponsor ceremonies in which the contributions of disabled and deceased veterans are recognized. For many years these ceremonies were only organized irregularly, but since 1967 they have been an annual occurrence (Pike 1986:318). They are also given extensive coverage in the popular media.

During the 1950s, the revolutionary government began implementing another policy that aimed to make war dead a part of the physical space of Vietnamese society by mandating the creation of "revolutionary martyr cemeteries" (*nghĩa trang liệt sĩ*). These could take varying forms. In some cases, officials designated an exclusive section in an existing cemetery for the burial of revolutionary martyrs, while in other cases new cemeteries were constructed that were to hold only revolutionary martyrs. The construction of such a cemetery, however, required that the remains of revolutionary martyrs be returned to their native communities, and as in many cases they were not, some communities did not construct such exclusive spaces. Regardless of whether they were present or not, virtually all communities have constructed monuments for revolutionary martyrs, generally referred to as *đài tượng niệm* or *đài liệt sĩ*. These take a variety of architectural forms, but they universally feature such slogans as "The Fatherland Remembers Your Sacrifice" (Tổ Quốc Ghi Công) or "Eternally Remember Our Moral Debt to the Revolutionary Martyrs" (Đời Đời Nhớ Ởn Người Liệt Sĩ).

These slogans were important means for communicating official appreciation for the deceased soldiers' sacrifices, but the state also wanted to further propagate the nobility and importance of the revolutionary martyrs by integrating the new cemeteries and commemorative monuments into people's lives. For example, officials in the northern province of Ninh Bình stated that "everyone has the responsibility to protect and care for the revolutionary martyrs' cemeteries in the cities and communes. People should display their remembrance and express their awareness of their debt to the heroic martyrs who have carried out their meritorious work for the revolution" (Ninh Bình, Cultural Service 1968:64). The same regulations encouraged communities to take local youth out to the cemeteries so that they could learn to care for the graves and appreciate the martyrs' sacrifices. Officials in Nam Hà Province came up with a unique innovation by mandating that weddings were to conclude with a visit to the local war dead cemetery so that newlyweds could place a bouquet of flowers on the monument to express their appreciation to the revolutionary martyrs (Vietnam, Ministry of Culture 1979:24). In contemporary Vietnam, revolutionary martyr cemeteries or commemorative monuments can be found in almost every community. Beyond these cemeteries and monuments, the government also began naming streets, schools, and other spaces after revolutionary martyrs. In the 1990s, the government augmented these preexisting policies by creating the new category of "Heroic Vietnamese Mothers" (Bà Mẹ Anh Hùng Việt Nam) to honor mothers who had lost several children in war. Taken in the aggregate, all of these policies served to help render noble and counter the potential meaningless of dying for the nation in battle.

OTHER WAR DEAD

War dead are a ubiquitous and readily visible part of contemporary Vietnamese society, but as should now be clear, it is those who died fighting for the socialist state and revolution who are given the greatest social prominence and are openly celebrated. Vietnam's wars, however, caused the deaths of millions of other Vietnamese, but in contemporary Vietnamese society, their deaths are not equally remembered or celebrated. One of the first such groups is composed of those who died noncombat-related deaths. Many soldiers, for example, died from disease while in the military, others died in accidents, and yet others died from such unexpected events as animal attacks. These individuals are referred to as "war dead" (tửsĩ), do not receive the revolutionary martyr designation, and thus are not accorded similar recognition. Beyond military personnel, however, large numbers of noncombatants were killed, and these individuals were referred to as "victims of war" (*nạn nhân chiến tranh*). In northern Vietnam, these victims were most commonly individuals who died as a result of American bombing, either accurate or errant. The most famous among this group were those killed on the night of December 26, 1972 when an American B-52 bomber released its bomb load over Khâm Thiên Street in the south of Hanoi, leading to the destruction of the area and the death of 283 civilians (Nguyễn Huy Phúc and Trần Huy Bá 1979:245). This assault is recognized as one of the great tragedies of the American War; its victims are remembered and honored in a monument built on the street. As innocent victims of American bombing, their deaths and the deaths of other such northern Vietnamese are easily integrated into the master narratives that the socialist state has propagated regarding war death, as they too are regarded as having given their lives as part of the broader struggle to defeat the American enemy.

Many northern Vietnam civilians were the innocent victims of warfare, but it is important to note that, comparatively, more noncombatants were killed in the southern and particularly the central regions of Vietnam. Indeed, scholars have estimated that more than one million civilians died in central and southern Vietnam during the American War. Nevertheless, the deaths of these individuals, as the anthropologist Heonik Kwon has described, created a set of difficulties and dangers distinct from those of the revolutionary martyrs and northern civilians, and this fact has necessitated its own set of unique responses (see Kwon 2006).

When describing noncombatant deaths in southern and central Vietnam, it is important to note that these victims of warfare were divided into two primary groups. First were those who were, like their northern counterparts, accidentally killed during military operations, notably in errant bombing, shelling, or shooting. A second category was composed of those deliberately killed in massacres. As Kwon describes, from 1966 onward, a large number of deliberate killings of civilians were carried out, notably by Marines from the Republic of Korea (ROK) operating in Quảng Ngãi province (ibid., 43). Early 1968 then witnessed two of the most infamous massacres of the war, the slaughter of 135 civilians by ROK Marines in Ha My in Quảng Nam province on February 24th, and the massacre of approximately 500 civilians by U.S. Army soldiers at Mỹ Lai in Quảng Ngãi province on March 16th.

Despite being victims of war, these massacre victims ended up in a socioculturally liminal or marginal position due to a number of characteristics. First, the majority of victims were definitively noncombatants, which made it difficult to even innovatively integrate them into the category of those who sacrificed their lives for the cause. For example at Ha My, of the 135 massacred, only three males were of combat age, while the other victims were women, children, village elders, and others (ibid., 45). The situation at Mỹ Lai and other locations was similar. Second, the nature of the war in southern and central Vietnam was riven with multiple ambiguities regarding residents' political loyalties. Unlike in conventional wars, in which uniformed military personnel face each other across a battlefield, both the French and American wars featured a combination of conventional warfare and guerrilla warfare. During the American War, most of the ground combat occurred in central and southern Vietnam, where soldiers of the Army of the Republic of Vietnam (ARVN) and its allies in the U.S., Korean, and other allied militaries fought a conventional war against the People's Army of Vietnam (PAVN, the army of North Vietnam), while also fighting a guerrilla war against the National Liberation Front (NLF), a guerrilla force allied with the Hanoi government and generally referred to as the Viet Cong (VC). NLF members were usually drawn from and supported by local communities, but they often did so in secret as they were operating in areas that were at least technically under enemy control. As a result, communities in these regions usually featured a mixture of those who supported the Saigon government and those who supported the NLF, but given the secretive nature of the latter, as well as the sense that many people's loyalties lay with whichever side would give them the greatest chance of survival, the nature of people's real loyalties remained uncertain. As such, when a massacre occurred, these uncertainties remained and thus a hesitance existed to publicly glorify these victims, as such a commemoration might also have honored enemy dead. Finally, once the war was over, the victorious northern side did not want to dwell on these difficult and complex aspects, but instead wanted to move the nation forward to its bright future; accordingly, no official attention was given to these victims (ibid., 66).

The consequences of these factors involving the massacre victims in the immediate post-1975 period has been a combination of marginalization and neglect. As Kwon notes, the victorious government was indeed interested in the dead, but its interests were restricted to locating the remains of and reburying revolutionary martyrs (the same effort existed in the north). The latter, in fact, became an important device for unifying the population, and thus the government encouraged residents to find their remains, which Kwon compellingly called a "sacred mission" (ibid.), and then combined this with the construction of revolutionary martyr cemeteries in the centers of communities. As Kwon commented, "The bodies of the fallen heroes, and the war cemeteries that kept these bodies, became a principal site of national memory of the unified struggle against a foreign power." He continued, "It was a central element of postwar body politics to place the heroic dead at the center of postwar village life and to promote civil interests in preserving their memory" (ibid.).

Unlike the care and solicitude shown toward the remains of revolutionary martyrs, the remains of massacre victims were treated much more dismissively. In Ha My, for example, massacre victims had initially been buried in shallow graves, but in the post-1975 period the government placed an emphasis on economic development; thus, remains were carelessly removed to open up fields for agriculture, and basically no effort was made to confirm identities. Kwon notes that some of the volunteers who came from the city of Đà Nẵng to participate in this work were regarded by the local community as having "shown no respect for the excavated bones when they helped to clear stray ammunition and land mines from the farm fields" (ibid.). More tellingly, when the bones were reburied, they ended up not in the center of the village, but in peripheral areas in what surviving relatives ultimately considered "improper graves" (ibid., 65). These realities are a source of continuing anguish for thousands of Vietnamese families.

Finally, it should be noted that one group that continues to be excluded from the official heroic narrative and remains uncommemorated in the public sphere are the dead of the Army of the Republic of Vietnam. During the war, hundreds of thousands of ARVN soldiers were killed in battle, but these soldiers were not granted public celebrations. In fact, many of their old cemeteries have been closed down and in some cases the bodies have been removed to make way for other construction. Such individuals can never be classified as revolutionary martyrs, nor can they be classified as having sacrificed their lives for the regime. From the current regime's perspective, official recognition of those they regard as enemy dead remains completely off-limits. Therefore, the families of those who lost loved ones while serving in the ARVN must content themselves with exclusively private commemorations.

THE ANGUISH OF THE MISSING

It goes without saying that the loss of family members in war has been and continues to be the source of tremendous and enduring anguish for millions of Vietnamese. Hundreds of thousands of Vietnamese families whose loved ones are missing in action or whose bones have never been recovered, however, experience a unique source of anguish. According to Vietnamese cultural ideas, when a person dies, his or her physical body ceases to function, but the "soul" (*linh hồn*) continues to exist. And, just as when the body was alive, the soul is a sentient being with consciousness, feelings, and emotions. As in other cultures, one of the main concerns for the living at an individual's death is that the deceased's soul find eternal peace. According to popular ideas, in order for the soul to attain ultimate peace, it must travel from the world of the living to what is known as the "other world" (*thế giới khác*). The "other world" is similar to the world of the living in that the dead are held to eat and drink, wear clothes, use money, own houses, and even drive cars, watch televisions, and sing karaoke. It is important to note, however, that once a soul has reached the "other world," its various needs must be provided by the living. Thus, mortuary rites commonly feature items needed by dead souls, such as food, money, and clothing, that are transmitted either through incense smoke, as in the case of the food, or through the smoke produced by burning votive paper items (*hàng mã*) that take the form of money, clothing, or other objects. The provisioning of these items to the soul in the "other world" keeps it happy, while the failure to deliver them makes the soul discontented and angry.

To reach the "other world," the soul is dependent upon the living to perform the proper funerary rites. Through these rites, the living help guide and send it to the "other world." However, to make this journey, the living need either to possess the deceased's remains or to know the location of the body. If the physical remains have been lost or the place where the deceased was buried is unknown, which was the case of hundreds of thousands of Vietnamese killed in the war, the soul is doomed to remain stranded in this world and can never pass to the "other world." It is also now culturally regarded as having become a "ghost" (*con ma*). Ghosts have several important characteristics. They are regarded as being angry for having died in an unexpected and unpleasant manner. Their anger is further compounded by the fact that, since they are stranded in the world of the living, their descendants cannot directly care for them. They must therefore provide for themselves, which they do by stealing from the ancestral rites performed for souls in the "other world" or by obtaining whatever humans leave out for them in special rites. Finally, given their defining anger, ghosts will often direct this anger toward the living, causing them illness or other misfortunes. Ghosts are constitutionally unhappy and are doomed to never finding peace unless living humans assist them.

The dangers that war deaths created for families are therefore apparent. Tens of thousands of young soldiers, primarily male, lost their lives in violent circumstances hundreds of miles from home. Most soldiers were buried near where they died or were lost completely. For the survivors, therefore, war deaths created the frightening possibility that their loved ones were doomed to become angry ghosts and that their souls could never be properly cared for.

The ways in which families have responded to these difficulties have varied. In some communities, such as in Thịnh Liệt Commune south of Hanoi, innovative rituals were created in order to cope with some of the difficulties distant war deaths entailed (see Malarney 2001). For many families, war death and the subsequent loss of the body marked the beginning of a decades-long search for remains so that the deceased could finally be put to rest and the family's burden lifted. Over the past several decades, a vast network has emerged to help facilitate the transmission of informal information about war dead, which is readily visible on television, newspapers, and such specialist publications as "War Veterans of Vietnam" (*Cựu Chiến Binh Việt Nam*), found at newsstands. Families have also turned to supernatural means of locating their lost loved ones. One novel innovation has been the creation of a new divinatory rite for identifying remains in a preexisting grave. Cemeteries for revolutionary martyrs across Vietnam have many "nameless" (*vô danh*) graves in which the identity of the interred soldier is unknown. Beginning in the mid-1990s, families that knew the location of the cemetery in which their loved one was buried could perform a rite involving the placement of one chopstick vertically into the ground near the grave and then attempting to balance an egg on top of the chopstick. If the egg fell to the ground, the grave did not hold their loved one's remains. An egg that successfully balanced on top of the chopstick, however, provided a positive confirmation that the remains in the grave were those of their loved one. This divinatory rite has been successful on numerous occasions, and according to an early article on this phenomenon in April 1996 in the magazine *Thế Giới Mới* (The New World), it even succeeded in locating the remains of one soldier who had been missing since the outbreak of the French War in December 1946 (Xuân Cang and Lý Đặng Cao 1996:8–11).

Another popular practice that has emerged over the past decade is known as *ngoại cảm*. It is difficult to provide a precise equivalent in English, but the word can be explained by breaking it down into its component parts. *Ngoại* means "external" or "outside," while *cảm* means "to feel" or "to be emotionally affected by something"; thus, *ngoại cảm* together designate having the ability to be emotionally affected by external entities. The *ngoại cảm* specialists, known in Vietnamese as *nhà ngoại cảm*, are said to have the ability to communicate with the souls of the dead, specifically those of the war dead. Vietnam has recently seen an explosion in the number of self-described *ngoại cảm* specialists, though it must be stated that many of them are charlatans who prey upon people's vulnerabilities. Having said that, there is a small group of *ngoại cảm* specialists who are recognized as legitimate and successful practitioners. Indeed, in July 2007, at an official ceremony entitled "Finding the Remains of Revolutionary Martyrs through Special Abilities" (*Tìm Hài Cốt Liệt Sĩ Bằng Khả Năng Đặc Biệt*), awards were presented to ten *ngoại cảm* specialists for their contributions in finding the graves of revolutionary martyrs in the period from 1997 to 2007. The group as a whole was credited with finding the graves of more than 15,000 revolutionary martyrs and others with revolutionary achievements during that decade. One *ngoại cảm* specialist, Nguyễn Thị Nguyện, was credited with having found the remains of more than five thousand revolutionary martyrs, while two others, Phạm Văn Lập and Trần Văn Tìa, had both discovered over one thousand graves. It is interesting to note that of the specialists, three were from Hanoi, three from Saigon, and one each from Hải Dương, Thái Nguyên, Bà Rịa-Vũng Tàu, and Điện Biên (Nguyên Bảng 2007).

Far from being a simply northern phenomenon, these specialists come from across Vietnam and provide an important service to those in anguish. By locating the remains of their loved ones, families finally resolve the dangers the ghosts presented by performing the proper funerary rites for them and putting their souls to rest. In a sense, by successfully locating their loved ones' remains, families can write the final chapter of their loved one's lives and bring the story to successful closure. In doing so, a tremendous burden of pain and grief is lifted. A powerful example of this was given in a 2006 BBC documentary on *ngoại cảm* entitled *Psychic Vietnam*. In the film, a family had been searching for the remains of a male family member for almost forty years and as a last resort consulted a well-known *ngoại cảm* specialist, named Nguyễn thị Minh Nghĩa, in the southern province of Bà Rịa–Vũng Tàu (she was another awardee). Nghĩa successfully provided the information on the deceased's location. After receiving the information, the deceased's widow commented, "My mind is at rest. This is all I have ever wanted. Now I can die happily" (Phua 2006). Her reaction has been shared by thousands of other Vietnamese families.

CONCLUSION

War dead are indeed ubiquitous in contemporary Vietnam, but as this chapter has shown, their mere existence conceals significant complexities. Some war dead are publicly celebrated in cemeteries and ceremonies, while others remain hidden from public view, only to be remembered and celebrated by their families. Regardless of political affiliation or circumstances of death, the war dead remain a source of pain and anguish for their close loved ones. For some, it is the simple fact of death that pains them, while for others, the absence of knowledge regarding the place of burial or the body itself creates a lingering fear and anxiety that their loved one has been doomed to become an angry ghost that will never find peace. Nevertheless, even for those who receive the greatest public celebration, the war dead represent for millions of Vietnamese families a continuing legacy of loss and anguish.

19

Producing the People: Exchange Obligations and Popular Nationalism

Elizabeth G. Traube

"If the national flag came from overseas," Fernando objected quietly, "it would mean that foreigners still ruled us." It was a Saturday afternoon in May 2001; we were talking with three Mambai elders in their ancestral origin village, in the mountains of central East Timor. Village members had gathered there to rebuild the sacred houses; one house had been destroyed during the violence of September 1999, when militias and departing Indonesian troops took revenge on the population for having overwhelmingly supported independence in a UN-sponsored referendum. The referendum had brought the Indonesian occupation (1975–1999) of the former Portuguese colony to an end and led to the establishment of the United Nations Transitional Administration on East Timor (UNTAET). In 2001, preparations were under way for the election of a constitutional assembly, as a prelude to the formal declaration of independence.[1]

In the mountains, people were anticipating the elections, but rebuilding their sacred houses was also a priority. The elders were supervising the ritual process when they took time to meet with me and my companions, Fernando and Mateus. Their spokesman opened the conversation by affirming the common ancestry of Timorese and Malaia, a category that includes various overseas foreigners. "We Timorese took the rock and tree," he said, and "you Malaia took the book and pen and went across the sea, but we all have one mother and one father." The Malaia had later returned from overseas, he said, with the Portuguese flag. How then, I asked, had East Timor's national flag been acquired? It had been "purchased," he responded, "with the suffering of the people," using a common formula for the independence struggle against Indonesia. When I continued to press, he replied that the national flag came from the sea; however, his reiterations of this claim prompted an objection from Fernando. Fernando's argument was based on the myth of the origins of colonial rule that he recounted for me a few days later.

I had first encountered this myth in 1973, when East Timor was a Portuguese colony and I was pursuing fieldwork for my doctoral dissertation.

The men who told me the story, Mau Bere and Mau Balen, were older brothers of Fernando and Mateus, respectively. I came to recognize the story as a variant of a widespread Austronesian theme: the stranger king. This narrative theme links political order to an encounter between an indigenous ruler and a newcomer who comes from somewhere beyond the borders of the realm, often from overseas. Typically, their encounter involves a transfer of power: the newcomer takes over political functions formerly vested in the original, autochthonous leaders. While the newcomer is installed as ruler of the realm, the original lords retain ritual or spiritual authority over the land (Fox 1995). Myths of this type can be used to legitimize the rule of foreigners (Henley 2002), but they make awkward vehicles for popular nationalism, as Fernando suggested.

Nevertheless, in participating in a struggle for national independence, Mambai did not entirely abandon their older worldview. In this paper I argue that Mambai have creatively reworked preexisting cultural ideas and symbols to express new political conditions and aspirations.

COLONIALISM, DECOLONIZATION, AND STRANGER KINGS

Early in 1973, I had settled in the administrative district of Aileu, some twenty kilometers south of Dili, the coastal capital of Portuguese Timor. I was living near Aileu-town, in the house of the headman of the subdistrict in which Mau Balen resided, and we met at the annual census. Mau Balen's ancestral origin house was located in a village named Raimaus, and he escorted me there to observe the opening of the annual agricultural rites. A priest from the neighboring village of Hohul presided over the Raimaus ritual. To explain the tie between the villages, many people invoked a story about two brothers, descendants of a mythic ancestor named Ki Sa, who once lived together in Raimaus. One day, the story goes, the older brother performed an agricultural ceremony while his younger brother was away. When the younger brother returned, he was so angry over this slight that he gathered up all the sacred ritual paraphernalia (metal disks, coral necklaces, drums, and gongs) and set off southward to Hohul, where he founded a new house which stands metaphorically as younger brother to the Raimaus house. People also portray the two villages as a single house, with Raimaus as the door and Hohul as the innermost, southern section, where sacra are kept. In this metaphor, visitors enter Hohul by way of Raimaus, and I followed that etiquette. Mau Balen and I "crossed over" to Hohul to attend a house-building ceremony. There I met a young Hohul man named Mau Bere who agreed to join Mau Balen and me. Over the remaining six months of my fieldwork we visited numerous ritual centers, and I became lastingly associated with the villages of Hohul and Raimaus.

My relationship to my Mambai hosts was widely represented in binary terms. People contrasted my "book and pen" with their sacred "rock and tree" as images of our respective ethnic identities. The technology of literacy marked me as a Malaia, a white overseas foreigner, while rock and tree stood for all the indigenous peoples of the land, represented as "Timorese." Much emphasis was placed on my status as a "returning outsider" who had come back to her ancestral homeland. Mambai are deeply invested in a mythology of common origins. Not only humankind but all the phenomena of nature are descended from Mother Earth and Father Heaven. Mambai identify Mount Ramelau in the central interior as the first dry land, where Mother Earth brought forth the diverse inhabitants of the land. Her firstborn were the nonhuman phenomena of nature, including rocks, trees, grass, animals, birds, who stand collectively as "elder siblings" to their human "younger siblings." At first, Mambai say, elder as well as younger beings were animated, and the trees and grasses screamed when people tried to cut them to build their houses. Then Father Heaven removed the power of speech from his elder children, so that the younger ones could use these nonhuman components of nature for their own livelihood.[2] Human beings, henceforth distinguished as "speaking mouths," are authorized to exploit the "silent mouths" for food and shelter, but they are also expected to show them respect.[3] According to an ethic of reciprocity, the "speaking mouths" should offer their silent elder kin restitution for the suffering they inflict. "We must repay them for their fatigue," Mambai say.

The human ancestors are differentiated by the gifts they receive from Father Heaven. To Au Sa, the firstborn, go the "nail and hammer, the bellows and forge," the equipment of the blacksmith; he wanders off to the west, and he plays little part in the stories I was told. These stories centered on the middle brother Ki Sa, who is the Hohul/Raimaus ancestor, and the lastborn, Loer Sa., Father Heaven bestows mystical powers on Ki Sa, referred to as Ki Sa's "luck and fortune." Meanwhile, the younger brother Loer Sa (from whom fair-skinned foreigners or Malaia descend) "rinses white, bathes clean" with water from a white spring; then he seizes all the regalia of political office provided by Father Heaven and disappears across the northern sea.

Storytellers from Hohul and Raimaus absorbed Portuguese colonial rule into the tale of world creation and wove it together with other stories about the ordering of the realm. In the latter, their ancestor Ki Sa engages with other mythic ancestors in a contest for precedence, which he wins through a cunning use of his mystical powers. However, "the rule is not heavy, the ban is not weighty," for the younger brother has left Ki Sa "with only rock and tree," the silent tokens of ritual authority. When he displays these to the realm, "women do not tremble and men do not fear, they stab one another and slay one another."

To end this anarchic, violent state, Ki Sa uses his mystical powers to cross the seas and confront his younger brother. On being informed of the situation in the homeland, Loer Sa hands over assorted regalia of sovereign power—named staffs, swords, drums, and a flagpole and flag. He promises that his descendants will follow later on. Ki Sa returns home, where "women and men tremble and fear" when he displays the new tokens. Storytellers conclude: "Then the rule was heavy and the ban was weighty."

Hohul and Raimaus people claimed precedence on the grounds that their ancestors had acquired symbols of rule from the Malaia, who later returned to Timor as the supreme political rulers, the paramount "stranger king." But the figure of the "stranger king" also has a local incarnation in the form of Mambai ancestors who come from outside Ki Sa's realm; Hohul and Raimaus people claim that their ancestors "turned over the rule" to these indigenous newcomers, the chiefs of Aileun.

Mambai asserted this claim repeatedly, with considerable passion, and they continue to invoke it today. Yet in contrast to the epic story about the Malaia, stories of these local events seemed thin. Once having structured the realm, Hohul and Raimaus people say, their ancestors simply grew old and weary; they "sat down to look after the rock and watch over the tree," retaining their ritual function, while they "handed over the rule," embodied in the named staffs, drums, and flags from overseas, to newcomers who had settled in an origin village known as Bandeira Fun. When an ancestor of this village died, a well-known story goes, his head turned into a twisted tree, *ai-leun,* from which the newcomers' kingdom takes its name, Aileun. The name was subsequently extended to the larger colonially created administrative district of Aileu.[4]

One way of understanding the indigenous political system is in terms of a binary relationship between a passive spiritual authority, who links the realm to life-giving cosmic forces, and an active political ruler, who regulates human affairs. Spiritual authority involves what I call "interiority": its representatives are oriented to the older, inner realm of silent, nonhuman persons, and they are immobilized by their vigil. "I go not to the east or to the west, to the north or to the south," ritual leaders chant; "I watch over the rock, I look after the tree," their silent elder siblings, whose immobility and fixity they share. Ritual leaders represent themselves as "stupid and dense," literally closed off to external events; their worldly ignorance, however, constitutes a deeper wisdom, a knowledge of origins that is implemented in ritual. Political chiefs, by contrast, are depicted in oral poetry as mobile, vigilant sentinels who patrol the realm; their portion of ritual sacrifices is the leg ("in order to walk"), and they are called "dog-nosed and bird-eyed" in formal ritual speech. Where spiritual wisdom involves a condition of impenetrability, political executives are portrayed as sharp-sensed, open, and receptive, attuned to the ever-changing outside world they oversee.

The imagery of complementary duties is widely shared, but political chiefs and sacral leaders tend to assess their relative importance in different ways. Aileun rulers recognize the spiritual authority of Hohul and Raimaus, but not, so far as I could ever ascertain, their claim to precedence as original donors of political rule. Yet Hohul and Raimaus people take pride in their imagined role as founders of the realm and believe that Aileun suspects them of a desire to "take back the rule" their ancestors "handed over." A story that Mau Bere's younger brother Fernando told me in 2001 conveys the ambiguities, as seen in Hohul.[5]

Some years before my first visit, Fernando recounted, Hohul had begun rebuilding its sacred houses. As is customary, they also planned to replace the flagpole, a token of their ancestor's quest overseas, and they had cut down a tree for this purpose. But the Aileun rulers protested: "Hohul is not Koronel," they said; "that office is ours," and they ordered Hohul to transport the fallen tree to their village.[6] When the people tried to obey, the tree turned into a snake and glided back toward Hohul, where it became a tree once more. They tried again to remove it, but it grew too heavy to lift, so they left it where it was and continued rebuilding their houses. When the houses were ready, the tree grew light, and so they brought it into the village, carved it, and erected it in its customary place.

In this story, the tree pole knows its proper place, literally and metaphorically. Hohul people refer to it as the "trunk of rule" and say it is their task to "steady the trunk." The word *fu*, "trunk, base, source, origin, cause," links the idea of origins to the image of a tree (Fox 1996:5–8). Hohul and Raimaus people often contrast their position as "trunk-holders" to that of political executives, the Aileun chiefs and above them the Malaia, who "hold the tip of rule," that is, the flag. One implication of the metaphor is that while rule may have many "tips," it has a single trunk. To Hohul and Raimaus people, their status as guardians of the trunk authorized them to legitimize new successors to office.

These ideas about the transmission of rule took on heightened significance after April 1974, when the Carnation Revolution overthrew the Caetano regime in Portugal and the new Portuguese government embarked on a program of rapid decolonization. In Dili, three political parties were rapidly formed, Fretilin, UDT, and Apodeti, their programs based respectively on national independence, federation with Portugal, and integration into Indonesia.[7] Both Fretilin and UDT sought support in the countryside, and a lively debate was soon under way. At the Raimaus house-building ceremony I was attending, people framed the political situation in terms drawn from myth, as a problem of succession. Their "younger brothers," people said, had "grown old and weary" and would have to "surrender the rule" to younger, fleeter heirs. Many people voiced fears of a return to the anarchic past; Hohul and Raimaus people warned that such fears would be realized unless all the parties assembled at their villages, for the guardians of the trunk to legitimize the chosen successor.

By November 1974, when I left Timor, the Aileun rulers had declared their support for Fretilin, but many people remained uncertain. A year later, a UDT coup disrupted the decolonization process. Aileu town was the site of a Portuguese military training center; Fretilin forces seized its arsenal and distributed the weapons to the local populace, who helped them turn back a UDT force advancing from neighboring Ermera.[8] The Portuguese colonial administration abandoned the island during the fighting and ignored repeated requests from the Fretilin victors to return and resume the decolonization process. Under the escalating threat of an Indonesian invasion, Fretilin unilaterally declared independence on December 3, 1975. Over the years that followed, Mambai learned that unlike other tokens of office, the national flag could not be bestowed by old leaders on new ones. It would have to be won through the suffering and sacrifice of "the people."

OCCUPATION AND RESISTANCE

At the time of the invasion, Indonesian authorities forced UDT leaders to sign a letter calling on Indonesia to restore order.[9] In fact, the civil fighting was over well before the Indonesians intervened, and the coerced character of the "invitation" was evident to the East Timorese. Rather then ending chaos, the invaders unleashed it, and the scale and force of their invasion undercut any effort to frame it as the arrival of peace-bringing stranger-kings.

The district of Aileu's reputation as a Fretilin stronghold put the population at high risk; the majority abandoned their homes and gardens and retreated into the mountains behind Fretilin's armed wing, Falantil. For the next three years, people moved between Fretilin base camps, homes of relatives, and their ancestral origin villages. My friends characterized the situation as living "in the forest," and they would list in detail the wild plants they ate to survive; they told harrowing stories of fleeing from place to place, describing their itineraries with the precision characteristic of ancestral origin narratives. Many Hohul men, especially those from houses that represent Hohul to the outside, joined the armed resistance.[10] Mau Bere led a small band of kinsmen, until an Indonesian squad trapped them on top of a cliff, without food or water, and forced them to surrender. Fernando told me that their captors were especially pleased with Mau Bere's hunting knife, a farewell gift from me.

In 1978, the Indonesians mounted a new campaign based on saturation bombing and encirclement of the population; unable to protect their civilian followers, Fretilin encouraged them to surrender and transformed itself into a guerrilla force (Taylor 1999; Dunn 2003). When they surrendered, people told me, they would emphasize their humble status, declaring that they had fled out of fear rather than allegiance to Fretilin, as anyone even suspected of Fretilin sympathies was at risk of being arrested and killed. The risk, however, persisted. Civilians were subjected to arbitrary arrests, torture, disappearances, intensive surveillance, and other forms of state terror, while immigrants from other islands were favored. Had the occupiers treated them well, many people assured me, they could have come to accept Indonesian rule in time. People readily acknowledged Indonesia's material contributions and contrasted them to Portugal's chronic neglect. Indeed, the Indonesians were determined to outdo their colonial predecessors, and they invested heavily in roads and schools, largely but not only for purposes of control (Anderson 1998:134–135). What precluded accommodation was the regime's murderous hostility toward the indigenous population. As one Mambai friend put it to me: "We saw that they wanted the land, but not its people."

On one occasion in 2001, I asked my old friend Mau Balen of Raimaus and my "sister" Fatima if they regarded Indonesians as "Malaia." The query elicited heated denials. They declared in unison that Indonesians were not Malaia because they are "black like us." When I observed that they referred to Africans as "black Malaia," Fatima countered that Africans came from overseas, like white Malaia, whereas Indonesians came "by land." But Indonesia, I protested, was comprised of many islands and was at least technically "overseas"; Fatima grudgingly conceded the point, but even so, she maintained, they referred to other islanders by their particular provenance, as "Javanese" or "Balinese," and so on, not as Malaia.[11] When I continued to look quizzical, they shifted to behavioral distinctions. Indonesians were not Malaia, they said, because they had brought war rather than peace to the land. Mau Balen pointed out that the invaders' claim to have come as helpers in 1975 was immediately belied by the sheer force of their arrival, with ships, planes, and guns that could fire from Dili to Aileu. Fatima, still pondering the sea–land distinction, added that they referred to the continuing stream of immigrants by the Indonesian term *pendatang*, "settlers," which she glossed as uninvited guests; people who "just come" and who "travel by land."

I repeated the exercise with various people who gave similar responses, excluding Indonesians from the category of Malaia and from the position of stranger-king. Another way people set the Indonesians apart was by identifying them as descendants of Au Sa, the blacksmith eldest brother. Like the Malaia, Au Sa's descendants are "returning outsiders," but they lack the qualifications of a ruler (which can be logically expressed as coming "by land" rather than from overseas). Au Sa, of course, is also black, like the peoples of the land. Even before the invasion, Mambai frequently rejected the idea of integration into Indonesia on the grounds that "black ruling black is no good." Such assertions, I think, have less to do with internalized racism than with the old ideology of rule, which posits the *difference* between the interiority of ritual leaders and the exteriority of political leaders as the condition of political order.

On the one hand, the Indonesian regime's systematic corruption and use of state-sponsored violence demonstrated its lack of the exteriority expected of a political ruler, who should be a perceptive and impartial arbitrator of

disputes. On the other hand, in place of the interiority of a properly immobilized ritual leader, Indonesians displayed negative forms of inwardness
that showed their intellectual and moral limitations. Fernando once compared the Indonesians to an eldest son who stays at home while his younger
sibling goes away to broaden himself through study. Mau Balen used poetic language to portray Au Sa as reclusive and inhospitable: "He fears the
whinny of the horse, fears the jangle of the bridle"; instead of welcoming
guests with generous gifts, he shuts himself in, refusing the spirit of reciprocity that organizes Mambai social life.[12]

Ideological legitimation of Portuguese colonial rule had never precluded
criticism of colonial attitudes and policies; indeed, people often criticized
the Portuguese for treating their Timorese kin like wild animals (Traube
1995). But the identification of the Indonesian occupiers with an ancestor
who was black, older, and of the land neatly amplified their categorical un-
fitness for political rule and provided symbolic resources for a particularly
bitter critique. In principle, Au Sa's identification as blacksmith elder brother
could have come to symbolize a benevolent, modernizing state, but under
the brutal conditions of the occupation it evoked the combination of material power with moral inferiority that many people perceived in the Indonesian regime.

Such symbolic practices helped deflect official efforts to instill a spirit of
Indonesian nationalism, which were admittedly weak at best, at the same
time as they strengthened an oppositional nationalist identity that might
otherwise have been diffused. Mambai portrayals of the occupiers belong
to the "arts of resistance" (Scott 1990), cultural forms through which the
dominant are portrayed in ways that reaffirm the moral superiority of the
dominated. Under the Indonesian occupation, moreover, local communities
of resistance came to imagine themselves as part of a wider national community, bound together by shared suffering. Once independence became a
reality, the ordeals that ordinary people had undergone during the occupation became a moral currency, empowering them to make claims on the new
state.

THE PURCHASERS OF THE NATION

I returned to Aileu in 2001, during the UN transitional administration. Sixteen parties, including Fretilin, had been recognized by UNTAET and were
authorized to compete in the upcoming constitutional election.[13] In this proliferation of parties, many Mambai professed to see not democratic freedom
but a troubling, potentially dangerous disunity. People were quick to point
out that party formation had led to violent conflict in 1975 and they expressed concern that the past would be repeated. Deep suspicion of political
elites fueled that anxiety. Party leaders or "big people" were widely accused

of pursuing status rather than the collective good. "They are merely looking for their own chairs," was the common and bitter assessment, and they had formed parties as a means to that end. Speakers often asserted that "the people" had not sacrificed themselves for parties, with their individual flags, but for the national flag, which they had "purchased" with their blood.

Mau Balen once offered a splendid commentary on the distinction. He began by comparing party flags to "white blood" or semen—a substance that, as he and Mau Bere had once labored to explain to me, is only productive when it is combined with female menstrual blood, *lar maten*, literally "dead blood." He went on to explain that behind party flags there is "just talk," the weightless discourse of elites who droned on about their programs and promises. Like white blood, he said, such discourse was unproductive by itself. It took the blood shed by "the people" to produce the flag of the nation.

Although Mau Balen's imagery was unique, the populist sentiment he expressed was widely shared and has persisted in the post-independence era. Mambai often use the idiom of differential suffering to evaluate belongingness to the nation. Recently returned diasporans were especially vulnerable to exclusion. It was understood that some exiles had been active in the resistance and had fled to save their lives, but the *capacity* to leave distinguished them from "the people." Mobility, in the form of access to planes, boats, and passports, was often framed as a mark of privilege. "The people" had no such resources, and for those who had remained behind, whatever suffering homesick exiles might have endured abroad could not equal their own. Nor was the charge that so-and-so had not truly suffered reserved for returned diasporans; it could be directed against any leader a speaker disapproved of, mistrusted, or opposed. With a few exceptions, party leaders were accused of "using the people's name" without having shared in their suffering.

Speakers who identified or affiliated with "the people" would often represent them as "stupid" (*beik*) in contrast to educated (*matenek*) elites. At one level, "stupidity" referenced the widespread illiteracy among the rural masses, which many people described as a social problem.[14] In figurative usage, however, the stupidity of "the people" took on positive connotations; it signified a form of popular wisdom or common sense, while formal learning was characterized as a mode of stupidity. The most egregious forms of elite stupidity, according to popular opinion, were evidenced in the competitive disunity that characterized *politika*—politics—a term used almost exclusively in the negative sense of maneuvering for power and advantage. Critics pointed to the squabbling and bickering among party leaders as symptomatic of the discord and division that resulted from the political pursuit of self-interest. By contrast, "the people" were said to understand the need for inclusive unity and to be already unified in their demands: what they expected from the state was assistance in securing "their livelihood," which depended on agriculture. "The people do not care about politics!" Mau Balen would often exclaim. "All they want is their livelihood."

In such everyday talk about "the people" who admonish political elites to put aside self-interest and see to the collective welfare, we hear an echo of old distinctions between political and spiritual leaders, but with "the people" in the latter's position. Both traditional ritual leaders and the people embody forms of "interiority," a condition that binds its possessors to the land and imposes on them a "stupidity" that is also a form of wisdom. Like ritual authorities, the people are symbolically associated with fixity, immobility, and constancy. Although they lack formal knowledge, they have a practical understanding of national needs, especially the need for unity. The people also understand that agricultural productivity is the precondition of a vibrant nation. Where the agricultural rites staged by sacral leaders symbolically reunited the realm, the people embody the unity of the nation constructed in the liberation struggle. Above all, the people resemble ritual authorities through their productive suffering. Their painful "purchase" of the national flag evokes the ideology of animist rituals wherein those who suffer to bring something forth must be repaid for their "fatigue."

On East Timor, the post-independence years have seen a breakdown of trust in the national leadership, which the 2007 parliamentary elections failed to overcome (McWilliam and Bexley 2008:79). Indeed, East Timorese political leaders face an ideological dilemma: whereas indigenous political culture once legitimized outsider-rulers, legitimacy now depends on claims to insider status that very few political elites can authenticate. But frustration with the state is one marker of the strength of popular nationalism. From the vantage point of the national community, the state is obligated to provide for the collective welfare; its perceived failure to do so leaves the people in the position of the donor and defines their suffering as an unreciprocated gift. Today the legitimacy of the national-state depends on its willingness to repay those who suffered and sacrificed to bring forth the nation.

NOTES

1. The Democratic Republic of Timor Leste (RDTL) was officially declared on May 20, 2002.

2. Mambai refer to Heaven's act as the "ban of the mountains"; it constitutes a cosmic law that people contrast with the rule over human beings that is brought back from the sea.

3. See Graham Harvey's (2006) usage of "animism" to designate codes of respectful behavior toward nonhuman persons.

4. I use *Aileun* to designate the kingdom and *Aileu* for the administrative district and its capital town. Mambai are fond of pointing out that *Ai-leun*, (that is, the twisted tree), "is not in Aileu (the administrative center), but in Bandeira Fun."

5. Mau Bere had died two years before my first return visit.

6. During the colonial period the Portuguese granted military patents to local chiefs as a means of establishing alliances; the term *koronel* derives from this practice.

7. Fretilin's acronym stands for the Revolutionary Front for the Independence of East Timor; the name was modeled on that of the Mozambican liberation movement Frelimo; UDT stood for Timorese Democratic Union, and Apodeti was the acronym for the Timorese Popular Democratic Association.

8. The founders of UDT were major landholders in Ermera, which became the party's base. To what extent the Aileu resistance to the Ermera force was motivated by nationalism or localism is difficult to say.

9. Dated November 30, 1975, the text had actually been prepared in Bali in August by the Indonesian secrete service and Timorese collaborators. The text demanded the integration of the territory into Indonesia and asked for help from the Indonesian government to this end. Many UDT leaders had fled to Indonesia after the failure of the coup; they were required to sign in order to be allowed to return to East Timor (Durand 2001:109).

10. Several Raimaus men (including Mau Balen's brother Mateus) also joined the armed resistance; but Raimaus became involved with a prophetic movement, and its leader promised to drive the Indonesians out through mystical means. I have described this movement elsewhere (Traube 2007).

11. Fatima, who is high school–educated, was certainly familiar with the geography of the region; Mau Balen is illiterate and, I suspect, the primary referent of "Indonesia" for him may be western Timor.

12. In a lighter vein, people professed to be offended by the Javanese practice of packing up food presented at ceremonies and taking it home to consume in private.

13. To UN "nation builders," a multiparty system is both a sign and instrument of democratization, and many East Timorese elites also believed that unless new parties were encouraged, Fretilin, with its immense cachet, would unduly dominate the political process. Popular opinion, however, remained largely antagonistic to party division.

14. Some individuals also portrayed their lack of formal educational qualifications as the result of their commitment to the resistance, on the dual grounds that their participation in resistance activities had taken time and energy away from schoolwork, and that the regime had awarded collaborators with educational opportunities while penalizing families suspected of supporting the resistance.

20

The Question of Collaborators: Moral Order and Community in the Aftermath of the Khmer Rouge

Eve Monique Zucker

AN EPILOGUE AS PRELUDE

It was near to the end of my fieldwork in Cambodia when Pu [Uncle] Thon offered to take me to see the sites that had comprised the old village of O'Thmaa before Pol Pot came and everything was destroyed.[1] The original village had consisted of four parts, each with its own place name and located at a distance from each other. Each part contained a group of households whose members were related by birth or marriage. Unlike today when the houses line the main road, the four parts formed a loose arc that together formed O'Thmaa village.

On the morning of the tour, we set off on the oxcart road behind my house passing the Thmaa Khmouch or ghost/spirit rock on our right. The base of this boulder is littered with old bottles and ancient ceramic jugs and bowls, which had been used as receptacles for the ash remains of ancestors that the villagers say lived perhaps a century ago. Turning westward, we continued until we reached a stretch of rice paddy where the first of these homesteads once stood. Pu Thon explained:

> This place was called Bung Srei. There were four houses here. . . . In the house of Yiey [Grandmother] Hom there were four people originally; now no one is left. Her two children, both Khmer Rouge soldiers from 1970 to 1972, were accused by someone from the village, not a Khmer Rouge, of being White Khmer and killed. One of these sons was married to Yiey Na, the daughter of Ta [Grandfather] Som.
>
> The next is the house of Yiey Na and no one is left. She was the daughter of Ta Sok. Her husband who was the son of Yiey Hom was a Khmer Rouge soldier but was killed after being accused by a villager of being White Khmer.

We continued westward toward the O'Thmaa creek and came to Ta En's garden near the giant mango trees and small stream:

This place is O'Ta Rom and is named after the ancestor guardian spirit named Rom. We believed in these spirits before the war. There were three houses here. The first was the house of Von. His wife is Yiey Oak.

Pu Thon told me that Von was a member of the Khmer Rouge who had his head cut off by the American-backed government under Lon Nol (1970–1975). The Lon Nol Government was at war with the Khmer Rouge, who were fighting a revolutionary war to seize power in the country and install an extremist Marxist-Leninist-inspired government that later decimated over one-fifth of the population (approximately 1.7 million people) in an effort to "cleanse" the nation. The Khmer Rouge Regime lasted from 1975 to 1979 under the leadership of Pol Pot.
Pu Thon's narrative continues:

> Lon Nol's soldiers cut off Von's head and sent it to their commander. It was the custom at that time. Von was a Khmer Rouge soldier who had gone to the "Struggle in the Forest" [he had joined the revolutionary movement that was based in the forests] with the Khmer Rouge in the late 1960s. He was the first cousin of Cheun. All of his family is dead except Yiey Oak and her son Som.
> Next is the house of Ta Chan. He was the village chief under Sihanouk [the monarch who held power before being ousted by Lon Nol] and first cousin of Ta Von. Chan's daughter married Ta En. Chan worked with Ta Kam who was the deputy village chief. Both were village chiefs for a long time. Chan was killed by Lon Nol. Everyone in his family is now dead except two daughters; one here in the village who is married to Ta En, and the other in Sre Ambel. His wife died of illness.

And so the tour continued, with each household having lost some, or all, of its members to the Khmer Rouge, Lon Nol, or each other. I tell this story here to start at the place where the old society ended. And now the story I tell begins.

INTRODUCTION

The villagers were only beginning to recover from the terror and devastation of the 1970s when the Khmer Rouge entered the highland village of O'Thmaa and its surrounding communities, having recently returned to their villages in late 1998. This homecoming has not been easy. In addition to having to physically rebuild their village, villagers also had to reestablish the village as a moral entity, a community based on sets of mostly kin ties, forming a reciprocal web of obligations among people.[2]
Much of the work on the aftermath of violence and the healing process that has followed has focused on the individual or collective "memory" of

violence (Antze and Lambek 1996; Rittner and Roth 1993; Robben and Suárez-Orozco 2000). I focused on how aspects of the moral order that were broken or damaged were being repaired in efforts to heal from the past. How were the actions and roles of collaborators linked to their social and moral position within the community, and how did this positioning vary across communities?

BACKGROUND TO RESEARCH

My research spanned two neighboring communities in a mountainous region of Kompong Speu province in southwestern Cambodia. The first of these two communes I call Prei Phnom and the second I call Doung Srei. Each of them consists of a collection of villages. I based myself in Prei Phnom's westernmost village, which I call O'Thmaa, bordering on the wilderness of the Cardamom mountain range. I made regular excursions to the other villages in Prei Phnom commune as well as to several in Doung Srei.

At the time of my research in 2003, O'Thmaa had a population of 175 people dispersed over 40 households. There were few elders in the community, especially men, because of the war and the large number of executions that had occurred within the village in the early 1970s. From 1970 until the mid-1990s, all men and many women old enough to become soldiers were conscripted by the Khmer Rouge, the government, or both. This lack of elders had significant repercussions for this community, where elders were considered the symbolic vessels of moral and traditional knowledge and therefore played important roles in the transmission and practice of religious and social events. Moral knowledge is acquired over a lifetime; such knowledge is considered to be wisdom in old age. Being morally wise means not only knowing right from wrong but also knowing the ways of the ancestors who are considered imbued with the best moral qualities, including honesty, wisdom, and virtue. An elder in Cambodia symbolically becomes like a living, and therefore accessible, ancestor.

The vast majority of villagers in the communities where I worked considered themselves Theravada Buddhists; however, 10 percent of O'Thmaa's population were Methodist Christians. Indigenous animist and Hindu "Brahman" practices interlaced the practices of villagers of both of these faiths. These villagers occupied the lowest ranks of Cambodia's socioeconomic ladder due to high illiteracy rates, continuous forced displacement since 1970, a shortage of arable land, and an overall lack of resources. Before the war they cultivated small rice paddies and gardens, and subsidized their living through trade in forest products such as resin, aloewood, and betel. Today people again tend rice paddies and gardens, but at the point of my study had been unable to grow sufficient rice and food to sustain them throughout the year. Instead, they relied on the illicit sale of forest products and aid from development agencies.

A HISTORY OF CONFLICT

The geographic locale of the community has also had significant historical consequences for its residents. The area is mountainous, forested, and only thirty km from the main highway, making it an ideal base for guerrilla warfare campaigns. The villagers explained to me that the area was put to this use in three separate historical instances. The first of these episodes took place in the late 1940s and early 1950s when the Khmer Independence movement (Khmei Issarak), with the support of the Vietnamese, used the area as a base from which to launch guerrilla attacks on the French colonial government. Later in the late 1960s and early 1970s, the area was taken again, this time by the Khmer Rouge and by the North Vietnamese. During this period, the Khmer Rouge established a base of operations in the area under one of their top leaders, famous for his brutality. The Khmer Rouge conscripted villagers at this time as soldiers and local leaders.

According to the villagers, the Vietnamese presence in the area lasted only a little more than a year, but the Khmer Rouge entrenched themselves and began implementing their insidious policies while continuing their fight through the American bombings of 1973, and onward. Between late 1970 and early 1972, the majority of villagers initially joined the Khmer Rouge up on a nearby mountain to flee the war and the Lon Nol government army. After a brief return to the village, most were forcibly evacuated by the Khmer Rouge to a cooperative where they were forced to eat, work, and sleep collectively. In April 1975, the civil war ended with a Khmer Rouge victory. They called their new state Democratic Kampuchea, which lasted four years until 1979 when Vietnam seized power. In its four years of existence, Pol Pot and his cohort exercised torture, mass executions, starvation, and devastation on the people of Cambodia, leaving close to two million people dead. When Vietnam took the country, the Khmer Rouge (including soldiers from the village) were forced to flee to the Thai border. However, by the late 1980s the Khmer Rouge had regained a foothold in this village region, making it a base and a battle zone up through the mid- to late 1990s.

The historical significance of the region is implied in the name the Khmer Rouge bestowed on it: Prei Brayut, or "The Forest of the Struggle," the place from which they launched and fought their revolution. Later the region became known as a "base" (*moulitan*) area, a place that came under Khmer Rouge control relatively early in the revolution, and from which they conscripted their soldiers and low-level leaders. These "base people" or "old people" were considered less corrupt than the "new people" of the urban centers, who were believed to have been contaminated by foreign ideologies (Him 2000; Kiernan 1996; Pin and Man 2000; Ung 2000).

Through all of this, most of the surviving people from the commune where I stayed were forcibly relocated numerous times. It was not until the 1990s that the residents resettled their villages; most villagers did not return to O'Thmaa until after 1998 when they began to rebuild their lives after nearly thirty years of absence.

TA KAM: THE STORY OF A VILLAGE ELDER

What follows is the story of one recent returnee to the village who I call Ta Kam. His story is told from three vantage points: mine, the villagers', and his own.

My Story of Ta Kam

It was on my first journey to O'Thmaa that I met Ta [grandfather] Kam. I found him constructing a bamboo platform for his thatched hut on the side of the village's northern slope. His face and body, both lean and angular from a lifetime of work and poverty, were topped by closely cropped silver hair that contrasted with the dark caramel of his skin. Ta Kam explained that he had only just returned to O'Thmaa. He had been born in this village and owned a parcel of land through his first wife, but lived in Doung Srei with his sister's family. He had returned to O'Thmaa to help his daughter farm.

At the time, I found his homecoming extraordinary for it brought into stark relief the rupture and continuity that seemed to characterize this village. I thought that it must have been a profound experience for him to return to see those he had known since his childhood and perhaps with whom he had had little contact for two or three decades. Ta Kam had said he was seventy-eight, and so I asked him about an old woman I had met earlier in the village, who appeared roughly the same age. He said only that he knew her and that she was a bit older than him. I found this strange in a village with such a small population. . . . Surely he must have more of a sense of connection with her. But he said little about her and seemed to dismiss the topic.

I did not meet Ta Kam again for four months. I made several attempts to visit him but was repeatedly told that he was away in the forest or the other commune. One rainy September evening I decided to try again. Remembering his hospitality, I was looking forward to seeing him and so I was quite pleased to find him at home that evening. Unfortunately Ta Kam was ill and my companion and I found him lying on the raised platform of his hut when we arrived. Even so, he welcomed us with warmth and grace. Ta Kam's manner was reminiscent of the archetypal traditional Khmer elder—

grandfatherly, self-effacing, wise, and kind. On a later visit, he agreed to tell me his life story.

After that I did not meet with Ta Kam for several months, but would catch occasional glimpses of him along the road with his worn red-and-white checked *kramar* (scarf) tied into a small bundle and slung over his shoulder. He was always dressed the same, in a threadbare white shirt, mid-length trousers, and wide-brimmed hat; he would be clutching a walking staff. Thin, gaunt, poorly attired, and making incredibly long treks under Cambodia's sweltering sun, he gave the appearance of an ascetic or pilgrim.

Over time, I learned a bit more about him. I was told that he often attended ceremonies at the temple in Doung Srei commune where he served as an *achaa* (Buddhist layman) and that he was related by blood (*sach-chiem*) as well as marriage (*sach-tlay*) to most of the people of the village. Nonetheless, I also observed that he had little or no interaction with the other villagers. No one seemed to show much interest or regard for him, unlike his daughter who seemed to enjoy good relations with most villagers. It was only much later that I was able to understand Ta Kam's peculiar relationship with the villagers.

Their Story of Ta Kam

In the final months of my fieldwork, the village development chief,[3] Sau, whom I knew quite well, and I were discussing the executions that had occurred in the village in the early 1970s after the Khmer Rouge had come to the area. I remarked how I had noticed there were a disproportionate number of widows (26 percent of village households at the time were headed by widows)[4] in O'Thmaa as compared to other villages in the area. Agreeing, Sau explained:

> During that time they had a chief like I am today. He wanted to have a good face and so he would issue complaints against people here to the commune leadership and they believed him. They would come then and catch these people and take them away to kill them. . . . Some of the people committed no wrong—but he accused them anyway to gain face (reputation). That village chief was Ta Kam.

Ta Kam, whom I had perceived as a warm, grandfatherly elder was in fact a killer—a collaborator.

After this it must not have taken long for word to spread that I now knew about this village secret, for I began to hear stories from other villagers as well. I learned that Ta Kam had been the vice village chief under Lon Nol and then was elected by the villagers to be the acting village chief under the Khmer Rouge. Ta Kam thus doubly betrayed the villagers. As leader he would have been expected to behave morally and offer the villagers some protection in exchange for their support. He not only failed to do this but also transgressed his role by sacrificing them to promote his own welfare and longevity. Ta Kam had now become in the words of one villager: "that Ta, who caught the people to take to kill."

Viewed as a killer of his own people, Ta Kam was shunned by the villagers. He did not speak or talk with anyone beyond his daughter and was notably absent at the annual village harvest festival. One former Khmer Rouge soldier who had lost his father to Ta Kam explained the present-day relationship between the villagers and Ta Kam as follows:

> That Ta, he doesn't dare to look at anyone young or old in the face. No one really likes him either. They don't want to be friendly with him; they hate him. If people wanted to they could take revenge (*songsuck*) against him at any time. But people think it is over now and so they don't want to fight and claim or demand (*tiem tia*) retribution for their parents' blood.

I now understood why no one would talk to Ta Kam when he came to the village and why he was rarely mentioned. People saw him as lacking morality and concerned only for his own promotion and welfare. In other words, they said he was ambitious in the negative sense, meaning that he willfully sought to better his position at the expense of others, was ignorant, and did not know right from wrong. Ta Kam sacrificed his neighbors and kinsmen to the Khmer Rouge and yet, remarkably, the children and wives of those he killed did not seek revenge. They said the past was behind them and they had no desire to continue fighting, suggesting that they have found a means by which to heal from their wounds, even if Ta Kam's living presence still continued to haunt them as a reminder of their lost loved ones.

Over time people were willing to share their stories with me, but they were still reticent about talking about Ta Kam. When they spoke about that terrible episode in the past they more often commented that the people of that generation committed evil deeds against one another for reasons that are not understood. One might anticipate that the villagers would also shun Ta Kam's daughter, but instead she enjoyed warm social relations with most villagers. This appeared antithetical to the idea that families are morally affiliated, an idea that informed the practice of arrests and executions under the Khmer Rouge in O'Thmaa when cadres and their entire families, including babies, were arrested and killed as traitors. This view of families seems to stem from broader Khmer beliefs about kinship ties in hierarchical relations of politics and violence. Not blaming the family as a whole provided villagers with another means of healing; the tear in the community was contained through their welcoming of the daughter. Because most villagers were related to Ta Kam by blood or by marriage, there was a vested interest in keeping his family within the community while surgically removing him.

Ta Kam's Story of Himself

It is important to humanize Ta Kam, for he is actually a real person and it is as such that villagers related to him, and because his story contextualizes the village's circumstances.

Ta Kam was born in O'Thmaa in 1923 to a family that had lived in the area for generations. Like other villagers at the time, most of his children died in infancy; later, a son taken by the Khmer Rouge died under Pol Pot. Ta Kam said he had relations in every village across the two communes, but when asked about his relations in O'Thmaa he said there was only his daughter and a couple of nephews. His account of his childhood was sparse. There was no school. He helped his parents tend their rice paddy and garden and helped collect forest products for consumption and trade. One of the significant events that Ta Kam remembers from his childhood was seeing a French hunter astride an elephant, accompanied by some Khmer soldiers. He explained that he hid himself in the forest at the time because he feared the Frenchman just as he would fear soldiers or policemen. In another act of evasion, he later avoided an encounter with a delegation sent from the district governor's office to conscript boys for military service. These encounters with outsiders of higher social rank and representing larger systems of power are important in understanding Ta Kam's later acts and the history of the village.

When Issarak and Vietnamese forces entered the area during the war of independence, Ta Kam was forced to flee with other villagers to the mountains in the north for four years. At age thirty-five, he went to work at a nearby mountain where the former king Norodom Sihanouk was building a residence. He recalls that there were twenty households in O'Thmaa when he left and twenty-five by the time the Khmer Rouge had entered the area in early 1970, when he was forty-seven. "Then," Ta Kam explained, "Pol Pot came to the area and they were killing everyone except me and a few others who managed to survive." He said he had not seen these other survivors since that time.

He continued with this period from 1970 to 1975, a particularly bloody chapter in O'Thmaa's history:

> Before 1975 I didn't do any work [meaning he held no special position]. I was just like other people, someone eking out a living. The war happened and some people fled to the forest, but I didn't. After that the Khmer Rouge pushed me to drive a cart and carry cloth, rice seed, and other stuff [again, he was not in a position of power].

Ta Kam later admitted that he had fled to the forest, but qualified this by saying: "Here we had a lot of trouble and had to flee to the mountains to live."

When I asked him whether he was ever made to be the village chief, he stated he had not, and that he had "always gone to the temple." He said he had never been a monk, but at the request of Doung Srei's temple monks and laymen he had served the monastery there as part of an effort to look after his next life.

THE PROBLEM OF THE COLLABORATOR AND A LACK OF ELDERS

In Ta Kam's life narrative he presented himself as a passive entity subject to the will of more powerful circumstances. The villagers do not agree. They said that he was elected by them to be village chief and he accepted the position. He was not forcibly conscripted by the Khmer Rouge. For them, he was not a victim but an opportunist who, motivated by ambition, perpetrated acts against his own people. Moreover, his actions were directed locally on his extended kin and community, violating the tacit collective identity of villagers as victims of outsiders and circumstance. Up to now, villagers had not talked openly about Ta Kam's place within village history. As a member of the former village he was one of them, and therefore his actions were in some sense viewed as a reflection on the villagers' character as a whole. Yet he was also no longer one of them, as he himself had chosen to live elsewhere. The villagers were apparently willing to see him socially erased. Ta Kam could not be forgiven as a victim of circumstance, for he violated the terms of this discourse by transgressing a boundary of insiders and outsiders.

Ta Kam's presence, however, is not the only obstacle to the village's recovery from the trauma of the past. There is also a problem of absence of elders—that is, moral elders. People say that Prei Phnom "lacks elders" after the war, and that traditional knowledge and practice in this commune is therefore relatively weak. This, they say, explains why the people of Prei Phnom have lost interest in traditional practices and knowledge and instead have turned toward "modern" ideologies and ways. The commune chief of Prei Phnom explained to me:

> The young people don't know much about the ancient traditions and the old people who did are dead now. These days the younger folks are into popular modern ideas.

Historical texts suggest that in Cambodia the restoration of order following chaotic historical episodes is sought not by innovation, but through a return to the ancestral traditions of the past (Chandler 1998). Prei Phnom has an inadequate number of elders to transmit the cultural heritage that might fill in and enrich the present. Ironically, Ta Kam is one of the few remaining elders of O'Thmaa. As one of the oldest members of the original village, he is well versed in its traditional knowledge, practices, myths, and stories. However, because of his own past, his knowledge is inaccessible to the next generation for it is tainted.

To sum up, Ta Kam represents a blockage to the remaking of moral order in several ways. First, his presence prevents people from forgetting the treacherous past of the village. Second, he blocks the transmission of an older moral order since he cannot legitimately pass on traditional knowledge. Third, he opposes the moral order itself by having inverted the structural order that places elders and ancestors in a morally elevated position. And finally, his presence reminds people of his role in the painful loss of their loved ones.

It may seem uncanny, then, that Ta Kam acts as a Buddhist layman in the neighboring commune, where he serves the needs of the monastery. Ta Kam himself describes no rupture in his telling explanation of his religious activities: "I am only looking after my next life." For him, it seems, the process of mending the moral order is less problematic than it is for the children of his victims, and one wonders whether he ever really perceived a breach in it in the first place.

CONCLUSION

Local collaborators such as Ta Kam pose difficulties to the process of rebuilding the social and moral order of villages such as O'Thmaa. However, villagers have found some means of reconstructing their communities and rebuilding trust in the wake of decades of violence, forced evacuations, destruction of families, and betrayal by members of their own community. Through such acts as forgiving soldiers on both sides by invoking a narrative of "victims of circumstance," or by practicing forgiveness through the acceptance of Ta Kam's daughter into the community, we see an effort to heal the wounds of the past. Finally and significantly, we also see that despite the opportunity to avenge the deaths of their loved ones by retaliating against Ta Kam, villagers have turned away from violence in an effort to allow healing and move on with their lives.

EPILOGUE

This chapter was based on fieldwork in 2001–2003. Having recently been back to the village (2010), I find that Ta Kam has now returned to the village and his presence is accepted by the villagers. He is now nearly ninety years old and is seen by the younger generation as an elder and a Buddhist layman. This younger generation does not carry the sentiments that the older generation does; to them the Khmer Rouge past is remote. There are very few living elders left in the village who are anywhere close to Ta Kam's age. In addition, the younger generation who were children and teenagers during the Khmer Rouge time are also significantly less in number than those who are now in their twenties.

NOTES

1. The names of all personages and places in the village area have been given aliases to protect their privacy.

2. For further reading, see also Ebihara 1968; Overing 2003; Yan 1996; and Zucker 2006.

3. The village development chief is elected as leader to represent the village in matters having to do with development projects initiated by development agencies and organizations. The development chief has de facto if not de jure responsibility for handling intervillage issues and politics.

4. This figure comes from data from the Lutheran World Federation and corresponds with data collected from the village chiefs and commune offices. O'Thmaa, as the most western village, has the highest percentage of widows, followed by its two neighbors immediately to the east. This is not coincidental, for all three of these villages fell under the same leadership and were moved to the same cooperative.

PART SEVEN

Global Processes and Shifting Ecological Relations

Processes of global change are not entirely new in Southeast Asia. It has long been cosmopolitan—as "the land below the winds" implies. Sea trade was an integral part of many of the early states of Southeast Asia. In addition, the upland areas of mainland Southeast Asia were sources of significant commodities for pre-modern states in Southeast Asia and in China (Frank 1998). Nevertheless, recent history has brought modernization and an increasingly rapid pace of change. Local resources are now traded not just regionally but globally. Demand and the pace of trade have increased. Items once used in the subsistence economy have become commodities, items sold for profit. Globalization has generally resulted in great increases in wealth gaps; while once the poor could at least "eke out a living," they now must find wage work or not eat at all. Commodification is also a feature of intimate human relations, as discussed by Chris Lyttleton (chapter 21) and Michele Ford and Lenore Lyons (chapter 23). In Part 7, we outline some of the local dynamics and consequences of globalization.

A significant problem for many of the diverse peoples of Southeast Asia has been alienation of land. We have previously mentioned the role of colonial-era mapping in the formation of modern Southeast Asian states. Mapping is increasingly a vehicle for the control of indigenous populations. It entails the designation of ownership of property—particularly the designation of individual private property as an extension of state bureaucratic control. In many countries, the state declared itself the owner of any unused land, or land of certain characteristics (such as in Thailand's uplands anything over thirty degrees in slope). Ultimately, what matters is not just the system of mapping, but who controls the maps (Fox 2002; Gillogly 2004). This has meant that local farmers who had farmed an area for hundreds of years might lose formal rights to their land by failing to register for title. Tribal peoples might not have been allowed to register their land at all. And people with extensive agricultural systems lost use of land that was left fallow for upwards of ten years as it was categorized as "unused" or "wasted" by state officials (swiddening entails a long fallow system, as discussed in Gillogly in chapter 6, and mentioned in Lyttleton, chapter 21; this underlies the issues raised by Jonsson in chapter 8). This is congruent with the lowland assessment of upland (tribal) land-use systems as irrational, uncivilized, unscientific, and unproductive. In some cases, states have attempted to manage land use through schemes of forced migration or resettlement. Lyttleton's contribution discusses one such form of migration. While the Lao government might, at times, encourage or compel upland farmers to move to the lowlands in order to preserve upland resources, it is also clear that road building and towns draw people into the lowlands, despite the precarious economic existence they face. In other cases not discussed in this book, governments have moved lowland wet-rice farmers from crowded regions to "underpopulated" forested and mountainous areas. Vietnam has encouraged lowland ethnic Vietnamese farmers to move into the uplands to cultivate these areas. Similarly, the transmigration scheme of the Indonesian government is a well-known example of this policy and its effects. In these processes, a wealth of indigenous knowledge of how to manage the land can be lost; indigenous peoples are removed from ancestral lands and, when the migrants know little of how to manage soil on slopes, disastrous erosion and downstream flooding can follow.

Ford and Lyons's chapter offers a fine-grained examination of a more widespread form of migration today, migrant labor and transnational interactions. Their interviews with women who migrate to the Riau Archipelago (a part of a growth triangle with Singapore and Indonesia that is a key site for large-scale manufacturing, tourism, transport, and service industries) movingly convey the choices and constraints these women experience. They may have started out as migrant domestic workers, but for varied reasons moved into working in the informal sector as sex workers. In some cases, they ended up as the wives of former clients. Through these women's stories we gain glimpses of how those with few choices strive to "exercise agency within the structural bounds of their particular circumstances, and with varying degrees of success, at each life stage" (Ford and Lyons, chapter 23).

Kathleen Gillogly has also observed the migration of ethnic minority people from Burma to Thailand as they flee war or seek ways to make a living. The life of an international migrant laborer is precarious. Without legal papers, the wages are low and workers are vulnerable to not even being paid at all; housing can also be difficult to find without residency papers. As Lyttleton points out, another element of labor migration is the increased use of certain drugs such as methamphetamines, which increase the worker's ability to continue toiling past the body's limits.

Often states claim land for the purpose of taking over shared resources such as forests. The discourse of this control is often over management of national resources such as watersheds, rational harvesting of forest as timber for the national economy, road building in order to integrate minority peoples into the state economy and political body, and (economic) development in general. Fishing is a highly significant common pool resource for coastal and island people. Eder (2008) has discussed the shifting relationships of fisherpeople to that resource in Palawan (Philippines). There, fisheries have been stressed by commercial fishing, both large-scale corporate fishing and local fishing for the Philippine market. Many of the people he studies are migrants from other regions of the Philippines and do not follow local tradition-based management regimes. Their household economic strategies allow more severe exploitation of coastal resources. The use of modern technology for fishing (types of nets, boats, use of blasting and poisons) is discussed by Gene Amarell in chapter 24. One response to these more destructive technologies has been to establish a marine park to ensure that fish nurseries in coral reefs are not so depleted that fish populations are unable to regenerate.

Use of natural resources can be distorted when items used for local subsistence are transformed into items that can be harvested and sold for cash. The teak industry of Britain and Thailand has already destroyed the forests of northern Thailand and Burma. To this day, Burma supplies huge quantities of timber to Thailand and China—countries that have destroyed much of their own forest and restricted access to what remains through the establishment of reserves and national parks. Burma's military junta's fight with upland minority groups is waged not just over democracy and representation, but also over control of natural resources—gold, silver, precious stones, and forests. The forcible education of Semang children in Malaysian state-run schools is also a means of extending state power over previous upland resources, as well as a form of disciplining the natives to labor (see Robert Knox Dentan, Juli Edo, and Anthony Williams-Hunt, chapter 22).

Another element of shifting ecological relations is the damming of rivers. Damming allows control of water for irrigation for lowland rice, which increases production and enables selling of surplus on world markets. Much of today's dam building, however, is for the purpose of generating hydroelectricity. In 2010, protests against damming became particularly sharp, as China opened up twelve new hydroelectric dams on the Upper Mekong River. News reports claim that farmers in Vietnam and Cambodia no longer have sufficient water for their rice crops. It remains to be seen if this can be scientifically verified (it had been a dry year at the point of the protests), but it does illustrate a key point about globalization and shifting ecological relations. As China industrializes and races to join the economic powerhouses of the world, it needs electricity. But state-level decisions affect an entire watershed that crosses national boundaries. While such expansion of resource use was a feature of state economics before the modern period, the levels of use appear to be far more intensive and far-reaching than ever before. We can see this in our own everyday lives.

21

When the Mountains No Longer Mean Home

Chris Lyttleton

In the past, the mountains of Muang Sing (a small district in northern Laos bordering China and Burma) were remote and undeveloped: they lacked electricity, roads, schools, and services. That is not to say the hills were unpopulated. Close to one hundred Akha villages were to be found in this area, built into hillsides at high elevation (in part, to protect from malarial mosquitoes) in clusters of around thirty to fifty households. Several years ago one could still venture a few hours' walk from small towns in the valleys and come across Akha men, women, and children tending to broad tracts of poppies in fields cut from hillside forests. Both the forests and opium were central to everyday Akha life. The Akha and other minority ethnic groups had been cultivating poppies for more than a hundred years after opium was introduced to the mountainous Upper Mekong region as part of complex colonial brinksmanship in the nineteenth century, and subsequently was encouraged by governments and local warlords as a source of profit.

In the new millennium, Muang Sing was briefly famous with Western tourists as travel books referred to it as the opium capital of the Golden Triangle. Drugs have not been the only attraction to these remote hills; traders from lowland Laos and nearby China still regularly traverse the highlands, seeking forest products for medicine and perfume as well as more obscure items such as women's hair to be used in China's booming wig industry. Whereas Akha largely used opium to exchange for lowland rice, they also earned small amounts of cash from these other forms of petty trade. Commodity culture remained scarce, however, for there were no shops and nothing to buy for many villagers; access to markets was, for many, at best a one- or two-day walk. Instead, daily routines were characterized by subsistence; local Akha families and communities gained everyday sustenance from the forest and small plots of land they sequentially cleared to plant rice (and poppies).

A few short years later, life here has changed dramatically. By 2008, remote is no longer a relevant description as new roads crisscross the Upper Mekong, bringing increased mobility and many people from different ethnicities and nationalities into regular contact with each other. Opium is barely grown in Laos anymore following strict government (and UN) mandates. The majority of local Akha no longer live in the mountains, having moved down into the valleys to engage in new livelihoods. Men do not make money from forest products to anywhere near the extent of the past. Women seldom sell their hair, instead selling old silver or newly made ethnic items to tourists, and a few occasionally gain money through more intimate contact with outside men, mainly Chinese visitors. More generally, many Akha now end up selling their labor to other ethnic groups in lowland fields, where they help to plant and harvest rice, sugar, and other market produce that mostly ends up across the nearby border in China.

In short, as subsistence fades as an adaptive strategy, modernization is bringing about a radically changed engagement with the world. In turn, subjective experience of what it means to be Akha, of what it means to pursue livelihood security, of what it means to reproduce both families and a social order, all take on new dimensions. Akha villagers actively seek certain options, such as economic accumulation. Other changes are less appealing: social hierarchy, exploitation, and ill health also accompany the difficult road to modernity in northwest Laos.

THE AKHA

The Akha are an ethnic minority group living throughout the hill areas of the Upper Mekong region. They speak a Tibeto-Burman language. Akha legend has it that they began to slowly migrate from their ancestral homeland in Tibet more than two thousand years ago into southern Szechuan and Yunnan in China. During the nineteenth and early twentieth century, they continued southward into northern Burma, northern Thailand, and northern Laos. The Akha collectively number nearly half a million (Kammerer 1998) including roughly 60,000 in the Lao provinces of Phongsaly and Luang Namtha. There are a number of different subgroups in Laos, but most speak similar dialects. In Luang Namtha, the Akha live in the forested hillsides of the Muang Sing and Muang Long districts. Overall, they are the predominant population in these districts but share valleys with lowland Lao, Tai-Lue, Tai-Dam, and a smattering of other minority groups such as Hmong and Lahu. They and a number of other ethnic groups who live in these border regions are immediately recognizable as they commonly are featured in large-scale glossy pictorial spreads in Lao, Thai, and Chinese tourist brochures due to their exotic attire, especially the women's silver-covered headdresses that can weigh up to two kg, and traditional customs such as annual fertility festivals.

Until recently Akha livelihoods in Luang Namtha were based almost entirely on highland swidden crops such as rice, opium, maize, and cotton. But since the 1990s, many Akha villages have relocated to lower slopes or valley lands, less than a day's walk to either Muang Sing or Muang Long towns. This has been partly due to a desire to access state services and markets, and partly is in response to opium prohibition and government policies that regulate shifting cultivation.

Akha social structure is patrilineal; a wife is incorporated into her husband's lineage after marriage. Sons are more desirable than daughters: "It is by producing a son that a man ensures not only the continuation of his direct patriline for at least one generation but also his own ascendance after death to the ranks of the ancestors in that patriline" (ibid., 566). In cases of divorce, children are considered to belong to the husband and to be under the protection of his ancestors. The traditional Akha house is divided into men's and women's sleeping rooms. Akha women typically eat only after the male householders have finished their meal. Villages that have moved to the lowlands and engage more closely with lowland Buddhist groups have begun to soften these mandates, but gender hierarchy is still evident in certain social roles.

Assimilation of ethnic minority groups within state-based forms of citizenship and national identity is seldom seamless, wherever it takes place, and movement into the lowlands affects the Akha in profound ways. Perhaps the most obvious is changing dress: Akha women now seldom wear their blue tunics and distinctive headdresses as they seek to identify more closely with lowland lifestyles. But integration is not simply about attire; it becomes more complicated when forces of globalization and donor-supported development bring different value systems into contact.

The changes the Lao Akha face reach to the deepest sense of ethnic identity. Similar processes have taken place in China, Burma, and Thailand, where decades of modernization have sharply altered everyday life for ethnic minorities. In Thailand and Burma, many Akha have converted to Christianity over the past fifty years. In China, the Akha endured the Cultural Revolution and subsequent national assimilation programs. In Laos, Akha have so far been relatively removed from far-reaching social change: the socialist government has not had the resources to reach them and foreign missionaries are forbidden to proselytize. But in the past ten years, development has become ubiquitous due to an opening up of the economy to donor aid (particularly from the West) and investment (particularly from China). As a result, many Akha have moved to the lowlands to take part in the opportunities that development offers: better health, better education, and, most important, a chance to dream of economic improvement and material consumption. It is too early to say precisely what the changes the Akha are embracing (or are forced to embrace) will deliver in terms of material wealth.

But we can say that lifestyle changes are already bringing radical new social formations and personal relations with a greater number of players, each angling for some sort of advantage in the charged world of market-based competition.

Akha in Thailand faced similar pressures several decades earlier. Tooker (2004) suggests they now adapt their sense of cultural identity to maximize opportunities in a capitalist context and that their previous protective sense of what constitutes a dangerous "outside" world has changed. The result is a "compartmentalization" of ethnic identity, which is used strategically at certain times, such as to organize events oriented to tourists so as to capitalize on the market value of ethnicity. Others point to more insidious outcomes of commercialization, as young Thai Akha are overrepresented in the urban underclass of prostitution and exploited labor (Kammerer 2000). In Laos, the outside–inside distinction preserving ethnic identity is also rapidly dissolving. In the past, changes due to modernization were limited by a sense of cultural and geographic isolation (for example, until recently very few Akha could speak Lao). But while not yet commodified to any large degree, as integration increasingly takes place Akha identity and cultural beliefs are both used by Akha and exploited by others in ongoing accommodation of modernity.

FROM EKING OUT LIVELIHOODS TO SEEKING EMPLOYMENT

Life in the Lao mountains is hard; in the past, average Akha life expectancy only reached the late forties and child mortality remains tremendously high. And while moving to the lowlands might have made access to services more convenient, the shift to market economy and wage labor carries its own difficulties. The Akha can no longer rely on access to forests for subsistence needs. Rather, in the lowlands where paddy land for rice cultivation is limited, they increasingly depend on selling labor. Usually this takes place with Tai-Lue who have long resided in the valleys, or Chinese who invest in market gardens. Recently relocated Akha also work for other Akha families who moved down earlier and purchased any available land.

All over the world, changing economic and technological structures reach deep into our subjectivities. "As our worlds change, so do we. As transnational trends, such as the latest phases of financial capitalism, remake the conditions of our lives and the parameters of our worlds, so too do they remake our most intimate inner processes: emotion, cognitive style, memory, our deepest sense of self" (Kleinman and Fitz-Henry 2007:55). The move from subsistence livelihood to capitalist styles of social and economic management brings new ways of relating to people and the environment. For the Akha, the shift to wage labor is about more than seeking cash to buy food: it creates a fundamentally different way of "being in the world." Now experience is more finely wrought by interpersonal relations premised on a market engagement. Embracing modernity thus also entails competition over resources and profits in contexts where certain people and ideas are privileged over others. Nowadays the Akha are becoming acutely aware of this process of marginalization, as some of them end up in positions of social subordination.

Relocation has altered mainstay communal livelihoods and more closely integrated the Akha into contemporary forms of modern citizenship with the moral obligations these entail to national governance and international programs for economic integration. The Akha are being swept along on this roller coaster of progress being promoted throughout the Upper Mekong. On the one hand, the sense of being actively engaged in an exciting new enterprise of market opportunity is pervasive. But others remain uneasy at the rapidity with which they are losing control of their future; control that in the past was firmly embedded in cultural structures that are now waning in their relevance. Some villages end up completely fractured. It is not uncommon to hear of long and heated debates in villages about the respective benefits of being in lowlands versus highlands; movement to lowlands has often been led by younger and more entrepreneurial cohorts, leaving behind older villagers far more ambivalent about the change.

Economic reformation is relatively new for post-socialist Laos, which has only recently embraced a free market economy. It has allowed China to provide large amounts of investment, where, as in Muang Sing, its use is often negotiated through local cross-border kin networks. With more relaxed border regulations, Chinese influence has brought dreams of modernity directly into Akha communities in ways hitherto not experienced. But with it comes an implicit awareness of a growing social hierarchy despite enduring socialist edicts of equality and solidarity.

Competition for resources within everyday life previously meant being skilled at gathering wood, skilled at hunting game, skilled at mountain rice cultivation, and skilled at reciting courting songs and ancestral traditions, but there seldom was direct rivalry within one's own community or with one's neighbors. In contrast, in the lowlands competition now takes new forms: currying favor with officials, finding the best connections for ongoing labor, learning to negotiate land use for water and rice, learning to find space for more highland Akha who move to the lowlands, and, most prominently these days, causing strong contestations over land to plant rubber. As a result, the Akha who have arrived more recently are dependent on others in ways that are in stark contrast to the situations existing in previous subsistence lifestyles, and a growing distinction is emerging between Akha who seek employment and those who employ them.

Obviously having even small amounts of cash means that families can purchase basic goods; a growing consumer consciousness brings its own pleasures. One can see this in the riotous evening gatherings as people crowd together to watch Chinese videos in the few houses with televisions. But on the other hand, labor is uncertain, subject to seasonal demand and carrying with it an implicit reliance on others to provide a wage. For the first time, the Akha without their own land are learning that they are dependent on systems outside their control. In the past they fought against an inclement climate and harsh environment. Now, Akha laborers must confront a system wherein they are being hired not for their own benefit but for someone else's gain—they are becoming, in Marx's terms, proletariats. Thus, in some instances, the younger and stronger men and women are first to be hired; or sometimes just women will be hired (by Chinese), for example, to plant watermelons, because they are supposedly more likely to work without complaint. As a result, competition emerges between groups from different villages. Those reliant on wages from labor or on hiring labor take on a quite different subjective relationship to the world. I recall sitting on a rough balcony in a recently relocated village as a group of women described how they were nowadays too demoralized to repeat the daily routine of going to a neighboring village to ask for work only to be rejected when limited demand meant that young men were the first to be recruited. The women stuck with sewing chores and said they much preferred their previous life in the mountains despite its arduous routine.

People cope with these changes in different ways and choose specific (and increasingly individualized) strategies to make their way in the new environment. For example, we see forms of drug use that assist with labor demands; we see the choices women make to take partners who might offer a new future.

"MODERN" DRUG USE

Opium is now hard to obtain in the Sing mountains. In the past, it was smoked by roughly 9 percent of the population, usually as a form of recreation, social courtesy (in hosting friends from other villages), or medicinal necessity (to lessen the symptoms of diarrhea, arthritis, tuberculosis, or the pain of childbirth). Most local Akha who habitually smoked opium have either undergone detox programs or simply have given it up "cold-turkey" style. But eradication of opium has not eliminated all drug problems. Huge amounts of amphetamines are produced in the Golden Triangle region (mostly in mobile factories in the upper Burma border areas). It is no coincidence that as opium use declined, amphetamine-type substances (ATS) usage has gone up among the Akha. This is not simply an issue of substitution, as amphetamines have radically different effects than narcotics. Rather, ATS usage has a broad appeal directly linked to value systems instilled by processes of modernization.

Demand for methamphetamines has emerged in sync with changing value systems fostered by development trajectories. It occurs for very clear reasons, as Grinspoon and Hedblom note: "Amphetamine use results to a large extent from the pressure many people feel to keep up the increasingly hectic pace of modern life, to cope with a world in which nothing seems predictable but change—constantly accelerating change" (1975:288). In both cities and rural areas throughout mainland Southeast Asia, ATS's growing popularity is based both on its performance-enhancing characteristics—it increases capitalist production among laborers, fishermen, truck drivers, students, and so on—and a growing demand for "designer drugs" among urban club-goers—perfect for conspicuous consumption (Lyttleton 2004).

Thus, even in the Muang Sing hills, ATS has become popular for its energizing effects. Rather than heroin use that exploded in neighboring countries after opium prohibition, the transition to methamphetamines is a highly charged sign of new social and material relations adopted by the Lao Akha as they enter into wage labor and capital accumulation. Taking ATS means being able to work harder and longer; it facilitates contract work where labor is hired for the job rather than by the hour. ATS has become a logical option if it means one can clear a field in fewer hours, earning money more quickly. ATS also has clear associations with modernity, whereas opium has been demonized as the drug of "backward" undeveloped "natives" characterized by lethargy and tardiness; ATS is also associated with energy, diligence, and productivity—characteristics of the "modern" citizen. Of course it is not so black and white. Heavy ATS use is also characterized by fits of paranoia and psychoses. Drug-associated crime has gone up and there have been stringent attempts by authorities to suppress its trade and use. Thus while current levels of ATS use are declining in face of heightened control (and opium use retains a small constituency), drug-use patterns remain a highly volatile indication of the stresses of social change. At the same time, new forms of social relationships arrive with a broader horizon of choices and become embedded in Akha lifestyles in more subtle ways.

INTIMACY AS THE TICKET TO PROGRESS

The Akha are aware of the changing ground rules and the difficult trajectory facing them now that they are entering a consumer culture. As one elderly man remarked to me: "In the mountains life was different, it was easier; we had money [from opium] but nothing to spend it on—here in the lowlands we have more desire to buy things but no money to do so." One option many Akha are embracing is the possibility of a future windfall to be gained from planting rubber for the booming Chinese market. Everywhere, both private and government land is being turned into rubber plantations as people dream of future fortunes. Market uncertainties and contractual difficulties aside, the headlong rush from both the Chinese and Lao side of the border to capitalize on rubber has meant a huge increase in the number of Chinese investors and agricultural advisors coming into numerous Akha villages in search of opportunities to invest in joint plantations—the locals have land, the Chinese have money and know-how.

New business opportunities for Akha involve more than land use and profit-margin negotiations. As mentioned earlier, capitalism deeply intrudes on one's sense of self and how to negotiate one's place in the world. These inevitably involve social relations. One example is the increased incidence of local Akha women marrying Chinese men who visit or temporarily work in Laos. Women indicate that such marriages offer them more chance of prosperity and well-being. They are aware of the dramatic difference in lifestyle just 2–3 km across the Chinese border, where all Akha villages have running water, electricity, and high levels of material consumption. Some village authorities (and the Lao government) have tried to actively control this marriage strategy, but to little avail. The practice has major repercussions for Lao Akha cultural reproduction. If a percentage of the marriageable women leave, the complex kin relations established between groups by marriage will be fractured by the presence of an international border (and childbearing policies) and there will be fewer potential wives for local men.

It is not only cross-border marriages that threaten the integrity of Lao Akha culture. Lao Akha culture permits premarital sexual relationships as a means of allowing young men and women to choose their ideal marriage partner. Such relations are often misrepresented in lowland Lao, Chinese, and Thai cultures as "primitive" and "promiscuous" ethnic practices (Lyttleton et al. 2004). Chinese Akha are aware of the traditional Akha cultural system that no longer exists in China or Thailand, which allows Akha men the opportunity to spend time alone with local women, and which in turn sometimes ends in sexual relations. The local Akha women have a choice as to whether to accompany non-Akha visitors, but in a noticeable shift from earlier times, Chinese Akha men and their lowland Chinese colleagues are introducing another bargaining chip. In the past, cigarettes and whiskey were given to young men in the village to facilitate introductions. Now gifts and money are given directly to the women. This, coupled with the potential prospect of cross-border marriage, promotes an increased number of commodified casual relationships. Increasingly, lowland Lao men are similarly seeking sexual access to Akha women. When we mentioned earlier that the inside–outside distinction is rapidly disappearing, the ways in which outside men are increasingly hoping to find Akha partners is one direct indication.

At face value, there should be no moral difficulty in recognizing young Akha women's desire for greater choices about how and with whom to further their engagement with modernity. For some, acquiring an outside partner is the most obvious strategy to bring this about. But nowadays the traditional system that allows local men a degree of control over women's sexuality also increasingly promotes sexual opportunism. Both married and single Lao Akha men are eligible sleeping partners for young women (men sometimes take more than one wife if she becomes pregnant). More recently, lowland Lao and Chinese men are seeking to exploit this system of orchestrated relations with single women. Following local mores, they ask village men to facilitate introductions for them. Some of these men, bringing money and gifts as the enticement, have no more than a short-term relationship on their minds.

This raises the issue of potential health threats that such broadening sexual networks represent. Mobility and the intersection of disparate groups of traders, travelers, truck drivers, and local communities are often a precursor to the spread of infectious diseases including HIV. The Akha in Muang Sing and Long have a history of high levels of STIs, in particular gonorrhea and chlamydia. No one knows if HIV is now part of the picture, as no testing has been done in this previously removed part of the world. It is certainly the case that the Akha are no strangers to health threats, in the past they commonly suffered from malaria and infectious waterborne epidemics when they moved out of the highlands. Given the rapidity of change and broadened social relationships, it remains an optimistic hope that new sexual diseases are not also part of an insidious underbelly accompanying modernization.

CONCLUSION

Throughout the world, immense social, political, and cultural shifts have accompanied the arrival of modernity over the past two centuries. In what is described as a compression of time and space that defines our contemporary era, globalization has brought many changes to the Akha in Laos. Regardless of whether local villagers choose to relocate closer to roads and markets, agree to state pressures that say they would be better removed from "threatened" forests, or decide they will stay in the higher slopes come what may, social change is rapidly altering daily life.

How Lao Akha identity is reproduced in the face of changing marriage patterns, new individualized work relations with lowland groups, and commercialization of traditional items and customs (much of the old silver used in adornment is being sold to outsiders) is a process still in play. Ethnicity is not readily dissolved, but its attributes change. The wealthier Akha in China are the role models most eagerly emulated. Already on the Lao side, active pursuit of material wealth is evident in new clothes, televisions, and a flood of other Chinese products in most villages. To gain access to this world of commodity culture, the Akha are bargaining with their future livelihoods, contracting local land for rubber planting to Chinese investors for up to fifty years. These changes have an impact on both the social and the individual bodies of the Akha. Changing drug patterns to accommodate new labor expectations, and strategic use of intimate relations are just two examples that show social change is never purely about rational decision making but inevitably introduces the more complex embodied realms of emotions and feelings.

Modernity has arrived with a rush in the Lao mountains, in a combination of opportunities (wage labor and agricultural expansion) and pressure (prohibitions on opium cultivation and forest use). One way or another, most Akha wholeheartedly embrace these new lives, most obviously indicated by material trappings such as motorcycles and televisions, but also underpinned by broadened options such as education and better health. But modernity is a fraught project; it cannot be presumed or adopted like a new suit of clothes. Akha make their choices and use their own cultural resources to seek the best negotiating position in this new landscape. No doubt some individuals and families will end up well off, but others will learn that they are part of an economic accumulation system that by no means benefits all. Cultural resilience is required to weather the sense of marginalization that, for some groups, inevitably accompanies roughshod modernization. As in neighboring countries, Akha in Laos are confronting the difficult situation of deciding what about being Akha is dispensable, and what is amenable, to their new lives as modern global citizens.

22

"They Do Not Like to Be Confined and Told What to Do": Schooling Malaysian Indigenes

Robert Knox Dentan, Anthony (Bah Tony) Williams-Hunt, and Juli Edo

In our efforts to develop the education for orang asli [*sic*], we must do away with the old style. The approach now is to make adjustments according to their culture and needs because their requirements are different from other communities.

—Deputy PM Datuk Seri Najib Tun Razak
(quoted in Mohamad 2007)

DR Bah Piyan Tan is the envy and pride of his Semai tribesmen in Tapah, Perak. He drives a big car and lives in a double-storey terrace house in a nice neighbourhood in Puchong, Selangor.

—*New Straits Times* 2007

This chapter concerns how Malaysian state-run schooling "disciplines the work force," a euphemism popular among advocates of "globalization." We draw parallels between how kidnappers treat kidnappees and how state agents treat children of Orang Asli, a Malaysian population occupying a status like that of U.S. Natives. They are the indigenous peoples of the Malaysian peninsula. Like U.S. Natives, they make up less than 1 percent of the current population. And, like U.S. Natives, they have lost or are losing most of their traditional territories; unlike U.S. Natives, they lack treaty rights or sovereignty.

The Malaysian state rests on "ethnicity." Malays rule because, the story goes, they are the indigenous people of Malaysia. That puts Orang Asli in an odd position, because *they* are the "indigenous people" according to the consensus of both ethnographers and the bureaucrats of international powers like the World Bank and the UN General Assembly, which the Malaysian government ostensibly supports (JOAS 2008). Indeed, *Orang Asli* is Malay for "indigenous people" (Dentan et al. 1997). Two authors of this paper are Semai, members of the famously peaceable and largest subcategory of Orang Asli.

Language is vital to this paper. Educatorspeak in any language obscures as much as it clarifies. We talk about "hidden curriculum" (knowledge and behavior schools inculcate without overt discussion, as in obedience and keeping still) and "schooling" (enforcing hidden curriculum) as well as "education" (widening people's horizons and giving them personally beneficial skills). Because children are the easiest people to victimize in any society (Office for Victims of Crime 2002:810), and because children encounter the state mostly in schools, observing how a particular state (in this case Malaysia) schools its poorest children (in this case Malaysian indigenes or Orang Asli) helps one evaluate the character of that state.

Compulsory education is a kind of kidnapping, a term we use instead of less vivid words such as "disembedding" (Boulanger 2008). The idea is to segregate impoverished kids from their unsatisfactory parents and supposedly retrograde "culture." We stress that no matter how attractive the kidnappers' blandishments, the consequences of refusing are dire. Force is the *ultima ratio regum,* the final argument of rulers. We agree that, in both criminal and legal kidnapping, kidnappers' motives may be lofty, kidnappees may go willingly with their abductors, and close emotional ties often develop between the two (by a process called "identification with the oppressor" [Dentan 2008]).

Kidnapping is central to maintaining globalized modernity—i.e., industrial capitalism, commercial slavery, or state-run education (Graeber 2007; Tilaar 2005). Rulers take subordinates-to-be from their homes, where the kidnapped have learned the complex skills needed to survive without alienating friends and neighbors (Macdonald 2008), and subject them to an ostensibly rationalized, simplistic, and universalistic meritocracy in which they must master the relatively simple skills needed to serve their new masters efficiently (Sukarman 2005; Dentan 2010, forthcoming). They go from rustic complexity into

forests of buildings and rivers of concrete where other men and women missed the stars at night and tended small plants on windowsills and kept tiny dogs and took them for walks along corridors in the endless procession of boxes and intersections and lights; where they rented space in other people's property so they had somewhere to sleep so they could get up and perform profit-related tasks they neither understood nor cared about, simply so they would be given tokens of exchange they needed in order to rent the space in which they slept and snarled and watched television, a society that was itself trapped in fracture and betrayal and despair; a culture turning into a Christmas bauble, gaudy beauty wrapped around an emptiness coalescing faster and faster into parking lots and malls and waiting areas and virtual chat rooms—non-places where nobody knew anything about any-body anymore. (Marshall 2002:284–85)

There, some quondam kidnappees, like Dr. Piyan (one of three current Orang Asli who hold PhDs), do well by the simple standards to which they have been assimilated enough to squelch the love of freedom to which Piyan referred in the phrase used in this chapter's title. Piyan's parents "learnt that education was the ticket to a better life from mixing with other people and estate officials" (*New Straits Times* 2007). Many Orang Asli now want schooling for their kids so that they can deal with non-Aslians without get-ting cheated and oppressed. The money isn't bad, either.

State ideologies construct state kidnappees as less competent and less complete than the people they are to serve: simple, ignorant, immature, thoughtless—"childish," in a word (Dentan and Juli 2008). The new rules obscure abductees' diversity and disrupt the skills that their "home" lives foster (Graeber 2007; Hickson 2010; Macdonald 2008). The process teaches Orang Asli abductees that they are inferior, so that, as Piyan says, "They do not have self-worth. They think that they are ugly and poor" (*New Straits Times* 2007).

There are dangers to watch out for in this discussion. First, if you're not Malaysian, don't feel superior. What compulsory Malaysian schooling in-volves goes on in compulsory schooling around the world (Gatto 2006). De-spite local peculiarities, the basic pattern is pretty much the same. Also, in a short chapter, it is easy to get lost in abstractions. This paper is about kids much like other kids. So let's start by introducing you to Bah Rmpent (Den-tan 2001).

SEMAI (ORANG ASLI) SCHOOLCHILDREN

If the kids don't go to school, if [my husband] doesn't take them [on his motorbike], if he doesn't yell at them, I'll yell at him. They get in trouble if they don't go to school. If [non-Semai] kids pick fights with them or their friends I tell them, "Don't mess with your schoolmates, be good to your schoolmates or you'll be sorry. If you're a bad friend, people won't want you around." Malay kids bully Semai kids all the time. They hit them, they take their books and papers. "Malay kids are bad," I say. "They'll pick fights with you. Don't hit them back. You'll just get in trouble."

—Kyah Grcaangsmother, 1992

Rmpent is about nine. He's "Semai," though Rmpent's people call them-selves *sng'ooy*, "people." To contrast themselves with other peoples, they call themselves *maay sraa'*, hinterland folk, or *maay miskin*, impoverished folk. If Pent were Malay, we'd tell you his father's name, too, what anthropologists call his "patronym," because Malay fathers officially head their families, so children are "sons of" or "daughters of" particular fathers. Arabic words, *bin* or *binte* respectively, indicate the relationship and also indicate that the child is Muslim, since Malays are by definition Sunni Muslim, and children's names are also usually Arabic.

Rmpent's official name (what Semai call *muh paspot*)—his identity card name—is Ali. The Malay registrar probably assumed he was doing Rmpent a favor by giving him a civilized Muslim name since the kid was bound to convert to Islam sooner or later and it would save everybody the paperwork. The patronym is a nudge toward what the government thinks is "development." POASM, the Orang Asli Association, has suggested all Malaysians use neutral terms for "child of," plus father's name.

Since Pent isn't Muslim, despite heavy pressure on Semai to convert, his official name uses the neutral patronym. Learning Malay patriarchal ways may eventually make patronyms seem "natural" for Semai. But Semai men in the old days were partners of their wives, not bosses. In those days, people used teknonyms, naming themselves after their children, the way American suburban parents do when they don't know the patronym: "You know, Mary, Susan's mother." Pent is a skinny, long-legged kid. When he hunkers down, his bony legs fold up on both sides of him, almost to his armpits, like a grasshopper's. Like most children in his settlement, he doesn't get a lot to eat. He and the other children sometimes use a slingshot to kill little birds or club wild rodents to death. In fruit season the kids hide slivers of bamboo coated with sticky tree sap among the leaves of fruit trees. When little birds light on the tree to steal the fruit, they get stuck in the sap and fall to the ground, where the children find them and wring their necks. The kids roast the meat in the ashes of the cooking fire for proteinaceous-filled snacks, the way U.S. kids eat candy. (They'd eat candy too, if they could afford it.) Otherwise, Rmpent's playmates don't get a lot of protein. Many Semai children are stunted for their age. That doesn't help them in fights at school. And traditional Semai are famous for avoiding fighting whenever possible, because they think it's stupid: you can get hurt (Dentan 2008). Fighting is a core course in the hidden curriculum of Malaysian schools. Rmpent fills his school notebook with images of tanks and bombers.

Today the sky is the flat grayish ivory color of rice gruel. Pent, raggedy green rucksack on his back, is off to school with his pal Tkooy. The boys must trudge a mile to the bus stop. The bus route dead-ends at the last Malay settlement down the road, like the electricity and the postal service. (The official rationale for moving Semai from the hill forests where they used to live was so that the government could deliver services to them, services like transportation, electricity, and mail. The rulers then gave the hereditary lands to non-Semai developers.) Sometimes, on gray days like this, rain squalls sweep in from the Indian Ocean to the west, sheet after sheet of chilly water shattering as the rain hits the asphalt, soaking the children's hair, clothes, and papers.

Figure 22.1. Asrama in Tapah, Perak, 2006. Photo by Colin Nicholas.

Figure 22.2. Semai kids listening, Cak Kuaak, Perak, 2006.

Figure 22.3. Homeschooling. "Playing the noseflute," pnsɔl Upper Teiw
War (Who River), November 14, 1991.

Figure 22.4. Homeschooling. Shucking maize. Teiw R'eis (Rias River), April 1992.

Wish we had one of those, the boys think as a Malay father gripping the handlebars of a 70 cc motorbike puttputts by, a little schoolboy upright between his knees, his wife riding sidesaddle in back so as not to shock prudish Malays by giving a glimpse of thigh, and a toddler resting on her lap in a sarong slung over her left shoulder. But the boys don't voice their desires: *No use in that.* Traditional Semai kids don't complain, though city kids are different, at least with their parents. Another motorbike passes, a Malay man in dark brown trousers driving, his wife in a high-necked, long-sleeved blouse riding sidesaddle behind him, clutching an open bright paisley parasol. Next comes a Chinese man in black shorts on a Vespa with half a dozen chickens, legs tied and slung on each side, their heads a handsbreadth over the cracked asphalt.

At the bus stop, near the little Chinese convenience store (where Semai who can't afford bus fare to the market in town buy most of their supplies), an older Malay boy sees the two relatively dark-skinned chums. "Sakai! Sakai!" he shouts to his buddies, and several Malay children elaborately pantomime holding their noses.[1] Some days the bigger boys beat the Semai kids up, for the hell of it. The Semai kids cluster separately from the Malay kids, just as their parents cluster away from the Malay adults.

When Semai parents complained about the bullying, the headmaster met with them. A plump middle-aged Malay man, with a high forehead and

Figure 22.5. Home from school. These boys speak Malay even at home, not wanting to sound *misKin,* a Malay-Arabic word meaning "impoverished and pathetic." April 30, 1992.

small chin that made his head almost globular, he listened with every appearance of respect and attentiveness, removing his rimless glasses and laying a finger alongside his nose as the parents recited incident after incident. Afterwards, he lectured all the children about the importance of living in peace, and the bullying let up for a while.

A few older Semai children from the area and yet more remote settlements go to a boarding school (*asrama*) in a small city a couple of dozen miles from home. A tall chain-link fence topped with three strands of barbed wire surrounds the buildings (see fig. 22.1). A uniformed male Malay guard occupies the guardhouse by the locked gate. A placard on the gate announces, in Malay:

Asrama SMK Sri Tapah
Arr. Visit Hrs.

1. When to visit[:] Saturday and Sunday, except in cases of emergency.
2. Visiting hours: 9AM to 6:30 PM.
3. Visitors are required to check in with the security officer before they are allowed to enter.
4. Visitors allowed to meet with students [only] in the room designated for that purpose.
   By direction of the principal

Advocates of long-term removal of Orang Asli children from their homes say that the elaborate security apparatus protects the children from those who might harm them. It also keeps them from fleeing to the homes and families for whom their yearning is more poignant than most Malays and Americans, who are inured to state-sanctioned kidnapping, can understand. The cement buildings differ starkly from traditional Semai houses—thatched roof, flattened-bamboo walls, floors three feet above the ground—in which, in the 1950s, a Semai cooperative would board kids from the hills who wanted to go to a city school (Dentan and Juli Edo 2008). The new (2007) "Orang Asli school" at Bandar Dua Puluh Hinai is a hostel. Eastman Chemical Malaysia provides computers, tuition, and "motivational talks" for this school. There are sixty-two students, only twenty-two of whom are Asli.

SEMAI SCHOOLCHILDREN IN MALAYSIAN SCHOOLS

The economic planners envisage the systematic elimination of the peasant.
For short term political reasons, they do not use the word elimination but the
word modernization. Modernization entails the disappearance of the small
peasant (the majority) and the transformation of the remaining minority into
totally different social and economic beings.

—Berger 1979:209

Besides offering the children a refuge (except from bullying by non-Asli kids and the beatings by teachers that affect all children in Malaysian schools), the *asrama* reflects a belief that the reason Orang Asli children do not "live up to their potential" in school is Orang Asli "culture." They and their parents, the story goes, don't appreciate the importance of schooling (Dentan and Juli 2008; Nettleton 2008).

Instead, the children get lonely, hate the bullying, take seriously the instances in which they are being told that they are stupid (as Dr. Piyan suggests), and play hooky to help their parents during fruit season (central to Semai agroforestry). Some 80 percent drop out before completing high school (Nettleton 2008). Despite the Malay proverb *Di-anjak layu, di-anggur mati* (Moved, things wither; transplanted, they die [Brown 1989:130]), the cure is kidnapping. But before discussing that process, common wherever governments undertake "modernization," we need to look at a seemingly academic question that was once common in introductory anthropology classes: what do people mean when they talk about "culture"?

The closest equivalent word for Malays comes from Arabic *adat*, found throughout Muslim Asia, although the underlying Malay concept antedates Islam (Wilkinson 1901, I:5–6). Narrowly, adat is "customary law," more generally the habitual behavior you expect from a particular category of people. Thus Malays say, "in the adat of fishermen, fish that get away were *really* big" (Brown 1989:77). And, like the English word *culture*, adat connotes "high culture," in which sense it connects with "proper speech." A person who is *berbahasa*, "well-spoken" (i.e., capable of speaking refined Malay), is civilized, unlike "crude" (*kasar*) people, who "are adat-deficient" (*kurang beradat*), and don't have real language but just cluck and squawk like chickens or Orang Asli (Dentan 1997).

Adat is central to the traditional Malay sense of self. *Kecil dikandung ibu; besar dikandung adat; mati dikandung tanah:* "Little, wrapped in mother's womb; grown up, wrapped in culture; dead, wrapped in earth." *Biar mati anak, jangan mati adat.* "Let your child die, not your culture" (Winstedt 1981:44). In this concept, ethnic identity and culture are *things* to formulate and preserve as is (see, e.g., the many Malay culture-and-etiquette books, such as Asiapac 2003; Alwi 1962; and Noor Aini 1991).

In the 1960s and 1970s, Orang Asli secluded from Malay influence often denied having any adat. "No, that's a Malay thing. We here, we just get up in the morning, we work, we go to bed, that's it," said an old Asli man in 1976. Still, to outsiders, this man's "culture" is striking enough and reified enough that the people have successfully commercialized it, exhibiting sculptures, inviting tourists to observe elaborate annual rituals, and generally treating it as a "thing" to manipulate.[2]

Ironically, in the 1970s and 1980s Malay officials and advocates of "economic development" decried efforts to preserve customary ways of living as elitist sentimentalism in which Orang Asli "culture" was valuable only

as a "museum piece." Orang Asli themselves asserted that such preservation efforts did not mean that they opposed "development," only development that involved dispossession without payment and "regroupment" (e.g.,
Veeranggan 2009) from their native land into smaller and smaller enclaves
on which they remained basically squatters (e.g., Center for Orang Asli Concerns n.d.; Dentan et al. 1997; Endicott and Dentan 2004:40–44; Lye 2004:19–
48; Swainson and McGregor 2008; Subramaniam 2008; Zawawi 1996). Since
Malaysian politics treats struggles over scarce resources as "ethnic," Orang
Asli have cast their resistance into Platonic ethnic terms, initially by defining themselves as opposite to Malays (Dentan 1975, 1976) and later by re-
casting the governmental administrative category "Orang Asli" as a grab-
bag "ethnic identity" based on being "more indigenous" than Malays, thus
undermining Malay supremacy (Nicholas 2000). The Malay solution is to as-
similate Orang Asli into the Malay population. As one old Semai man said,
"Once Orang Asli [= 'indigenous people'] become Malays, then Malays will
really be indigenous people." Along with Islamicization, public schooling
mostly works toward that goal (Dentan et al. 1997; Juli, Williams-Hunt, and
Dentan 2009; Nicholas 2000).

Struggles over land forced Orang Asli to recast general understandings that underlay local communities' access to communal resources into
terms of adat, in the sense of customary law. International law then allowed
them to resist whimsical dispossession by politically more powerful ethnic
groups (JOAS 2008). In the area of education, the Orang Asli situation parallels that faced by nineteenth-century German minorities in Buffalo (Dentan's city):

> (1) language maintenance was essential to ethnic identity and cultural pres-
> ervation; (2) knowledge of English [and Malay] essential for achieving pros-
> perity; [but there was] (3) interethnic debate over the propriety of public in-
> stitutions encouraging cultural diversity; and (4) prejudice among politicians
> and school officials. (Gerber 1984:31)

Under international pressure (e.g., UNICEF 2008; Subramaniam 2008),
bolstered by Semai nongovernmental organizations such as POASM and
Sinui Pai Nanek Sengik (Tijah and Joseph 2003), the Malaysian bureaucracy
recently authorized an elementary-level course in the Semai language (Kementerian Pendidikan Malaysia 2003) and included mention of Orang Asli
in textbooks. Several Orang Asli churches are developing texts, helped by
Tim Phillips, a student from the Summer Institute of Linguistics. But official
support for these courses is unreliable, and Dr. Piyan (the successful Semai
we introduced at the start of this chapter) speaks Chinese at home.

Any improvement in the situation Semai schoolchildren face is laudable.
But we argue that cultures and identities are not *things* to be preserved but
skills for dealing with the world. They change in response to changing cir-

cumstances (Carneiro da Cunha 1995). In the mid-1970s, when Dentan first visited Btsisi', a coastal group of Orang Asli, they were in the midst of a spectacular explosion of sculpture in response to outside demands. These new market-oriented sculptures had developed from Btsisi' traditional disposable sickness figures. But now, apparently, these Semai make sculptures according to strict "classical" (1970s) models. Instead of letting the culture of carving develop autonomously, perceived market forces have reified it, making it into a Platonic *thing*. A course in one of the more than forty dialects of Semai, which is one of more than a dozen Orang Asli languages, is a valuable token of respect and may help the minority of Semai who are able to enroll in it when and where it is actually offered. But it will not "save" the language in the long run, any more than the Germans immigrants in Buffalo succeeded in preserving German.

The appropriate goal, far harder to achieve than token jiggering with the curriculum by the ruling Malays, is for Orang Asli to control their children's curricula and to educate them in what will then be an Orang Asli way. It is unlikely that that project is even a possibility. The hidden curriculum of schooling in "modern" societies is unlikely to change for the children of poor people, and those who institute and benefit from such programs are unlikely to abandon kidnapping, whatever country they live in.

NOTES

1. This word can be translated as "nigger." *Sakai* means dark, ignorant, stupid, sexually incontinent former slaves. For a more nuanced and detailed account see Dentan 1997.

2. E.g., Department of Museums and Antiquities, n.d. [a] and n.d. [b]; JOAS 2008; Shahrum 1969; Werner 1973. Outsiders have censored and secularized performances of reified Asli culture to make them more acceptable to non-Asli (see Department of Museums and Antiquities, n.d. [c]; Rashid 2007).

23

Narratives of Agency: Sex Work in Indonesia's Borderlands

Michele Ford and Lenore Lyons

"Some people do this kind of work because they are forced to, but others do it because they want to live the high life," said Lia earnestly, responding to a question about the prevalence of trafficking in the sex industry on Karimun, an island on the western edge of the Riau Archipelago in Indonesia.[1] An extremely attractive young woman in her mid-twenties, Lia is the image of middle-class Indonesian respectability in her modern, loose-fitting clothes and bright colored *jilbab* (headscarf) modestly fastened over her head and shoulders. Her comment neatly sums up the dichotomous thinking that dominates both public and scholarly discussions about sex work in Indonesia.[2] According to this logic, sex workers are either forced into prostitution by circumstance (including instances of force or deception), or they freely choose to sell their bodies for financial gain.

Lia has lived in Karimun for more than a decade and is familiar with the circumstances that have given rise to a large sex industry on the island and elsewhere in the archipelago. The Riau Islands form the borderland between Singapore and Indonesia, at the periphery of the Indonesian state. The islands have been part of a growth triangle with Singapore and Malaysia since the early 1990s, resulting in large-scale foreign and joint-venture investment in manufacturing, tourism, transport, and service industries. An influx of migrant workers to the region, combined with the ease of travel from economically powerful Singapore, has created the conditions for the proliferation of vice industries such as sex work and gambling on many of the islands. The sex industry caters predominantly to men from nearby Singapore (and to a lesser extent Malaysia), and is fueled by geographical proximity, comparative cost, and the relative anonymity afforded by travel to a foreign country (Ford and Lyons 2008). Local islanders always say that sex workers come to the Riau Islands from other parts of Indonesia—from Sumatra, Kalimantan, and Sulawesi, but mainly from Java—and this is supported by our research. While some scholars claim that women are trafficked to the Riau Islands following false promises of good jobs in factories or restaurants (Agustinanto 2003:179), activists from some local NGOs argue that many of the women who end up in the industry have previous experience as sex workers in Jakarta or elsewhere.

Trafficked women attract some sympathy from the local community even as they endure continued public stigmatization. However, both groups are equally shunned, marginalized by a discourse that positions them as both victims and "immoral women" (*wanita tuna susila*, a common term for sex workers). But this does not mean that sex workers conceive of their lives only in oppressed terms. Attention to the local and historical specificities of sex work reveals that normative constructions of sexuality and gender are often partial (cf. Kempadoo 1999). Lia's appearance and demeanor, in fact, belie her own experience. Her carefully crafted middle-class persona is part of a deliberate strategy designed to distance herself from the stain of her past life as a sex worker. Even when talking with foreign researchers, she is initially careful about keeping to a socially approved script that positions her as a good wife and mother who was deceived and then trafficked into prostitution, a situation from which she eventually escaped. Reality, however, is much more complex. Later, Lia's narrative changes to one of decisiveness and initiative, as she describes the personal qualities that have allowed her to shape her life during and after commercial sex.

Lia's story—like the stories of many of her former colleagues—demonstrates the choices and constraints that sex workers face as they actively seek alternative lives. Yet each of these stories is as individual as it is similar. Ani has also experienced life in Karimun's brothels. Like Lia, she is now also a model of middle-class decorum. She, too, makes careful, strategic decisions about her new life in order to fit the image of a modern housewife. We meet far away from her home in a middle-class residential area of the city, beyond the gaze of prying neighbors. Ani has consciously adjusted her lifestyle to suit her new neighborhood, copying the way her neighbors dress and talk and avoiding any actions that might draw attention to her past. But unlike Lia, in recalling her previous life as a sex worker, Ani frequently invokes a discourse of victimhood and immorality. Her story is nevertheless also a story of agency.

Lia's and Ani's narratives raise questions about how we can theorize the "*constrained* choice to become a sex worker, without moralisingly declaring all sex work to be exploitation or violence against women" (Schotten 2005:230). The latter view is espoused by those writers who, writing from an abolitionist stance, argue that prostitution is the ultimate expression of male dominance and thus the cornerstone of all sexual exploitation (cf. Barry 1996). According to this argument, there is no place for sex workers to claim that their work is *not* harmful or alienating. Such a totalizing perspective provides little space for alternative accounts of the intersection between structure and agency and overlooks the ways in which women themselves understand and explain their life histories. The stories that Lia and

Ani, two women who became labor migrants, then sex workers, and finally the wives of ex-clients, tell about their lives demonstrate these complexities and challenge commonsense understandings about women's agency.[3]

MARRIED WOMEN TO LABOR MIGRANTS

Lia and Ani are both ethnic Javanese. They grew up in similar circumstances in very different geographical settings. Ani was born in 1977 in the province of Lampung on the southern tip of Sumatra, while Lia was born two years later in Deli Serdang in the province of North Sumatra. Their parents are poor Javanese peasants who were relocated to Sumatra as part of Indonesia's transmigration program, under which millions of Indonesians—mostly Javanese and Balinese—were resettled to the less populous "outer islands." Under the objectives of the program, transmigrants were expected to introduce more intensive cultivation techniques and thus boost the nation's food production. However, the land they were allocated often proved unsuitable for these techniques and resulted in environmental degradation and continuing poverty. Unable to secure a livelihood from farm work, large numbers of transmigrants have relied increasingly on nonfarm income. While Lia's parents continue to eke out a living on their small-hold farm, Ani's parents have become petty traders.

Ani married a local man soon after dropping out of junior high school, and immediately became pregnant, giving birth to a son. But Ani's dreams of becoming a wife and mother were short-lived. By the time she was nineteen, she was single again, having left her violent and unfaithful husband. Lia managed to finish junior high school but was unemployed for a time before marrying a man from her village, with whom she had a son in 1999 and a daughter a year later. Her husband died not long after the birth of her daughter, leaving Lia with the difficult task of having to find work to support her two children. When their marriages ended, both women faced an uncertain future. Economically, as single mothers, they faced the prospect of raising their children with no savings and little prospect of deriving a secure income in their villages; and socially, as a *janda* (divorcee or widow), they were the object of community distrust.

The lack of local jobs meant that both women had to look beyond their communities for employment opportunities. After her divorce, Ani left her young son with her mother in Lampung and moved to Jakarta to work in a biscuit factory. It was the first time she had stepped outside her hometown. The work was grueling and life in the factory was highly disciplined. Ani's earnings were much higher than she could have earned in her village, but they were barely enough to meet the cost of living in Jakarta. Nevertheless, she managed to send some money back to her mother to help pay for her son's milk and food. Lia chose a different path. She joined the thousands of

Indonesian women who are recruited each year to work overseas as domestic workers. She was employed in Singapore to look after the elderly relative of a Chinese family. In addition to her duties as a caregiver, she was expected to clean the house, wash the car, and tend the garden. When her six-month bond expired, Lia decided to break her contract and return home. Her decision to do so was not easy. For the entire time she had worked in Singapore, Lia had received no income because all her wages were paid to the employment agent who had arranged her travel. But even her more recent experience of sex work has not made her look back more favorably on her time abroad:

> I'll never forget what it was like to be a servant in Singapore. It was really hard. If you're just five minutes late they totally lose it. There's absolutely no time to rest. It's exhausting . . . I never want to do that kind of work again.

Nothing was worse, Lia believed, than the total lack of control she had as a domestic worker.

LABOR MIGRANTS TO SEX WORKERS

Ani's and Lia's experiences as labor migrants in the formal economy provided the conditions for them to undertake another form of labor migration—this time into the informal sector as sex workers in the Riau Islands. Their experiences of entering the sex industry represent two ends of the spectrum. Ani was tricked into the sex industry by an acquaintance. In late 1997, her neighbor, Ibu Eka, approached her while she was waiting at the Raja Basah bus terminal in Lampung City to return to her job in Jakarta. Ibu Eka suggested that Ani join her in Malaysia where she was working in a factory earning a monthly wage almost fifty times what Ani was getting. The promise of so much money was irresistible and Ani accepted the invitation. But Ani never made it to Malaysia. Ibu Eka brought her to Karimun, supposedly a transit site for the next leg of their journey. Not long after she arrived, Ani was taken to work in a brothel complex that housed around six hundred sex workers. Ani worked there for two years. During that time she never managed to send any money to her family. She explained that "women like her" became trapped in the industry:

> The trouble is once you're working here, it's hard to move on. Most sex workers have a really low level of education and their only work experience is in the sex industry. They can't go into [petty] trade because they don't have any capital, and they can't work in the supermarket because they don't meet the educational requirements. . . . It's impossible to leave [the brothel] if you're not a good talker, if you don't stand up for yourself. Like me—I wanted to get

out but I couldn't. Most of my friends were afraid too. In fact, most people who do that sort of work aren't brave people. I'm not sure what we were all scared of really.

Unlike Ani, Lia was a "good talker," who could "stand up for herself." After leaving Singapore, Lia returned briefly to her village, but soon decided to work in the Riau Islands. She was employed in a small brothel run by a local Malay woman. Lia resented having to share her takings with the madam, who deducted large amounts of money for food and lodging on top of her 50 percent cut. Eventually Lia decided to leave:

> After four months I decided to run away. I was sick of working in a high-risk job without making any money. I figured I'd be better off on my own, finding my own clients and keeping all the money for myself. That's what I was thinking. . . . She [the madam] threatened me, you know. She said she'd report me to the police and all that. I said, "I don't care if you report me to the police here. Even if you report me to the police in Jakarta I'm not scared. Prostitution isn't permitted in this world." That's what I said to her. I might not be very educated, but I know that prostitution is illegal, so I didn't care where she reported me.[4]

Lia had amassed a file containing the contact details of those clients she had liked when working in the brothel, and used this list to establish herself as a freelance sex worker. While she met most of her clients in one of Karimun's numerous hotels, some of her regulars would ask her to meet them in Singapore. These arrangements were mutually beneficial. All Lia's costs were covered and she went home with four times the going rate for an overnight booking in Karimun; meanwhile, her clients received twenty-four hours of service without the annoyance of a ferry trip and at considerably less cost than had they hired a Singaporean-based sex worker.

Ani's and Lia's experiences of sex work initially appear to be quite different. While Ani was sold and trafficked into prostitution, Lia made a conscious decision to travel to the Riau Islands to become a sex worker. They also experienced different degrees of autonomy in negotiating sex work—Ani was bonded to a brothel where the madam dictated her working conditions, while Lia decided to strike out on her own as a freelancer. Lia's freedom to pick and choose the clients whom she "liked" provided her with more freedom to negotiate the conditions of her work. However, both women were subject to the whims and fancies of their clients and to the inevitable risks of violence and sexually transmitted diseases. While Lia's freelance status provided her with greater financial rewards, she was much more vulnerable to harassment by local authorities and had to work hard to maintain her client base. By contrast, while Ani earned much less than Lia, she had some protection under her contractual arrangement with her madam.

FROM SEX WORKERS TO BATAM WIVES

Ani married her second husband, a fifty-seven-year-old Singaporean Chinese client, just three months after they first met in the brothel where she was working. Before they could marry, Ah Huat paid SGD 2,000[5] to Ani's madam to release her debt with the brothel. After their marriage, Ah Huat bought a two-bedroom house for them in Tanjung Balai Karimun, the main city on the island. Ani later brought her parents and child to Karimun to meet her husband and to see her new home:

> When my mother first came to visit she cried until she passed out. I was still young, you see, and my husband was old. I just said to her—as I told you she doesn't know about my background—I said to her, "Mum, he's the one I'm meant to be with. What's the point of marrying a young man if he treats me badly, he's not responsible, and he doesn't care for my family, especially as I have a child? Yes, he's old, but he takes responsibility for everything, he is caring. And the main thing is that he's responsible. He cares for my child, for you and father, for everyone." She found it so hard to accept because I am still young. That was the problem for her. But eventually she got used to it. She even became fond of my husband.

Ani's son now lives with her in Karimun and her parents have become reconciled to her marriage. She feels safe with her husband because he is so different from her violent first spouse. Ah Huat continues to live and work in Singapore but visits Ani regularly and provides her with Rp.4,000,000 housekeeping money per month. He plans to retire to the Islands in a few years and live there permanently with his new wife and her child.[6]

Since her marriage, Ani has had the chance to lead a middle-class lifestyle unavailable to all but the well-to-do in Jakarta. She has her own home and motorcycle, sufficient income to buy expensive clothes and food, and has traveled to Singapore, Malaysia, and Thailand:

> My life's really different. Really different—just so different. I used not to have anything. I couldn't afford to buy anything! Now I can go to Malaysia, to Thailand. I can go anywhere, buy anything. Best of all because my husband loves me, he gives me anything I ask for. . . . Before I couldn't even buy a dress worth Rp.20,000. I hardly had enough money to buy food.

Ani is no longer the naïve country girl who was tricked into sex work, but a financially savvy woman who makes important decisions about her family's future. This transition has involved careful, strategic decisions about her new life in order for her to fit the image of a middle-class housewife.

Lia also married a former client, Farid, a Malaysian whose first wife is infertile. Farid has rented a house for Lia in Tanjung Balai Karimun and sends her 1,500 Malaysian Ringgit[7] per month to cover her living costs. Like Ah

Huat, he visits regularly but continues to live and work in Malaysia. If he is too busy to come to the Islands, Lia sometimes goes to Malaysia, where they meet in a hotel. Farid's first wife knows he has married again, but the two wives have never met.[8] Unlike Ani, Lia's decision to marry was not about reconstructing an idealized nuclear family with the children from her previous marriage, who have remained with their grandparents in Deli Serdang. Instead, she dreams of establishing a new family with her second husband.

Lia pragmatically acknowledges that women married to nonresident non-Indonesians face a range of problems, not least of which is the threat of being abandoned by their husbands. She believes that women have the power to make or break their relationships with foreigners:

> It really depends on us. If we're good to them, they'll be even better to us. But if we're bad, well, that's what happens. Lots of my friends are stuck in the brothels because they have taken money from their Singaporean or Malaysian clients and given it to their boyfriends here. . . . Eventually their Singaporean "husbands" dump them, even though those Singaporeans are actually quite nice men. [These women] really overstep the mark. They get a good one, and they go and do that. There are plenty of those. They don't realize that their boyfriends are just using them. They get dumped [by their Singaporean client], the money stops, and then the boyfriend disappears. Then they are all on their own again.

Although Farid has professed a desire for a child, Lia worries that he might abandon her and the baby. If that were to happen, she matter-of-factly asserts that she would go back to freelance sex work to support her children. Her willingness to return to sex work reflects Lia's sense of herself as an independent woman who can make choices about her future, as well as her knowledge that paid sex can be a lucrative form of work.

Unlike Ani, Lia does not profess to be "in love" with her new husband. But this does not mean that she views her relationship as any less authentic than any other marriage. The concept of a "love marriage" is relatively new in Indonesia, and it is commonly asserted that in an arranged marriage love will grow between the couple (Smith-Hefner 2005; Munir 2002). Although marriage to a foreigner has provided Lia with a more secure economic future, her decision to marry Farid was not solely based on money. She rejected a Singaporean suitor (who could have offered her greater wealth and the chance to live in a developed country) because of their different religious beliefs and because of the greater autonomy that life as a second wife living alone in Karimun offered her. Like Ani, Lia has modified her behavior and dress to approximate the life of a middle-class housewife and is generally successful in "passing" within the community. Both women acknowledge that their economic and social mobility is a matter of both luck and hard work.

CONCLUSION

Ani's and Lia's stories throw into sharp relief the false dichotomy between "force" and "choice" in the debate over women's involvement in sex work. Both women have experienced choice and constraint throughout their lives—as young married women, as single mothers, as labor migrants, as sex workers, and as women married to foreign men. They have exercised agency within the structural bounds of their particular circumstances, and with varying degrees of success, at each life stage. Their marriage to foreigners has catapulted them from their status as poor transmigrants firmly into the lower middle classes, where they are able to consume a lifestyle unattainable for most Indonesian women of their class background. The anonymity afforded by their lives on the outer fringes of the Indonesian nation-state has allowed them to conceal the nature of their involvement in sex work from their families. However, the moral and social sanctions placed on women's sexuality leave an enduring mark on their lives. While the border zone has provided them with prospects that they would not have had elsewhere, it also imposes risks and other costs. For women seeking new futures on the border, hard-won respectability can all too easily disappear. The physical distance between marriage partners gives the women a high level of autonomy, but leaves them vulnerable should their husbands tire of the commute. And, while their husbands are aware of their "history," their families and neighbors are not, leaving them constantly fearful that the truth about their social mobility may be discovered.

We are not suggesting that all working-class women (or sex workers) have these same opportunities by virtue of being present in the islands, as class mobility is contingent upon many factors and must be actively and consciously achieved. Ani and Lia have shaped a future for themselves far different from that available to them in the transmigration villages where they grew up, a future in which they have the moral protection of a married status and ample economic resources, while maintaining a level of day-to-day autonomy unimaginable to most Indonesian women. Yet although they have benefited from the fluid nature of class formation and community structures in the borderlands, as former sex workers, Lia and Ani continue to carry the stain of the past with them as they navigate the often treacherous path between structure and agency.

NOTES

1. The fieldwork on which this article is based was funded by an Australian Research Council (ARC) Discovery Project grant *In the Shadow of Singapore: The Limits of Transnationalism in Insular Riau* (DP0557368).

2. Wardlow (2004:1037) reminds us that use of the term *sex work* is "potentially problematic because it assumes particular kinds of subject positions, motivations,

and gendered identifications that may not be accurate for all women who exchange sex for money." However, we use it here (in contrast to the alternative "prostitution") in order to draw attention to the criminal and legal dimensions of women's labor. As a discursive strategy it also "opens up a space for the formation of new identities not based on passivity, or sexual exploitation and sexual victimhood" (Sullivan 2003:78).

3. The stories of Ani and Lia are based on in-depth interviews conducted in August 2006. Pseudonyms are used at the request of the informants.

4. Indonesia's national criminal code does not prohibit sex work. It is illegal, however, to participate in the trade of women or underage males; or to earn a profit from the prostitution of women (Sulistyaningsih 2002).

5. In 1999, SGD 2,000 was worth approximately USD 1,135.

6. The pattern of cross-border marriage described here is not unusual in the Riau Islands and is a reflection of both economic and social imperatives. For further discussion of why couples live on separate sides of the border see Lyons and Ford (2008).

7. September 2006, MYR 1,000 = USD 274.

8. In Malaysia, Muslim men may marry up to four wives.

24

Just Below the Surface: Environmental Destruction and Loss of Livelihood on an Indonesian Atoll

Gene Ammarell

Early one morning in March 1992, I was sitting at my desk, getting ready for another day of fieldwork on the remote and generally peaceful Indonesian island of Balobaloang, one of dozens of coral islets scattered near and far along the coast of South Sulawesi. Lost in my thoughts, I was startled by the sound of a distant bomb going off. Running out of my house and down to the shore, my next-door neighbor, a military officer posted to the island, sensed that I was off to find the source of the sound. He waved to me and pointed in the direction of a fishing boat just beyond the edge of the reef flat.

"They are bombing for fish," he explained.

"What?" I exclaimed.

"They threw a bottle bomb from the boat." He looked at me and then back out at the boat rocking back and forth in the distance. "The bomb goes off under water and stuns the fish. Then they swim and dive to gather the fish. They catch a lot all at once in this way."

Although I knew very little about blast fishing at that time, I understood that it was highly destructive to the aquatic environment. In fact, the fishermen had dropped the bomb in a place where I often snorkeled, captivated by the luxuriant variety of colorful and exotically shaped corals and tropical fishes.

"Isn't that illegal? Why don't you stop them?" I wanted to ask the officer, but thought better of it. I was, after all, an American graduate student and guest of the Indonesian government and the local villagers. I was living on the island for a year and a half to study navigational knowledge and practice among the island's ethnically Bugis seafarers, long renowned across Southeast Asia as deep-water navigators and interisland traders. I had been trained as an anthropology student to be a "dispassionate observer," and I had been warned by my local host that I should stay out of politics or risk being asked to leave the country before my research was completed. In 1992,

Indonesia was still ruled by President Suharto, a former army general who held dictatorial control of the military and country and who allowed little dissent. No, challenging an army officer would not be a good idea. After a few more minutes observing the blast-fishing boat, I took leave of my neighbor and went back to my house to finish preparing my list of questions for that day's fieldwork.

I had been on the island for nearly a year by then, and I did feel comfortable asking those villagers with whom I felt closest about the blast fishing. During that time, it became clear to me that many of them were concerned about the practice, but no one dared speak out about it. I learned that blast fishing was only rarely practiced by the villagers of Balobaloang, and that the blast fishers came from other islands. Just before leaving the island for my return to the United States, I took a telephoto picture of a boat whose crew was gathering up fish stunned by a bomb they had detonated. I gave this photo to a trusted friend who had grown up on the island and had moved to the capital city of Makassar, where he was employed as a civil servant. He said he would show it to people and not reveal its source, but, as far as I know, nothing ever came of this.

After completing my doctorate and assuming a teaching position at Ohio University, I returned to Balobaloang in 1997 and again in 2000 to record the life histories of several retired senior Bugis navigators. On those occasions, I stayed in the home of Pak Razak, the captain who had first brought me to Balobaloang aboard his then new 40-ton *lambo*.[1] One morning in 2000, we were standing on the front deck of his house and were startled by the sound of a bomb being detonated beyond the reef flat opposite his house. Without being asked, he offered that this was, indeed, blast fishing and that its occurrences were increasing at a troubling rate, destroying the fishery near the island, and forcing village fishers to travel great distances to find enough fish to feed their families and sell to neighbors.

Further discussions with Razak and others revealed that the local fishers had been forced after more than nine years of destructive fishing to give up their indigenous and ecologically sustainable dugout boats equipped with outriggers and powered by paddle. Now they fished from narrow plank boats inspired by Western designs. Larger than dugouts and powered by diesel engines, these boats, called *joloro'*, are capable of traveling far enough from the island and covering enough ground to make fishing more profitable.

Disturbed by what I now saw as an attack on the very lives and livelihoods of the people who had been my gracious hosts and friends for more than a decade, I returned to the United States and made plans to spend my sabbatical year studying the impact of destructive fishing practices on the people of Balobaloang and the marine environment surrounding the island.

My plan was to carry out ethnographic research among the local fishers and their families, learning all that I could about their knowledge of the surrounding reefs and marine life as well as the technologies they employed in foraging for fish and other marine life for subsistence and trade. I would also record their stories of the history of destructive fishing in the area and their responses to it.

I would not be doing this alone. I was joined by graduate students from Ohio University and Hasanuddin University, Makassar. One team from both schools carried out a survey of the health of the surrounding reef, while Amelia Hapsari, an Indonesian graduate student in Telecommunications at Ohio University, produced a "participatory" documentary video, one that allowed the fishers and their families to tell their own story about the impact of destructive fishing practices on their own lives.

In Indonesia as elsewhere, bombs used for fishing are made from plastic drinking bottles filled with explosives illegally obtained on the black market.[2] Such a bomb is tossed from a dugout into a school of reef fish. The dugout is quickly paddled away while the weighted bomb sinks to a predetermined depth and explodes. The fishing boat then moves in and divers using "hookah" rigs and goggles descend with empty sacks to collect the stunned and dead fish. They then load the fish aboard the boat and take them to a nearby island to be dried before taking them into port, or, if they are close to port, the fish will be ice-packed aboard the "mother ship" and sold "fresh" in local markets and restaurants.

The major long-term destruction from blast fishing, beyond the killing of juveniles and noncommercial species (or "by-catch"), results from the impact of the explosion on the corals that comprise the reef. Recall that corals are huge colonies of tiny living organisms called "polyps" of the class Anthrozoa and the hard "skeletons" they create around them. These corals provide the foundation for complex marine ecosystems and are homes to hundreds of species of fish and other marine life. When a bomb explodes on or above a coral reef, it smashes the coral skeletons to bits, killing the polyps and leaving only coral gravel behind. Because this gravel shifts with the waves, no new colonies can establish themselves, and the area can no longer support abundant life.

While blast fishing yields dead fish for local markets, potassium cyanide is used to drug valuable reef fish so that they can be easily captured alive and without injury for international markets, where they wind up as dinner in high-end restaurants or as pets in saltwater aquariums. Fishermen dive with plastic bottles filled with potassium cyanide solution, squirting it into holes and crevices in the coral where the targeted fish live. The fish then drift out and are kept alive in floating nets or holding tanks until they are picked up by the "mother ship" and taken into port. Meanwhile, the poison kills any polyps with which it comes into contact as it drifts with the current. This "bleached" coral is essentially dead, and, while new polyps may eventually recolonize the old substrate, these bleached skeletons are fragile and easily destroyed by strong waves or, in the worst cases, subsequent blast fishing. And even if corals aren't destroyed, breeding stocks of fish such as groupers are often wiped out by cyaniders who have learned that these and other fish return to their birth places to spawn at the same time each year. When cyaniders return to the spawning grounds year after year for several years, whole generations of adult fish are lost, and eventually there are no more young fish being born at those locations. Interestingly, several fishermen on Balobaloang told me that grouper are "lazy feeders" when they are spawning; the effect is that they are highly unlikely to be overfished using traditional weighted hand lines with baited hooks.

On the island of Balobaloang, I was told, blast fishing was practiced up until about 1990 but only at times when large quantities of fish were needed for weddings, circumcisions, and other ritual events where large numbers of people were expected to be fed. On one occasion in the 1980s, a local fisherman was caught and arrested for blast fishing by the police officer stationed on the island; in those days, such an arrest meant a promotion and salary increase for the police officer and shame for the perpetrator and his family. Since then, I was assured, no one on Balobaloang has made a living from either blast fishing or cyanide poisoning.

By the early 1990s, however, fishermen from other islands, nearby and distant, began to exploit for profit the rich fishing grounds of the Sabalanas with both explosives and cyanide. Because key materials are illegal and, thus, expensive and hard to obtain, and because it is difficult for an individual to get his own larger catch to market, those who practice destructive fishing usually work for a patron, referred to locally as a *pongawa* or *bos*. Such patron–client relationships have a deep history in Southeast Asian social organization (see, for example, Scott 1979; Errington 1989; Pelras 1996; Robinson 1998; Chozin 2008). In this case, I learned over time, the boss provides, on credit, the needed illegal materials, as well as other fishing equipment. He also pays the requisite bribes to the police and other local officials to protect the fishermen from being arrested; if someone gets arrested and their boat impounded, the boss will pay the judge to have the case dismissed. The boss also buys the fish from the fishermen, taking out a large percentage of the profit plus payment on the debt. While the fishermen may freely enter into these arrangements, because of their ongoing indebtedness to the boss, it is often hard for fishermen to terminate the relationship.

When we arrived in September 2003, the first thing my wife and I set about was having a small house built in the village on the island's oceanward side. This would be our home and house for other researchers for the duration of our stay; later on it would become a research center for studying Sabalana Islands coral reef management. While it was being built, I began work with my longtime research associate and principal of the village elementary school, Supriady Daeng Matutu, interviewing local fishers in order to learn about their fishing knowledge and practices, past and present.

About three weeks after our arrival, I was sitting on the porch of our temporary home on the south side of the island, looking out across the exposed reef flat. Preoccupied with getting our own house built but anxious to start my research, I spotted a dugout and some men fishing just beyond the flat. I picked up my camera and notebook, and ventured out to learn all I could about what these men were doing. As it turned out, there were four men, one pair fishing with a net from the dugout and the other pair diving for fish with home-crafted goggles and spear guns. Because I was on foot, I could only stand and watch both operations from the edge of the flat. After a time, however, the latter pair of men emerged with fish on their spears and more in a dugout they had anchored while they fished, one of them inviting me to photograph their catch and shouting proudly, "and we caught these with our own hands, not with bombs!" These two men, Mama' and Saleh, were among only about ten men on the island of about six hundred residents who made their living entirely from fishing. Within the following few weeks, I got to know more of them through conversations, interviews, observations, and participation aboard their fishing boats. I will now introduce a few of them and their individual stories as fishermen.

A close neighbor of both Mama' and Saleh, MuLammadong, better known as "Dadong," started fishing full time around 1985 when he was in his mid teens. Unlike his neighbors, Dadong never fishes with spear guns nor gathers other sea products like trepang.[3] Rather, he relies almost exclusively on the commonly used weighted hand lines of monofilament wound onto homemade wooden spools. Like others, when setting out in his boat to fish the reefs, Dadong first trolls for baitfish with homemade aluminum lures while heading for favorite spots, usually next to a patch of corals where specific species of fish are known to congregate during certain seasons. If the fishing looks promising, the anchor is dropped onto the sandy bottom and the boat is allowed to drift over the corals. Often, boats will join one or two others from the village, fishing near one another for a time and even sharing bait. If the fish are not biting, the boats will, one by one, move on to other areas.

While others like Saleh and Mama' prefer to fish for anywhere from several hours to up to three days at a time, depending on their fishing success, Dadong often goes fishing for up to three weeks before returning home. On these occasions, Dadong sells fresh fish to villagers on another island and dries the rest for subsequent sale to an agent after returning home; the agent then carries the fish to Makassar for resale. Others, like Saleh, prefer to carry their own baskets of dried fish into port aboard local trading ships, cutting out the middleman and realizing higher profits.

While at their peaks the east and west monsoons bring high wind and waves, Dadong will set out any time of year when the weather is good. When he first started fishing in the mid-1980s, fishermen usually needed only to travel to the edges of nearby reefs in dugouts powered by paddle and sail to secure large catches (see Figure 24.1). However, with the growing use of destructive practices by outsiders since the early 1990s, those fish stocks have been rapidly depleted, forcing Dadong and others to travel farther and farther across the Sabalanas in diesel-powered *joloro'* to ply their

Figure 24.1. Fishing from a dugout or *lépa-lépa*.

Figure 24.2. Fishing from a *joloro'*.

trade. Where once it took a dugout up to twenty-four hours to travel across the Sabalanas to reach the island of Saregé, 30 nautical miles from Baloba-loang, Dadong can get there in just four hours in his *joloro'*.

With the reduction in travel time came much larger catches per trip, and while fuel prices have risen dramatically in recent years, so has the price of fish. So, until the use of blast fishing and cyanide poisoning became a common occurrence and spread to the far reaches of the Sabalanas, Dadong and others were, for a while, still realizing reasonable profits. Still, they understood that blast and cyanide fishing were driving them further and further from the island and that the entire fishery was rapidly being destroyed.[4]

Why, I wondered, in the face of this wanton destruction of their precious resource, hadn't the people of Balobaloang stood up against the blast and cyanide fishermen? Over several months of interviews and participation with them onboard their boats, local fishermen gradually revealed the history of their attempts to halt the destruction and the extensiveness of the corruption that blocked change.

The first thing I learned in 2003, after I had begun my research project of fishing, was that the majority of blast fishermen in the area came from nearby Sumanga' Island, while fleets of cyaniders traveled nearly 100 nautical miles to fish the Sabalanas from their home island of Lai Lai, just off of the coast of Makassar. While these were different operations run by separate bosses in Makassar, the cyaniders parked their boats at Sumanga' and got fresh water there. This relationship had evolved because while both bosses paid protection money to the village head living on Balobaloang, shares were distributed to the local leader on Sumanga' as well as the resident police and military officers. While only a decade earlier they had resided on the main island of Balobaloang, both now chose to reside on Sumanga', out of sight of the residents of Balobaloang, who had made it clear that they were opposed to the practice and wanted it to stop.

Initially, Dadong and others had hoped that, as in the past, the police would enforce the law if they had the evidence presented to them. Thus, a few years earlier Dadong boldly stole cyanide from the boat of one of the offenders and took it to the police as evidence, hoping they would lock up the illegal fishermen. Instead, due to endemic corruption among government officials, Dadong was threatened with arrest for possession of an illegal substance. Reluctantly, he dropped his case and returned to Balobaloang to fish rather than face possible prison time himself.

About a month after Dadong told me this, a boat carrying ice and a crew from Sumanga' detonated a bomb just a few hundred yards offshore from our house, not far from a spot where villages had recently begun a small reef rehabilitation project.[5] This had been the first bombing in a while in the area. A few people sat on the beach and watched, and a couple of dug-outs from Balobaloang went out to share in the spoils by gathering fish that were floating dead on the surface. I had a hard time understanding this, wondering again why villagers just looked on without protest and even took advantage of the situation.

Later, in an interview discussion with one of the local fishermen, I was told that as far as the bombers from Sumanga' were concerned, all one has to do is paddle out and ask them to not come so close to the island. This is what he and others had done on the south side: they explained that previous bombs had shaken and cracked the concrete walls and tall minaret of the village mosque, and the bombers agreed to stay away. As fellow Muslims, they consider the mosque a sacred place and one that cost the villagers large sums of money to build and maintain. As for the larger question of why they didn't impede blast and cyanide fishers from elsewhere, I was told that several years earlier, men from Balobaloang had boarded a boat from Lai Lai whose crew were fishing with cyanide and told them to leave the area. The captain agreed but went back on his word and simply continued sending out divers with cyanide. Angered by this, the villagers reboarded the boat and towed it to the adjacent island of Sabaru, where they discharged the crew and burned it. When the rest of the fleet returned to Lai Lai with their story, the *pongawa* was outraged that the authorities on Balobaloang and Sumanga', whom he had paid off, hadn't prevented this act of aggression. In retaliation, he sent word to the captains of the trading ships from Balobaloang, who were loading cargos in the harbor at Makassar, that should they try to leave the harbor, he would burn and sink their ships. Pragmatically, it makes sense that the value of a large ship laden with valuable cargo is many times that of a simple fishing boat, and that the act of destroying a cargo ship would immediately deprive the families of the owner and crew of their livelihoods. Seen another way, a ship owner had far greater political and economic power than the owner/operator of a small fishing boat. However, when the captains of the cargo ships went to the police, they said that there was nothing they could do; their superiors were already on the payroll of the *pongawa*. Thus, after several days of negotiations, the *pongawa* "forgave" the villagers on the promise that the ship owners and village leaders would never again allow the villagers to interfere with his operation.

By now, I was identifying with the fishermen who had been blocked at every turn from saving the reef and their livelihoods, not to mention that a major source of nutrition for all the villagers was being depleted. With the help of colleagues in the city, I met with an officer in the maritime police who appeared to be incorruptible and who had already led several sting operations against illegal fishing operations. As zealous as he was in his desire to end destructive fishing in South Sulawesi, he simply lack the money he needed to launch more than two or three raids per year. And, even with these sting operations, perpetrators and their boats had been released from custody by local judges who were in the pockets of the bosses. He did, however, manage to carry out one operation, capturing the mother ship with a cargo of live grouper from the Sabalanas to Makassar. Covered on television news and in local newspapers, this event delighted the villagers with whom I spoke, but, understandably, did not overcome their lack of trust in the system. What it did accomplish was to rid the area of cyanide fishers for several weeks.

Soon after this, Amelia Hapsari, a graduate student and videographer from Ohio University, came to Balobaloang to produce a participatory video with the villagers.[6] Hapsari, a native of the city of Semarang on the island of Java, had never been to such a remote part of her own country, and, as an urban, middle-class ethnic Chinese, had to work hard to develop rapport with the relatively ethnocentric and class-conscious Bugis villagers. Inspired by the work of Paulo Freire, an influential Brazilian educator and philosopher, Hapsari believed that if oppressed people were provided the opportunity to tell their own story, they could start the process of becoming liberated from their oppression.[7] She was determined, therefore, to involve villagers in every major decision regarding the video, starting with the subject matter. This did not take long; after the second open meeting, it was clear that the fishermen and even several ship owners who were not allied with the village head wanted her to document the lives of the fishermen and the destructive fishing practices that were increasingly making life harder for everyone on the island.

By her shear dedication and risk-taking (she even traveled aboard a local fishing boat on a choppy sea to film a blast fishing operation and interview the fishermen aboard their boat while the fish were being loaded on board), Hapsari was soon able to gain the trust of many villagers. In the process, we learned about yet another obstacle to resolving the problem. Standing opposed to the "individualism" that Americans, in particular, take for granted as "human nature," most Indonesians have traditionally placed greater value on social "harmony" (Geertz 1961; Mulder 1996; Tobing 1961). This, in itself, is a complex idea and one that expresses itself in a variety of ways. In this case, we were immediately warned against inviting villagers to "go public" by discussing the problem of illegal fishing on a film that would later be viewed and commented upon by other villagers. By doing so, we risked upsetting the social harmony of the village and the complex web of social relationships upon which villagers rely to ensure that, no matter what, their material and social needs are met. Operating together with "patron–client" relationships, this meant, for example, that a fisherman who needed a loan to repair or buy a new boat or engine could go to a ship owner with the understanding that should the ship owner subsequently require help, he could rely on the fisherman and his family to provide it. For example, if the ship owner eventually needed assistance with a wedding celebration for his child, he could rely upon the fisherman and his kin to provide fish, help build the wedding stage, and prepare the food for the guests. Because almost everyone in the village was related to one another either by blood or marriage, and many had relatives scattered across the Sabalanas, including on the island of Sumanga', openly criticizing or accusing any particular individual patron could tear at the very social fabric that held the small society together.

Hapsari and I saw this ethic of reciprocity or "sharing" manifesting itself in many ways among the fishermen themselves. For example, aboard local fishing boats, if the captain caught many fish while someone else caught few or none, the captain always shared part of his catch with the other fisherman. If, however, the accompanying fisherman had a particularly good day, he would share his catch with the captain to help defray the cost of fuel. Less benign than this, when blast fishers came close to Balobaloang, they always shared some of their catch with village fishermen, thus obligating them to put up with the destruction they were causing. And, on a larger scale, the village head could claim that if it were not for the bribes that he and other officials accepted from the bosses, he would have to raise revenue to build and maintain infrastructure—or to simply float a fisherman a needed loan—through taxation of the catches of the village fishermen.

It is all the more surprising, then, that in spite of this ethic, people did speak out, asking Hapsari to take the video to the mainland to show it to the authorities, believing that once they had the evidence, the authorities would feel compelled to intervene. Even after she had done so and had shown them footage of the noncommittal responses of the authorities, many villagers were pleased that their voices had finally been heard. When I returned to Balobaloang in 2006, the rapidly escalating cost of fuel, coupled with the reduced fish stocks, had forced at least one fisherman to take his family and move to an island further south where, it was said, laws were enforced and fish were more plentiful. By now only seven full-time fishermen remained in the village, but they and other villagers were happy to see an edited version of Hapsari's video. Still hopeful that it might force the government to act, they asked that it be broadcast on national television. I promised them that I would convey their message to Hapsari.

However, when Hapsari, herself, returned to the village a few months later to gather footage for the final cut of the video, she felt the full brunt of the ethic of harmony and sharing when none of the fishermen who had earlier spoken out on film allowed her to film follow-up interviews. Off camera, Dadong said that he could no longer participate in the project because he was afraid the village head would see him as a *pagar makan tanaman* or "fence eating the crops" (someone who is insincere, taking [from] both sides), saying on camera that the leaders were receiving bribes from the *pongawa* but then going to the village head to ask for money. He affirmed, however, that he and others like him who had little capital and wanted to remain independent would neither join the blast or cyanide operations and become bound by debt to the *pongawa*, nor would they buy larger trading ships and take on the responsibility, as patrons, of guaranteeing the livelihoods of crew

314 / *Gene Ammarell*

members and their families. He said that he and others had to decide carefully when and where to fish so as to not waste expensive fuel. Finally, he said he would continue to fish and, perhaps, explore other technologies such as mariculture (raising fish in enclosures in the ocean), and he believed he could remain an independent fisherman through ingenuity and hard work.

Across Indonesia—indeed, around the world—people and communities are facing grave and complex challenges to their lives and livelihoods. Whether we obtain our food by foraging on land or at sea, farming, and/or buying it in a shop or supermarket, in our daily choices each of us helps to collectively transform our environment at an ever-accelerating rate. These transformations, in turn, both limit and create future opportunities for procuring sustainable livelihoods.

For the people of Balobaloang, the choices seem rather limited at this point. As much as many of the residents would like to create a just and sustainable fishery, choices made by more powerful government officials have continually frustrated local efforts at resolving the growing environmental crisis facing them and their neighboring islanders. Traditional values of harmony and sharing help bind this community together, while global capitalism assumes that economic progress is the result of individual competition in a free market. With increasing demand for seafood in regional and world markets and lack of enforced regulations, fisheries like those surrounding Balobaloang are rapidly being depleted and even destroyed. In the meantime, stories like these are increasingly focusing international attention upon the need to foster sustainable fisheries and curtail the destruction of coral reefs worldwide. In Indonesia as elsewhere, this increased attention is forcing governments to respond with new regulations and development projects. However, even if fisheries can be saved and, over time, restored, questions remain as to whether people like Dadong, Saleh, and Mama' will be able to continue to rely on fishing as a sustainable source of livelihood for themselves and their families and as a source of sustenance for their neighbors.

NOTES

1. *Lambo* are a type of cargo ship that is used by petty traders across eastern Indonesia. Built according to traditional construction techniques and European design, they are powered by both sails and auxiliary diesel engines (see, for example, Southon 1995; Ammarell 1999).

2. An explosive mixture of ammonium nitrate fertilizer and kerosene plus detonator, and wick. To learn more about blast fishing in this region, see Chozin 2008.

3. Trepang (*Holothuria* spp.) are also know as sea cucumbers or sea slugs. They are gathered from the reef, dried, and sold in local markets or exported as an expensive delicacy.

4. As of 2006, the price of fuel was so high and the catches so small that Dadong and others were experiencing significant losses in spite of their hard work, and several men had either moved away or stopped fishing and found other work.

5. Funded and organized by a visiting graduate researcher from Ohio University, villagers had constructed and launched a small cement "reef ball" to provide substrate for new coral growth and habitat for fish.

6. The video *Sharing Paradise* was recently released by Documentary Educational Resources.

7. *Pedagogy of the Oppressed* by Paulo Freire was first published in 1968 and has sold more than 750,000 copies to date. Freire has widely been recognized as a founder of what has come to be known as "critical pedagogy" and "liberation theology."

REFERENCES

Adams, Kathleen M. 1993. "The Discourse of Souls in Tana Toraja (Indonesia): Indigenous Notions and Christian Conceptions." *Ethnology* 32(1):55–68.

———. 1998. "More Than an Ethnic Marker: Toraja Art as Identity Negotiator." *American Ethnologist* 25(3):327–351.

———. 2006. *Art as Politics: Re-crafting Identities, Tourism, and Power in Tana Toraja, Indonesia.* Honolulu: University of Hawai'i Press.

Aditjondro, George Junus. 2007. "Reciprocal Gratitude without 'Thank You.'" *Jakarta Post*, October 27.

Agence France Presse. 1995. "US Imperialism Killed Over 10% of Vietnamese Population During War." Hanoi, April 29, 1995.

Aguilar, Filomeno V. 1998. *Clash of Spirits: The History of Power and Sugar Planter Hegemony on a Visayan Island.* Honolulu: University of Hawaii Press.

Agustinanto, Fatimana. 2003. "Riau." In *Trafficking of Women and Children in Indonesia,* edited by R. Rosenberg, 178–182. Jakarta: International Catholic Migration Commission and the American Center for International Labor Solidarity.

Alatas, Alwi, and Fifrida Desliyanti. 2002. *Revolusi Jilbab: Kasus Pelarang Jilbab di SMA Negeri Se-Jabotabek, 1982–1991* (The Jilbab Revolution: The Prohibition of Headscarves in State Schools in the Jabotabek Region, 1982–1991). Jakarta: Al-I'tishom, 2002.

Alwi Sheikh Alhady. 1962. *Malay Customs and Traditions.* Singapore: Eastern Universities Press.

Ammarell, Gene. 1999. *Bugis Navigation.* New Haven, Conn: Yale University Southeast Asia Studies Monograph Series.

Andaya, Leonard. 2001. "The Search for the 'Origins' of Melayu." *Journal of Southeast Asian Studies* 32(3):315–330.

———. 2008. *Leaves of the Same Tree: Trade and Ethnicity in the Straits of Malacca.* Honolulu: University of Hawai'i Press.

Anderson, Benedict. 1991 [1983]. *Imagined Communities: Reflections on the Origin and Spread of Nationalism* (rev. ed.). London: Verso.

———. 1998. "Gravel in Jakarta's Shoes." In *The Spectre of Comparisons: Nationalism, Southeast Asia and the World*, 131–138. Verso: London & New York.

Anderson, E. N. 1988. *The Food of China*. New Haven, Conn.: Yale University Press.

Antze, Paul, and Michael Lambek. 1996. *Tense Past: Cultural Essays in Trauma and Memory*. New York: Routledge.

Apinan Poshyanand. 1993. "Thai MODERNism and (Post?) Modernism, 1970s and 1980s." In *Tradition and Change: Contemporary Art of Asia and the Pacific*, edited by C. Turner, 222–236. St. Lucia, Queensland: University of Queensland Press.

———. 1996. "Roaring Tigers, Desperate Dragons in Transition." In *Contemporary Art in Asia: Traditions/Tensions*, edited by A. Poshyananda, 23–53. New York: Asia Society.

———. 2003. "Montien Boonma: Paths of Suffering (*Dukkha*)." In *Montien Boonma: Temple of the Mind*, edited by Apinan Poshyananda, 9–39. New York: Asia Society.

Aragon, Lorraine V. 2000. *Fields of the Lord: Animism, Christian Minorities, and State Development in Indonesia*. Honolulu: University of Hawai'i Press.

Arumugam, Indira. 2002. Sociology of the Indians. In *The Making of Singapore Society: Society and State*, edited by Tong Chee kiong and Lian Kwen Fee, 320–250. Singapore: Times Academic Press, and Leiden: Brill Academic Publishers.

Ashkenazi, Michael, and Jeanne Jacob. 2000. *The Essence of Japanese Cuisine: An Essay on Food and Culture*. Richmond, Surrey: Curzon.

Asiapac Editors. 2003. *Gateway to Malay Culture*. Singapore: Asiapac Books.

Avieli, Nir. 2007. "Feasting with the Living and the Dead." In *Modernity and Re-Enchantment: Religion in Post-War Vietnam*, edited by P. Taylor. Singapore: ISEAS Press.

Bachtiar, H. W. 1973. "The Religion of Java: A Commentary." *Majalah Ilmu-Ilmu Sastra Indonesia* 5(1):85–118.

Bangkok Post. 1998. "Setting the Past in Stone." October 12. Available at http://geociti.es/RainForest/7813/9/9shrine.htm, accessed August 13, 2009.

Bao Ninh. 1993. *The Sorrow of War*. English translation by Frank Palmos, based on the translation from the Vietnamese by Vo Bang Thanh and Phan Thanh Hao, with Katerina Pierce. London: Secker & Warburg.

Barry, Kathleen. 1996. *The Prostitution of Sexuality: The Global Exploitation of Women*. New York: New York University Press.

BBC Online. 2005. Burma's Confusing Capital Move. BBC News. November 8. http://news.bbc.co.uk/2/hi/4416960.stm. Accessed October 25, 2010. Copy in possession of author.

Bello, David A. 2005. *Opium and the Limits of Empire: Drug Prohibition in the Chinese Interior, 1729–1850*. Cambridge, Mass.: Harvard University Press.

Bellwood, Peter. 1997. *Prehistory of the Indo-Malaysian Archipelago*. Honolulu: University of Hawai'i Press.

Bendtz, N. Arne. 1986. "Some Reflections about the Batak People and Their

Beliefs." In *Horas HKBP! Essays for a 125-year-old Church,* edited by A. A. Sitompul and Arne Sovic. Pematangsiantar, Sumatera Utara, Indonesai: SekolahTinggi Teologi.

Benedict, Ruth. 1934. *Patterns of Culture.* London: Routledge.

Bennett, Tony. 1995. *The Birth of the Museum: History, Theory, Politics.* New York: Routledge.

Berger, John. 1979. "Historical Afterword." In *Pig Earth.* New York: Pantheon.

Bernama. 2008. "Suhakam Urges Govt to Protect Orang Asli Rights." http://www.malaysianbar.org.my/legal/general_news/suhakam_urges_govt_to_protect_orang_asli_rights.html/, accessed November 19, 2008.

Bigalke, Terry. 1981. A Social History of "Tana Toraja" 1870–1965. Ph.D. diss., University of Wisconsin–Madison.

Bishop, Claire. 2006. Introduction/Viewers as Producers. In *Participation,* edited by Claire Bishop, 10–17. London: Whitechapel.

Blackburn, Susan. 2004. *Women and the State in Modern Indonesia.* Cambridge: Cambridge University Press.

Blackwood, Evelyn. 2000. *Webs of Power: Women, Kin and Community in a Sumatran Village.* Lanham, Md.: Rowman and Littlefield.

Boulanger, Clare L. 2008. *A Sleeping Tiger.* Lanham, Md.: University Press of America.

Bourchier, David. 2010. *Dynamics of Dissent in Indonesia: Sawito and the Phantom Coup.* London: Equinox Publishing.

Bourdieu, Pierre. 1984. *Distinction: A Social Critique of the Judgment of Taste.* London and New York: Routledge and Kegan Paul.

Bourriaud, Nicolas. 2006. "Relational Aesthetics, 1998." In *Participation,* edited by Claire Bishop, 160–171. London: Whitechapel.

Bowie, Katherine. 2008. "Standing in the Shadows: Of Matrilocality and the Role of Women in a Village Election in Northern Thailand." *American Ethnologist* 35(1):136–153.

Boxing Act. 1999 [2542]. Phra Ratcha Banyat Kila Muai Pho. So. 2542 [Boxing Act 1999]. 1999. *Ratcha Kitchanubeksa [Royal Gazette]* 116, 128 (December 16): 11–25.

Braudel, Fernand. 1996 [1949]. *The Mediterranean and the Mediterranean World in the Age of Philip II.* Vol 1. *(La Méditerranée et le Monde Méditerranéen a l'époque de Philippe II).* Berkeley: University of California Press.

Brenner, Suzanne A. 1996. "Reconstructing Self and Society: Javanese Muslim Women and 'the Veil.'" *American Ethnologist* 23(4):673–697.

———. 1999. *The Domestication of Desire: Women, Wealth, and Modernity in Java.* Princeton, N.J.: Princeton University Press.

Brown, C. C. 1989. *Malay Sayings.* Singapore: Graham Brash.

Bua Nin-Archa. 1989. "Muai Thai Boran: Tamnan Silapa Kan Tosu Khong Thai [The Traditional Thai Boxing: A History of Thai Martial Art]." Mimeograph.

Bubandt, Nils. 2001. "Malukan Apocalypse: Themes in the Dynamics of Violence in Eastern Indonesia." In *Violence in Indonesia,* edited by Ingrid

Wessel and Georgia Wimhöfer, 228–253. Hamburg: Abera Verlag Markus Voss.

Bulliet, Richard W. 1990. "Process and Status in Conversion and Continuity." In *Indigenous Christian Communities in Islamic Lands: Eighth to Eighteenth Centuries*, edited by Michael Gervers and Ramzi Jibra Bikhazi, 1–14. Toronto: Pontifical Institute of Mediaeval Studies.

Bunnag, Shane. 2005. *Breast Stupa Cookery Project*. Video.

Caldwell, John C. 1976. "Toward a Restatement of Demographic Transition Theory." *Population and Development Review* 2(3 & 4):321–366.

Cambodian Genocide Program. 2010. Cambodian Genocide Program of the Yale University's Genocide Program, MacMillan Center for International and Area Studies. http://www.yale.edu/cgp/, accessed October 23, 2010. Copy in possession of author.

Carlisle, Steven G. 2008. "Synchronizing Karma: The Internalization and Externalization of a Shared, Personal Belief." *Ethos* 36(2):194–219.

Carneiro da Cunha, Manuela. 1995. "Children, Politics and Culture: The Case of Brazilian Indians." In *Children and the Politics of Culture*, edited by Sharon Stephens, 282–291. Princeton, N.J.: Princeton University Press.

Cate, Sandra. 1999. "Cars-Stuck-Together: Tourism and the Bangkok Traffic Jam." In *Converging Interests: Traders, Travelers, and Tourists in Southeast Asia*, edited by Jill Forshee, Christina Fink, and Sandra Cate, 23–50. Berkeley, Calif.: Center for Southeast Asia Studies, Monograph No. 36.

———. 2003. *Making Merit, Making Art: A Thai Temple in Wimbledon*. Honolulu: University of Hawai'i Press.

Causey, Andrew. 2003. *Hard Bargaining in Sumatra: Western Travelers and Toba Bataks in the Marketplace of Souvenirs*. Honolulu: University of Hawai'i Press.

Center for Orang Asli Concerns. n.d. *Drowned Forests, Damned Lives*. [CD] Subang Jaya, Selangor: COAC.

Chandler, David. 1998. "Songs at the Edge of the Forest: Perceptions of Order in Three Cambodian Texts." In *Facing the Cambodian Past*, edited by D. Chandler, 76–99. Chiang Mai: Silkworm Press.

Chang K.-C. (ed.). 1977. *Food in Chinese Culture: Anthropological and Historical Perspectives*. New Haven, Conn.: Yale University Press.

Chang Noi. 2009. "Red and Yellow and Shades of Grey," *The [Bangkok] Nation*, May 4. http://www.nationmultimedia.com/2009/05/04/opinion/opinion_30101903.php, accessed October 14, 2010.

Cheng Zu. 2006. "Uncomfortable Realities: Historical Disparity, Social Dysfunction and Collective Responsibility." *Bangkok Post*, August 30. www.bangkokpost.com archives, accessed January 7, 2009.

Chia, Felix. 1980. *The Babas*. Singapore: Times Books International.

Choo, Simon. 2004. "Eating Satay Babi: Sensory Perception of Transnational Movement." *Journal of Intercultural Studies* 25(3):203–213.

Chozin, Muhammad. 2008. Illegal but Common: Life of Blast Fisherman in the Spermonde Archipelago, South Sulawesi, Indonesia. Master's thesis, Center for Southeast Asian Studies, Ohio University.

Chua Beng Huat. 2005. *Life Is Not Complete without Shopping: Consumption Culture in Singapore*. Singapore: Singapore University Press.

Clammer, John. 1980. *Straits Chinese Society: Studies in the Sociology of the Baba Communities of Singapore and Malaysia*. Singapore: Singapore University Press.

———. 1993. "Deconstructing Values: The Establishment of a National Ideology and Its Implications for Singapore's Political Future." In *Singapore Changes Guard: Social, Political and Economic Directions in the 1990s*, edited by Garry Rodan, 34–51. Melbourne: Longmans Cheshire, and New York: St. Martin's Press.

———. 1997. "Framing the Other: Criminality, Social Exclusion and Social Engineering in Developing Singapore." In *Crime and Social Exclusion*, edited by Catherine Jones Finer and Mike Nellis, 136–153. Oxford: Blackwell.

———. 1998. *Race and State in Independent Singapore: The Cultural Politics of Pluralism in a Multiethnic Society*. Aldershot and Brookfield, Vt.: Ashgate.

Clark, John. 1998. *Modern Asian Art*. Honolulu: University of Hawai'i Press.

Coedès, Georges. 1968. *The Indianized States of Southeast Asia*, translated by Susan Brown Cowing; edited by Walter F. Vella. Honolulu: The University of Hawai'i Press/An East-West Center Book.

Cohen, Erik. 1987. "Hmong Cross: A Cosmic Symbol in Hmong (Meo) Textile Designs." *RES* 14(Autumn):27–45.

———. 2001. *The Chinese Vegetarian Festival in Phuket: Religion, Ethnicity and Tourism on a Southern Thai Island*. Bangkok: White Lotus.

Cohen, Paul T. 1984. "Are the Spirit Cults of Northern Thailand Descent Groups?" *Mankind* 14(4):293–299.

———. 2000. "Resettlement, Opium and Labor Dependence: Akha–Tai Relations in Northern Laos." *Development and Change* 31:179–200.

Coleman, Simon. 2000. *The Globalisation of Charismatic Christianity: Spreading the Gospel of Prosperity*. Cambridge: Cambridge University Press.

Condominas, Georges. 1977. *We Have Eaten the Forest: The Story of a Montagnard Village in the Central Highlands of Vietnam* (Nous avons mangé la forêt de la Pierre-Génie Goô). Translated by A. Foulke. New York: Hill and Wang.

———. 1990. From Lawa to Mon, from Saa' to Thai: Historical and Anthropological Aspects of Southeast Asian Social Spaces, translated by Stephanie Anderson, Maria Magannon, and Gehan Wijeyewardene. An occasional paper of the department of anthropology, in association with the Thai-Yunnan project. Canberra: Department of Anthropology, Research School of Pacific Studies, Australian National University.

Connell, Robert W. 1995. *Masculinities*. Oxford: Polity Press.

Constable, Nicole. 2003. *Romance on a Global Stage: Pen Pals, Virtual Ethnography, and "Mail Order" Marriages*. Berkeley: University of California Press.

———. 2007. *Made to Order in Hong Kong: Stories of Migrant Workers*, 2nd ed. Ithaca, N.Y.: Cornell University Press.

Coté, Joost (trans.). 1995. *Letters from Kartini: An Indonesian Feminist.* Monash, Australia: Monash Asia Institute.

Cowlishaw, Gillian. 2004. *Blackfellas Whitefellas and the Hidden Injuries of Race.* Cornwall, Blackwell Publishing.

Critcher, Chas. 2003. *Moral Panics and the Media.* New York: Open University Press.

Cumings, Bruce. 1997. "Boundary Displacement: Area Studies and International Studies during and after the Cold War." *Bulletin of Concerned Asian Scholars* 29(1):6–26.

Cunningham, Clark E. 1964. "Order in the Atoni House." *Bijdragen tot de Taal-, Land-en Volkenkunde* 120:34–68.

Darlington, Susan M. 1990. Buddhism, Morality and Change: The Local Response to Development in Thailand. Ph.D. diss., University of Michigan.

———. 2003a. "Buddhism and Development: The Ecology Monks of Thailand." In *Action Dharma: New Studies in Engaged Buddhism*, edited by Christopher Queen, Charles Prebish, and Damien Keown, 96–109. London: Routledge Curzon Press.

———. 2003b. "Practical Spirituality and Community Forests: Monks, Ritual and Radical Conservatism in Thailand." In *Nature in the Global South: Environmental Projects in South and Southeast Asia*, edited by Paul Greenough and Anna L. Tsing, 347–366. Durham & London: Duke University Press.

———. 2003c. "The Spirit(s) of Conservation in Buddhist Thailand." In *Nature across Cultures*, edited by Helaine Selin, 129–145. Dordrecht: Kluwer Academic Publishers.

———. 2005. "Thai Buddhist Monks." In *Encyclopedia of Religion and Nature*, Vol. 2, 1629–1630. New York: Continuum International Pubs.

———. 2007. "The Good Buddha and the Fierce Spirits: Protecting the Northern Thai Forest." *Contemporary Buddhism* 8(2):169–185.

———. 2009. "Translating Modernity: Buddhist Response to the Thai Environmental Crisis." In *TransBuddhism: Transmission, Translation and Transformation*, edited by Abraham Zablocki, Jay Garfield, and Nalini Bhushan, 183–207. Amherst: University of Massachusetts Press.

———. Forthcoming. *The Ordination of a Tree: The Thai Buddhist Environmental Movement.* Albany: SUNY Press.

Davis, Erik. 2009. Buddhism Makes Brahmanism: Entities and Erotics in Cambodian Religion. Talk given at the Southeast Asian Summer Studies Institute, Madison, Wis. July 25.

Delcore, Henry D. 2004. "Symbolic Politics or Generification? The Ambivalent Implications of Tree Ordinations in the Thai Environmental Movement." *Journal of Political Ecology* 11(1):1–30.

Dentan, Robert Knox. 1975. "If There Were No Malays, Who Would the Semai Be?" In *Pluralism in Malaysia*, edited by Judith Nagata. *Contributions to Asian Studies* 7:50–64.

———. 1976. "Identity and Ethnic Contact: Perak, Malaysia, 1963." In *Intergroup Relations: Asian Scenes*, edited by Tai S. Kang. *Journal of Asian Affairs* 1(1):79–86.

———. 1997. "The Persistence of Received Truth: How the Malaysian Ruling Class Constructs Orang Asli." In *Indigenous Peoples and the State*, edited by Robert Winzeler. Monograph 46/Yale University Southeast Asia Studies. New Haven, Conn.: Yale University.

———. 2001. "A Vision of Modernization." *Anthropology and Humanism* 26(1):3–15.

———. 2008. *Overwhelming Terror.* Boulder, Colo.: Rowman and Littlefield.

———. 2010. "Nonkilling Social Arrangements." In *Nonkilling Societies*, edited by J. C. Evans-Pym. Honolulu: Center for Global Nonkilling.

———. Forthcoming. "Childhood, Familiarity and Social Life among East Semai." In *Anarchic Solidarity: Autonomy, Equality, and Fellowship in Southeast Asia*, edited by Thomas Gibson and Kenneth Sillander. New Haven, Conn.: Yale Southeast Asian Studies Publications.

———, and Juli Edo. 2008. "Schooling vs. Education, Hidden vs. Overt Curricula." *Moussons* 12(1–2):3–34.

———, and Robert Knox, Kirk Michael Endicott, Alberto G. Gomes, and M. Barry Hooker. 1997. *Malaysia and the "Original People."* Boston: Allyn and Bacon.

Department of Museums. n.d. (a). *Worshipping Ceremony of the Mah Meri Aboriginal Tribe.* (CD) Kuala Lumpur: Ministry of Culture of Malaysia.

———, n.d. (b). *The Art of Wood Carving of the Orang Asli.* (CD) Kuala Lumpur: Ministry of Culture of Malaysia.

———, n.d. (c). *Sewang (Semai Ethnic).* (CD) Kuala Lumpur: Ministry of Culture of Malaysia.

Dessaint, Alain Y. 1972. "Lisu Settlement Patterns." *Journal of the Siam Society* 60:195–204.

Dessaint, William, and Alain Y. Dessaint. 1992. "Opium and Labor: Social Structure and Economic Change in the Lisu Highlands. *Peasant Studies* (Salt Lake City) 19(3):147–177.

Djamour, Judith. 1965. *Malay Kinship and Marriage in Singapore.* London: Athlone Press.

Drowned Forests, Damned Lives. n.d. (CD). Center for Orang Asli Concerns. Subang Jaya, Selangor: COAC.

DuBois, Cora. 1944. *The People of Alor: A Social-Psychological Study of an East Indian Island.* Minneapolis: University of Minnesota Press.

Dunn, James. 2003. *East Timor: A Rough Passage to Independence.* Double Bay, New South Wales: Longueville Books.

Duplatre, L. 1933. Review of *L'esclave privé dans le vieux droit Siamois,* by R. Lingat. *Journal of the Siam Society* 26:103–124.

Durand, Frédéric, 2001. "Timor Lorosa'e 1930–2001: Partis politiques et processus électoraux à hauts risques." *Aséanie* 8:103–126.

Durrenberger, E. Paul. 1971. The Ethnography of Lisu Curing. Ph.D. diss., University of Illinois.

———. 1976. "Law and Authority in a Lisu Village: Two Cases." *Journal of Anthropological Research* 32(4):301–325.

———. 1989. *Lisu Religion.* De Kalb: Northern Illinois University, Center for Southeast Asian Studies.

Dzuhayatin, Siti Ruhaini. 2001. "Gender and Pluralism in Indonesia." In *The Politics of Multiculturalism: Pluralism and Citizenship in Malaysia, Singapore, and Indonesia,* edited by Robert W. Hefner, 253–267. Honolulu: University of Hawai'i Press.

Eberhardt, Nancy. 2006. *Imagining the Course of Life: Self-Transformation in a Shan Buddhist Community.* Honolulu: University of Hawai'i Press.

Ebihara, May Mayko. 1968. Svay, a Khmer Village in Cambodia. Ph.D. diss., Columbia University.

Echols, John M., and Hassan Shadily. 1989. *An Indonesian-English Dictionary,* 3rd ed. Ithaca, N.Y.: Cornell University Press.

Eder, James F. 2008. *Migrants to the Coasts: Livelihood, Resource Management and Global Change in the Philippines.* Series on Contemporary Social Issues. Belmont, Calif.: Wadsworth Cengage.

Edwards, Penny. 2007. *Cambodge: The Cultivation of a Nation, 1860–1945.* Honolulu: The University of Hawai'i Press.

Eggan, Fred. 1960. "The Sagada Igorots of Northern Luzon." In *Social Structure in Southeast Asia,* edited by George P. Murdock, 24–50. Viking Fund Publications in Anthropology, No. 29. Chicago: Quadrangle Books.

Eliade, M. 1959. *Cosmos and History: The Myth of the Eternal Return.* New York: Harper.

Embree, John F. 1950. "Thailand, a Loosely Structured Social System." *American Anthropologist* 52:181–193.

Emmerson, Donald K. 1984. "'Southeast Asia': What's in a Name?" *Journal of Southeast Asian Studies* XV(1):1–21.

Endicott, Kirk Michael, and Robert Knox Dentan. 2004. "Into the Mainstream or into the Backwater?" In *Civilizing the Margins,* edited by Christopher R. Duncan, 24–55. Ithaca, N.Y.: Cornell University Press.

Errington, Shelly. 1989. *Meaning and Power in a Southeast Asian Realm.* Princeton, N.J.: Princeton University Press.

Ezra, Markos. 2003. Factors Associated with Marriage and Family Formation Processes in Southern Ethiopia. *Journal of Comparative Family Studies* 34(4):509–530.

Federspiel, Howard. 2007. *Sultans, Shamans and Saints: Islam and Muslims in Southeast Asia.* Honolulu: University of Hawai'i Press.

Feillard, Andrée. 1995. *Islam et Armée dans l'Indonésie Contemporaine.* Paris: Editions l'Harmattan in association with Association Archipel, Cahier d'Archipel 28.

Ford, Michele, and Lenore Lyons. 2008. "Making the Best of What You've Got: Sex Work and Class Mobility in the Riau Islands." In *Women and Work in Indonesia,* edited by M. Ford and L. Parker, 173–194. London: Routledge.

Foster, George M. 1961. "The Dyadic Contract: A Model for the Social Structure of a Mexican Peasant Village." *American Anthropologist* 63:1173–1192.

Foucault, Michel. 1988. "Technologies of the Self." In *Technologies of the Self: A Seminar with Michel Foucault*, edited by Luther Martin et al., 16–49. Amherst: University of Massachusetts Press.

———. 2002. *The Order of Things: An Archeology of the Human Sciences* [1973]. London: Routledge.

Fox, C. E. 1925. *The Threshold of the Pacific: An Account of the Social Organization, Magic, and Religion of the People of San Cristoval in the Solomon Islands*. New York, N.Y.: Alfred A. Knopf.

Fox, James J. 1993. *Inside Austronesian Houses: Perspectives on Domestic Designs for Living*. Canberra: Comparative Austronesian Project, Research School of Pacific Studies, Australian National University.

———. 1995. Installing the Outsider Inside: The Exploration of an Epistemic Austronesian Cultural Theme and Its Social Significance. Paper presented at the first Conference of the European Association for Southeast Asian Studies, *Local Transformations and Common Heritage in Southeast Asia*, Leiden University, June 29 to July 1, 1995, revised draft.

———. 1996. Introduction. In *Origins, Ancestry and Alliance: Explorations in Austronesian Ethnography*, edited by James J. Fox and Clifford Sather, 1–17. Canberra: Research School of Pacific and Asian Studies, The Australian National University.

Fox, Jefferson. 2002. "*Siam Mapped* and Mapping in Cambodia: Boundaries, Sovereignty, and Indigenous Conceptions of Space." *Society and Natural Resources* 15:65–78.

Frank, Andre Gunder. 1998. *Re-Orient: Global Economy in the Asian Age*. Berkeley: University of California Press.

Frazer, James George. 1910. *Totemism and Exogamy*. London.

Freire, Paulo. 1993 [1970]. *Pedagogy of the Oppressed*, translated by Myra Bergman Ramos. New York: Continuum.

Freud, Sigmund. 1918. *Totem and Taboo: Resemblances between the Psychic Lives of Savages and Neurotics*, translated by A. A. Brill. New York: Moffat.

Fry, Gerald W. 2002. The Evolution of Educational Reform in Thailand. Paper presented at the Second International Forum on Education Reform, September 2–5, Bangkok. Available at http://www.worldedreform.com/intercon2/fly.pdf, accessed August 19, 2009.

Furnivall, J. S. 1956 (1948). *Colonial Policy and Practice: A Comparative Study of Burma and Netherlands India*. New York: New York University Press.

Gatto, John Taylor. 2006. *The Underground History of American Education*. New York: Oxford Village Press.

Geertz, Clifford. 1973. *The Interpretation of Cultures: Selected Essays*. New York: Basic Books.

———. 1976 [1960]. *The Religion of Java*. Chicago: The University of Chicago Press.

Geertz, Hildred. 1961. *The Javanese Family: A Study of Kinship and Socialization*. Prospect Heights, Ill: Waveland Press.

————. 1994. *Images of Power: Balinese Paintings Made for Gregory Bateson and Margaret Mead.* Honolulu: University of Hawai'i Press.

————, and Togog, Ida Bagus Made. 2005. *Tales from a Charmed Life: A Balinese Painter Reminisces.* Honolulu: University of Hawai'i Press.

Gell, Alfred. 1998. *Art and Agency: An Anthropological Theory.* Oxford: Clarendon Press.

George, Cherian. 2008. *Singapore: The Air-Conditioned Nation: Essays on the Politics of Comfort and Control.* Singapore: Landmark Books.

Gerber, David A. 1984. "Language Maintenance, Ethnic Group Formation, and Public Schools." *Journal of American Ethnic History* (Fall):31–61.

Gillogly, Kathleen A. 2004. "Developing the 'Hill Tribes' of Northern Thailand." In *Civilizing the Margins: Southeast Asian Government Policies for the Development of Minorities,* edited by Christopher Duncan, 116–149. Ithaca, N.Y.: Cornell University Press, Southeast Asian Studies Program.

————. 2006. Transformations of Lisu Social Structure under Opium Control and Watershed Conservation in Northern Thailand. Ph.D. diss., University of Michigan.

Goldenweiser, Alexander A. 1910. "Totemism: An Analytical Study." *Journal of American Folklore* 23:179–293.

Gomez, James. 2000. *Self-Censorship: Singapore's Shame.* Singapore: Think Centre.

Gouda, Francis. 1995. *Dutch Culture Overseas: Colonial Practice in the Netherlands Indies, 1900–1942.* Amsterdam: Amsterdam University Press.

Graeber, David. 2007. "Turning Modes of Production Inside Out: Or, Why Capitalism Is a Transformation of Slavery (Short Version)." In *Possibilities: Essays on Hierarchy, Rebellion, and Desire,* 85–112. Oakland, Calif.: AK Press.

Green, Maia. 2000. "Participatory Development and the Appropriation of Agency in Southern Tanzania." *Critique of Anthropology* 20(1):67–89.

Gridthiya Gaweewong. 2001. "On Thai Artists and an Issue of Cultural Identity." apexart, Conference in Rio de Janiero, Brazil, July. Available at http://www.apexart.org/conference/Gaweewong.htm, accessed December 8, 2008.

Grinspoon, Lester, and Peter Hedblom. 1975. *The Speed Culture: Amphetamine Use and Abuse in America.* Boston: Harvard University Press.

Guggenheim, Y. K. 1985. *The Development of the Science of Nutrition from Ancient to Modern Times.* Jerusalem: Magnes, The Hebrew University Press (in Hebrew).

Hainley, Bruce. 1996. "Where Are We Going? And What Are We Doing? Rirkrit Tiravanija's Art of Living." *Artforum International* 34(6):54–98.

Hanks, Jane R. 1965. "A Yao Wedding." In *Ethnographic Notes on Northern Thailand,* edited by Lucien M. Hanks, Jane R. Hanks, and Lauriston Sharp, 47–66. Ithaca, N.Y.: Cornell Southeast Asia Program Data Papers.

Hanks, Lucien. 1962. "Merit and Power in the Thai Social Order." *American Anthropologist* 64 (6):1247–1261.

Hapsari, Amelia, and Gene Ammarell. 2008. *Sharing Paradise* (videorecording). Watertown, Mass.: Documentary Educational Resources.

Haraway, Donna. 1991. "A Cyborg Manifesto: Science, Technology, and Socialist-Feminism in the Late Twentieth Century." In *Simians, Cyborgs and Women: The Reinvention of Nature*, 149–181. New York: Routledge.

Hart, Gillian. 1978. Labor Allocation Strategies in Rural Javanese Households. Ph.D. diss, Cornell University.

Harvey, Graham. 2006. *Animism: Respecting the Living World*. New York: Columbia University Press.

Hassan, Fuad. 1975. Kita *and* Kami: *An Analysis of the Basic Modes of Togetherness*. Jakarta: Bharatara.

Hayslip, Le Ly (with Jay Wurts). 1989. *When Heaven and Earth Changed Places: A Vietnamese Woman's Journey from War to Peace*. New York: Penguin Books.

Hefner, Robert W. 1993. "Islam, State, and Civil Society: ICMI and the Struggle for the Indonesian Middle Class." *Indonesia* 56(Oct):1–35.

———. 2000. *Civil Islam: Muslims and Democratization in Indonesia*. Princeton, N.J.: Princeton University Press.

Henley, David. 2002. *Jealousy and Justice: The Indigenous Roots of Colonial Rule in Northern Sulawesi*. Amsterdam: VU University Press.

Higham, Charles. 2001. *The Civilization of Angkor*. Berkeley: University of California Press.

Hill, A. H. 1970. *The Hikayat Abdullah: Abdullah Bin Abdul Kadir. An Annotated Translation*. Kuala Lumpur, Singapore, London, New York: Oxford University Press.

Him, Chanrithy. 2000. *When Broken Glass Floats: Growing Up under the Khmer Rouge, a Memoir*. New York: W.W. Norton.

Hirsch, Marianne. 1997. *Family Frames: Photography, Narrative and Postmemory*. Cambridge, Mass.: Harvard University Press.

Hirsch, Philip. 1996. "Environment and Environmentalism in Thailand: Material and Ideological Bases." In *Seeing Forests for Trees: Environment and Environmentalism in Thailand*, edited by Philip Hirsch, 15–36. Chiang Mai: Silkworm Books.

Hoa, Dien Diep, Kathleen Gillogly, Le Thi Van Minh, Nguyen Quang Minh, and Nguyen Hong Long. 1993. "Autonomy and Solidarity." In *Too Many People, Too Little Land: The Human Ecology of a Wet Rice-Growing Village in the Red River Delta of Vietnam*, edited by Le Trong Cuc and A. Terry Rambo, with the assistance of Kathleen Gillogly, 51–82. Occasional Paper No. 15, Program on the Environment. Honolulu: East-West Center.

Hoskins, J. 2010. "Seeing Syncretism as Visual Blasphemy: Critical Eyes on Caodai Religious Architecture." *Material Religion* 6(1):30–58.

Hull, Terence, and Gavin W. Jones. 1994. Demographic Perspectives. In *Indonesia's New Order: The Dynamics of Socio-economic Transformation*, edited by Hal Hill, 123–178. Honolulu: University of Hawai'i Press.

Hull, Valerie L. 1996 [1982]. "Women in Java's Rural Middle Class: Progress or Regress?" In *Women of Southeast Asia*, edited by Penny Van Esterik, 78–95. Dekalb, Ill.: Northern Illinois University Press.

Hutheesing, Otome Klein. 1990. *Emerging Sexual Inequality among the Lisu of*

Northern Thailand: The Waning of Dog and Elephant Repute. Leiden: E. J. Brill.

Ileto, Reynaldo. 1979. *Pasyon and Revolution: Popular Movements in the Philippines, 1840–1910.* Quezon City: Ateneo de Manila University Press.

Ishii, Yoneo. 1986. *Sangha, State, and Society: Thai Buddhism in History,* translated by Peter Hawkes. Monographs of the Center for Southeast Asian Studies, Kyoto University, No. 16. Honolulu: University of Hawai'i Press.

Jamieson, Neil. 1995. *Understanding Vietnam.* Berkeley: University of California Press.

Jay, Robert. 1969. *Javanese Villagers: Social Relations in Rural Modjokuto.* Cambridge, Mass.: MIT Press.

Jerryson, Michael. 2010. "Militarizing Buddhism: Violence in Southern Thailand." In *Buddhist Warfare,* edited by Michael Jerryson and Mark Juergensmeyer, 179–209. New York: Oxford University Press.

JOAS [Indigenous People's Network of Malaysia]. 2008. Press Statement: Orang Asli Call for the Application of the Declaration of Rights of Indigenous Peoples to Malaysian Law and Policies, September 4.

Jones, Gavin W. 1994. *Marriage and Divorce in Islamic South-east Asia.* New York: Oxford University Press.

Jonsson, Hjorleifur. 2001. "Does the House Hold? History and the Shape of Mien (Yao) Society." *Ethnohistory* 48(4):613–654.

———. 2004. "Mien Alter-Natives in Thai Modernity." *Anthropological Quarterly* 77(4):675–706.

———. 2005. *Mien Relations: Mountain People and State Control in Thailand.* Ithaca, N.Y.: Cornell University Press.

Juli Edo, Anthony Williams-Hunt, and Robert Knox Dentan. 2009. "'Surrender,' Peacekeeping, and Internal Colonialism: A Neglected Episode in Malaysian History." *Bijdragen tot de Taal, Land en Volkenkunde* 165 (2–3): 211a–240.

Kammerer, Cornelia. 1998. "Descent, Alliance, and Political Order among Akha." *American Ethnologist* 25(4):659–674.

———. 2000. "The Akha of the Southwest China Borderlands." In *Endangered Peoples of Southeast and East Asia,* edited by L. Sponsel, 37–53. Westport, Conn.: Greenwood Press.

Kau Ah Keng, Tambyah Siok Kuan, and Tan Soo Jiuan. 2006. *Understanding Singaporeans: Values, Lifestyles, Aspirations and Consumption Behaviours.* London and Singapore: World Scientific.

Keane, Webb. 1997. *Signs of Recognition: Powers and Hazards of Representation in an Indonesian Society.* Berkeley: University of California Press.

Keeler, Ward. 1984. *Javanese: A Cultural Approach.* Athens: Ohio University Monographs in International Studies, Southeast Asia Series, No. 69.

Keesing, Roger. 1989. "Creating the Past: Custom and Identity in the Pacific." *The Contemporary Pacific* (1–2):19–42.

Kementerian Pendidikan Malaysia. 2003. *Sukatan Pelajaran Bahasa Semai:*

Kurikulum Bersepadu. Sekolah Rendah. Kuala Lumpur: Pusat Perkembangan Kurikulum, Kementerian Pendidikan Malaysia.

Kempadoo, Kamala (ed.). 1999. *Sun, Sex, and Gold: Tourism and Sex Work in the Caribbean.* Lanham, Md.: Rowman and Littlefield.

Kessler, Christl, and Jürgen Rüland. 2008. *Give Jesus a Hand! Charismatic Christians: Populist Religion and Politics in the Philippines.* Quezon City: Ateneo de Manila University.

Keyes, Charles F. 1987. *Thailand: Buddhist Kingdom as Modern Nation State.* Boulder, Colo.: Westview Press.

Khet Sriyaphai. 2007. *Parithat Muai Thai* [An Overview of Thai Boxing]. Bangkok: Matichon.

Kiernan, Ben. 1996. *The Pol Pot Regime: Race, Power, and Genocide in Cambodia under the Khmer Rouge, 1975–79.* New Haven, Conn.: Yale University Press.

———. 2003. The Demography of Genocide in Southeast Asia: The Death Tolls in Cambodia, 1975–79, and East Timor, 1975–80. *Critical Asian Studies* 35(4):585–597.

King, Victor T. 2005. *Defining Southeast Asia and the Crisis in Area Studies: Personal Reflections on a Region.* Working Papers in Contemporary Asian Studies Series, No. 13. Lund University, Sweden: Centre for East and South-East Asian Studies.

———, and William D. Wilder. 2003. *The Modern Anthropology of Southeast Asia: An Introduction.* London: Routledge Curzon.

Kingshill, Konrad. 1965 [1960]. *Ku Daeng—The Red Tomb.* Bangkok: Bangkok Christian College.

Kipp, Rita Smith. 1993. *Dissociated Identities: Ethnicity, Religion and Class in an Indonesian Society.* Ann Arbor: University of Michigan Press.

Kirsch, A. Thomas. 1977. "Complexity in the Thai Religious System." *Journal of Asian Studies* 36(2):241–266.

Kleinman, Arthur, and Erin Fitz-Henry. 2007. "The Experiential Basis for Subjectivity: How Individuals Change in the Context of Societal Transformation." In *Subjectivity,* edited by João Biehl, Byron Good, and Arthur Kleinman, 51–65. Berkeley: University of California Press.

Klima, Alan. 2002. *The Funeral Casino: Meditation, Massacre, and Exchange with the Dead in Thailand.* Princeton, N.J.: Princeton University Press.

Kwon, Heonik. 2006. *After the Massacre: Commemoration and Consolation in Ha My and My Lai.* Berkeley: University of California Press.

Lansing, J. Stephen. 1983. *The Three Worlds of Bali.* Santa Barbara, Calif.: Praeger Publishers.

———. 2006. *Perfect Order: Recognizing Complexity in Bali.* Princeton Studies in Complexity. Princeton, N.J.: Princeton University Press.

Leach, Edmund R. 1965 [1954]. *Political Systems of Highland Burma.* Boston: Beacon Press.

Ledgerwood, Judy. 1997. The Cambodian Tuol Sleng Museum of Genocidal Crimes: National Narrative. *Museum Anthropology* 21(1).

Lehman, F. K. 1963. *The Structure of Chin Society: A Tribal People of Burma Adapted to Non-Western Civilization.* Illinois Studies in Anthropology, No. 3. Urbana: University of Illinois Press.

Leshkowich, Ann Marie. 2008. "Fashioning Appropriate Youth in 1990s Vietnam." In *The Fabric of Cultures: Fashion, Identity and Globalization,* edited by Eugenia Paulicelli and Hazel Clark, 92–111. London and New York: Routledge.

Levi-Strauss, Claude. 1963. *Totemism.* Boston, Mass.: Beacon Press.

———. 1983. *The Way of the Mask,* trans. S. Modelski. London: Jonathan Cape.

Levy-Bruhl, Lucien. 1966 [1922]. *The "Soul" of the Primitive.* Chicago: Henry Regnery Company.

Li, Tania Murray. 1989. *Malays in Singapore: Culture, Economy and Ideology.* Kuala Lumpur and Singapore: Oxford University Press.

Liddle, William. 1996. "The Islamic Turn in Indonesia: A Political Explanation." *The Journal of Asian Studies* 55(3):613–634.

Local Development Institute. 1992. *Community Forestry: Declaration of the Customary Rights of Local Communities. Thai Democracy at the Grassroots.* Bangkok: Local Development Institute.

Lockhard, Craig. 1998. *Dance of Life: Popular Music and Politics in Modern Southeast Asia.* Honolulu: University of Hawaii Press.

Low, Patrick. 1972. "Trends in Southeast Asia." No. 2. *Paper of Seminar Trends in Malaysia.* Singapore: Institute of Southeast Asian Studies.

Lowe, Setha M. 2000. *On the Plaza: The Politics of Public Space and Culture.* Austin: University of Texas Press.

Lye Tuck-Po. 2004. *Changing Pathways.* Lanham, Md: Lexington Books.

Lyons, Lenore, and Michele Ford. 2008. "Love, Sex and the Spaces in-between: Kepri Wives and their Cross-border Husbands." *Citizenship Studies* 12(1): 55–72.

Lyttleton, Chris. 2004. "Relative Pleasures: Drugs, Development and Modern Dependencies in Asia's Golden Triangle." *Development and Change* 35(4): 909–935.

———, Paul Cohen, Houmphanh Rattanavong, Bouakham Thongkhamhane, and Souriyanh Sisaengrat. 2004. *Watermelons, Bars and Trucks: Dangerous Intersections in Northwest Laos.* Rockefeller Foundation. Vientiane: Institute for Research on Culture.

Macdonald, Charles. 2008. "Order against Harmony: Are Humans Always Social?" *Anthropologi, Journal of the Finnish Anthropological Society* 33(2):5–21.

Madrid, Robin. 1999. "Islamic Students in the Indonesian Student Movement, 1998–1999: Forces for Moderation." *Bulletin of Concerned Asian Scholars* 31(3):17–32.

Malarney, Shaun Kingsley. 2001. "'The Fatherland Remembers Your Sacrifice': Commemorating War Dead in North Vietnam." In *The Country of*

Memory: Remaking the Past in Late Socialist Vietnam, edited by Hue-Tam Ho-Tai, 46–76. Berkeley: University of California Press.

Manit Sriwanichpoom. 2003. *Protest*. Bangkok: Manit Sriwanichpoom.

———. 2008. "Died on 6th October, 1976." In *Flashback '76: History and Memory of October 6 Massacre*, Exhibition Catalog, Pridi Banomyong Institute.

Mannikka, Eleanor. 1996. *Angkor Wat: Time, Space, Kingship*. Honolulu: University of Hawaii Press.

Marshall, Michael. 2002. *The Straw Men*. New York: Jove.

Martens, Michael. 1988. *Focus or Ergativity? Pronoun Sets in Uma*. Papers in Western Austronesian Linguistics, no. 4, edited by H. Steinhauer, 263–277. Pacific Linguistics Series A, no. 79. Canberra: Australian National University.

Matisoff, James A. 1983. "Linguistic Diversity and Language Contact in Thailand. In *Highlanders of Thailand*, edited by John McKinnon and Wanat Bhruksasri, 56–86. Kuala Lumpur and New York: Oxford University Press.

Mauss, Marcel. 1990. *Essay on the Gift*. New York: W.W. Norton.

McKean, Philip. 1976. "Tourism, Culture Change and Culture Conservation in Bali." In *Changing Identities in Modern Southeast Asia*, edited by David Banks, 237–247. The Hague: Mouton Publishers.

McKhann, Charles. 1998. "Naxi, Rerkua, Moso, Meng: Kinship, Politics and Ritual on the Yunnan-Sichuan Frontier." In *Naxi and Moso Ethnography*, edited by M. Oppitz and E. Hsu, 23–45. Zurich: University of Zurich Press.

McWilliam, Andrew, and Angie Bexley. 2008. "Performing Politics: The 2007 Parliamentary Elections in Timor Leste." *The Asia Pacific Journal of Anthropology* 9(1):66–82.

Mead, Margaret. 1937. *Cooperation and Competition among Primitive People*. New York: McGraw-Hill Book Co., Inc.

Miller, Daniel. 2005. "Materiality: An Introduction." In *Materiality*, edited by Daniel Miller, 1–50. Durham and London: Duke University Press.

Mills, Mary Beth. 1999. *Thai Women in the Global Labor Force: Consuming Desires, Contested Selves*. New Brunswick, N.J., and London: Rutgers University Press.

Moerman, M. 1965. "Ethnic Identification in a Complex Civilization: Who Are the Lue?" *American Anthropologist* 67(5):1215–1230.

———. 1966. "Ban Ping's Temple: The Center of a 'Loosely Structured' Society." *Anthropological Studies in Theravada Buddhism*, edited by M. Nash, 137–174. New Haven, Conn.: Yale University, Southeast Asia Studies.

Mohamad, Roslina. 2007. "First K9 School for Orang Asli Children Launched." *The Star*, September 9.

Montesano, Michael J. 2009. "Contextualizing the Pattaya Summit Debacle: Four April Days, Four Thai Pathologies." *Contemporary Southeast Asia* 31(2): 217–48.

Muai Siam [Siam Boxing Magazine]. 2008. *News* 23, Issue 1812 (July 9–15):5–8.

Mulder, Niels. 1996. *Inside Indonesian Society.* Amsterdam: Pepin Press.

Munir, Lily Zakiyah. 2002. "'He Is Your Garment and You Are His . . .': Religious Precepts, Interpretations, and Power Relations in Marital Sexuality among Javanese Muslim Women." *Sojourn: Journal of Social Issues in Southeast Asia* 17(2):191–220.

Murdock, George P. 1960. "Cognatic Forms of Social Organization." In *Social Structure in Southeast Asia,* edited by George P. Murdock, 1–14. Viking Fund Publications in Anthropology, No. 29. Chicago: Quadrangle Books.

Nagata, Judith. 1974. "What Is a Malay? Situational Selection of Ethnic Identity in a Plural Society." *American Ethnologist* 1(2):331–350.

———. 1976. "Kinship and Social Mobility among the Malays." *Man: The Journal of The Royal Anthropological Institute.* New Series, II(3):400–411.

———. 1979. *Malaysian Mosaic: Perspectives from a Poly-Ethnic Society.* Vancouver: University of British Columbia Press.

———. 1984. *The Reflowering of Malaysian Islam.* Vancouver: University of British Columbia Press.

———. 1995. "Modern Malay Women and the Message of the 'Veil.'" In *"Male and Female" in Developing Southeast Asia,* edited by Wazir Jahan Karim, 101–119. Oxford: Berg.

Nettleton, Steve. 2008. "Giving an Early Boost to the Next Generation of Malaysia's 'Original People.'" http://www.unicef.org/infobycountry/malaysia_39246.html, accessed November 1, 2010.

New Straits Times. 2007. "Malaysian Potpourri: The Orang Asli Community: Education is the Ticket to a Better Life." September 25.

Nguyên Bảng. 2007. *Nhiều Nhà Ngoại Cảm Tìm Mộ Liệt Sĩ Được Khen Thương* (Many *Nhà Ngoại Cảm* Who Have Found Revolutionary Martyr Graves Receive Commendations). July 23. *Tiền Phong* Online. http://www.tienphong.vn/Tianyon/Index.aspx?ArticleID=90529&ChannelID=46, accessed November 1, 2010.

Nguyễn Huy Phúc and Trần Huy Bá. 1979. *Đường Phố Hà Nội* (The Streets of Hanoi). Hanoi: Nhà Xuất Bản Hà Nội.

Nguyen, V. H. 1995 [1944]. *The Ancient Civilization of Vietnam.* Hanoi: The Gioi Publishers.

Nhung Tuyet Tran. 2008. "Gender, Property, and the 'Autonomy Thesis' in Southeast Asia: The Endowment of Local Succession in Early Modern Vietnam." *The Journal of Asian Studies* 67(1):43–72.

Nicholas, Colin. 2000. *The Orang Asli and the Struggle for Resources.* Copenhagen: International Work Group for Indigenous Affairs.

Niessen, S. A. 1985. *Motifs of Life in Toba Batak Texts and Textiles.* Dordrecht: Foris Publications.

Ninh Bình, Cultural Service. 1968. *Công Tác Xây Dựng Nếp Sống Mới, Con Người Mới và Gia Đình Tiền Tiến Chống Mỹ, Cứu Nước* (The Task of Building the New Ways, New Person and Progressive Family in the Struggle against the Americans to Rescue the Nation). Ninh Bình: Tỷ Văn Hóa Ninh Bình.

Noor Aini Syed Amir, Datin. 1991. *Malaysian Customs and Etiquette.* Singapore and Kuala Lumpur: Times Books.

Nooy-Palm, C. H. M. 1979. *The Sa'dan Toraja: A Study of Their Social Life and Religion,* Vol. 1. The Hague: Martinus Nijhoff.

Oey-Gardiner, Mayling. 1991. "Gender Differences in Schooling in Indonesia." *Bulletin of Indonesian Economic Studies* 27(1):57–79.

Office for Victims of Crime. 2002. "Children as Victims and Witnesses." In *Victims and Victimization,* edited by David Shicor and Stephen Tibbetts, 81–102. Prospect Heights, Ill: Waveland Press.

Olson, Grant. 1991. "Cries over Spilt Holy Water." *Journal of Southeast Asian Studies* 22:75–85.

Ong, Aihwa, and Michael C. Peletz. 1995. *Bewitching Women, Pious Men: Gender and Body Politics in Southeast Asia.* Berkeley: University of California Press.

Overing, Joanna. 2003. "In Praise of the Everyday: Trust and the Art of Social Living in an Amazonian Community." *Ethnos* 68(3):293–316.

Pandit Chanrochanakit. 2006. The Siamese Diorama and the Thai National Imaginary in Contemporary Thai Art. Ph.D. diss., University of Hawaii.

Panya Kraitus and Pitisuk Kraitus. 1988. *Muay Thai: The Most Distinguished Art of Fighting.* Bangkok: P. Kraitus.

Papanek, Hanna. 1973. "Purdah: Separate Worlds and Symbolic Shelter." *Comparative Studies in Society and History* 15:289–325.

Parkin, Harry. 1978. *Batak Fruit of Hindu Thought.* Madras, India: Christian Literary Society.

Pattana Kitiarsa. 2003. *Lives of Hunting Dogs: Rethinking Thai Masculinities through an Ethnography of Muay Thai.* Nakhon Ratchasima, Thailand: Suranaree University of Technology.

———. 2005. "Lives of Hunting Dogs: *Muai Thai* and the Politics of Thai Masculinities." *South East Asia Research* 13 (March 1):57–90.

Peacock, James L. 1987. *Rites of Modernization: Symbolic and Social Aspects of Indonesian Proletarian Drama.* Chicago: University of Chicago Press.

Pedersen, Lene. 2007. "An Ancestral *Keris,* Balinese Kingship and a Modern Presidency." In *What's the Use of Art? Asian Visual and Material Culture in Context,* edited by Jan Mrazek and Morgan Pitelka, 214–237. Honolulu: University of Hawai'i Press.

Pedersen, Paul B. 1970. *Batak Blood and Protestant Soul: The Development of National Batak Churches in North Sumatra.* Grand Rapids, Mich.: Wm. B. Eerdmans Publishing Co.

Peletz, Michael G. 1996. *Reason and Passion: Representations of Gender in a Malay Society.* Berkeley: University of California Press.

Pelras, Christian. 1996. *The Bugis.* Cambridge, Mass.: Blackwell.

Pettifor, Steven. 2007. Interview by author, Bangkok, Thailand, November 27.

Phillips, Herbert P.. 1957. Bang Chan field notes. Unpublished.

——. 1966. *Thai Peasant Personality: The Patterning of Interpersonal Behavior in the Village of Bang Chan*. Berkeley and Los Angeles: University of California Press.

——. 1987. *Modern Thai Literature with an Ethnographic Interpretation*. Honolulu: University of Hawai'i Press.

Phua, Joe. 2006. "Communicating with Vietnam's War Dead." May 17. http://news.bbc.co.uk/2/hi/programmes/this_world/4989480.stm, accessed November 11, 2009.

Picard, Michel. 1996. *Bali: Cultural Tourism and Touristic Culture*. Singapore: Archipelago Press.

Pike, Douglas. 1986. *PAVN: People's Army of Vietnam*. New York: Da Capo Press.

Pin, Yathay, and John Man. 2000. *Stay Alive, My Son*. Ithaca, N.Y.: Cornell University Press.

Pinaree Sanpitak. 2007. Interview by author, Bangkok, Thailand, November 29.

——. 2008. Talk on *Breast Stupa Cookery Project*, Mills College, May 1.

Pino, E., and T. Wintermans. 1955. *Kamus Inggeris (English Dictionary), Part 1: English-Indonesian*. Jakarta, Indonesia: J. B. Wolters.

Poewe, Karla (ed.). 1994. *Charismatic Christianity as Global Culture*. Columbia: University of South Carolina Press.

Polanyi, Karl. 1944. *The Great Transformation*. New York: Rinehart.

Pongpet, Mekloy. 1991. "Stopping the Chainsaws with Sacred Robes." *Bangkok Post*, March 29, 27–28.

Potter, Jack. 1976. *Thai Peasant Social Structure*. Chicago: University of Chicago Press.

Prajuab Tirabutana. 1958. *A Simple One*. Southeast Asia Program, Data Paper No. 30. Ithaca, N.Y.: Cornell University.

"The Prophet of Profit: El Shaddai's Mike Velarde Brings Religion down to Earth." 1996. *Asiaweek*, Sept. 20.

Queen, Christopher S., and Sallie B. King (eds.). 1996. *Engaged Buddhism: Buddhist Liberation Movements in Asia*. Albany: State University of New York Press.

Rafael, Vicente L. 1988. *Contracting Colonialism: Translation and Christian Conversion in Tagalog Society under Early Spanish Rule*. Ithaca, N.Y.: Cornell University Press.

Rahmat, Andi, and Mukhammad Najib. *Gerakan Perlawanan dari Masjid Kampus* (The Opposition Movement from the Campus Mosque). Surakarta: Purimedia, 2001.

Rambo, A. Terry. 1983. "Fire and the Energy Efficiency of Swidden Agriculture." *Asian Perspectives* 23:309–316.

——. 1984. "No Free Lunch: A Reexamination of the Energetic Efficiency of Swidden Agriculture." In *An Introduction to Human Ecology Research on Agricultural Systems in Southeast Asia*, edited by A. T. Rambo and E. Percy, 154–163. Honolulu: East-West Environment and Policy Institute.

Rashid, Esa. 2007. *Bunga Moyang: Seni Lipatan Daun Mah Meri* [Ancestral Flowers: Mah Meri Woven Leaf Art]. Siri Buku Seni Kraf Orang Asli. Kuala Lumpur: Kementerian Kebudayaan, Kesenian dan Warisan Malaysia.

Rebac, Zoran. 1989. *Thai Boxing Dynamite: The Explosive Art of Muay Thai.* London: Paul H. Crompton.

Reid, Anthony. 1988. *Southeast Asia in the Age of Commerce 1450–1680.* Vol. One. *The Lands Below the Winds.* New Haven, Conn., and London: Yale University Press.

Renan, Ernest. 1990 [1882]. What Is a Nation? Reprinted in *Nation and Narration,* edited by Homi K. Bhabha, 8–22. New York: Routledge.

Renard, Ronald D. n.d. Using a Northern Thai Forest: Approaches by a Conservationist Monk, Thai Lowlanders, Hmong Highlanders, and International Development. Unpublished paper.

Reuters, "Thai Policeman Pays to Stop Bride Suicide." 1998. November 18.

Reynolds, Frank E. 1977. "Civic Religion and National Community in Thailand." *Journal of Asian Studies* 36(2):267–282.

———. 1994. "Dhamma in Dispute: The Interactions of Religion and Law in Thailand." *Law and Society Review* 28(3):433–451.

Riddell, Peter. 2001. *Islam and the Malay-Indonesian World.* Honolulu: University of Hawai'i Press.

Rittner, Carol Ann, and John K. Roth. 1993. *Different Voices: Women and the Holocaust.* New York: Paragon House.

Robben, Antonius C. G. M., and Marcelo M. Suárez-Orozco. 2000. *Cultures under Siege: Collective Violence and Trauma in Interdisciplinary Perspectives.* Cambridge and New York: Cambridge University Press.

Robinson, Kathryn. 1998. "Traditions of House-building in South Sulawesi." in *Living through Histories: Culture, History and Social Life in South Sulawesi,* edited by Kathryn Robinson and Mukhlis Paeni, 168–195. Canberra and Jakarta: Anthropology Australian National University in collaboration with the Indonesian National Archives.

———. 2000a. "Gender, Islam and Nationality: Indonesian Domestic Servants in the Middle East." In *Home and Hegemony: Domestic Work and Identity Politics in South and Southeast Asia,* edited by Kathleen M. Adams and Sara Dickey, 249–282. Ann Arbor: University of Michigan Press.

———. 2000b. Indonesian Women: From *Orde Baru* to *Reformasi.* In *Women in Asia: Tradition, Modernity and Globalisation,* edited by Louise Edwards and Mina Roces, 137–169. Ann Arbor: University of Michigan Press.

Roff, William. 1967. *The Origins of Malay Nationalism.* Kuala Lumpur: University of Malaya Press.

Ross, Alan O. 1962. "Ego Identity and the Social Order: A Psychosocial Analysis of Six Indonesians (Bataks)." In *Psychological Monographs: General and Applied* 76(23):1–33.

Russell, Susan. n.d. Christianity in the Philippines. http://www.seasite.niu.edu/crossroads/russell/christianity.htm, accessed October 23, 2010.

Rydstrøm, Helle. 2003. *Embodying Morality: Growing Up in Rural Northern Vietnam*. Honolulu: University of Hawai'i Press.

Salazar Parreña, Rhacel. 2001. *Servants of Globalization: Women, Migration, and Domestic Work*. Stanford, Calif.: Stanford University Press.

Sandhu, K. S. and A. Mani (eds.). 1993. *Indian Communities in Southeast Asia*. Singapore: Institute of Southeast Asian Studies.

Saneh Chamrik and Yos Santasombat (eds). 1993. *Paa Chumchon nai Prathetthai: Naewthaang kaan Phadthanaa* [Community Forests in Thailand: The Direction for Development]. Vols. 1, 2, 3. Bangkok: Local Development Institute.

Schipper, K. 1993. *The Taoist Body*. Berkeley: University of California Press.

Schotten, C. Heike. 2005. "Men, Masculinity, and Male Domination: Reframing Feminist Analyses of Sex Work." *Politics and Gender* 1(2):211–240.

Schwenkel, Christina. 2006. "Recombinant History: Transnational Practices of Memory and Knowledge Production in Contemporary Vietnam." *Cultural Anthropology* 21(1):3–30.

———. 2009. *The American War in Contemporary Vietnam: Transnational Remembrance and Representation*. Bloomington: Indiana University Press.

Scott, James C. 1979. *The Moral Economy of the Peasant: Rebellion and Subsistence in Southeast Asia*. New Haven, Conn.: Yale University Press.

———. 1990. *Domination and the Arts of Resistance: Hidden Transcripts*. New Haven, Conn.: Yale University Press.

———. 2009. *The Art of Not Being Governed: An Anarchist History of Upland Southeast Asia*. Yale Agrarian Studies Series. New Haven, Conn.: Yale University Press.

Seear, Lynne, and Suhanya Raffel (eds.) 2006. *The 5th Asia-Pacific Triennial of Contemporary Art*. Brisbane: Queensland Art Gallery Publishing.

Shahrum Bin Yub. 1969. *Mah Meri Sculpture*. Kuala Lumpur: Museums Department.

Sharp, Lauriston. 1957. Thai social structure. Paper read at the Ninth Pacific Congress (Bangkok). Unpublished.

Sherman, D. George. 1990. *Rice, Rupees, and Ritual: Economy and Society among the Samosir Batak of Sumatra*. Stanford, Calif.: Stanford University Press.

Shiraishi, Saya. 1997. *Young Heroes: The Indonesian Family in Politics*. Ithaca, N.Y.: Cornell University Press.

Sibeth, Achim. 1991. *The Batak: Peoples of the Island of Sumatra*. London: Thames and Hudson.

Siddique, Sharon, and Nirmala Purushotam. 1984. *Singapore's Little India*. Singapore: Times Books for the Institute of Southeast Asian Studies.

Sidel, John. 2001. "Riots, Church Burnings, Conspiracies: The Moral Economy of the Indonesian Crowd in the Late Twentieth Century." In *Violence in Indonesia*, edited by Ingrid Wessel and Georgia Wimhöfer, 47–63. Hamburg: Abera Verlag Markus Voss.

Sihombing, T. M. 1986. *Filsafatbatak: Tentangkebiasaan-Kebiasaanadatistiadat*. Jakarta: Balaipustaka.

Sinaga, Anicetus B. 1981. *The Toba-Batak High God: Transcendence and Immanence*. Sankt Augustin, Germany: Anthropos Institute.

Singh, Ajay, and Julian Gearing. 2000. "The Murky Events of October 1973: A Book Proposal Reopens Thailand's Wounds." *Asiaweek.com*, January 28. http://www-cgi.cnn.com/ASIANOW/asiaweek/magazine/2000/0128/as .thai.history1.html, accessed August 15, 2009.

Sizemore, Russell F., and Donald K. Swearer. 1990. "Introduction." *Ethics, Wealth and Salvation: A Study in Buddhist Social Ethics*, edited by Russell F. Sizemore and Donald K. Swearer. Columbia: University of South Carolina Press.

Smith-Hefner, Nancy J. 2005. "The New Muslim Romance: Changing Patterns of Courtship and Marriage among Educated Javanese Youth." *Journal of Southeast Asian Studies* 36(3):441–459.

Sneddon, James. 2003. *The Indonesian Language: Its History and Role in Modern Society*. Sydney: University of New South Wales Press.

Somboon Suksamran. 1987. *Kaanphadthanaa Taam Naew Phuthasaasanaa: Karanii Phra Nak Phadthanaa* [A Buddhist Approach to Development: The Case of 'Development Monks']. Bangkok: Social Science Institute of Thailand.

———. 1988. "A Buddhist Approach to Development: The Case of 'Development Monks' in Thailand." In *Reflections on Development in Southeast Asia*, edited by Lim Teck Ghee, 26–48. Singapore: Institute of Southeast Asian Studies.

Southon, Michael. 1995. *The Navel of the Perahu: Meaning and Values in the Maritime Trading Economy of a Butonese Village*. Canberra: Research School of Pacific and Asian Studies, The Australian National University.

Spiro, M. E. 1966. "Buddhism and Economic Action in Burma." *American Anthropologist* 68(5):1163–1173.

Sponsel, Leslie E., and Poranee Natadecha. 1988. "Buddhism, Ecology, and Forests in Thailand: Past, Present, and Future." In *Changing Tropical Forests*, edited by John Dargavel, Kay Dixon, and Noel Semple, 305–325. Canberra: Centre for Resource and Environmental Studies, Australian National University.

Stevens, Alan M., and A. E. Schmidgall-Tellings. 2004. *A Comprehensive Indonesian-English Dictionary*. Athens, Ohio: Ohio University Press.

Stoler, Ann L. 1976. "Garden Use and Household Consumption Patterns in a Javanese Village." *Masyarakat Indonesia* 3.

Subramaniam, Yogeswaran. 2008. "A Wish List Too Far?" *Aliran Monthly* 28(8):15–17.

Suchira Payulpitack. 1992. "Changing Provinces of Concern: A Case-Study of the Social Impact of the Buddhadasa Movement." *Sojourn* 7(1):39–68.

Sudarat Musikawong. n.d. "Art for October: Thai Cold War State Violence in Trauma Art." *positions: east asia cultures critique* 18(1):19–50.

Sukatan Pelajaran Bahasa Semai: Kurikulum Bersepadu Sekolah Rendah. 2003. Kuala Lumpur: Pusat Perkembangan Kurikulum, Kementerian Pendidikan Malaysia.

Sukarman, Widigdo. 2005. *Sikap Dunia Pendidikan dalam Era Globalisasi* [The Character of World Education in the Era of Globalization]. *Jurnal Studi Amerika* 10(2):33–40.

Sulistyaningsih, Endang. 2002. *Sex Workers in Indonesia: Where Should They Go?* Jakarta, Indonesia: Manpower Research and Development Center Ministry of Manpower and Transmigration.

Sullivan, Barbara. 2003. "Trafficking in Women: Feminism and New International Law." *International Feminist Journal of Politics* 5(1):67–91.

Sun, Laichen. 2003. "Chinese Military Transfers and the Emergence of Northern Mainland Southeast Asia, c. 1390–1527." *Journal of Southeast Asian Studies* 34(3):495–517.

Sutee Kunavichayanont. 2008a. Interview by author, Bangkok, Thailand, August 8.

—— 2008b. "Selective History/Memory." In *Flashback '76: History and Memory of October 6 Massacre*, Exhibition Catalog, Pridi Banomyong Institute.

Swainson, Luke, and Andrew McGregor. 2008. "Compensating for Development." *Asia Pacific Viewpoint* 49(2):155–167.

TalkAsia. 2008. Interview with Thai Prime Minister Samak Sundaravej, www.cnn.com, February 19. http://edition.cnn.com/2008/WORLD/asiapcf/02/18/talkasia.samak/index.html#cnnSTCText, accessed December 31, 2008.

Tambiah, Stanley J. 1970. *Buddhism and the Spirit Cults in North-east Thailand.* Cambridge: Cambridge University Press.

——. 1977. "The Galactic Polity: The Structure of Traditional Kingdoms in Southeast Asia." *Annals of the New York Academy of Sciences* 293:69–97.

Tan Chee Beng. 1993. *Chinese Peranakan Heritage in Malaysia and Singapore.* Kuala Lumpur: Penerbit Fajar Bakti.

Tan Yong Soon. 2008. *Living the Singapore Dream.* Singapore: SNP Editions.

Tannenbaum, Nicola. 2000. "Protest, Tree Ordination, and the Changing Context of Political Ritual." *Ethnology* 39(2):109–127.

——. 2009. "The Changing Nature of Shan Ritual and Identity in Maehongson, Northwestern Thailand." *Contemporary Buddhism* 10(1):171–184.

Taylor, John, 1999. *East Timor: The Price of Freedom.* London and New York: Zed Books.

Taylor, Keith W. 1983. *The Birth of Vietnam.* Berkeley: University of California Press.

——. 1998. "Surface Orientations in Vietnam: Beyond Histories of Nation and Region." *Journal of Asian Studies* 57(4):949–978.

Taylor, Philip (ed.). 2008. *Modernity and Re-enchantment: Religion in Post-Revolutionary Vietnam.* Singapore: ISEAS.

Teh, David. 2006. "Growing Pains." *Art and AsiaPacific* 48:38–39.

Textor, R. B. 1960. An Inventory of Non-Buddhist Supernatural Objects in a Central Thai Village. Ph.D. diss., Cornell University.

Thai Inter-Religious Commission for Development and the International Network of Engaged Buddhists. 1990. *Radical Conservatism: Buddhism in the Contemporary World*. Bangkok: The Sathirakoses-Nagapradipa Foundation.

Thairath Online. 2008. *Ruab nak muai Thai chue dang kha ya* [Arrest of a famous Thai boxer selling drugs], July 4. Available at http://www.thairath.co.th/online.php?section=newsthairathonline&content=95784, accessed July 4, 2008.

Thanom Chapakdee. 2007. Interview by author, Bangkok, Thailand, November 27.

Thích Nhất Hạnh. 1987. *The Miracle of Mindfulness: A Manual on Meditation*. Boston: Beacon Press.

Thongchai Winichakul. 1994. *Siam Mapped: A History of the Geo-Body of a Nation*. Honolulu: University of Hawaii Press.

———. 2002. "Remembering/Silencing the Traumatic Part: The Ambivalent Memories of the October 1976 Massacre in Bangkok." In *Cultural Crisis and Social Memory: Modernity and Identity in Thailand and Laos*, edited by S. Tanabe and C. F. Keyes, 243–283. Honolulu: University of Hawaii Press.

Thrift, N. J., and D. K. Forbes. 1985. "Cities, Socialism and War: Hanoi, Saigon and the Vietnamese Experience of Urbanisation." *Environment and Planning D: Society and Space* 3:279–308.

Tijah Chopil, and Jerald Joseph. 2003. *Creating Knowledge for Change*. Mumbai: Asian South Pacific Bureau of Adult Education (ASPBAE).

Tilaar, H. A. R. 2005. Adaptasi dan Adopsi Masyarakat terhadap Pendidikan Modern [Popular Adaptation and Acceptance of Modern Education]. *Jurnal Studi Amerika* 10(2):4–12.

Tobing, Ph. L. 1961. *Hukum Pelayaran Amanna Gappa* [Amanna Gappa Navigational Law]. Ujung Pandang: Yayasan Kebudayaan Sulawesi Selatan dan Tenggara.

———. 1994. *The Structure of the Toba-Batak Belief in the High God*. Jakarta: South and South-East Celebes Institute For Culture.

Tomkins, Calvin. 2005. "Shall We Dance? The Spectator as Artist." *The New Yorker*, October 17, 82–95.

Tooker, Deborah. 2004. "Modular Modern: Shifting Forms of Collective Identity among the Akha of Northern Thailand." *Anthropological Quarterly* 77(2):243–288.

Tran, Nhung Tuyet. 2006. "Beyond the Myth of Equality: Daughters' Inheritance Rights in the Lê Code." In *Vietnam Borderless Histories*, edited by Nhung Tuyet Tran and Anthony J. S. Reid, 121–145. Madison: The University of Wisconsin Press.

Traube, Elizabeth G. 1995. "Mambai Perspectives on Colonialism and Decolonization." In *East Timor at the Crossroads: The Forging of a Nation*, edited by Peter Carey and G. Carter Bentley, 42–55. London: Social Science Research Council.

———. 2007. "Unpaid Wages: Local Narratives and the Imagination of the Nation." *The Asia Pacific Journal of Anthropology* 8(1):9–25.

Tréglodé, Benoit de. 2001. *Héros et revolution au Viet Nam: 1948–1964*. Paris: L'Harmattan.

Trocki, Carl A. 2006. *Wealth, Power and the Culture of Control*. New York: Routledge.

Turner, Caroline, 1993. "Introduction: Internationalism and Regionalism: Paradoxes of Identity." In *Tradition and Change: Contemporary Art of Asia and the Pacific*, edited by Caroline Turner, xiii–xvii. St. Lucia, Queensland: University of Queensland Press.

Ung, Loung. 2000. *First They Killed My Father: A Daughter of Cambodia Remembers*. New York: HarperCollins.

UNICEF. 2008. *UNICEF Using Folklore to Promote Education in Malaysia*. (Video) http://youtube.com/watch?v=LV7Jxt8f7kA.

Vail, Peter. 1998. "Modern Muai Thai Mythology." *Crossroads: An Interdisciplinary Journal of Southeast Asia Studies* 12(2):75–95.

Vandergeest, Peter, and Nancy Lee Peluso. 1995. "Territorialization and State Power in Thailand." *Theory & Society* 24(3):385–426.

Veeranggan, Athi. 2009. "Orang Asli Want Traditional Land Reserved for Them." http://www.malaysiakini.com/news/97139, accessed January 25, 2009.

Vella, Walter F. 1957. *Siam under Rama III, 1824–1851*. Locust Valley, N.Y.: J. J. Augustin.

Vergouwen, J. C. 1964. *The Social Organization and Customary Law of the Toba-Batak of Northern Sumatra* [1933]. KITLV Translation Series Number 7. The Hague: Martinus Nijhoff.

Vickery, Michael. 1984. *Cambodia, 1975–1982*. Boston: South End Press.

Vietnam, Ministry of Culture. 1979. Những Văn Bản Về Việc Cưới, Việc Tanh, Ngày Giỗ, Ngày Hội [Documents on weddings, funerals, death anniverseries and public festivals]. Hanoi: Văn hòa.

Vietnam Institute of Philosophy. 1973. Đảng Ta Bàn Về Đạo Đức (Our Party Discusses Ethics). Hanoi: Ủy Ban Khoa Học Xã Hội Việt Nam.

Wacquant, Loic J. D. 1995. "Through the Fighter's Eyes: Boxing as a Moral and Sensual World." In *Boxing and Medicine*, edited by Robert Cantu, 129–174. Champaign, Ill.: Human Kinetics.

Waddell, J. R. E. 1972. *An Introduction to Southeast Asian Politics*. Sydney: John Wiley.

Wales, Quaritch H. G. 1931. *Siamese State Ceremonies: Their History and Function*. London: Bernard Quaritch Ltd.

Walker, Andrew. 2006. "Matrilineal Spirits, Descent and Territorial Power in Northern Thailand." *The Australian Journal of Anthropology* 17(2):196–215.

Wardlow, Holly. 2004. "Anger, Economy, and Female Agency: Problematizing 'Prostitution' and 'Sex Work' among the Huli of Papua New Guinea. *Signs* 29(4):1017–1040.

Warner, Michael. 2002. "Publics and Counterpublics." *Public Culture* 14(1): 49–90.

Waterson, Roxana. 1990. *The Living House: An Anthology of Architecture in Southeast Asia.* Singapore, Oxford, and New York: Oxford University Press.

——. 1995. "Houses and Hierarchies in Island Southeast Asia." In *About the House: Levi-Strauss and Beyond,* edited by Janet Carsten and Stephen Hugh-Jones, 47–68. Cambridge: Cambridge University Press.

Werner, Roland. 1973. *Mah-Meri Art and Culture.* Kuala Lumpur: Muzium Negara.

White, Benjamin. 1976. Production and Reproduction in a Javanese Village. Ph.D. diss., Columbia University.

White, Erick. 2009. "PAD's Last Day at Government House." *New Mandala: New Perspectives on Mainland Southeast Asia,* posted online on January 29, 2009 at http://asiapacific.anu.edu.au/newmandala/2009/01/29/pads-last-day-at-government-house, accessed August 5, 2009.

Wiegele, Katharine. 2005. *Investing in Miracles: El Shaddai and the Transformation of Popular Catholicism in the Philippines.* Honolulu: University of Hawaii Press.

——. Forthcoming. "Mass and Mass Mediated Spaces of Religious Community in Manila, Philippines." In *Mediating Faiths: Religion and Socio-Cultural Change in the Twenty-First Century,* edited by Michael Bailey, Anthony McNicholas, and Guy Redden. Farnham, UK: Ashgate Press.

Wilkinson, R. J. 1901. *A Malay-English Dictionary.* Singapore: Kelly and Walsh.

Wilson, Ara. 2004. *The Intimate Economies of Bangkok: Tomboys, Tycoons and Avon Ladies in the Global City.* Berkeley: University of California Press.

Wilson, David A. 1959. "Thailand." In *Government and Politics of Southeast Asia,* edited by George McT. Kahin, 1–72. Ithaca, N.Y.: Cornell University Press.

Wilson, H. E. 1978. *Social Engineering in Singapore.* Singapore: Singapore University Press.

Winstedt, Richard. 1981. *Bidalan Melayu. Malay Proverbs,* rev. ed., translated and edited by Tan Chin Kwang. Singapore: Graham Brash.

Wit Pimkanchanapong. 2008. Interview by author, Bangkok, Thailand, August 4.

Wolff, John U., and Soepomo Poedjosoedarmo. 1982. *Communicative Codes in Central Java.* Ithaca, N.Y.: Cornell University Press.

Wolters, O. W. 1999. *History, Culture, and Region in Southeast Asian Perspectives.* Rev. edition. Southeast Asia Program Publications, Studies on Southeast Asia No. 6. Ithaca, N.Y.: Cornell University.

Wong, Deborah. 2001. *Sounding the Center: History and Aesthetics in Thai Buddhist Performance.* Chicago Studies in Ethnomusicology. Chicago: University of Chicago Press.

Woodside, Alexander. 1971. *Vietnam and the Chinese Model: A Comparison of Vietnamese and Chinese Government in the First Half of the Nineteenth Century.* Cambridge, Mass.: Harvard University Press.

——. 2006. *Lost Modernities: China, Vietnam, Korea, and the Hazards of World*

History. The Edwin O. Reischauer Lectures 2001. Boston, Mass.: Harvard University Press.

Woodward, Hiram W., Jr. 1993. "The Thai 'Chedi' and the Problem of Stupa Interpretation." *History of Religions* 33(1):71–91.

Woodward, Mark. 1989. *Islam in Java: Normative Piety and Mysticism in the Sultanate of Yogyakarta.* Tucson: University of Arizona Press.

Worathep Akkabootara. 2008. "From Imperfect Aesthetics to the Proactive Politics of Art Intervention: How Getting Stuck in Bangkok Traffic Could Change a Person's Perception of Art." In *Navin's Sala: Navin Production's International Art and Life Magazine*, edited by Navin Rawanchaikul, 140–143. Chiang Mai, Thailand: Navin Production Co., Ltd.

Xuân Cang, and Lý Đặng Cao. 1996. *Tìm Mộ Liệt Sĩ Bằng Phương Pháp Mới?* (Finding Revolutionary Martyr Grave with a New Method?). *Thế Giới Mới* (October): 8–11.

Yan, Yunxiang. 1996. *The Flow of Gifts: Reciprocity and Social Networks in a Chinese Village.* Stanford, Calif.: Stanford University Press.

Yao, Souchou. 2007. *Singapore: The State and the Culture of Excess.* New York and Abingdon: Routledge.

Yeoh, B. S. A., S. Huang, and J. Gonzalez. 1999. "Migrant female domestic workers: Debating the Economic, Social and Political Impacts in Singapore." *International Migration Review* 33(1):114–136.

Zainah Anwar. 1987. *Islamic Revivalism in Malaysia: Dakwah among the Students.* Petaling Jaya: Pelanduk Publications.

Zawawi, Ibrahim (ed.). 1996. *Kami Bukan Anti-Pembangunan.* Kuala Lumpur: Persatuan Sains Sosial Malaysia.

Zheng, Yangwen. 2005. *The Social Life of Opium in China.* New York: Cambridge University Press.

Zialcita, Fernando N. 2003. "Is Southeast Asia a Jigsaw Puzzle or a Collage?" In *Globalization in Southeast Asia: Local, National and Transnational Perspectives*, edited by Shinji Yamashita and J. S. Eades, 21–41. New York and Oxford: Berghahn Books.

Zucker, Eve Monique. 2006. "Transcending Time and Terror: The Re-emergence of Bon Dalien after Pol Pot and Thirty Years of Civil War." *Journal of Southeast Asian Studies* 37(3):527–546.

The documentary and commercial films listed below are recommended by the editors and chapter contributors as potential accompaniments to various chapters in this volume. (If the rental source is unlisted, the film is widely available via commercial outlets such as Netflix.)

Forest Monks:

-*Forest Monks*. (2010) By Religion and Ethics Newsweekly, a PBS series. Available online: http://www.pbs.org/wnet/religionandethics/episodes/january-15-2010/forest-monks/5472/.

Muay thai in Thailand:

-*Ong Bak: Muay Thai Warrior* (2003)

-*Beautiful Boxer* (2003)

Island reef-bombing issues in South Sulawesi, Indonesia:

-*Sharing Paradise*. (2008). Available from Documentary Educational Resources (www.der.org).

Timor Leste:

-*Children of the Crocodile*. (Subtitled). (2001). Available from Women Make Movies: http://www.wmm.com/filmcatalog/pages/c582.shtml

Cambodia, genocide and recovery:

-*The Killing Fields* (1984)

-*S21 The Khmer Rouge Killing Machine* (2002)

-*Sleepwalking through the Mekong* (2009).

Minority issues in Thailand:

-*Mien Sports and Heritage, Thailand* (2001). Avaiable online: http://shesc.asu.edu/jonsson

Religion in Indonesia:

-*The Long Search: Religion in Indonesia: The Way of the Ancestors* (1978). BBC.

-*The Three Worlds of Bali*. Odyssey Series. (1979). Available from Documentary Educational Resources (www.der.org)

On Orang Asli foraging lifestyles in Malaysia:

-*The Batek: Rainforest Foragers of Kelantan, Malaysia*. Sold as an accompaniment to the book *The Headman Was a Woman: The Gender Egalitarian Batek of Malaysia,* by Kirk M. Endicott and Karen L. Endicott. 2008. Long Grove, Ill: Waveland Press.

On Vietnam:

-*Indochine* (1992)

-*Psychic Vietnam,* BBC (2006). Film clip available online at Communicating with Vietnam's War Dead, BBC Online http://news.bbc.co.uk/2/hi/programmes/this_world/4989480.stm

On migrant workers and livelihoods:

-*B.A.T.A.M.* (2005) Available from Documentary Educational Resources (www.der.org)

-*Bangkok ZigZag.* (2003) Available from Immersion Films: http://bangkokzigzag.com/projects.html.

CONTRIBUTORS

KATHLEEN M. ADAMS is professor of anthropology at Loyola University Chicago. She is author of *Art as Power: Re-crafting Identities, Tourism, and Power in Tana Toraja, Indonesia* and coeditor of *Home and Hegemony: Domestic Work and Identity Politics in South and Southeast Asia.*

GENE AMMARELL is associate professor of anthropology in the department of sociology and anthropology at Ohio University. He is author of *Bugis Navigation* and executive producer of the documentary film *Sharing Paradise.*

LORRAINE V. ARAGON teaches anthropology and Asian studies at the University of North Carolina, Chapel Hill, and is a 2010–2011 Fellow at the National Humanities Center. She is the author of *Fields of the Lord: Animism, Christian Minorities, and State Development in Indonesia* and numerous other publications about Indonesian religion, ritual arts, minorities, intellectual property law, and intergroup conflicts.

NIR AVIELI is an assistant professor in the department of sociology and anthropology at Ben Gurion University, Israel. His book *Rice Talks: Food and Community in Hoi An, Vietnam* is forthcoming from Indiana University Press.

SANDRA CATE, anthropologist and folklorist, explores tourism, concepts of heritage, and the expressive culture of Southeast Asia. She is the author of *Making Merit, Making Art: A Thai Temple in Wimbledon* and co-editor of *Converging Interests: Travelers, Traders, and Tourists in Southeast Asia.* She teaches anthropology at San José State University.

ANDREW CAUSEY is associate professor of anthropology in the department of humanities, history, and social sciences at Columbia College Chicago. He is author of *Hard Bargaining in Sumatra: Western Travelers and Toba Bataks in the Marketplace of Souvenirs.*

JOHN CLAMMER is director of international courses at the United Nations University, Tokyo. He has written widely on Southeast Asia and Japan.

HAROLD C. CONKLIN is emeritus professor of anthropology and the Franklin Muzzy Crosby Professor Emeritus of the Human Environment at Yale University. His books include *Hanunóo Agriculture* and *Ethnographic Atlas of Ifugao*.

SUSAN M. DARLINGTON is professor of anthropology and Asian studies at Hampshire College. Her research, based on extensive fieldwork in Thailand, examines the work of Buddhist monks engaged in rural development, environmental conservation, and other forms of social activism.

ROBERT KNOX DENTAN is professor emeritus at the State University of New York at Buffalo. He has written many chapters, articles, and books, including *The Semai: A Nonviolent People of Malaya* and *Overwhelming Terror: Love, Fear, Peace and Violence among Semai of Malaysia*.

JULI EDO is an associate professor of anthropology at the University of Malaya and the first Orang Asli to receive a Ph.D. degree in anthropology. He is also past director of the Centre for Malaysia Pribumi Studies at the University of Malaya. He is the author of *The Senoi of Perak* and *Tradisi Lisan Masyarakat Semai* [Semai Oral Tradition], among other writings. His research interests include educational, development, social change, and human rights issues of the Orang Asli and the Penan.

MICHELE FORD chairs the department of Indonesian studies at the University of Sydney. She is author of *Workers and Intellectuals: NGOs, Trade Unions and the Indonesian Labour Movement* and coeditor of *Women and Work in Indonesia; Women and Labour Organizing in Asia: Diversity, Autonomy and Activism*; and *Indonesia Beyond the Water's Edge: Managing an Archipelagic State*.

KATHLEEN A. GILLOGLY is assistant professor of anthropology at the University of Wisconsin-Parkside. She has done fieldwork in Thailand, Laos, Vietnam, the Solomon Islands (South Pacific), and the south side of Chicago, focusing on social structure, kinship, agricultural development, state policies toward upland ethnic minorities, and environmental anthropology.

LUCIEN M. HANKS, JR. was trained in psychology, but taught anthropology at Bennington College for most of his career. He is the author of *Rice and Man*, a pioneering study of the agricultural ecology of lowland Thailand and (coauthored with Jane Hanks) *Tribes of the Northern Thailand Frontier*. He died in 1988.

HOLLY HIGH lectures in anthropology at the University of Sydney. Her research in Laos has dealt with the tensions of poverty and development and the dynamics of everyday political economy.

HJORLEIFUR JONSSON has done research in Thailand, Cambodia, and Vietnam, and most recently among Southeast Asian refugee immigrant communities in Oregon and California. He is author of *Mien Relations: Mountain People and State Control in Thailand.*

PATTANA KITIARSA is assistant professor in the Southeast Asian studies program, National University of Singapore. He has published in Thai and English on Thai popular Buddhism, transnational labor migration, Thai boxing, and Thai films. He is editor of *Religious Commodifications in Asia: Marketing Gods.*

LENORE LYONS is research professor in Asian studies at the University of Western Australia. She is recognized as the leading scholar on the feminist movement in Singapore and is author of *A State of Ambivalence: The Feminist Movement in Singapore.*

CHRISTOPHER LYTTLETON is associate professor of anthropology at Macquarie University, Australia. He is author of *Endangered Relations: Negotiating Sex and AIDS in Thailand,* and *Mekong Erotics: Men Loving/Pleasuring/Using Men in Lao PDR.*

SHAUN KINGSLEY MALARNEY is professor of cultural anthropology at International Christian University, Tokyo. He is author of *Culture, Ritual and Revolution in Vietnam* and of a translation and annotation of Vũ Trọng Phung's *Lục Xì: Prostitution and Venereal Disease in Colonial Hanoi.*

JUDITH NAGATA is professor emerita of anthropology and senior research fellow at the York Centre for Asian Research at York University, Toronto. Her books include *Malaysian Mosaic: Perspectives from a Poly-ethnic Society* and *The Reflowering of Malaysian Islam.*

CHRISTINA SCHWENKEL is assistant professor of anthropology at the University of California, Riverside. She is the author of *The American War in Contemporary Vietnam: Transnational Remembrance and Representation.*

NANCY J. SMITH-HEFNER is associate professor of anthropology at Boston University. She is the author of *Khmer American: Identity and Moral Education in a Diasporic Community.*

ELIZABETH G. TRAUBE did research in the early 1970s in what was then Portuguese Timor with Mambai people of the central highlands. She is the author of *Cosmology and Social Life: Ritual Exchange in an Eastern Indonesian Society* and numerous articles on Mambai society and culture.

KATHARINE L. WIEGELE is adjunct assistant professor of anthropology at Northern Illinois University. She is the author of *Investing in Miracles: El Shaddai and the Transformation of Popular Catholicism in the Philippines.*

ANTHONY WILLIAMS-HUNT (BAH TONY KNOON BAH JANGGUT), a lawyer, has published articles on Orang Asli indigenous law and political struggles.

EVE MONIQUE ZUCKER is a visiting scholar in the department of anthropology at the University of California, San Diego. She has lived and worked in an upland Khmer village in southwestern Cambodia, where she studied memory, morality, social change, and post-conflict recovery.

INDEX